AF608260

PRIVACY IN THE AGE OF SHAKESPEARE

RONALD HUEBERT

Privacy in the Age of Shakespeare

UNIVERSITY OF TORONTO PRESS
Toronto Buffalo London

Toronto Buffalo London
www.utppublishing.com

ISBN 978-1-4426-4791-6

Library and Archives Canada Cataloguing in Publication

Huebert, Ronald, 1946–, author
Privacy in the age of Shakespeare / Ronald Huebert.

Includes bibliographical references and index.
ISBN 978-1-4426-4791-6 (bound)

1. English literature – Early modern, 1500–1700 – History and criticism.
2. Privacy in literature. I. Title.

PR428.P68H83 2016 820.9'003 C2015-907182-8

This book has been published with the help of a grant from the Federation for the Humanities and Social Sciences, through the Awards to Scholarly Publications Program, using funds provided by the Social Sciences and Humanities Research Council of Canada.

University of Toronto Press acknowledges the financial assistance to its publishing program of the Canada Council for the Arts and the Ontario Arts Council, an agency of the Government of Ontario.

Conseil des Arts
du Canada

Funded by the Government of Canada | Financé par le gouvernement du Canada

To
Rachel and David

Contents

Illustrations

Preface

The creation of this book has been supported by Dalhousie University and the University of King's College, where I regularly practise my craft; by Clare Hall, Cambridge University, where I was a Visiting Fellow in 2007–8; and by the Social Sciences and Humanities Research Council of Canada, through the award of a Standard Research Grant for the period 2003–6. A great deal of the material printed here has been ventured orally in many different venues: as matter for discussion in a graduate seminar on Early Modern Privacy at Dalhousie; as informal presentations in an undergraduate seminar on Picture and Poetry in Early Modern Culture at King's; as talks in the Friday afternoon speaker series in the Department of English at Dalhousie; as conference contributions at meetings of the Canadian Society for Renaissance Studies/Société canadienne d'études de la Renaissance, of the Association of Canadian College and University Teachers of English, of the Centre for Seventeenth-Century Studies at the University of Durham, and of the Icons and Iconoclasts Conference at the University of Aberdeen; as contributions to the Arts/Society/Humanities (ASH) Colloquia held at Clare Hall; and as visiting lectures at the University of Saskatchewan and the University of Cork. I must offer collective thanks to the many people who provoked my thinking about privacy on these various occasions by means of their comments and questions; I hope they will continue the dialogue begun orally by reading and commenting on the written text.

In addition, I want to single out people who have supported my work in more than the usual ways. Four scholars have read this book from beginning to end. Two of them are the readers selected by the Press, whose identities are not disclosed to me, but whose comments I have nonetheless found extremely helpful, especially as guides to revision; my book has been positively nurtured by both of them. The other two scholarly readers are Christina Luckyj, my long-term colleague and friend at Dalhousie, and John L. Lepage of Vancouver Island University, a relatively new acquaintance who has rapidly become a close friend and a trusted intellectual ally. Both of these friends read my typescript with unrelenting patience; both saved me from numerous errors, great and small; and both gave me the generous benefit of their critical judgment. In revising my typescript I have not always done exactly what Christina or what John suggested I do, but I have made hundreds of changes in response to their comments, and I remain deeply indebted to them both.

Many other individuals have given this work their generous support. Joanne H. Wright read an early draft of chapter 6 and helped me to improve it. John E. Crowley read a very early version of chapter 5 with similar results. John Baxter repeatedly heard me speak about privacy, an event he further extended by inviting me to address his Shakespeare class. Since John has the rare talent of sharpening the critical focus of everyone he listens to, I am deeply grateful for his many thoughtful responses to my work. David McNeil and I have developed a close working relationship during the last five years, and I have no doubt that this book has profited from our collaboration. Roberta Barker, William Barker, Lyn Bennett, Jennifer Brady, Hélène Cazes, Peter O. Clarke, Judith Rice Henderson, Brenda Hosington, Krista Kesselring, Joseph Khoury, Andrew King, Robert M. Martin, Ian McAdam, Kathryn Morris, Cynthia Neville, Edward Pechter, Dosia Reichardt, Paul Stevens, Tonny van den Broek, Nicholas von Maltzahn, and Roy Wolper have been supportive in many different ways, all of them generous and all of them deeply appreciated. William W.E. Slights offered invaluable encouragement at a time when that was what I most needed. The late Camille Wells Slights took an interest in my work that mattered a great deal to me, and I will never forget our conversations. Michael Ursell proved to me that a research assistant who knows his way around libraries, both virtual and substantial, can make a very great difference indeed. Sharon Brown and Thomas Haggerty provided expert technical assistance with the illustrations. Barbara Porter and James Leahy offered much-needed editorial advice in the months leading up to publication. And Suzanne Rancourt was an exemplary editor at every stage of the process.

Elizabeth Edwards shares my private life, and she too has been deeply supportive of my work, sometimes (I am sure) at the expense of her own. My most heartfelt thanks are to her. The dedication gives the names of our two children, and I considered adding to their names the phrase, "whose privacy I have tried to foster." But they are now responsible adults no longer in need of the paternal good I would be claiming to have given. So the gesture of dedicating this book to them can be read as a way of releasing them, of setting them free.

RH
Halifax, Nova Scotia
1 March 2015

Bibliographical Note

Whenever I quote from old-spelling texts, whether in print or in manuscript, usage of *i/j*, *u/v*, and long *s* has been silently modernized. When quoting from printed texts I have likewise corrected obvious typographical errors and expanded archaic abbreviations. When quoting from manuscripts, however, I have tried to retain as much of the idiosyncratic flavour of the source material and to represent it as faithfully as today's typography will allow.

The official reckoning of dates in early modern England was still governed by the Julian calendar, which designates 25 March as the first day of the year. To avoid confusion, I therefore cite dates between 1 January and 24 March as follows: 30 January 1648/9. The slash separates the Julian (Old Style) reckoning from the Gregorian (New Style) now adhered to in most jurisdictions.

PRIVACY IN THE AGE OF SHAKESPEARE

Privacy: The Early Social History of a Word

I want to begin with a particular appeal to the idea of privacy, for reasons that will soon become apparent. The circumstances under which the appeal was made can be outlined with some confidence: the time is around 1610 or later, quite certainly within the last five years of the life of Sir John Harington (1560–1612), the author of the words I am about to quote; the place is the manor of Kelston, in Somersetshire, the country estate to which Harington retired (in about 1607) after it became obvious that his bid for a serious appointment in the court of King James wasn't going to get the results he wanted. At some point in this last phase of his life Harington wrote a prose treatise, *The Prayse of Private Life*, which was never published in his lifetime nor for the next 320 years or so, that is, until Norman Egbert McClure decided to append it to his meticulous edition of Harington's letters and epigrams.[1]

In keeping with the intellectual habits of his literary community, Harington constructed his treatise by borrowing from models: in this case, quite explicitly from earlier humanist writing (by Petrarch) and from Latin classics (by Virgil, among others). The Petrarchan model was *De vita solitaria*, a text in which Petrarch set out to explain why, rather than accepting employment offered him by the papal court at Avignon, he preferred to maintain his own intellectual agenda. Harington's text is often described as a translation of Petrarch's, and this is a tempting but misleading designation. While Harington ponders the nostalgic

1 *The Letters and Epigrams of Sir John Harington together with "The Prayse of Private Life,"* ed. Norman Egbert McClure (Philadelphia: University of Pennsylvania Press, 1930). Subsequent Harington references, unless otherwise noted, are to this edition.

principle, "Sweete is yt to remember passed perrills" (349), he is indeed translating Petrarch.[2] And he goes on to quote the very same line of the *Aeneid* that Petrarch uses to illustrate the point that great prosperity may contain the seeds of disgrace. This thought, according to both Petrarch and Harington, led Anchises ("the lamentinge father") to say to Aeneas, "quam metui ne quid Libyae tibi regna nocerent!"[3] a notion that Robert Fitzgerald renders in English as follows: "How much I feared the land of Libya/Might do you harm."[4] To follow up this pastiche of translation and quotation, Harington ventures a further idea: "Whereunto he addeth, in howe great pleasure and securitie are they that live a private life" (349). This comment does not seem to originate from any of the layers of intertextual material that I have been citing. Indeed, I find it impossible to identify securely the "he" who is adding this thought. Is it Anchises? Is it Aeneas? Is it Petrarch? None of these is an obvious candidate, and I am left with the strange intuition that this valorization of "private life" is Harington's own.[5]

If I am right, then this is an interesting development in a number of ways. First, it is culturally meaningful, as part of a long-term historical change which I will be frequently suggesting (and sometimes explicitly describing) in many of the chapters of this book. Crudely stated, Harington's remark participates in the coming into positivity of the idea of privacy. I will be noticing later (in chapter 6) the huge gap which separates the abolition of privacy in More's *Utopia* (1516) from its divinely sponsored construction in Milton's *Paradise Lost* (1667). The 151 years of cultural history between these two dates, the large landscape which I am referring to in the title of this book as the age of Shakespeare, were the site of crucial renegotiations in the meaning and value of privacy. That

2 Namely, "dulce nonnunquam est amara recordari demulcentque animum transmissa pericula quamlibet in partem"; see *De vita solitaria/La vie solitaire*, ed. Nicholas Mann and Christophe Carraud (Grenoble: Éditions Millon, 1999), 142.

3 *The Aeneid of Virgil*, ed. R.D. Williams (London: Macmillan, 1972), 6.694.

4 *The Aeneid*, trans. Robert Fitzgerald (New York: Vintage Classics, 1990), 184.

5 The passage by Petrarch which corresponds most closely to Harington's observation has been rendered into modern English as follows: "How great therefore is the joy and the sense of safety in the solitude of one who has passed through everything that was to be dreaded and counts all evils behind him." See Petrarch, *The Life of Solitude*, trans. Jacob Zeitlin (Urbana: University of Illinois Press, 1924), 167. Notice that the word "private" does not appear in Petrarch's sentence, nor in the title of his treatise, as Zeitlin translates them.

Harington should need the idea of "private life" to counterbalance the dangers faced by the hero in the public sphere is in itself a mark of how the negotiation is being played out.

The reference to "a private life," like Harington's choice of a title for his treatise, namely, *The Prayse of Private Life*, is of lexical interest too. The word "private" is doing work for Harington that it was not called upon to do in his source materials. Indeed, there is a sense in which Harington has deliberately replaced Petrarch's "solitaria" with the partly overlapping but not entirely synonymous "private." This change is a stylistic choice, of course, but it is a change deeply embedded in the definitions of the idea of privacy that I will soon be outlining, and in the usage preferences of early modern writers of English that I will be citing in some detail.

And Harington's remark is of biographical interest too. Though he inherited Kelston while still in his early twenties, and married a young woman (Mary Rogers) shortly thereafter,[6] Harington was eager to play a conspicuous role as a courtier. Since Queen Elizabeth herself was his godmother, his expectations must have been both ample and credible. His reputation as a wit only made him more attractive to the queen, and his translation of *Orlando Furioso* (1591) may have been completed in response to her express command. But his next major literary achievement, *A New Discourse of a Stale Subject, Called the Metamorphosis of Ajax* (1596), a work of satire which makes indiscreet allusions to various Elizabethan courtiers under cover of proposing to improve hygiene by means of a rudimentary version of the flush toilet, caused him considerable trouble.[7] His association with Essex was also an adventure in ambivalence: whatever dignity Essex conferred upon Harington by knighting him (along with many others) on the Irish campaign only raised the suspicions of the queen and led at length to banishment from court. Harington did his utmost to recover his standing under King James, going so far as to propose (to Sir Robert Cecil and Charles Blount, whom he hoped could influence the king) that he be appointed Archbishop of Dublin and Lord High Chancellor of Ireland.[8] When another man was

6 See Jason Scott-Warren, "Harington, Sir John (bap. 1560, d. 1612) courtier and author," *Oxford Dictionary of National Biography* (2008).

7 See the "Introduction" to *A New Discourse of a Stale Subject, Called the Metamorphosis of Ajax*, ed. Elizabeth Story Donno (London: Routledge, 1962), 41.

8 See McClure, "Introduction," *Letters and Epigrams*, 30.

appointed to these offices, Harington must have realized, however gradually, that his ambitions for a conspicuous public role were not going to be rewarded. So his praise of private life is in part a strategy of compensation. He shares this ambivalence towards privacy with other capable men of his time and place (with Edmund Spenser, for example, or with John Donne),[9] partly because he depends on the same unpredictable system of patronage. Harington was luckier than most of his competitors, in the sense that his private life – the Kelston estate, which he could share with his wife and seven children, to say nothing of servants and friends – was always waiting for him.

What Harington's situation makes clear, I think, is that the idea of privacy and the word which names it were of genuine importance in the age of Shakespeare and should therefore be of some interest to readers of early modern English texts. Indeed, I am making assumptions here that run counter to the prevailing critical orthodoxy, which would claim that there's no such thing as the private in early modern culture, and that even if there is, it's by definition a bad thing. The first of these assumptions is made by Lena Cowen Orlin, who argues "that 'private life' is a conceptual construct" and that, "in the early modern period, the private was, after all, public in consequence."[10] The patriarchal family, in Orlin's view and that of many other scholars,[11] was a commonwealth writ small in which the paterfamilias monitored the behaviour of all members of the household and his wife discharged her duties in relation to publicly declared objectives. Orlin's more recent book, *Locating Privacy in Tudor London*, is a copiously documented study of all of the direct evidence and a great deal of supplementary information relating to the upwardly mobile family of Francis Barnham and his wife Alice.[12] The occasion for

9 On Spenser see Richard Rambuss, *Spenser's Secret Career* (Cambridge: Cambridge University Press, 1993), 7–24 and 114–16; on Donne see Ronald Huebert, "'Study our Manuscripts': John Donne's Problems with Privacy," *The Seventeenth Century* 26, no. 1 (2011): 1–21.

10 See *Private Matters and Public Culture in Post-Reformation England* (Ithaca, NY: Cornell University Press, 1994), 18, 73.

11 See, for example, Susan Dwyer Amussen, *An Ordered Society: Gender and Class in Early Modern Europe* (Oxford: Blackwell, 1988); and Alan Stewart, "The Early Modern Closet Discovered," *Representations* 50 (Spring 1995): 76–100.

12 See *Locating Privacy in Tudor London* (Oxford: Oxford University Press, 2007), 24–39. Francis Barnham was a member of the Drapers' Company, Alderman of Farrington Without the Walls, and Master of the Drapers' Company (1569, 1571); Alice Barnham (née Bradbridge) married him (probably in 1574) and bore him four children, all of them boys.

this enquiry is Orlin's claim (very plausibly supported) that the subjects of a portrait formerly known as *Lady Ingram and Her Two Boys* (1557) are really Alice Barnham and her two elder sons, Martin and Stephen. The virtues of Orlin's book are ample, but her treatment of the question of privacy is not one of them. She has no coherent position on privacy, except a desire to deny that it really made much of a difference in the sixteenth century, and an eagerness to refute claims that privacy was an emergent and growing concern for the inhabitants of London during this period. Orlin's book turns a blind eye to the rich archive of *literary* evidence about what privacy might have meant to Shakespeare and his contemporaries, and therefore leaves open the opportunity to propose a much more wide-ranging synthesis of questions relating to early modern privacy than anything now available.

Even where privacy is granted a meaningful existence, as it is in Francis Barker's brilliant but tendentious book, its role has often been to underline the thesis that progression towards greater interiority in early modern literature is really a regression: a sad decline towards the birth of the dreaded "bourgeois subjectivity."[13] Barker places a quotation from Pepys at the very beginning of his account, and then moves quickly to a denunciation of "private, sick sexuality" (8). Thus he manages to impose a coloration of naughtiness and guilt upon the idea of privacy itself. David Cressy's work is less polemical and more persuasive, but even here we encounter a mistrust of privacy, now embedded in the scholarly cliché that, in the early modern period, "any distinction between public and private spheres is slippery and unstable, for the two domains intermeshed."[14]

My own research would suggest that a serious rethinking of some of the assumptions governing the study of early modern privacy is in order. The view that privacy did not matter to Shakespeare's contemporaries, or that it was simply unavailable to them, or that the boundary between the public and the private was nebulous, should not be allowed to stand without challenge. The line between public and private was not drawn in precisely the same place by early modern writers as it would be today, but it was drawn and it did matter. Furthermore, while privacy was by no means equally available to everyone, it was a highly desirable objective (in

13 *The Tremulous Private Body: Essays on Subjection* (London: Methuen, 1984), 10.

14 *Birth, Marriage, and Death: Ritual, Religion, and the Life-Cycle in Tudor and Stuart England* (Oxford: Oxford University Press, 1997), 476.

different ways) for women and men, for Puritans and Anglo-Catholics, for aristocrats, merchants, and even servants. I do not assume that privacy is an absolute good, or that it is uninflected by historical change. But I do think that privacy mattered to a great many early modern people – all the more so, I suspect, because of the religious and social pressures to conform and the efforts taken by authorities at various levels to monitor personal behaviour.

For at least a generation, I would argue, the dominant trend among scholars of English Renaissance literature has been towards reading each literary text as a discursive action within a system of political, social, and historical forces, subject to the constraints of ideology, censorship, patronage, and so on. Such critical strategies, while immensely valuable, have tended to favour texts with an overt (or hidden) public agenda. Still, the evolution of a distinctively private space in the literature of the sixteenth and seventeenth centuries has been discussed by scholars, often as an enquiry into a particular author[15] or genre.[16] In addition, Katharine Eisaman Maus has written an excellent and suggestive account of "inwardness" as represented in some of the canonical authors and cultural writings of the Renaissance,[17] and Cecile M. Jagodzinski has traced the ways in which the silent reading of printed texts promoted the valorization of privacy.[18] My intention is to build on these enquiries so as to address the question of privacy in a more comprehensive and systematic way.

---

15 See for example Barbara Everett, "Donne and Secrecy," *Essays in Criticism* 51 (2001): 51–67; and Alexander Sackton, "Donne and the Privacy of Verse," *Studies in English Literature, 1500–1900* 7 (1967): 67–82.

16 See Élisabeth Bourcier, *Les journaux privé en Angleterre de 1600 à 1660* (Paris: Publications de la Sorbonne, 1976); Anne Ferry, *The "Inward" Language: Sonnets of Wyatt, Sidney, Shakespeare, Donne* (Chicago: University of Chicago Press, 1983); Viviana Comensoli, *'Household Business': Domestic Plays of Early Modern England* (Toronto: University of Toronto Press, 1991); Patricia Fumerton, *Cultural Aesthetics: Renaissance Literature and the Practice of Social Ornament* (Chicago: University of Chicago Press, 1991); and Jacqueline Pearson, "The Least Certain Boundaries: Gendered Bodies and Gendered Spaces in Early Modern Drama," *Sederi* 3 (2003): 163–81.

17 *Inwardness and Theater in the English Renaissance* (Chicago: University of Chicago Press, 1995).

18 *Privacy and Print: Reading and Writing in Seventeenth-Century England* (Charlottesville: University of Virginia Press, 1999).

One of the indispensable resources for my project is volume 3 of *A History of Private Life* (1986; 1989), edited by Roger Chartier.[19] Among the chapters of this work which I have found most useful are Madeleine Foisil's "The Literature of Intimacy" (327–61) and Jean Marie Goulemot's "Literary Practices: Publicising the Private" (363–95), but there is a great deal else in this compendium, including ample and helpfully arranged documentation. There are occasional references to English texts in this volume, but the real object of study is French literature and culture. My practice has been to learn whatever I can from *A History of Private Life*, bearing in mind that what is true for France in the mid-seventeenth century may not hold at all for England. The importance of Protestantism for English culture, the prevalence of Puritan thought and practice, led at length to the view that religious allegiance and affiliation were questions that could only be settled by appealing to the private judgment of the individual Christian; some of these developments are discussed at length in chapter 2, and they are also alluded to elsewhere, in relation to the thinking of Milton and Marvell, for example. *A History of Private Life* is therefore not so much a direct competitor to my own work, as an extremely useful ally, and it is in this spirit that it will be cited in the chapters that lie ahead.

A Working Definition

What exactly *is* privacy? My answer to this unavoidable question will unfold in two stages. First I adopt what might be called an Aristotelian strategy in defining my key term: that is, I distinguish it, as clearly and precisely as I can, not only from its radical opposite (the public, in this case), but from its near neighbours (the solitary, the intimate, and the domestic, for example) with which it might be confused. The second stage in my essay in definition might be designated, with some accuracy, as an answer to the question, What exactly *was* privacy in the century and a half that separates *Utopia* from *Paradise Lost*? The second phase of my concern with definition therefore gives the whole enquiry the historical inflection it needs if we are ever to be in the position of

19 *Passions of the Renaissance*, ed. Roger Chartier, trans. Arthur Goldhammer, vol. 3 of *A History of Private Life*, gen. eds Philippe Ariès and Georges Duby (Cambridge, MA: Harvard University Press, 1989).

understanding what early modern writers meant when they used the words "private" and "privacy."

Just how careful do we need to be in drawing the distinction between the public and the private? Every reader of this book will be able to use the distinction with complete confidence, when she or he acknowledges the difference between making a presentation at an academic conference (a public event) and having a conversation with family or friends in one's own living room (a private occasion). It is easy of course to imagine many liminal scenarios between these two extremes: going out for lunch with a former student, for example, or visiting a museum in the company of a colleague from another university. But such liminal cases do not for a moment undermine the meaningfulness of the distinction between public and private. Indeed, if we did not have a secure sense of the primary distinction to begin with, the scenarios I have suggested would not strike us as belonging somewhere between the extremes.

Because privacy has been and continues to be a hotly contested legal question, however, there are bound to be circumstances under which the public/private distinction needs to be made in precise and unambiguous language. I am not going to rehearse the many attempts that writers and thinkers have made in the hope of reaching the goal of precision; readers who wish to consult such an overview can find it readily elsewhere.[20] For my purposes, it is preferable to cite the single definition in which I place the greatest confidence, and to offer both my reasons for endorsing it and some reservations. The formal definition I have chosen is by Jeffrey Reiman, who advances the view, in "Driving to the Panopticon," that privacy is "the condition in which other people are deprived of access to either some information about you or some experience of you."[21] I agree with this definition because it (like many of its rival formulations) places appropriate emphasis on *access* to the person; because it includes both information about (medical records, for example) and experience of (touching or listening to) the person; and because of the sense in which privacy is maintained only by means of a restriction (others are *deprived* of access). The only modification I would want to make is to

20 See, for example, Shaun MacNeil, "A Philosophical Definition of Privacy," *The Dalhousie Review* 78 (1998): 437–57; and Tony Doyle, "Privacy and Perfect Voyeurism," *Ethics and Information Technology* 11 (2009): 181–9.

21 *Critical Moral Liberalism: Theory and Practice* (Lanham, MD: Rowman and Littlefield, 1997), 172.

include in the definition the positive idea of *control*, as it appears for example in Charles Fried's analysis: "The person who enjoys privacy is able to grant or deny access to others."[22] I think this notion of control is easily compatible with Reiman's definition, even though he doesn't want it to be.[23] Indeed, the notion of who controls access to my personal self is crucial not only to the scenarios I alluded to earlier to distinguish between public and private events, but also to our evaluation of the liminal spaces which stand between the two extremes. Let me return briefly to these imagined occasions to explain what I mean.

When I'm presenting a paper at an academic conference I know that I'm in the public domain and that I cannot appeal to the various protections of privacy. To begin, I cannot control who attends my talk; perhaps I can influence friends and supporters to attend by networking with this in mind, but I cannot (and must not be able to) exclude my harshest critics from the audience if they wish to be there. This reading of the situation would bear out the fundamental requirements of the most common definition of "public": "Open to general observation, view, or knowledge; existing, performed, or carried out without concealment, so that all may see or hear" (*OED adj.* 1a). True, you may need to be a member of the academic society I am addressing if you want to be informed of or invited to my talk in advance. But it is still a public performance, much as the concert given by your string ensemble is a public event, though open only to persons who have paid for tickets. The radical extreme of a public event would perhaps be the attack on Sunday shopping by the orator who mounts his soapbox at Speakers' Corner in Hyde Park. But even here the audience is restricted to persons able to afford the pleasures of Sunday morning in London. There is, in my view, sufficient similarity connecting the academic talk, the string ensemble concert, and

---

22 "Privacy [A Moral Analysis]," in *Philosophical Dimensions of Privacy: An Anthology*, ed. Ferdinand D. Schoeman (Cambridge: Cambridge University Press, 1984), 210.

23 See Reiman's claim that, "If we include control in the definition of privacy we will find the value of the sort of privacy we want in the bedroom, but not of the sort we want in the bathroom" ("Driving," 173). His point is that control (I decide who enters) and prohibition (nobody else can enter) are different in kind, but I think this is a tenuous distinction. Putting up a "Do not enter" sign is indeed the exercise of control (supported, in the case of bathrooms, by various kinds of social taboo). But anyone who has used a urinal in a public washroom will know that, even when we are using the bathroom, control is neither absolute nor unimportant.

the soapbox oration to allow us to identify all three of these as public performances. Perhaps the most significant likeness is the fact that the performers, in all three cases, do not control access to the performance.

And this is precisely what distinguishes the public event(s) from a private conversation among family and/or friends in the living room of my home. The salient difference is that, on this occasion, I *do* control who has access. This may not be absolute control, in the sense that I have discussed the matter with my wife beforehand, and it may not be complete control, in the sense that the two persons invited to join us may (unexpectedly) bring a third person with them. Still, there is a sense in which I control access, however indirectly, nonetheless. The unexpected third person is very unlikely to be my harshest critic and is very likely to be someone who my friends think will be a congenial part of the mix. Let us assume for the sake of argument that all of the guests have strongly developed academic interests, and even that the main topic of our conversation (the early modern public execution as a theatrical event) is the very same as the topic of my conference paper. The overwhelming difference, therefore, is the distinction between a public occasion (in which I do not control access) and a private event (in which, with some qualifications, I do).

Perhaps the liminal scenarios I imagined earlier will now raise no further problems, but let me make sure, by revisiting one of them, namely, going out for lunch with a former student. This event may have some of the earmarks of a private meeting: let's say that I have made the invitation and decided on the venue. So the two of us meet at a well-known Halifax restaurant at 1:30 on Tuesday and are promptly seated at a table next to a window offering us a generous view of a downtown promenade. We carry on conversation to our mutual satisfaction and without interruption (except by the waiter, as he makes appropriate explanations and asks the necessary questions). This may look like privacy, until you consider how tenuous my control of access to this occasion might turn out to be. The waiter at the next table could indeed be a graduate student whose work I am supervising, and he might take the trouble to engage me in conversation. My wife's best friend might be passing by on the promenade and, noticing us, might wave her greetings. Let's suppose that, though I didn't see the wave, my former student did. There are now a number of ways in which I have failed to control access to my person, if that is what I wanted to do. But I don't think any of these will be troublesome, either to me or to my companion, because both of us will make the assumption that a quiet lunch in an agreeable restaurant, while provisionally private in some important respects, nevertheless takes place in the public domain, and therefore qualifies as a liminal scenario in which the participants make most (but not all) of the decisions about access to themselves.

If the idea of privacy needs to be distinguished from its polar opposite, the public, it is probably in greater need of separation from the nearly synonymous concepts with which it might be confused. Here I begin with solitude, because the difference between Petrarch's treatise on this subject and Harington's adaptation of it has already implied that, while solitude and privacy may overlap in some instances, each has lexical inflections of which the other is unaware.

There are plenty of situations in everyone's life where privacy and solitude will occur simultaneously. When I am alone in my study, engrossed in a book that I have been longing to read for some time, my experience can rightly be described as both private and solitary. When my children were young, I often enjoyed the experience of reading aloud to them, sometimes together, but mostly one at a time. When I read a chapter of *Black Beauty* to my daughter at her bedtime, there were two of us in the room, so neither of us could be designated as solitary. Indeed, we were sharing the profound experience of being alone together, an experience which belongs unambiguously to the private life of both participants. The paradoxical phrase "alone together" is a signal that, although the experience in question is shared, it has some of the special qualities that we associate with solitude, though in this instance the situation has another inflection that we might call intimacy. About this quality I will have more to say shortly, but for now I am satisfied with the inference that privacy need not be a solo performance.

When we distinguish between privacy and solitude, questions about the quality of one's experience are likely to arise, and I think it is right that they should do so. As everyone knows, it is possible to feel profoundly solitary even when surrounded by numerous people. It is the brilliance with which T.S. Eliot captures the experience of isolation that has made "The Love Song of J. Alfred Prufrock" such an enduring poem. But to call Prufrock's experience a representation of privacy would simply confuse matters, and it would be inaccurate too, because the poem offers no reasons for supposing that access to Prufrock is restricted or that he himself is in control of access. I would suppose that a young woman performing a vocal solo in a nightclub might feel pretty desperately alone too, isolated by the glare of the spotlight, and not at all reassured by the many pairs of eyes focused on her; and this might hold true even if she herself wrote the song to mark the occasion of her boyfriend's birthday. But I think the same young woman, when singing the very same notes and lyrics in her own apartment for the person she has chosen to bring into her private world, might feel deep gratification and pride in the pleasure she is able to share. Even if her notes and lyrics are the same, however, there is a sense in which she is not giving the same performance: in the first case she is providing entertainment, and in the second she is offering her lover the gift of her voice.

As this last example implies, there is a strong connection between privacy and intimacy, a connection that is often and I think accurately described by observing that privacy is a precondition for the development of intimacy.[24] A relationship of true intimacy, whether sexual or otherwise, is likely to flourish only if an environment of privacy has already been established. Because a special intensity is thought to be characteristic of intimacy, this is likely to be achieved only between two participants. In the case of sexual lovers, the ecstatic rapture they are capable of reaching in private would be spoiled or tarnished or perhaps even prevented from occurring at all if a third person were to observe them. The same holds true, less obviously and perhaps less emphatically, for close friends.[25] The introduction of a casual acquaintance into the middle of a conversation *entre nous* would certainly change and most likely hamper the experience. Privacy would ensure that such interruptions not be the norm, and would therefore enable the friendship to prosper. As readers of chapter 2 will observe, intimacy for the early modern Christian was often a much-desired outcome of the relationship between the soul and God. Here too it was thought, by some influential writers at least, that observation by a third party should be avoided; it is the teaching of Christ that

24 See, for example, Robert S. Gerstein, "Intimacy and Privacy," in *Philosophical Dimensions of Privacy: An Anthology*, ed. Ferdinand D. Schoeman (Cambridge: Cambridge University Press, 1984), 265–71; James Rachels, "Why Privacy Is Important," in *Philosophical Dimensions*, 297–8; and Jeffrey Reiman, "Privacy, Intimacy, and Personhood," *Critical Moral Liberalism: Theory and Practice* (Lanham, MD: Rowman and Littlefield, 1997), 151–67.

25 For this kind of intimacy in particular, see Kathy Eden's copiously researched book *The Renaissance Rediscovery of Intimacy* (Chicago: University of Chicago Press, 2012), especially her account of the friendship between Montaigne and Étienne de la Boétie (99–100).

designates those who pray conspicuously as "hypocrites" and that offers the pious Christian this advice: "But thou, when thou prayest, enter into thy closet, and when thou hast shut thy door, pray to thy Father which is in secret; and thy Father which seeth in secret shall reward thee openly" (Matthew 6:5, 6). This idea deserves and will get much more detailed attention in its scheduled place. I raise it now only to suggest that, in at least three parallel situations – sexual love, close friendship, and pious prayer – privacy would appear to be a necessary condition for achieving intimacy. It is not a sufficient condition, of course; in all three situations a degree of commitment is required that will be described variously as caring, trusting, transcending self-interest, and so on. But without privacy these emotional charges, however strongly felt, are unlikely to create the experience of intimacy.

In order to distinguish between the private and the domestic, it will be helpful to draw upon the thinking of Jürgen Habermas, whose analysis of this issue is embedded in a vast and subtly nuanced map of historical change. Among the questions that interest Habermas is the self-presentation of the family in European bourgeois culture. He begins his study not with the fully developed image, but with its dark and ancient shadow. In the Greek city state, he claims, citizens occupied "the public sphere" (the *polis*), which they understood to be "a realm of freedom and permanence." But the autonomy of each citizen rested on his dominance of a household (the *oikos*), in which the labour of women and slaves was required to ensure his standing: "The reproduction of life, the labor of the slaves, and the service of the women went on under the aegis of the master's domination; birth and death took place in its shadow; and the realm of necessity and transitoriness remained immersed in the obscurity of the private sphere."[26] The private and the domestic are comparable in one vital respect: both are not and cannot aspire to be the public sphere, in which everything that really matters takes place.

Habermas begins with this gloomy account of the *oikos*, I would imagine, because he wants a foil against which the self-advertising lustre of the bourgeois family will stand out in bold relief. Under the implicit influence of capitalism, though never directly acknowledging this debt,

26 *The Structural Transformation of the Public Sphere: An Inquiry into a Category of Bourgeois Society*, trans. Thomas Burger and Frederick Lawrence (Cambridge, MA: MIT Press, 1989), 3–4.

the bourgeois family was able to make a remarkable impression: "It seemed to be established voluntarily and by free individuals and to be maintained without coercion; it seemed to rest on the lasting community of love on the part of the two spouses; it seemed to permit that non-instrumental development of all faculties that marks the cultivated personality" (46–7). With the repetition of "it seemed" Habermas provides a hint to the enigmatic meaning of his description. The bourgeois family only *appeared* to have these three wonderful qualities because they were the ideological markers that capitalism required. Once established, however, they became "more than just ideology" (48) in the sense that people believed in them and made them part of their lived reality.

If Habermas is right about either of these paradigms – the shadowy *oikos* or the showy and self-conscious liberalism of the bourgeois family – then there's not much fundamental similarity between the domestic and the private. In both models domestic activities are not undertaken by the subjects who develop and value their autonomy. The domestic realm in either case is maintained by a system of mandatory service so that a person of privilege is able to participate in a democratic culture or cultivate his personal interests. In our own time it is easy to conflate the domestic and the private, and to believe that everybody's domestic life affords the opportunity for *some* privacy. Indeed, we have come to believe in a *right* to privacy, however vaguely defined such a belief may be. I don't think such a belief could take hold in a culture where simple domestic tasks (cooking, laundry, removal of excrement) were taken care of by large numbers of servants. The domestic and the private could come into proximity only after technology had enabled them to do so.

The question, What exactly *is* privacy? can therefore be answered as follows. Privacy is the condition in which other people are deprived of access to either information about or experience of my person to the extent that I decide to exercise control of access. It should be distinguished from solitude (in the sense that privacy can be shared with other persons), from intimacy (in the sense that privacy is a necessary but not a sufficient condition for intimacy), and from domesticity (in the sense that domestic activities may be subject to a regulatory regime from which privacy ought to be free), though it has affinities with all three of these lexical cousins. But the definition outlined here, however cogent it is taken to be, does not yet address my second fundamental question, namely, what *was* privacy in the cultural landscape which I have designated as the age of Shakespeare?

Early Modern Usages

There were no privacy laws in Shakespeare's time. There could have been no reliable expectations of anonymity, since people of all classes were likely to encounter the same bartender, cheesemonger, laundress, or oyster wench over and over again in their daily or weekly routines. Travel was virtually unavailable for most people, who lived their entire lives within a fifty-mile radius of their places of birth; even for the privileged few it was painfully slow (by our standards), and anything but impersonal. The behaviour of the privileged was incessantly monitored by servants and retainers, whose loyalty and devotion were of course the subject of surveillance by their superiors. Under these circumstances it's tempting to infer that privacy couldn't protect anyone: that the all-seeing eye of Providence was really the personification of a social system that left no corner unmolested.

What bothers me about this easy inference is that early modern writers refer to the distinction between the public and the private with great regularity, and they presume that the distinction makes sense. In response to the gap which appears to separate the material circumstances and the linguistic practices of Shakespeare's time I propose to outline some of the changes and transvaluations that affected the words "privacy" and "private" in the sixteenth and seventeenth centuries. This exercise will at very least help us to distinguish between what early modern writers are saying when they use these words and what we might wish they were saying.

The word "privacy" is a relative newcomer to the English vocabulary. Chaucer doesn't use it, and it appears to have been rare in the Middle Ages – so rare, in fact, that the *Middle English Dictionary* has no entry for it. The earliest example given by the *Oxford English Dictionary*, 2nd ed., is from a mid-fifteenth-century metrical life of St Cuthbert. An old man flees from Ireland to Britain, taking with him a group of orphan children over whom he wishes to retain custody: "To kepe thaim in privace,/ Whil eftirwarde better myght be."[27] The word "private" is a little more

27 *The Life of St Cuthbert in English Verse*, ed. J.T. Fowler, Publications of the Surtees Society 87 (Durham: Andrews, 1891), 18. Interestingly, this example does not survive in the online version of the *OED*, to which I refer in parenthetical citations.

likely to occur in medieval texts, though it too is absent from Chaucer. Among the species of penance described in *The Clensyng of Mannes Sowle* (ca 1400), the third is called "a private penaunce or a secrete penaunce"; it is transacted not in public or in the presence of a congregation, but only in relation to the sinner's confessor, or "shrifte fadir."[28] Aside from rare and relatively late instances like these, medieval scribes and authors managed to do without the words "privacy" and "private." Not that they suffered this absence as a great impoverishment; they did have the words "privity" and "privy" ready to hand to do most of the work that would later be taken over by their more modern cousins. In *The Miller's Tale* Chaucer gets along quite handily with the old system. When Alisoun decides that, yes, given the right opportunity she will have an affair with her lodger Nicholas, she tells him that circumspection and planning are essential:

> "Myn housbonde is so ful of jalousie
> That but ye wayte wel and been privee,
> I woot right wel I nam but deed," quod she. (1.3294–6)

Nicholas now has the task of manipulating the old husband, John, so as to make it easy to cuckold him. He approaches John with a fabricated story that requires strict confidentiality: "Fecche me drynke,/And after wol I speke in pryvetee/Of certeyn thyng that toucheth me and thee" (1.3492–4).[29] These medieval instances are linked with subsequent Renaissance usage, especially the one strand of it which has to do with secrecy, intimacy, and surreptitious behaviour. But the widespread use of "privacy" and "private" from the sixteenth century on does register an important change as well. In the Renaissance privacy was emerging as a category of experience in its own right. No longer merely an attribute attached to a certain kind of behaviour, privacy was beginning to require a vocabulary of its own.

The early modern meanings of the words "privacy" and "private" tend to arrange themselves into four distinct though sometimes overlapping

28 See Mark H. Liddell, "A New Source of *The Parson's Tale*," *An English Miscellany Presented to Dr Furnivall in Honour of his Seventy-Fifth Birthday* (Oxford: Clarendon, 1901), 263–4.

29 *The Works of Geoffrey Chaucer*, ed. F.N. Robinson, 2nd ed. (Boston: Houghton Mifflin, 1957), 49, 51.

clusters, which I will now discuss one at a time. The first such semantic cluster has to do with status, most often with the absence of status. Under this rubric what is distinctive about the private is a deficiency, a lack: the private is *not* the public (see *OED* private *adj.* 4). This cluster of meaning hints at the links between the private and some etymological relatives: the privative, privation, and deprivation. Such linkages are even stronger in French, where the adjective "privé/e" (meaning "private") and the verb "priver" (meaning "deprive") are homonyms. In military language, then as now, "private" designates the absence of any particular rank in the hierarchy; that's why, as Leonard Digges observes, "Coronelles, Captaines, and suche principall persons oughte not to be thruste in Ranke as Private Souldiours."[30] In religious terms, at least for a devout Roman Catholic like Thomas Stapleton, there's an inescapable affinity between the private and the heretical. It is not enough, Stapleton argues, to "embrace and beleve his [i.e., God's] holy worde after some privat and peculiar fashion, as al heretikes do." The heretic is by definition one who lacks the authority which only the church can confer: "he interpreteth it [i.e., scripture] after his owne liking and privat judgement, and letteth go the hold of the Catholike consent, and authoryte."[31] In pedagogical terms, Richard Mulcaster, the celebrated headmaster of the Merchant Taylors' School, argues that "*private education*" (by which I think he means instruction by private tutors) simply lacks the manifest virtues of the English public school. Education, after all, must train individuals to live "amongest others" in society. So the private realm is at best a supplement to what really matters: "All the functions here be publike and regard every one, even where the thinges do seeme to be most private, bycause the maine direction remaineth in the publike, and the private must be squared, as it will best joyne with that."[32] This first cluster of meanings is clearly hierarchical; in warfare, in religion,

---

30 *An Arithmeticall Militaire Treatise, named Stratioticos* (London: Henry Bynneman, 1579), T4–4^{v}.

31 *A Fortresse of the Faith First Planted Amonge Us Englishmen, and Continued Hitherto in the Universall Church of Christ: The Faith of Which Time Protestants Call, Papistry* (Antwerp: Jhon Laet, 1565), B1^{v}–2.

32 *Positions, Wherein Those Primitive Circumstances Be Examined, Which Are Necessarie for the Training Up of Children, Either for Skill in Their Booke, or Health in Their Bodie* (London: Thomas Vautrollier for Thomas Chare, 1581), 2A1.

and in education, public consensus prevails over private initiative or intuition. Although widespread, this pattern of emphasis isn't universal. Sometimes the private is the preferred alternative, by virtue of its exclusiveness, its elitism. When the title page of James Shirley's *The Lady of Pleasure* (London: Tho[mas] Cotes, 1637) notes that the quarto is printed "As it was Acted by her Majesties Servants, at the private House in Drury Lane," a claim is being advanced, implicitly, on behalf of a better sort of theatre, something that will appeal to gentlemen able to spend a shilling or more for an afternoon's entertainment. Perhaps it's fitting that the theatre, where clowns can be kings and vice versa, should once again be inverting the established hierarchy of value.

A second cluster of meaning has to do with ownership and property (see *OED* private *adj.* 5). The English translation of *Sleidanes Commentaries,* a book which advances a moderate but still firmly Lutheran interpretation of the Reformation, contains the following comment on the Anabaptists: "They teache howe it is not lawful for the christians to go to the law, nor to beare office, nor to take an othe, neither to have any thynge private, that al things ought to be common unto al men."[33] The utopian agenda is claiming adherents in a real society, and the moment it does so it becomes not only foolish but threatening. Here private property is not the source of every social ill, but well on its way to becoming a refuge from the chaos of public life. This, at any rate, is what it has become in the rhetoric of Peter Heylyn, an outspoken royalist and supporter of Laud who lost his status and influence as an Anglican divine as a result of Cromwell's ascendancy and therefore turned to writing books about geography. In the prefatory statement to one such book, Heylyn points out that he now has plenty of time for writing, but he's unsure about the value of his work: "perhaps I could have spent those times of leisure, which the change of my affairs hath given me, with greater benefit to my self, and more to the advantage of my private fortunes." Heylyn may not be thinking of property exclusively, but the idea of private ownership is strongly implied. And the sense of the private sphere as a refuge from the public is quite eloquently expressed: "Nor have we only time enough to spend, but some time to spare; some privacies and retreats

33 Johann Sleidan, *A Famouse Cronicle of Oure Time, Called Sleidanes Commentaries, Concerning the State of Religion and Common Wealth, During the Raigne of the Emperour Charles the First,* trans. John Daus (N.p.: n.p., [1560]), 2A1.

from business; some breathing fits from the affairs of our *Vocations*."[34] For a high-church royalist in the mid-seventeenth century, private reserves of wealth (both material and mental) are required to offset public losses.

A third semantic grouping, which I've mentioned already in connection with medieval usage, draws an implicit equation between privacy and secrecy of various kinds (see *OED* private *adj.* 6). Sir Jerome Horsey, who served on diplomatic missions to the Russian court in the late sixteenth century, has more reasons than most to insist on confidentiality. He records one occasion on which he expressly "wished all secreacie might be used, for that som other privacies committed to my charge had ben so whispered owt, not of my self, as not longe after it came to the prince and Emporis ears, whereat grew no small jeloucie and displeasur."[35] If "privacy" can refer to the item concealed, as in the example just quoted, it can also refer to the place of concealment. Robert Plot finds room in his book on Staffordshire to tell an anecdote about the preservation of the future King Charles II after the Battle of Worcester (1651). Allegedly Charles disguised himself in rustic garments, cut off his hair, rubbed soot on his hands and face, and climbed into an oak tree near Boscobel House in Wales. "Having rested at *Boscobel* two days," the account continues, "one in the *Oak*; the night in a *privacy* behind the *Chimney* in one of the Chambers; and the other in the house and garden; the night following he removed to *Moseley*."[36] This meaning of privacy is now obsolete; indeed, I believe that the association between privacy and secrecy is not nearly as strong as it used to be, though it survives in such formulaic phrases as "private and confidential."

A special case of the link between privacy and secrecy is encoded in the phrase "private parts," an expression which had many variations in the early modern period. Thomas Herbert, in an account of his travels to East India around 1630, observes that in some of the kingdoms he visited "the women goe most part naked, except a cloth which should cover those parts, made to be private." A stranger coming to this paradise of nearly naked women, Herbert alleges, "shall presently have his choice of

34 *Cosmographie in Four Books: Containing the Chorographie and Historie of the Whole World, and All the Principal Kingdoms, Provinces, Seas, and Isles Thereof*, 2nd ed. (London: Henry Seile, 1657), A2.

35 *His Travels, Imploiments, Services and Negociacions*, in *Russia at the Close of the Sixteenth Century*, ed. Edward A. Bond (London: Hakluyt Society, 1856), 236.

36 *The Natural History of Staffordshire* (Oxford: The Theater, 1686), 2Q2.

many Virgins, and choosing one he fancies, for a small price; she guides him to a lodging, and performes his domestique affaires what ever, at bed and board, all the time of his abode their discharging her duty and privacie very punctually."[37] The context here would suggest that privacy is a sexual activity rather than a body part, but obviously the two are related in any case. An anecdote about Catherine Sforza insists on the equation between privacies and sexual organs. Following the murder of her husband, and after yielding up her children as hostages, she is said to have stood upon the castle walls in order to berate her political enemies; unmoved by their threats, "but plucking up her clothes, and shewing them her privacies, she bad them do what they would with her children, for she had still the mould to cast others in."[38] I don't presume to judge the truth of these accounts; they are written by men about the sexuality of women; indeed they are recorded by Englishmen observing the sexual behaviour of women from cultures thought to be exotic, and are therefore very likely to be inflected by gender, ethnicity, and race. What I am claiming here is that "privacy" and "private" gave speakers of English a fairly acceptable way of alluding to the female organs in particular. The male organ was referred to in a more old-fashioned way. When Frances Howard decided that she wanted nothing more to do with her husband, the 3rd earl of Essex, she approached the astrologer Simon Forman, who designed, among other things, a wax model of her husband with a thorn "*stuck* upon the *privity* of the said *picture*."[39] Both verbal methods, the old and the new, the male and the female, offer ways of naming the secret parts of the body while, nominally at least, leaving their secrecy intact.

The fourth and final cluster of meaning that I have been able to identify has to do with various kinds of interiority. Evidence for this meaning in early modern usage is indirect but nonetheless persuasive. The *OED* gives a brief but telling entry to the rare and obsolete word "privancy," which it glosses as "intimacy" on the basis of a single example, a translation of the Spanish word *privanza* by James Mabbe. The narrator of the

37 *A Relation of Some Yeares Travaile, Begunne Anno 1626* (London: William Stansby and Jacob Bloome, 1634), F4^v–G1.

38 Trajano Boccalini, *I Ragguagli di Parnasso: Or Advertisements from Parnassus*, trans. Henry Carey, 2nd earl of Monmouth (London: Humphrey Moseley and Thomas Heath, 1656), K1^v.

39 *Truth Brought to Light and Discovered by Time, or a Discourse and Historicall Narration of the First XIIII Yeares of King James Reign* (London: Richard Cotes, 1651), D2–2^v.

passage in question is describing the relationship between Ozmin and Don Alonso de Cuniga: "a kind of friendship was begun betweene them, (if any such thing may be found betweene master and man:) notwithstanding, inasmuch as man is compatible, it is commonly called by the name of Privancie or Inwardnesse."[40] Stephen Gosson, in advancing one of his many arguments against the theatre, advises introspection as a way of resisting theatrical blandishments: "Enter every one into your selves, and whensoever you heare that playe againe, or any man els in private conference commend Playes, consider not, so much what is spoken to colour them, as what may bee spoken to confounde them."[41] The "private conference" is in fact part of the temptation here, because it allows the advocate of stage plays to enter into the mind of the prospective theatregoer. Another kind of interiority preoccupies the poet Eliza, who speaks of her poems as if they are children: "my *Babes* ... were obtained by vertue, borne with ease and pleasure," she claims. Creativity thus occurs in the inner self, though destined for the outside world; Eliza is at length persuaded "that those desires were not given me, to be kept in private, to my self, but for the good of others."[42] Eliza is reclaiming for womankind, and of course for God, the metaphor of pregnancy and childbirth by which male poets (like Sidney and Donne, for example) had represented their creative labours.[43]

To return once more to my point of departure, it should now be apparent that the verbal landscape of Shakespeare's time is densely populated with users of the word "privacy" and its cognates, and that many voices both shape and are shaped by the social history of this word in the early modern period. If you were to rearrange the examples I have cited in strict chronological sequence, it would also become apparent that, generally speaking, there is a progression from suspicion of or hostility to privacy in the earlier texts to acceptance of and even a cherishing of privacy in the later ones. This would by no means be a smooth, linear development, but the overall trend would hold true nonetheless. It would

40 Matheo Aleman, *The Rogue: Or the Life of Guzman de Alfarache*, trans. James Mabbe (London: Edward Blount, 1623), H4[v].

41 *Playes Confuted in Five Actions* (London: Thomas Gosson, [1582]), G2[v].

42 *Elia's Babes: or The Virgin's Offering (1652): A Critical Edition*, ed. Liam Semler (Madison, NJ: Fairleigh Dickinson University Press, 2001), 57–8.

43 See Maus, "A Womb of One's Own: Male Renaissance Poets in the Female Body," *Inwardness and Theater*, esp. 182–3.

also be possible to observe a preponderance of material interpretations of privacy (property, status) in the earlier texts, and spiritual interpretations (secrecy, interiority) in later ones. The study of a particular word, in this instance, bears the marks of a series of cultural changes, among them the movement away from a universal church committed to prohibiting private interpretation and towards the division of religious practice into many sects and denominations, most of them committed to fostering private access to deity. To put it crudely, the Reformation was a good thing for privacy, and the articulations of Puritan thought in its various forms were a particularly good thing.

But articulations of private thought, whether Puritan or not, are always in danger of entering the public domain. This is the paradox known as the publication of privacy.[44] Anyone who advocates the value of privacy in a context where more than two or three people are gathered has in a sense chosen to make privacy public. Puritan strategies of celebrating and promoting the private realm tended, in fact, and virtually by definition, to border on contradiction at the best of times: the new spiritual value conferred upon the personal act of worship went hand in hand with a strict and voyeuristic appraisal of outward behaviour. Once privacy has gone public, so to speak, it runs the double risk of not quite living up to the standards of the public domain on the one hand, or of ceasing to be private on the other. But this is a paradox we still have to live with; insofar as privacy is a word in the language we all use it becomes an experience that, in our separate ways, we share.

Looking Ahead

Now a word about the structure of this book as a whole, as articulated in the chapters which follow. Each of the next eight chapters addresses its own topic and was designed to stand alone as a discussion of some aspect of early modern privacy. But if each chapter has a degree of autonomy, that is not the same thing as complete independence. Taken together, chapters 1 through 8 form a pattern (or better still, a series of interlocking patterns), as I am about to explain in a provisional way, and as my conclusion will underscore.

---

44 See Jean Marie Goulemot, "Literary Practices: Publicising the Private," in *Passions of the Renaissance*, 363–95.

I have arranged the eight chapters so as to bring about four pairs, with each of the four commenting in significant ways on the four clusters of meaning that I have just identified. For reasons that are not quite arbitrary, I have given the subsequent chapters the inverse order to the one I chose when describing the meaning clusters themselves. This arrangement allows me to begin with some of the more familiar nuances of privacy and to move gradually to some of the more recondite usages.

Chapters 1 and 2, in strikingly different ways, highlight the linkage between privacy and interiority. In chapter 1 I will be exploring theatrical representations of interiority (in *Hamlet* and *Twelfth Night* especially), while in chapter 2 I will be arguing that a remarkably parallel turn inward is observable in the devotional practices of early modern Christians, to judge by the prose and verse that recommend and celebrate such piety. Taken together, these two chapters show privacy to have been a subject of great interest to early modern people, both in their most secular activities (attending the Globe Theatre) and in their most religious moments (at meditation or prayer).

Chapters 3 and 4 are both concerned with privacy and secrecy, partly but not exclusively with the strand of meaning in which the human sexual organs are referred to as "private parts." The very activity of voyeurism is called into being by the taboo which tells us that these parts should be hidden. Chapter 3 begins with visual representations of voyeurism (by Titian, Tintoretto, and Artemisia Gentileschi among others), and then explores the widely divergent colorations of voyeurism in poetry (mostly by Robert Herrick) and drama (*Much Ado about Nothing* and *The Duchess of Malfi*). Chapter 4 draws exclusively on manuscripts that were created and read by early modern people (mostly men), and were therefore repositories of what we might think of as shared secrets. These might take the form a crude joke or a beautiful poem or anything in between. The point of highlighting these items here is that they show us, at times, the kinds of private materials that couldn't (or at least didn't) find acceptance in the public domain.

The idea of ownership, as in the phrase "private property," is inescapably visible in chapters 5 and 6. Gender is the point of contention in chapter 5, where it quickly becomes apparent that the cultivation of a private life was more difficult for early modern women than for their male counterparts. The difference had a great deal to do with the kind of ownership that I would describe as entitlement. If aristocratic marriage partners had separate closets, for example, the man's room was referred to as *his* closet, the woman's as simply *the* closet. In chapter 6 Sir Thomas

More addresses the question of private property head-on, by removing it from Utopia. But his view of privacy doesn't prevail in subsequent constructions of the perfect world; indeed, I argue that Milton's valorization of privacy in *Paradise Lost* is diametrically opposed to More's position.

I should add here that the boundaries between the four pairs I am now describing are quite permeable, and that interiority, which I described as characteristic of the first pair, can and does arise as an issue in, for example, chapter 6. That is one of the ways in which the chapters can be said to be interlocking. But each of the pairs is separate from the others nonetheless by virtue of a distinctive emphasis. In chapters 7 and 8 this emphasis falls on the first cluster of meaning, in which privacy was defined as the absence of official status. The treatment of early modern dissidents, as I describe it in chapter 7, characteristically led to their loss of status, and in extreme cases to the loss of life. Privacy was on the whole an insufficient protection against surveillance. The case of Andrew Marvell, the subject of chapter 8, brings many of the same conflicts into play. But for Marvell the retreat from public life into private worlds of various kinds is both desirable and deliberate. His career marks an early stage in the evolution of privacy as a right that one's culture ought to respect.

Readers of this book may notice that I tend to begin a new chapter with a question. See, for example, the beginning of chapter 6 ("When early modern thinkers and writers tried to imagine the perfect world, what role did they assign to privacy in it?") or chapter 7 ("In early modern culture, did privacy protect the heterodox?"). Even where not made explicit, the implied opening question will be easy to identify. This tendency is no mere stylistic tic, but rather part of an intellectual strategy. I have come to believe with some confidence that, when you ask the right question about a text or a cultural practice or about the relationship between the two, a crucial part of the enquiry has already been accomplished. With the help of scholarly research, critical analysis, and imaginative speculation (when required), answers are bound to present themselves, some of course more plausibly than others. Each of the following chapters, therefore, raises a central question and offers some provisional answers to it. But I have not tried to harmonize these various answers or to impose an artificial similarity upon them. I do hope to arrive at a synthesis that is greater than the sum of the various parts, but that will be the work of the conclusion.

And finally, a word about what I will describe as the texture of this book. This is the product of my own intellectual habits and practices, which are those of a literary critic rather than those of a social theorist.

What this means in part is that I love working with texts: reading them, interpreting them as best I can, imagining them in the cultural context in which they originated, challenging them if need be by finding out if there are important questions they don't ask but might have been expected to, and so on. Someone with my habits of mind is very likely to get carried away with a text, especially if it is a particularly beautiful or troublesome one. So indeed there are many occasions in this book where the question of privacy recedes into the background, though it is never forgotten entirely. And when it is addressed head-on, as is often the case at key transitional points in each chapter, and as is always the case as the conclusion approaches, the inferences I am able to draw from the texts I interpret will tend to be suggestive rather than definitive. I am not apologizing for the methodology on display here; I'm just trying to account for it. Readers who require quantifiable information about early modern populations, housing conditions, illegitimacy rates, and so forth (all of which could have a conceivable bearing on the question of privacy) will want to turn to the work of social historians. But readers who want to develop a sense of how people thought about privacy in the age of Shakespeare, of the expectations they brought to the experience of privacy, and of the language they used to speak and write about it – these readers will understand why I proceed as I do. It is for them that this book has been written.

Chapter One

Invasions of Privacy in Shakespeare

Readers of Shakespeare today have almost no access to his private life. If he wrote letters, none of them has survived, and any letters he received have perished too, either by accident or design. If he engaged in casual table talk over drinks, he either prevented himself from saying anything indiscreet, or else nobody made it his business to record his conversation. If he kept a diary, or even an account book, there's no surviving evidence of these. So we approach Shakespeare without the kinds of evidence I will be using at every turn in subsequent chapters, and without the complicated set of clues about the ambivalent attractions of privacy that are available in the case of a writer like Andrew Marvell (see chapter 8).

Scholars confronted with the absence I have just described have of course not been prudent in response to it. The biographical appeal of Shakespeare's "sugred Sonnets among his private friends," as Francis Meres described them in *Palladis Tamia* (1598),[1] has been virtually irresistible: hence the various and repeated efforts to find the real-life identities of the Fair Young Man and the Dark Lady of the sonnets in particular. Never mind that Shakespeare invested no discernible effort in the publication of these poems, either before or after their unauthorized printing by T.T. in 1609. In fact, Shakespeare's reticence here makes the notion that the sonnets are *une sequence à clé* all the more

1 See S. Schoenbaum, *William Shakespeare: A Documentary Life* (New York: Oxford University Press, 1975), 140. I quote from Schoenbaum's reproduction of the original text.

tantalizing. The behaviour of readers and scholars on this question, and on many more like it, is inflected by the fact that Shakespeare isn't just an author but a celebrity.

When an author is also a celebrity there's a good chance that any material object thought to reach into his private life will become a fetish object. This is exactly (and understandably) what has happened to the various portraits that may be likenesses of Shakespeare (notably the Chandos portrait, NPG 1 in the National Portrait Gallery) and the commemorative images (the monument in Holy Trinity Church, Stratford-upon-Avon, and the Droeshout engraving on the title page of the First Folio) based on presumably accurate visual evidence.[2] Even these few examples will trigger heated arguments about the prominence of the receding hairline (visible in all three) or the significance of the gold earring (in the Chandos portrait only). But when we debate these questions, I think we should remind ourselves that we are behaving not so much like historical scholars as like fans.

And the same process of fetishization can happen with textual objects too, whether in manuscript or in print. A highly engaging instance of what I mean is Charles Nicholl's *The Lodger: Shakespeare on Silver Street*, a book which takes its point of departure from the records of a litigation in the Court of Requests, 11 May 1612 and subsequently, in which Christopher Mountjoy of Silver Street is being sued by his son-in-law and former apprentice, Stephen Belott, and Shakespeare (among others) is asked for his testimony. It turns out that Joan Johnson, a former maidservant in the Mountjoy household, will refer in her testimony to "one Mr Shakespeare that laye in the house,"[3] and at this point (roughly 1604) Shakespeare becomes the lodger. Now Nicholl's very considerable set of skills as a research scholar are put to work, and he is able to reconstruct a great deal of what must have/might have/may have happened. And reconstruction is the right word: Silver Street no longer exists, except in sixteenth-century maps and descriptions which locate it where the London Wall car park is now situated, under the A1211 (50). But Nicholl brings the street, its houses, and its ambience back to life. The house Shakespeare lived in was occupied by a French immigrant family all of

2 For handsome reproductions of the items just mentioned, and commentary on the evidence about their status, see Tarnya Cooper, *Searching for Shakespeare* (New Haven, CT: Yale University Press, 2006), 48–61.

3 *The Lodger: Shakespeare on Silver Street* (London: Allen Lane, 2007), 288.

whom seem to have been engaged in the thriving trade of tire making, that is, creating flashy and expensive headdresses for women of fashion. In addition to Christopher Mountjoy, his apprentices, and servants, the household included his wife, Marie, and their only child, Mary. Now we have a landlady for Shakespeare and, to judge by the evidence Nicholl assembles, a fairly exotic one: someone who speaks French, visits the astrologer Simon Forman, attracts the erotic attention of the mercer Henry Wood (123–5), provides a headdress for Queen Anne (143), and so on. Throughout Nicholl's account there is the poorly suppressed wish that the Shakespeare/Marie Moutjoy connection be so much more than just a tenant/landlady relationship. Nicholl asks, "What did this apparently amorous and adulterous Frenchwoman mean to Shakespeare, and he to her?" (246) Clearly, he wants to imply that they were lovers, but historical research won't take him where he wants to go: "If I had to sum up the relationship between Shakespeare and Marie Mountjoy I would say only that she was his friend – a description of her at once bland and deeply resonant. If there was something more, it remains a secret between them" (248). So we are back once again where we started: denied access to whatever may have happened in Shakespeare's private life.

The list of celebrity fetish objects could be extended indefinitely were we to include items from Shakespeare's professional life: the various printed quartos (both good and bad), images of the Globe Theatre on engraved maps (identified both correctly and incorrectly), comments in verse and prose (both admiring and spiteful) by his contemporaries, and so on. But I will restrict myself to just one further example: the words "Item I gyve unto my wife my second best bed with the furniture" inserted as an interlinear addition on the final page of Shakespeare's last will and testament, dated 25 March 1616.[4] If you care about Shakespeare at all, it's difficult to maintain cool indifference when you read these words, especially when you realize that they were added later to a document that otherwise doesn't mention a wife. These are words, moreover, chosen and presumably dictated by someone deeply familiar with the powers of language. So scholars can't resist speculating, as Stephen Greenblatt does quite memorably in this comment about how and why Shakespeare may have added the interlinear bequest:

4 Schoenbaum, *Documentary Life*, 245.

> Someone – his daughter Susanna, perhaps, or his lawyer – may have called this erasure, this total absence of acknowledgment, to his attention. Or perhaps as he lay in his bed, his strength ebbing away, Shakespeare himself brooded on his relationship to Anne – on the sexual excitement that once drew him to her, on the failure of the marriage to give him what he wanted, on his own infidelities and perhaps on hers, on the intimacies he had forged elsewhere, on the son they had buried, on the strange, ineradicable distaste for her that he felt deep within him.[5]

Germaine Greer quotes exactly these two sentences in *Shakespeare's Wife*, a book in which she sets herself the daunting task of persuading us that Ann Shakespeare was in all likelihood a perfectly lovely person, and that her marriage to William was, for all we know, a delightful experience for both of them. Along the way she identifies and critiques, with characteristic brilliance, the various kinds of masculine condescension which have given us the more usual and more dismal story of Shakespeare's matrimonial life. What we are given by "Greenblatt and his ilk" is certainly not something we should wish to have: "It is to be hoped that the truth is less contemptible."[6] But if the truth is closer to what Greer wants us to believe, then we're left wondering why, after her husband's burial, "Ann had to endure the opening and reading of the will" (314). I'm inclined to agree with the judgment planted in the nicely chosen verb "endure," but I don't think it helps to rescue Ann Shakespeare from a truth that must indeed have been painful.

What I am arguing, implicitly, is that attempts to invade Shakespeare's own privacy will bring mixed results at best. Even very fine scholars and critics, like those I've been citing, will find that they are not so much discovering Shakespeare's private life as inventing it. But we need not throw up our hands in despair at the prospect of learning nothing about privacy from Shakespeare. We need only admit that his best thinking on this question, as on most others, is embedded in his most public work: the plays he wrote for performance by the Lord Chamberlain's and the King's men. So I propose turning to these dramatic scripts to discover some of the ways in which Shakespeare wanted the actors in his company

5 *Will in the World: How Shakespeare Became Shakespeare* (New York: Norton, 2004), 145.

6 *Shakespeare's Wife* (London: Bloomsbury, 2007), 321.

to use the word "private," and to watch some of the scenes in which the concept of privacy was of particular interest to him.

Privacy in the Playhouse

The word "private" as Shakespeare assigns it to the actors who speak his lines appears to be distributed through all four of the clusters of meaning that I described in the introduction. The first strand of meaning, having to do with the absence of official status and hence lacking authority in the public domain, is resonantly present in *Henry V* in the speeches of both Michael Williams and King Harry during the scene which shows us Harry disguising himself as a citizen in order to survey the morale of his troops. Williams points out that a soldier's danger far exceeds the king's and that there's no room for redress: there's precious little "that a poor and private displeasure can do against a monarch" (4.1.189–90).[7] Williams rightly takes his private status to be a kind of deprivation. Harry will of course put his own spin on this distinction when he has the stage to himself:

> What infinite heartsease
> Must kings neglect that private men enjoy?
> And what have kings that privates have not too,
> Save ceremony, save general ceremony? (4.1.224–7)

As he so characteristically does, Shakespeare offers us two competing claims about the value of the term under discussion, and here he situates these claims with great social precision.

The cluster of meaning most frequently at play in Shakespeare's drama is the one which has to do with secrecy of various kinds (identified as the third strand in the introduction). Sometimes this meaning is obvious and meant to be so, as in Iago's insinuating question, "What,/To kiss in private?" (*Othello* 4.1.1–2), or in Coriolanus's promise to the citizens (never fulfilled, it turns out), "I have wounds to show you which shall be yours in private" (2.3.72–3). But secrecy may imply the absence of

7 *Henry V*, ed. Gary Taylor, Oxford Shakespeare (Oxford: Clarendon, 1982). Unless otherwise noted, quotations from Shakespeare's plays and poems are from the individual volumes of the Oxford Shakespeare, as identified under Shakespeare's name in the bibliography.

official sanction, and therefore meaning clusters one and three often overlap, as they seem to do routinely when "private" has the sense of "undeclared": Somerset's warning to Richard Duke of York, "Your private grudge, my lord of York, will out,/Though ne'er so cunningly you smother it" (*1 Henry VI*, 4.1.109–10), alludes to both the secrecy of York's intentions and the implicit declaration York is making in this scene by carrying a white rose rather than a red.

Surprisingly, Shakespeare seldom uses "private" to imply ownership, in the way that phrases such as "private property" or "private enterprise" have led us to expect. Perhaps his closest approach to this meaning cluster (identified as the second strand in the introduction) happens in *Julius Caesar* when Antony points out to the plebeians that Caesar's will leaves to them "His private arbours, and new-planted orchards,/On this side Tiber" (3.2.241–2). But even here, because we are hearing about a conspicuously public figure, "private arbours" may designate those places he owned as an individual rather than those he controlled as head of state. In *Henry VIII*, when Katherine resists Wolsey's suggestion that she and the cardinals "withdraw/Into your private chamber" (3.1.27–8), we have another example of a place designated for private use, but this occurs in a scene that most scholars would assign to Fletcher.

Does Shakespeare use the word "private" to suggest various kinds of interiority? The answer is clearly yes, even though examples are not frequent. In *The Two Gentlemen of Verona* Valentine remarks that "The private wound is deepest" (5.4.71) when he discovers that Proteus has betrayed him. But this sounds like a mere formula, especially when it is cancelled a few seconds later by Valentine's forgiveness of Proteus and his notorious offer to surrender Sylvia to his friend. It would be tempting to argue that Julia creates a far more subtle sense of interiority when she speaks to her maid Lucetta about "the inly touch of love" (2.7.18). In *The Rape of Lucrece*, though Shakespeare is not working with the goal of theatrical performance in mind, he sets himself the demanding task of representing the heroine's inner state after her violation. All four of the instances of the word "private" in this text are spoken by Lucrece, the first of them in a specific attempt to describe her humiliation: "O unseen shame, invisible disgrace!/O unfelt sore, crest-wounding private scar!" (827–8). The crest that is wounded is the reputation of her husband, Collatine. But there can be no doubt that the location of the "private scar" is Lucrece's inner self. In *Troilus and Cressida* Ulysses claims to have heard a splendidly favourable description of Troilus's many virtues from Aeneas, who knows Troilus "Even to his inches, and with private soul/

Did in great Ilium thus translate to me" (4.5.111–12). We should be wary of Ulysses; irony is the very water he swims in. But the designation of someone's "private soul," even if it's just a ruse to take us in, is surely also an allusion to a profoundly felt interiority.

Shakespeare's preferred senses of "private," however, have to do with social status or secrecy, and not with psychological depth. Still, it doesn't follow that he shows little interest in the states of mind and being associated with the inner self. In fact, his practice as a playwright shows a growing attraction to exactly this question, especially in the plays he wrote in mid-career, when his abilities as a theatre artist were already at the height of their development and his grasp of the human predicament was both ample and subtle. Most of what follows in this chapter will be a discussion of Shakespeare's take on the question of privacy in two of these mid-career plays: *Hamlet* and *Twelfth Night*.

The Heart of Hamlet's Mystery

The credit for locating a distinctive inwardness in the character of Hamlet, or the blame for doing so if you prefer, belongs to the German Romantics. I am thinking in part of the famous reflections on *Hamlet* in *Wilhelm Meister's Apprenticeship* by Johann Wolfgang von Goethe. While he struggles to make his mark in the acting profession, Wilhelm has the opportunity to play the role of Hamlet, and he takes this assignment very seriously indeed. He studies the text for every scrap of evidence about Hamlet's character before the death of his father and the hasty remarriage of his mother. He believes that Hamlet, as we first see him, is carrying a burden of "reflection and sorrow"[8] that he is not capable of bearing or at least not ready to bear. He finds the key to Hamlet's situation expressed in the couplet which all but ends Act 1: "The time is out of joint; O cursed spite/That ever I was born to set it right" (1.5.186–7).[9] And he explains his view to Serlo, the director of his theatre troupe: "To me it is clear that Shakespeare meant, in the present case, to represent the effects of a great action laid upon a soul unfit for the performance of it"

8 *Wilhelm Meister's Apprenticeship*, trans. Thomas Carlyle (London: John C. Nimmo, 1903), 1:303.

9 *Hamlet*, ed. Ann Thompson and Neil Taylor, Arden Shakespeare (London: Methuen Drama, 2006), 227. Subsequent references are to this edition and will be made in parentheses.

(1:304). If Hamlet's soul is like a "costly jar," then the obligations now demanded of him are like an oak tree planted within him; as the roots of the tree expand, the jar will be shattered. "A lovely, pure, noble, and most moral nature, without the strength of nerve which forms a hero, sinks beneath a burden it cannot bear and must not cast away" (1:304).

The rich archive of commentary on this interpretation of Hamlet's character includes repeated warnings that we ought to distinguish between Goethe's own position (whatever that may have been) and the position he assigns to a fictional character, Wilhelm (who demonstrates his limits and blind spots on many occasions).[10] Still, even if Wilhelm's eventual performance of the part and his company's performance of the whole play can be subjected to critical scrutiny that Goethe himself may have encouraged, Wilhelm's view of Hamlet's basic character seems to me a projection of Goethe's own. This indeed was the assumption made by August Wilhelm von Schlegel when he lectured on *Hamlet* to an admiring audience in Vienna over 200 years ago, and specifically distanced himself from what he saw as Goethe's too "favourable"[11] assessment of Hamlet's nature.

The thesis of Schlegel's *Hamlet* lecture has had a remarkable afterlife; he calls *Hamlet* "a tragedy of thought" (404),[12] a claim that appears to conflate psychological, aesthetic, and epistemological meaning. First, there is Hamlet's habit "Of thinking too precisely on th'event" (4.4.40), which stands between his intentions and his ability to act. Here we have the first stirrings of the question, Why does Hamlet delay? – a question which would find its classic exposition in A.C. Bradley's *Shakespearean Tragedy*.[13] Schlegel goes on to claim that the inconclusive "perplexity"

10 See for example William Diamond, "Wilhelm Meister's Interpretation of Hamlet," *Modern Philology* 23 (1925–6): 91–2; Linwood R. DeLong, "Reflections on a Remarkable Performance of *Hamlet*: A Re-examination of the *Hamlet* Scene in Goethe's *Wilhelm Meisters Lehrjahre*," *Man and Nature/L'Homme et la Nature* 5 (1986): 80; and Jane V. Curran, *Goethe's "Wilhelm Meister's Apprenticeship": A Reader's Commentary* (Rochester, NY: Camden House, 2002), 154.

11 *Course of Lectures on Dramatic Art and Literature*, trans. John Black and A.J.W. Morrison, 2nd ed. (1846; repr., New York: AMS Press, 1965), 405.

12 In the German original, "ein Gedankentrauerspiel"; see *Vorlesen über dramatische Kunst und Literatur*, in *Kritische Schriften und Briefe* (Stuttgart: W. Kohlhammer Verlag, 1966), 6:168.

13 *Shakespearean Tragedy: Lectures on "Hamlet," "Othello," "King Lear," "Macbeth,"* 2nd ed. (London: Macmillan, 1905), 70–86.

represented on stage is "calculated to call forth the very same meditation in the minds of the spectators" (404). With this judgment he anticipated the many controversies about audience response that may be alluded to by quoting one sentence of Stephen Booth's brilliant essay: "*Hamlet* is the tragedy of an audience that cannot make up its mind."[14] And for Schlegel, "thought" is an epistemological category too, as for example in his interpretation of Hamlet's quip to Rosencrantz, "there is nothing either good or bad, but thinking makes it so."[15] Schlegel infers that "the poet loses himself here in labyrinths of thought, in which neither end nor beginning is discoverable" (406). The problem of knowledge is persistently foregrounded in *Hamlet*, without any resolution that could prevent humanity from falling into "the abyss of scepticism" (406). And this line of argument signals the pattern of epistemological enquiry that *Hamlet* will provoke, notably in a work such as Eric P. Levy's "'Things Standing Thus Unknown': The Epistemology of Ignorance in *Hamlet*."[16]

I am of course deleting many of the intermediate steps by which the views of the German Romantics came to be adopted as essential to the culture of Shakespeare interpretation. Among the first of these would be Coleridge's lectures on Shakespeare, which, whether or not they are rightly regarded as examples of plagiarism, certainly had the effect of promoting Schlegel's views in the anglophone world.[17] Among the most widely disseminated would be Laurence Olivier's film version in which the soliloquies are delivered by voice-over so as to suggest that we are not hearing Hamlet speak (overtly), but are listening to the unravelling of his thoughts.

I do not wish to imply that the turn inward has been unproblematically endorsed by everyone engaged in *Hamlet* interpretation. Nothing in *Hamlet* interpretation is unproblematic. So there have of course been

---

14 "On the Value of *Hamlet*," in *Reinterpretations of Elizabethan Drama: Selected Papers from the English Institute*, ed. Norman Rabkin (New York: Columbia University Press, 1969), 152.

15 This remark occurs only in the Folio text, and is therefore relegated to Appendix 1, 466, by the current editors of the Arden Shakespeare.

16 In Levy's *Hamlet and the Rethinking of Man* (Madison, NJ: Fairleigh Dickinson University Press, 2008), 121–36.

17 See, for example, Coleridge's description of Hamlet's predilection for "great, enormous, intellectual activity, and a consequent proportionate aversion to real action"; in Coleridge, *Shakespearean Criticism*, ed. Thomas Middleton Raysor, 2nd ed. (London: Dent, 1960), 1:34.

dissenting voices and counter-arguments. I am not going to outline and comment on these positions one at a time; to do so would prevent me from doing anything more. So instead I will hold up for admiration the opening pages of Katharine Eisaman Maus's *Inwardness and Theater in the English Renaissance.* Maus begins by quoting at some length from Hamlet's rather testy first speech to Gertrude, in which he distinguishes between his outward display of mourning, "the trappings and the suits of woe," and the real grief he harbours in his heart: "that within which passes show" (1.2.85–6). She then shows how this speech participates in a widespread rhetoric of inward versus outward in the culture of Shakespeare's time, a rhetoric which tended to privilege the inward (by implying its authenticity) over the outward (by pointing out its ability to mislead). In her opening gambit Maus shows quite elegantly how and why inwardness matters when we're interpreting *Hamlet,* and at the same time she tactfully responds to some of the critiques of the assumption she is making.[18]

Still, inwardness is not identical to privacy; scholars who acknowledge the artfulness by which Shakespeare crafts the inner workings of Hamlet's mind seldom use the concept of privacy in order to do so. Sometimes privacy is explicitly removed from the category of notions that ought to concern us. In his book-length study of *Hamlet* Stephen Greenblatt, for example, declares imperiously: "There is no strict dividing line for Shakespeare between the private and the public, between the bedchamber and the throne room, between the imaginary and the actual."[19] This pronouncement is completely unearned, in the sense that it is not supported by evidence of any kind; it is, I would suggest, a cliché circulated by critics who used to be known as new historicists, a cliché that owes its currency to its compatibility with new-historicist objectives rather than to anything in the plays of Shakespeare or the culture which nurtured them.

My objective, then, in the argument that follows, is to convince you that the distinction between the private and the public does matter to Hamlet himself, and therefore mattered, apparently, to the writer who created and, presumably, to the spectators who first encountered the play.

18 *Inwardness and Theater in the English Renaissance* (Chicago: University of Chicago Press, 1995), 1–6.

19 *Hamlet in Purgatory* (Princeton, NJ: Princeton University Press, 2001), 174.

I have already alluded to Hamlet as we first see him, and to his assertion of the value of "that within." All we need to add to this picture is Hamlet's unwillingness to grant other people access to his inner self, and we have the portrait of someone fiercely protective of his own privacy. Having manoeuvred Guildenstern into admitting that he cannot play the recorder, Hamlet rounds on him with this: "Why, look you now how unworthy a thing you make of me: you would play upon me! You would seem to know my stops, you would pluck out the heart of my mystery, you would sound me from my lowest note to my compass. And there is much music, excellent voice, in this little organ. Yet cannot you make it speak. 'Sblood! Do you think I am easier to be played on than a pipe?" (3.2.355–62). A first principle in defining privacy is the question of access: if I decide who can enter my room, then it is a private space; if others make the decision for me, or are able to enter without my consent, then it is not. Yes, Rosencrantz and Guildenstern are on a spying mission, but that doesn't change the equation: they are seeking access to "that within," to the "mystery" which Hamlet declares is private and therefore unavailable to them.

When he is dealing with us, the spectators, Hamlet is far more generous with himself. I am thinking here of his great soliloquies, only one of which opens with what we might call rhetorical punctuation, "Now I am alone" (2.2.484), but all of which contribute to the uncanny bond between Hamlet and the spectators. We take it as a special privilege that Hamlet, who guards his private thoughts so jealously against the enquiries of Rosencrantz and Guildenstern, or the peering of Polonius, or even the loving entreaties of Gertrude and Ophelia, should be so ready to confide in us. And when he does confide, he speaks in the language of interiority. The setting for "To be, or not to be" is "in the mind"; that is where "the will" is confronted by "conscience"; that is where "the native hue of resolution/Is sicklied o'er with the pale cast of thought" (3.1.55–84). The language here is too familiar to allow further quotation; everyone can quote what Hamlet says here. And everyone who has watched even a competent theatrical production will remember the thrill of being able to see right into Hamlet's inner self. The spectators may not be able to pluck out the heart of Hamlet's mystery, but at times they feel almost close enough to do so.

For someone so deeply committed to defending his own privacy, Hamlet is remarkably unwilling to respect the privacy of others. This is high on the list of what makes his treatment of Ophelia look so cruel. Polonius has heard that Hamlet has "Given private time" (1.3.91) to his daughter, an allegation that she confirms and a situation she clearly relishes. Indeed, she makes her most private space, her closet, accessible to Hamlet. What she gets in return is not the whispers of love that she longs for, but a demonstration of something she doesn't understand:

> My lord, as I was sewing in my closet
> Lord Hamlet, with his doublet all unbraced,
> No hat upon his head, his stockings fouled,
> Ungartered and down-gyved to his ankle,
> Pale as his shirt, his knees knocking each other,
> And with a look so piteous in purport
> As if he had been loosed out of hell
> To speak of horrors, he comes before me. (2.1.74–81)

The behaviour of women, especially of young aristocratic women, was of course subject to surveillance of many kinds, as I will show at length in chapter 5. Even so, a young woman's closet should be a refuge of sorts, where she can escape from the pressure of being watched. Hamlet not only enters her closet, as if he had free access to it, but displays himself in a way that she is bound to find disruptive. The unbraced doublet, the ungartered stockings, and the hatless head were associated with love-melancholy, but here they seem more like the signs of a man's body about to escape from its careful wrap of Elizabethan clothing. That Ophelia finds the incident unsettling is apparent from the way in which she tells her father about it.

The nunnery scene is a further assault on Ophelia's private self, an assault that leaves her in the position "of ladies most deject and wretched" (3.1.154). But I pass over it in order to observe the treatment Hamlet gives her in public, in the moments just before the dumbshow which introduces *The Murder of Gonzago.* As the courtiers assemble, Gertrude calls for Hamlet to "sit by me" (3.2.105), but he chooses Ophelia instead, and asks her: "Lady, shall I lie in your lap?" (3.2.108). There's no right answer to this, as Ophelia quickly learns; while she seeks to minimize the damage at every turn, he only escalates the attack: "Do you think I meant country matters?" (3.2.110). When she tries to sidestep this with "I think nothing, my lord" (111), he is relentless: "That's a fair thought to lie between maids' legs" (113). While she tries her best to retreat behind conventional modesty, he insists on demonstrating that he can and will speak in public about what she would have referred to as her private parts. If this last point seems strained, recall that Hamlet gets Rosencrantz and Guildenstern to admit that they live near Fortune's "waist, or in the middle of her favours" (2.2.227–8), a description then capped by Guildenstern's line, "Faith, her privates we" (229). A conversation of this kind can seem innocent enough, if spoken by adolescent boys; and it is no worse than banter in bad taste when spoken by men. What makes Hamlet's use of the rhetoric of women's private parts offensive is that he uses it in public to humiliate a woman who is still deeply in love with him.

Soon we will find him in Gertrude's closet, though this time he has at least been invited. This is a justly famous and in its way a very busy scene, and I will be all but ignoring some of the big questions that arise from it (why Hamlet feels so little remorse after having killed Polonius, why Gertrude can't see the Ghost when Hamlet clearly can, and so on) in order to focus on the issue of privacy. It would appear that, in his original instructions to Hamlet, the Ghost urged him explicitly to respect Gertrude's privacy:

> Taint not thy mind nor let thy soul contrive
> Against thy mother aught; leave her to heaven
> And to those thorns that in her bosom lodge
> To prick and sting her. (1.5.85–8)

Hamlet clearly ignores this part of his mandate when, upon entering her closet, he accuses her of speaking "with a wicked tongue" (3.4.11) and says he will expose her secrets:

> You go not till I set you up a glass
> Where you may see the inmost part of you. (3.4.18–19)

This belligerent opening move leads, with blinding speed, to Gertrude's cry for help, to a similar cry from Polonius, and then to the perfectly guided rapier thrust which impales Polonius.

You'd think that all the excitement might distract Hamlet, but no. His mind is deeply tainted by loathing of his mother's current sex life, which he describes as living

> In the rank sweat of an enseamed bed,
> Stewed in corruption, honeying and making love
> Over the nasty sty – (3.4.90–2)

At this point the Ghost appears in order to "whet" Hamlet's "almost blunted purpose" (3.4.107), and for a few minutes he treats his mother more gently. Only for a few minutes, however, because he cannot let go of her sexual behaviour: "but go not to my uncle's bed," he begs her; "Refrain tonight,/And that shall lend a kind of easiness/To the next abstinence" (3.4.157–65). What arouses disgust about Hamlet's treatment of Gertrude in this scene is the vividness of his sexual imagination, and the alacrity with which he returns to the images which it feeds him. At the end of the scene when Gertrude, now reduced to passivity, asks "What shall I do?" (3.4.178), he prefaces his answer with more of the same:

> Not this, by no means, that I bid you do –
> Let the bloat King tempt you again to bed,
> Pinch wanton on your cheek, call you his mouse,
> And let him for a pair of reechy kisses,
> Or paddling in your neck with his damned fingers,
> Make you to ravel all this matter out
> That I essentially am not in madness,
> But mad in craft. (3.4.179–86)

These lines remain shocking, even after Freud and Ernest Jones,[20] perhaps not so much for what they say about Hamlet as for what they do to Gertrude: that is, they treat her sex life as if it is her son's business, subject to his management, without a scruple of respect for her privacy.

Hamlet's willingness to be invasive is not confined to women and their closets. Aboard ship he intercepts the "packet" carried by Rosencrantz and Guildenstern and retreats to his "own room" so as "to unfold/Their grand commission" (5.2.15–18), a document that in our day would certainly be classified "top secret." I'm not blaming Hamlet for taking an action that saves his life; I'm pointing out, however, that it is an invasive action, an action that requires rashness – "And praised be rashness for it" (5.2.7) – rather than respect for the private and confidential. To observe that Hamlet takes such liberties because he's (rightly) convinced that he's the centre of an espionage plot changes the morality but not

20 Freud, *The Interpretation of Dreams*, trans. Joyce Crick (Oxford: Oxford University Press, 1999), and Ernest Jones, *Hamlet and Oedipus* (1949; repr., Garden City, NY: Doubleday Anchor Books, 1954).

the meaning of what he does. Indeed, it might be fair to say that all of his assaults on privacy are based on his conviction that former friends, allies, and indeed his own mother are cosying up to Claudius and are therefore no longer deserving of his trust. This would provide him with motivation for, but it doesn't excuse him from, humiliating Ophelia, browbeating Gertrude, or (for that matter) sentencing Rosencrantz and Guildenstern to death.

The case of Laertes is slightly different, though it certainly includes Hamlet's violation of his privacy. I am alluding to the scene at Ophelia's graveside where Hamlet breaks cover not when he learns the identity of the person being buried, but when he sees Laertes leap into her grave so that he may hold her "once more in mine arms" (5.1.239). Laertes's action provokes a desperately competitive reaction: the declaration, "This is I, Hamlet the Dane" (246–7), a physical struggle with Laertes, and then the amazing claim:

> I loved Ophelia – forty thousand brothers
> Could not with all their quantity of love
> Make up my sum. (5.1.258–60)

Even if this is true, it is an amazingly selfish and self-centred position to be holding. In a play so fundamentally concerned with mourning, Hamlet chooses to disrupt the one opportunity Laertes has to mourn his sister. And what he seems to attack with special violence is the private bond of intimacy between brother and sister.

The spectators of course have just seen Laertes make a shady deal with Claudius that will lead (and is designed to lead) to Hamlet's death. But Hamlet can know nothing about this. Perhaps that is why he uncharacteristically, and in the Folio text only, feels "sorry" (Appendix 1, 472) for the way he treated Laertes. This is the one case in which he cannot excuse his violation of another's privacy by pointing the finger at the other's political opportunism or corruption. The spectators can excuse him, but he can't excuse himself.

Among the major players – aside from the company of players, about whom I will have a word to say in due course – that leaves only Claudius and Horatio. It is worthwhile to ask briefly of each of these in turn whether Hamlet respects (or invades) the space they might consider private.

Claudius of course is the most conspicuously *public* figure in the play. He is represented almost always as engaged in official business: speaking to his assembled courtiers, debriefing ambassadors, hearing advice from his trusted allies, defusing an attempted rebellion, and so on. For this reason the effort to invade his private self will be different in kind, and perhaps also in degree. From the outset it would seem that Claudius is trying to invade Hamlet's privacy, as he turns to him with the sound of kinship in his voice: "But now, my cousin Hamlet, and my son – " (1.2.64). Hamlet replies by refusing intimacy: "A little more than kin, and less than kind" (65). In effect Hamlet is saying that Claudius will be unable to invade his private space, try as he may. And this is perhaps the first indication that the struggle between these two "mighty opposites" (5.2.61) will be, on the question of privacy as with so much else, a stand-off for most of the play.

Certainly Hamlet will try to invade the private space of Claudius's guilty conscience. This is exactly what he is up to when he stages *The Murder of Gonzago* and asks Horatio to help him watch the king. And it's equally clear that Claudius is eager to discover the reliable truth about Hamlet's private self; the strategy of spying that he repeatedly endorses could have no other motive. After the interruption of *The Murder of Gonzago* the stalemate I have been describing has been reinforced rather than broken. Hamlet rightly thinks that he has observed evidence of the king's guilt: "O good Horatio, I'll take the Ghost's word for a thousand pound" (3.2.278–9). But Claudius, having been careful to observe Hamlet while he himself is being observed, and perhaps alarmed by the tactics of "Lucianus, nephew to the king" (3.2.237), decides that Hamlet is too much of a threat, and makes the hasty arrangements to send him to England.

This leads to the scene in which Claudius tries to pray and Hamlet passes up his golden opportunity to do the deed. What strikes me as interesting about this scene is that it perpetuates the stalemate which keeps these two bound to one another. Claudius reveals his bad conscience, and his inability to repent, to the spectators. But Hamlet, observing his uncle in the posture of prayer, does not enquire deeply enough into the state of his soul. When Hamlet says, "That would be scanned" (3.3.75), he refers only to his own reasoning, and not to the private utterances of Claudius which the audience has just heard. It's as if there's an agreement of sorts which keeps these enemies from looking too deeply into one another. When you've identified your mortal enemy, the last thing you want to engage with is his private self.

The Players of course have no private lives, or so at least Hamlet pretends when he calls them "the abstract and brief chronicles of the time" (2.2.462–3). Their identity rests on what they do, not on who they are, and what they do is represent "actions that a man might play" (1.2.84). Hamlet is of course keenly interested in what the Players have to offer, and he's eager to use their skills to his own advantage. But he doesn't assume, even when the 1st Player "has tears in's eyes" (2.2.458), that he's watching anything more than a performance. "What's Hecuba to him, or he to her,/That he should weep for her?" (2.2.494–5). Theatrical performance, to Hamlet, is the diametrical opposite of the private self which enfolds the heart of his mystery.

I'm tempted to say that Horatio, like the Players, has no private self and is therefore not vulnerable to invasion. This would hold true in general, but it would not explain the deep and lasting bond that holds Hamlet and Horatio together. Hamlet expresses his need for solidarity with his friend in metaphors of inwardness:

> Give me that man
> That is not passion's slave, and I will wear him
> In my heart's core – ay, in my heart of heart –
> As I do thee. (3.2.67–70)[21]

In Act 5, while Hamlet is most vulnerable, Horatio is constantly at his side. Yet we learn next to nothing about him, certainly not enough to imagine a private life for him. We don't know his family background, his social standing, his erotic preferences, his literary tastes. All of these are qualities that Shakespeare is capable of signalling, with admirable celerity, even in minor characters. (Think of Hastings in *Richard III* or Don Pedro in *Much Ado about Nothing*.) Horatio, despite the favour shown him by Hamlet, remains surprisingly neutral.

That is because, I believe, Horatio is our representative, he is a stand-in for the audience, he is the spectator par excellence. The most important tasks he undertakes are exercises in watching. First he is brought along by Marcellus "to watch the minutes of this night" (1.1.26) for the appearance of the Ghost. At the performance of *The Murder of Gonzago* Hamlet gives him a similar assignment: "Even with the very comment of thy soul/Observe my uncle" (3.2.75–6). And since Horatio has been in the uniquely privileged position of going along with Hamlet to his

21 William W.E. Slights quotes and comments with great subtlety on this passage as he approaches the end of his wide-ranging study *The Heart in the Age of Shakespeare* (Cambridge: Cambridge University Press, 2008), 179–80.

final reckoning, of hearing Hamlet address that final speech to him until "The rest is silence" (5.2.342), he remains in the position of spectatorship to the end, with the added responsibility of telling Hamlet's story to the "yet unknowing world" (5.2.363). The spectator's role is not empty after all, but it is filled with an inwardness other than his own.

Partly because Horatio is our representative, but for a great many other reasons too, we as spectators confer greater authority upon Hamlet than upon any other Shakespearean character. Among the reasons for this phenomenon are the sheer number of lines he speaks, the brilliance and beauty of his language in both prose and verse, the subtlety of the judgments he makes especially but not only in his soliloquies, the quickness and amplitude of his mind, and the growing conviction that Claudius, no matter what he says, will do everything he can to disinherit his nephew. This is a necessarily incomplete list of reasons, but it is long enough to suggest how urgently we as spectators want to be on Hamlet's side in any conflict. The results of this partiality are also numerous, but I will mention only two. One is the stigma of incest which we follow Hamlet (and the Ghost of his father) in attaching to the marriage between Gertrude and Claudius. We tend not to ask ourselves whether Gertrude and Claudius are blood relations, or how incest was defined in medieval Denmark. We just think of the relationship as incestuous because Hamlet himself does. Even more remarkably, we refuse to blame him for sending Rosencrantz and Guildenstern to their inglorious execution. When he hears Hamlet's account of this matter, Horatio does ask for a slight pause: "So Guildenstern and Rosencrantz go to't" (5.2.56). But Hamlet picks up the pace with hardly more than a stutter step: "They are not near my conscience. Their defeat/Does by their own insinuation grow" (5.2.57–8). And I think we as spectators follow Hamlet again, with almost scandalous ease, into thinking that Hamlet acted in self-defence (which indeed he did) and that therefore the question of how he acted needn't even arise. I suspect we would also fail to remember that the death of this pair is reported by an English Ambassador in the closing moments of the play, if Tom Stoppard hadn't conferred a posthumous immortality upon them.

But, while Hamlet charms us as spectators into seeing it his way, the impression he makes on other characters in the play is remarkably different. He seems to have a talent for making those around him feel defensive, or hostile, or stupid, or some combination of all three. The conspicuous mourning costume he wears when we first see him makes both Claudius and Gertrude uncomfortable, and the effect is amplified when he deigns to speak to his elders. When Gertrude dares to use the word "seems" in addressing him, he makes her pay a heavy price: "'Seems' madam – nay, it is – I know not 'seems'" (1.2.76). And at this point he begins his lecture about the difference between outer and inner, the sham and the authentic. In fact he lectures other people, often belligerently, whenever he wants to. Polonius, often ridiculed for prolixity himself, has to endure Hamlet's insults about the incapacities of old men, his tactless allusions to Jephthah's daughter, and his instructions to identify a cloud as camel-shaped, but also "like a weasel" and "like a whale" (3.2.370–2). I've already drawn attention to the ways in which he humiliates Ophelia, hectors Gertrude, and shouts defiance at Laertes. Yes, Hamlet makes Claudius desperately uncomfortable, to the point that he fears for his life. But, in one way or another, Hamlet makes everyone at Elsinore very nervous. Everyone except Horatio, that is, whose special placement I have already tried to describe.

The ways in which privacy is asserted, defended, violated, and shared turn out to tell us a great deal about the double perspective I have just been outlining. When Hamlet chooses to open his private thoughts to you, as he does to Horatio, as he once did (apparently) to Ophelia, and as he does repeatedly to the spectators, you will be taken in, charmed, and seduced by his charisma. But if he chooses not to share his inner self with you, don't try to invade his privacy. The results will be ungratifying at best, and probably catastrophic, because Hamlet will defend the heart of his mystery with a fierceness that you have to respect. Looked at in this way, the distinction between public and private matters a great deal to Hamlet himself and should matter as well to everyone who wants to join Horatio in retelling his story.

A clear-minded appraisal of privacy and its invasions may offer us a new approach into the world of *Hamlet*, but I think the converse is also true. Because of the way in which it is organized, *Hamlet* teaches us something of great interest about the nature of privacy, or at least about the way in which we experience it. Privacy is by definition a two-way street, and each person's experience of it is inflected by the direction in which he or she is going. On this side of the street there's *my* privacy, and (like Hamlet) I regard it as profoundly important. I will protect it from fools and enemies, and share it only with those I love. On the other side of the street is *your* privacy, marked out as such by the sign "private and confidential." Does this nomenclature incline me to offer you the respect you deserve, or does it tempt me to ask: I wonder what he's trying to hide? *Hamlet* creates an awareness of both sides of the street: the *my* side is clearly Hamlet's, and the *your* side is that occupied by the many people at Elsinore who fear, suspect, and misunderstand him. Since Hamlet has in our culture been virtually given iconic status as the subject position, it should not be surprising to find that he has something to tell us about privacy.

The Price of Privacy in Illyria

The relationship between *Hamlet* and *Twelfth Night* is not just a matter of chronological proximity. A phrase such as *theatrical proximity* would be a slight improvement, if it could be taken to imply that the two plays rotated through the repertory of the Lord Chamberlain's men at the same time, and that spectators who went to the Globe to see *Hamlet* on a given afternoon in 1601 might be able to return to the same theatre just days later to see the same actors perform *Twelfth Night*. Under these circumstances, it would be easy to notice a surprising number of similarities between the two productions. Perhaps the most striking parallel would be the ability of the man in black to attract the spectators' attention. This coincidence relied in part on a casting decision: the charismatic Richard Burbage in all likelihood played both parts, Hamlet and Malvolio.[22] Both plays are concerned with acts of mourning: Hamlet's grief at his father's death, Ophelia's at hers, Laertes's at his sister's; Olivia's mourning vow and costume in response to the deaths of her father and her brother. Both plays require and indeed showcase the actorly skills of swordsmanship, singing, and mimicry. But now I am belabouring the obvious point that both scripts are designed to exploit the talents and resources of the Lord Chamberlain's men in the very early years of the seventeenth century.

So let me press beyond these adventitious connections by suggesting that, in both plays, Shakespeare is deeply worried about, indeed

22 The assumption that Burbage played Hamlet is uncontroversial; see, for example, Andrew Gurr, *The Shakespeare Company, 1594–1642* (Cambridge: Cambridge University Press, 2004), 222; the view that he also played Malvolio is persuasively argued by David Grote, *The Best Actors in the World: Shakespeare and His Acting Company* (Westport, CT: Greenwood Press, 2002), 105–6. T.W. Baldwin had suggested earlier that Malvolio was played by Augustine Phillips, with Burbage taking Orsino (see *The Organization and Personnel of the Shakespearean Company* [Princeton, NJ: Princeton University Press, 1927], 238, 255), but this view is no longer tenable.

tormented by, the consequences of misinterpretation. Feste gives an explicit signal of this concern when he cries out, in response to Olivia's order to take him away, "Misprision in the highest degree!" (1.5.50). Feste has been manipulating language to suggest that, since the real fool is Olivia herself, the servants must understand her command as an order to have herself taken away; when Olivia corrects this with "Sir, I bade them take away you" (1.5.49), Feste claims he has been misinterpreted. "Misprision" is his way of calling for a review of the evidence; etymologically dependent on the verb "misprize," Feste's word implies "contempt, scorn; failure to appreciate or recognize the value of something" (*OED n.*[2]). The arguments he now uses to support this claim are, as always, full of wit and therefore fun to follow. But I resist the temptation in order to suggest, simply, that much of my subsequent discussion of the play will highlight scenes in which characters are tricked into arriving at false interpretations, scenes in which characters believe they are being misinterpreted, and scenes in which erroneous interpretations are spectacularly corrected by the arrival of new information.

Anxiety about misinterpretation is, if anything, even more obvious in *Hamlet*, as the previous analysis has already shown. Why does Hamlet write extra lines for *The Murder of Gonzago* and instruct Horatio to observe the reaction of Claudius to the performance? Because he needs to be certain that his interpretation of his uncle's guilt is the right one. To act on the wrong interpretation would be "Misprision in the highest degree" because it would drain the ethical meaning from Hamlet's whole project. And, as will soon become apparent, anxiety about misinterpretation has a great deal to do with privacy (and its invasions) in both plays. I have already quoted Hamlet's dismissive words about Guildenstern's presuming that he has the right and the ability to pluck out the heart of Hamlet's mystery. The desire to protect the inner self from exposure and hence the likelihood of misinterpretation is expressed rather differently in *Twelfth Night*: by means of Olivia's protective veil, for example, or by Malvolio's insistence on taking the high moral road in his dealings with the members of Olivia's household. What each of these strategies aims to protect is the kind of privacy that includes and requires interiority. In comedy, however, spectators are less likely to concede the absolute value of the inner self.

So much could be inferred even from the setting of *Twelfth Night*: the country of Illyria, a name that Shakespeare could have found on a map (roughly where we might expect to find Croatia), but which he clearly intended to designate a never-never land of the kind where the quasi-magical and spectacularly improbable events of comedy are all taken in stride. Even so, Illyria has its own rules and conventions, some of which were traced with admirable precision by Camille Wells Slights in *Shakespeare's Comic Commonwealths.* In particular, Slights was able to invoke, with great skill and subtlety, the principle of recompense: "To give is to create an obligation; to take is to imply a willingness to pay that debt."[23] She observed this principle at work in the behaviour of Feste, who, though always willing to offer another performance, is persistent and clever in demanding payment once, twice (if he's lucky), and three times (if he dares). But the concern for who's paying for what extends right to the top of the social ladder, as we can infer from Olivia's undertaking to sponsor the double wedding that will soon take place, "Here at my house and at my proper cost" (5.1.310). The play as a whole is therefore a network of reciprocity, and we respond to its inhabitants by noticing how adroitly (or how clumsily) they play their parts within it.

Before returning to the question of privacy, I want to inflect Slights's description of this world by noticing that wealth doesn't mean quite the same thing to all of the characters of the commonwealth. Most of them have to earn their wealth, or at least the minimal access to it that will keep body and soul together. Members of this group include the Sea-Captain, the Clown, and all of the servants from Viola and Curio to Maria and Malvolio. But some of the characters are aristocrats who live off the proceeds of inherited wealth, namely land, and will never have to earn a living. The notable members of this class are the two landowners, Orsino and Olivia, but it includes Sir Andrew Aguecheek, whose "three thousand ducats a year" (1.3.20) would imply a very considerable fortune; and it includes Sir Toby Belch as well, insofar as he determines to exploit his position as Olivia's uncle and his friendship with Sir Andrew to ensure that he never does anything to pay for his drinking habit. When the culture of Illyria is described in this way, it starts looking a lot more like the London Shakespeare knew: a city in which the aristocratic occupants of magnificent houses (the Herberts of Baynard Castle, for example) would rub shoulders with highly successful members of the Guilds (Francis Barnham of the Drapers' Company, for example) and condescend without apology and only as occasion served to the large supporting cast of servants, shopkeepers, and paupers.

23 *Shakespeare's Comic Commonwealths* (Toronto: University of Toronto Press, 1993), 223.

Not all of the members of this world – or, should we say, of these two partly overlapping worlds – will experience privacy in the same way. If you're situated at the top of the social hierarchy, then your privacy is an entitlement that goes without saying, and your retainers are variously occupied in protecting it. Orsino would seem to be acting on this assumption when, having enjoined Cesario to press his suit to Olivia, he adds these instructions to his other courtiers: "Some four or five attend him,/ All if you will, for I myself am best/When least in company" (1.4.35–7). Before we meet Olivia we learn that she has vowed to live "like a cloistress" (1.1.27) for seven years, and before Cesario can enter we see her insisting on this vow by putting on her veil. While Olivia's brother was alive, he was presumably the landowner himself, and because his consent would have been required before any courtship scenario could succeed, her brother was implicitly the guarantor of her privacy. Now that she can make real decisions all by herself, Olivia needs a strategy that will keep her suitors at arm's length: the vow and the veil in effect do for her what the three caskets do for Portia in *The Merchant of Venice.* If the vow and the veil are not enough, Olivia can use irony to supplement them, as in this description of her own beauty: "It shall be inventoried and every particle and utensil labelled to my will, as *item,* two lips, indifferent red; *item,* two grey eyes, with lids to them; *item,* one neck, one chin, and so forth" (1.5.234–7). These are the words of a woman who values her privacy more than anything Orsino has on offer.

Of course we will see her remove the veil and drop the ironic tone soon enough, but she will persist in wanting to protect her privacy. Now her privacy is no longer solitude, but something she emphatically wants to share with the man (as she thinks) with whom she has fallen in love (as she thinks). She explicitly sends her attendants offstage so as to allow for intimate conversation with Cesario: "Let the garden door be shut," she says, "and leave me to my hearing" (3.1.90–1). Her insistence on a privacy that she shares with one other person will extend to her marriage, which, as first undertaken, is a secretive event. She urges Sebastian to accompany her and the Priest she has in tow to a chantry, where they may exchange vows without interference; the Priest has apparently promised to "conceal it" until Sebastian is "willing it shall come to note" (4.3.28–9). The concealment cannot last long, however, because Cesario's emotional stand-offishness will soon provoke Olivia into insisting that he is her "husband" (5.1.139–40). Now the secret is out, and confirmed by the testimony of the Priest, but not understood until the arrival of Sebastian completes the "natural perspective, that is and is not" (5.1.210). Olivia has done everything she can to protect her privacy, but she is tricked by the structure of comedy itself into moving beyond private satisfactions and into the world of shared gratifications. For her, the price of privacy reconfigures itself as the very considerable expense of staging the double wedding that the plot of comedy now requires.

But the cost of insisting on privacy is the most glaring in the case of Malvolio. In his very first scene Malvolio shows such open hostility to Feste that Olivia reprimands him: "O, you are sick of self-love, Malvolio, and taste with a distempered appetite" (1.5.85–6). In effect, Malvolio is protecting his private self with such relentless discipline as to rule out any chance of becoming "generous, guiltless, and of free disposition" (1.5.86–7) as Olivia recommends. Far from following her advice, Malvolio merely hardens his selfishness when Olivia isn't there to restrain him.

When Feste, Sir Toby Belch, and Sir Andrew Aguecheek get well into their cups, Maria warns them that Olivia will send Malvolio to remind them of the house rules. But the revellers are past caring, and the "caterwauling" (2.3.68) escalates until Malvolio does enter. There will surely be a pause now as everyone tries to anticipate what will happen next. And what does happen is that Malvolio, far from calming things down, explodes: "My masters, are you mad?" he begins, and after a bit of name-calling he poses another question which is really an accusation: "Is there no respect of place, persons, nor time in you?" (2.3.81–5).

Of course he has a point. Those of us who have been both scholars and the parents of teenagers will know exactly what he's trying to accomplish. He's protecting his private space against the incursion of the revellers. Still, however much we may respect Malvolio's position, it is impossible (in the theatre at least) to resist the adroitness of Sir Toby's recompense: "Art any more than a steward? Dost thou think because thou art virtuous there shall be no more cakes and ale?" (2.3.106–8). The revellers are going to make Malvolio pay for the stridency of his rebuke, not once, not twice, but three times.

It begins of course with the letter scene, orchestrated by Maria with great care to ensure that Malvolio will interpret the text the way she wants him to: "I do not now fool myself, to let imagination jade me; for every reason excites to this, that my lady loves me" (2.5.154–6). Attempts to defend Malvolio's reading of the letter as hermeneutically sound,[24]

24 See for example Sean Benson, "'Perverse Fantasies'? Rehabilitating Malvolio's Reading," *Papers on Language and Literature* 45, no. 3 (2009): 261–86.

however persuasive as textual discourse, fail to account for the psychological cul-de-sac in which Malvolio is trapped, and the gross misinterpretation of his own situation that he constructs. Even his erotic script has room for only one star performer, and that is Malvolio himself.

That's why, when he comes to Olivia next in yellow stockings and cross-gartered, he can see only himself. Despite his history of privileged access to Olivia, he shows not the slightest skill at interpreting her behaviour towards him in this scene. When she asks, out of concern for his health, "Wilt thou go to bed, Malvolio?" (3.4.27), he interprets her question as a sexual come-on. As for "Sir Toby and the lighter people" (5.1.330), who are now in charge of Malvolio's rehabilitation, he pretends they are of no importance to him: "Go off, I discard you. Let me enjoy my private" (3.4.86). The appeal to privacy here, as if it were the only solution to the social mess in which Malvolio now finds himself, is oblique justification for Maria's earlier claim that he is "sometimes … a kind of puritan" (2.3.130). To valorize the private self in the way that Malvolio shows himself willing and eager to do is to run the risk of becoming a social outcast.

And this of course is what Malvolio quickly becomes in the rest of the play. He is thrown into a dark cell, tormented without mercy by Feste, and given no way of defending himself against accusations of madness. The degree to which he has been stigmatized can be inferred from his exit line in Act 5: "I'll be revenged on the whole pack of you" (5.1.368). There are of course as many ways of interpreting this line as there are actors willing to play the part of Malvolio. But I think that all interpretations will acknowledge that, because he insists on his own privacy as if it were an absolute value, Malvolio bears at least some responsibility for his own exclusion from the social formation at the close.

Among the qualities Malvolio shares with his Puritan contemporaries is a reliance on the written word that borders on both the ridiculous and the sublime. I am alluding again to his interpretation of the letter he thinks Olivia wrote him. But I am drawing attention also to his repeated request for "a candle and pen, ink, and paper" (4.2.82) by which he hopes to gain release from his dungeon. If only I could write down a sincere account of the injustices I suffer, and send this account to Olivia, Malvolio thinks, she will be obliged to deliver me from this dark humiliation. Eventually he is given the tools of his trade, and he does write the letter he has been planning in his heart. But when it is read out in extenso by Fabian in Act 5, it does not achieve the desired effect. So Malvolio produces the piece of writing from his archive which he knows will trump all: the original letter in which Olivia had given him "such clear lights of favour" (5.1.327). Now Malvolio has to learn that Olivia didn't write the letter after all, and that his proleptic ascent to a greatness thrust upon him has been no more than a private delusion.

Despite his celebrated brilliance as a creator of clowns *and* kings, Shakespeare, even the mature Shakespeare, does not always give what we might think of as subjective character to the players of minor parts, including important minor parts. This is surely the point that Stoppard is making in *Rosencrantz and Guildenstern Are Dead.* Within *Hamlet* his protagonists have a function, but nothing we could legitimately call character. So I am going to end this consideration of *Twelfth Night* by looking briefly at three minor roles, those of Maria, Antonio, and Feste. In each case I will be asking: Does this character have anything that we could identify as a private life?

In Maria's case the answer is clearly yes, although we might not have known this before we discover, almost as an afterthought, that Sir Toby has married her to reward her for creating the letter scene. In other words, Maria has done exactly what Malvolio wanted to do: she marries *up* so as to escape the limits of her position as a servant. Nobody saw this coming, because in fact Maria has been far more skilful at protecting her privacy than are most of her social superiors. The first time she's on stage Sir Toby urges Sir Andrew to accost her, and when Sir Andrew learns the meaning of this word, he seems a bit scandalized. Maria now responds with a "Fare you well, gentlemen" (1.3.56) as if to suggest that the sexually inflected banter has gone far enough, thank you very much. But she turns out to be less prudent and more enterprising than she lets on; Maria does have a private life, but it's one that she lives when she's not onstage.

Antonio is a problem, and that should be expected, because Antonio is a problem on any reading of the play. From the moment he enters he seems pathetically reluctant to allow Sebastian to leave his sight, even when Sebastian says: "I shall crave of you your leave that I may bear my evils alone" (2.1.5–6). Antonio can't comply with this, so he goes out in search of his love object, hoping to persuade him to return to his "lodging" (3.3.20) before he has taken so much as a tour of the town. Add to this the insinuation of piracy and the hostility between Antonio and Orsino, and we have the makings of a very confusing role. He's reduced at length to begging Viola for some of the money he gave Sebastian; he's led away by officers, the first of which claims (later) that they arrested him "In private brabble" (5.1.59). When at last he is restored to Sebastian, who now calls him "my dear Antonio" (5.1.211) and claims to have been tormented by their separation, it is already too late, because Sebastian has just married Olivia. Perhaps Antonio does have a private life, but if he does, it's not enough to give coherence to his part.

Does Feste have a private life? I'm inclined to think not. The very beautiful song with which he ends the play seems to me not a personal biography at all but a generic description of and lament for the fate of mankind. So what is Shakespeare up to when he gives us a Fool who isn't that funny, but who sings beautiful sad songs, and who seems to be adept at encouraging other people in their merriments and excesses? Perhaps the best answer is still the one devised many years ago by Northrop Frye: Feste and Malvolio are polar opposites in that their function is to focus the comic and the anti-comic moods respectively.[25] Malvolio's insistence on privacy sets him apart from the revels to which comedy aspires; and Feste's transcendence of privacy allows him to invite us into a world of holiday: a world in which we too can forget our private objectives in the interests of a communal "what you will."

What value then should we attach to the experience of privacy in the world of Illyria? Most inhabitants of this world seem to assign it considerable value, to judge by the efforts they take to protect their own privacy or to share it with carefully selected others. But many of the same inhabitants work just as hard to invade the privacy of others, so there is never a fully secure answer to the question I have posed. In Illyria, privacy is not absolute, nor does it come at a fixed price. It is something of real value nonetheless, even if its price is subject to constant renegotiation.

Privacy and Spectatorship

By way of conclusion, let me revisit the now-familiar notion of the inherently perspectival quality of privacy, and the metaphor of the two-way street which I used earlier to explain this concept. Privacy may seem to be pretty much the same thing to Malvolio as it was to Hamlet: an absolute right that requires vigilant protection, the locus of introspection that I have been calling interiority, and (when violated and disrespected by others) the matrix in which a desire for revenge can take root and flourish. But this description requires that we see matters uniformly from

25 See *A Natural Perspective: The Development of Shakespearean Comedy and Romance* (New York: Columbia University Press, 1965), 92–3.

Hamlet's point of view and from Malvolio's; in fact this is not the case, because Shakespeare is situating us as spectators on opposite sides of the street in the two instances.

Hamlet, as I have already remarked, has an amazing capacity for claiming our loyalty; as spectators, we want to be on his side in virtually every conflict. In the case of Malvolio the opposite is true either for most of the play or for all of it. Like Hamlet, Malvolio draws attention to his alienation from the society to which he belongs, and he is willing to judge the behaviour of his enemies with similar passion. But Malvolio judges people not for murdering his father, disinheriting him, and seducing his mother, but for persisting in the noisy consumption of cakes and ale at all hours of the night. In the comic world of Illyria we are dealing with "human follies," as Ben Jonson puts it, as opposed to tragic "crimes."[26] So a moral response that seems called for in tragedy can look curiously out of place in comedy.

But the difference is not simply one of moral magnitude. It is also a difference of artistic strategy which places us as spectators right beside Hamlet but curiously distant from Malvolio. When Hamlet speaks about himself, he is alone, and we listen to his words as if they were the unmediated signifiers of his thoughts. When Malvolio opens up his heart, as in the letter scene, he is accompanied by a chorus of commentators (Maria, Sir Toby, Sir Andrew, and Fabian) who have nothing to do but make him look ridiculous. That he is unaware of their presence only makes him that much more vulnerable to their irony.

It's true of course, as critics of audience response have shown,[27] that Malvolio's position is much more susceptible to pathos in the dungeon scene (4.2), when the comic revellers lock him into a helpless position, and he has to do the utmost to convince them that he is not mad. Even here, there's a wonderful asymmetry between his part and that of Hamlet, who tries to persuade the court of Elsinore that he *is* mad. The point, however, is that Malvolio's claim for the integrity of his inner self, for the absolute value of privacy, is treated in the long run as a form of madness.

26 See the Prologue (l. 24) to *Every Man in His Humor*, ed. Gabriele Bernhard Jackson, Yale Ben Jonson (New Haven, CT: Yale University Press, 1969), 38.

27 See for example Ralph Berry, "*Twelfth Night:* The Experience of the Audience," *Shakespeare Survey* 34 (1981): 111–19.

I have argued earlier that Horatio is a stand-in for the spectators in *Hamlet*. If there is a similar part in *Twelfth Night*, it would have to be Fabian. His is the most neutral and least individuated of all the comic parts, and yet he is there as an observer whenever Malvolio is being humiliated. At the very end, when Olivia asks Feste to read out the letter that Malvolio wrote to her from prison, Feste cannot resist performing its language in a style that parodies the voice of its author. Olivia therefore reassigns the task to Fabian, who carries it out with a greater care for the unvarnished truth of the matter. Later on it is Fabian who confesses how the trick to gull Malvolio came about, and in this confession he is once again a representative of the spectators. The whole purpose of the ruse, if Fabian can be trusted, is to "rather pluck on laughter than revenge" (5.1.357). This is a perspective that invites us to see Malvolio's insistence on privacy as pathetic, perhaps, but as indefensibly risible too.

Chapter Two

Private Devotions

The growing need for privacy as the locus for early modern piety cannot be understood without reference to the great upheavals which altered, challenged, prescribed, prohibited, compromised, and subverted various forms of public worship. I am of course thinking of events such as the separation of the Church of England from papal authority (1534), the burning of Protestant heretics during Queen Mary's reign, the execution of Jesuit missionaries and their accomplices during Elizabeth's, the appointment of William Laud as Archbishop of Canterbury (1633), the ejection of clergy with royalist affiliations from their churches during the Commonwealth, and the ejection of Puritan clergy after the Restoration. I do not propose to narrate or reinterpret these events, all of which have been studied in detail by historians. Rather, I hope to show the degree to which these external pressures led to a spiritual turning inward, parallel with but of course not identical to the inward turn of Hamlet as described in the previous chapter. The new spiritual inwardness was cultivated by Protestants and Catholics alike, as the subsequent argument will show. Most of the texts I will be citing are by British authors, but where necessary I will refer to texts by continental Europeans as well.

The Prayer Closet

Near the end of the period of cultural history I am designating as the age of Shakespeare, and in the aftermath of several generations of public instability on matters of religion, Edward Wetenhall, a young and well-placed clergyman in the Church of England, opens his devotional manual, *Enter into Thy Closet* (1666), with the following remarkable if completely understandable claim: "That person can no wise be esteemed a serious and th[o]rough Christian, uprightly and cordially discharging his duty towards God, who is a stranger unto privacy."[1] I will set aside for now the levels of religious and social meaning of this assertion in order to follow Wetenhall's quite literal instructions for the creation of a prayer closet.

Ideally, it should be a cheerful room, with plenty of natural light, in the top storey of one's house; this location would ensure separation from the daily business being carried on below, "and besides that," Wetenhall writes, "some secret Property there is in such high and eminent places, whence we may behold the heavens and overlook the earth" (B3^{v}), thus following the examples of Christ (who went up onto a mountain to pray), of St Peter (who prayed from a housetop), and of the disciples (who assembled in an upper room). The prayer closet should be separated from more utilitarian spaces by at least two closed doors, so as to ensure that the meditating Christian's voice won't be overheard. The furniture should be sparse but appropriate: the table, stool, and candlestick "of *Elisha's* chamber" should be supplemented by a "hard *Couch* or great chair" (B4) on which to rest, on occasion for the whole night.

The table visualized by Wetenhall will be equipped with textual material to support meditation: a Bible and a copy of *The Book of Common Prayer*, two blank manuscript books in which to record the results of devotional work, plus pen and ink to carry out this task. If the person in charge keeps in the closet any materials not dedicated to devotions, "as Students do Books, Gentlemen writings, and Ladies Medicines, &c." (B4), these extraneous objects should be off to one side, and should definitely not be placed on the table, or "*Praying desk*" (B4^{v}) as Wetenhall now calls it. The wall above this desk should be decorated with a monochrome hanging (Wetenhall prefers green) so as to provide the eye with no distractions.

Wetenhall knows that only people of ample means will be able to afford the appointments he has described, and only they moreover will have the leisure to commit as many hours to devotions as he prescribes. People who "get their living by their daily labour, whose abilities of mind are therefore meaner, and whose privacy more difficult" (C6) can still be expected to perform morning and evening prayers. But more privileged

---

1 *Enter into Thy Closet: Or, a Method and Order for Private Devotion*, 5th ed. (London: John Martyn, 1676), B1. All of my quotations are from this edition, but they have been checked against the readings of the first edition (1666).

people are held to a much stricter standard, on the grounds that more is expected of those to whom more is given. Men and women of ample means should therefore be withdrawing to their closets twice a day (morning and evening) to engage in the three-phase devotional exercise of "*Reading, Meditation* and *Prayer*" (C6^{v}). The detailed assignments laid out for each of these phases leave little doubt that devotions are going to be time-consuming, especially if the results are conscientiously recorded. "If I am able," Wetenhall recommends, "I shall find it an incredible benefit, in the end of these my meditations to use my pen, whensoever by any reading I have gained more remarkable benefit, and to register in one of my Paper books (reserved ever for this purpose, which for distinctions sake I may know by the name of my *Memorial*) that particular which I have gained" (D4). Wetenhall proposes reading substantial passages of scripture, morning and evening, so that virtually the whole text of the Bible is read over three times a year. Favourite books may be read more frequently, and less engaging passages (the minor prophets, say, or Deuteronomy) only occasionally. But the reading and rereading project is both ample and serious; the note-taking should be organized so as to record whether a particular reading of 1 Corinthians 13, for example, makes any advance upon earlier readings of this text. For the fully literate Christian, private devotions turn out to be a scholarly undertaking that relies upon and promotes many of the same habits of mind that would come to characterize literary criticism three centuries later.

It goes almost without saying that the prayer closet as Wetenhall describes it is a decidedly Protestant place. It contains no graven images, no rosary beads, nothing even resembling the shape of the cross. I make this point partly to raise one of the inescapable questions that will shape this chapter, namely, what were the differences, if any, between Protestant and Catholic approaches to devotional life? The superficial differences I've just noted may be no more than that, or they may suggest radically incompatible ways of leading the life of piety. The argument I advance here will suggest, at least indirectly, ways of deciding between these alternatives.

Surprisingly perhaps, the closet as Wetenhall imagines it is not an all-male preserve. Recall that he relegates to the fringes those typical objects of attachment: books for students, writings for gentlemen, medicines for women. No, this is not egalitarian thinking, nor could it be, for reasons that I will outline at some length in chapter 5. But if he doesn't give women equal standing, Wetenhall certainly imagines that they might have closets of their own. So much is at least implied by the frontispiece to his book, an engraving which pictures a stylishly dressed young woman,

Figure 1 Frontispiece to Edward Wetenhall, *Enter into Thy Closet: Or, a Method and Order for Private Devotions*, 5th ed. (London: John Martyn, 1676), Cambridge University Library

kneeling at her prayer desk, her hands held together, her eyes open and her gaze directed upwards. Directly behind her is a man-sized angel with powerful wings, his right hand reaching out so as to almost touch her bottom, his left hand extended in the direction of her gaze, which is also the direction from which spiritual illumination pours into the room. Perhaps I have given this image more attention than it deserves; it is not a work of art so much as a means of advertising. But what it advertises is definitely the female Christian engaged in devotions in the presence of nobody but the divine.

The appointments of the prayer closet presuppose that devotions are carried out not exclusively by the Christian soul, but by the body too, at least insofar as it aids and abets the soul's devotional exercise.[2] I have already mentioned Wetenhall's assumption that prayers will be spoken out loud, and hence the need for soundproofing. The couch he includes in his ideal prayer closet is a provision that anticipates fatigue; it will be more effective if the room includes "A Chimney, against Winter's cold" (B4). Although he doesn't want to be absolutely prescriptive about the physical methods of devotion, Wetenhall dedicates a chapter (Book 2, Chapter 8) to outlining "*the best outward manner of Prayer, in fit postures and fit words*" (E3). He approaches the question with apparent nonchalance: "Now though the posture of the body seem to be a small matter, yet methinks my prayers want their due solemnity, if not performed in a posture of worship" (E3^{v}). True, one could pray while "riding upon his horse back" (E3^{v}), as Donne did so beautifully on Good Friday, 1613, but in the prayer closet Wetenhall prefers to "bow" his "knees" (E4) and to lift up his hands. This is not a formula so much as a preferred practice, and it does not rule out more extreme gestures, such as "*Prostration*, or casting my self on the earth before God" (E4^{v}) when the situation calls for drastic demonstrations.

These then are the three polarities which will help to organize what follows: Protestant and Catholic, male and female, body and soul. In each of these cases I hope to be alert and flexible enough to notice and account for pious practices that transgress or evade these binary oppositions,

2 This point is eloquently made by Richard Rambuss in *Closet Devotions* (Durham, NC: Duke University Press, 1998), 127–31. Although I am indebted to Rambuss's provocative book, not only here but throughout this chapter, I will also indicate, where appropriate, some of the ways in which I believe his study misses the mark.

but the polarities are nonetheless indispensable categories in the discussion that follows. And while my overall aim here is to discover the ways in which early modern devotional practice shaped and enhanced the experience of privacy, I do not want to preclude finding evidence to the contrary. Suppose that the practice of piety offered only an illusion of privacy: an illusion that disguised the degree to which the eye of Providence was ever on the watch and ceaselessly aware of even the tiniest human shortcomings. Is this the enhancement of privacy, we should be willing to ask, or its constant invasion?

These are big issues, and they arise from a textual field already well studied. There would be no hope of reaching any conclusions at all, however provisional, if I were to attempt a comprehensive review of the vast early modern literature of devotion in the English language alone. So I will focus my attention, largely but not exclusively, on two celebrated paradigms for meditation: the agony of Christ in the garden, and the allegorical positioning of the Christian soul as the bride of Christ. This strategic decision will exclude a great deal of potentially interesting material, but it will still allow for discussion of a wide variety of texts in both verse and prose, some of them written by authors with names as familiar as Robert Southwell and George Herbert, some of them by less obvious choices: Francis Rous, for example, or Sarah Davy. If I have given Edward Wetenhall rather artificial prominence in these opening pages, that is because he usefully frames many of the questions that I believe ought to be addressed. In a roughly symmetrical way, John Saltmarsh will have a conspicuous place near the end, partly because his unusual career helps to point the way to conclusions, even while it makes them problematic.

Prayer in the Garden

Medieval Christianity produced a vast archive of devotional literature, of which the *Imitation of Christ* (1418), probably by St Thomas à Kempis, and Nicholas Love's *Mirror of the Blessed Life of Jesus Christ* (ca 1410) are important examples. But it was the work of St Ignatius of Loyola, specifically *The Spiritual Exercises* (1548), that would place devotional life onto what we might call a scientific footing. Long before his book was published, Ignatius had founded the Society of Jesus (1534), had gained papal approval for this initiative (1540), and had been chosen the first Superior General of the order. He was clearly a charismatic figure, able to inspire loyalty and veneration for the divine in the many people willing to follow him. To encourage and assist his followers and admirers in aspiring to ever-higher levels of piety, Ignatius organized retreats at which an authoritative leader (Ignatius himself, no doubt) would, over a period of weeks, instruct a group of retreatants in the arts of meditation and prayer. *The Spiritual Exercises* are not a coherent record of one such event, and even less are they a sequential account of Ignatius's own devotions. Rather, they read like an instructor's manual; Ignatius appears to be giving the instructions his followers will find essential if they are to carry on the task (as team leaders, so to speak) of spreading Christian piety of the kind endorsed by the Society of Jesus around the world.

In the preliminary "Notes" to his book, Ignatius points out that his program as a whole is divided into four phases, which he then speaks of as four weeks, even though he doesn't require that each phase be mechanically limited to exactly seven days. The retreat-giver must remain constantly sensitive to the retreatant's particular needs, and he will therefore adjust the pace according to the abilities of the individual or the group he is leading. But in general the four weeks are dedicated to meditations upon (1) sin, including the sinfulness of the retreatant; (2) the incarnation and life of Christ up to Palm Sunday; (3) the passion of Christ from the last supper to the crucifixion and burial; and (4) the resurrection and subsequent events, including the ascension. Even a casual browser could infer this fourfold structure from the text of *The Spiritual Exercises*, but the retreatant himself should not be aware of it, at least not in advance. "It is a good thing for the retreatant in the first week not to know anything about what he will be doing in the second week."[3] It appears that Ignatius wants the retreatant to develop the habit of taking a great deal on trust, even blind trust, so as to authorize the retreat-giver to decide what's best for him and when.

A great deal more could be (and has been) said about Ignatius's approach to meditation: about his division of the soul into faculties of memory, reason, and will; of his exploitation of the five senses in calling forth vivid scenarios both physical and spiritual; of his influence in furthering the cause of the Catholic Reformation.[4] But I want to narrow the focus at this point to test what he has to say about the first of my

3 *The Spiritual Exercises of Saint Ignatius*, trans. Thomas Corbishley, SJ (London: Burns and Oates, 1963), 15.

4 See, for example, Louis L. Martz, *The Poetry of Meditation: A Study in English Religious Literature*, rev. ed. (New Haven, CT: Yale University Press, 1962), 25–39.

paradigm cases: the agony of Christ in the garden. Initially it seems that Ignatius rushes past this event very quickly in the Second Contemplation of the Third Week. Christ brings his eleven remaining disciples with him after the last supper, and, in Ignatius's account: "Leaving eight of them in one part of the Valley, and three more in one part of the Garden, He betakes Himself to prayer, His sweat turning to drops of blood" (69). True, this is merely a summary of "the story" and will presumably provoke the retreatant into far more detailed contemplation. A few more tips are provided in what looks like an appendix listing "Events of the Life of our Lord Christ." Here is Ignatius's more detailed account:

> *First.* At the end of Supper and after singing a hymn, our Lord sets out for the Mount of Olives, with His terrified disciples. He leaves eight of them in Gethsemani, with the words: "Sit down here, while I go in and pray."
>
> *Second.* Taking with Him Peter, James and John, He prays three times to God, in the words: "My Father, if it is possible, let this chalice pass me by; only as thy will is, not as mine is." In His agony, He prayed all the more earnestly.
>
> *Third.* He fell into such dread that He said: "My soul is ready to die with sorrow." And He sweated blood so abundantly that St Luke tells us: "His sweat fell to the ground like thick drops of blood," implying that His garments were already soaked. (97–8)

Now we have much more circumstantial detail, but even here the story is given almost in shorthand: the three separate prayers, for instance, are narrated only once. The sweat resembling drops of blood Ignatius takes with acknowledgment from the gospel of Luke, but he says nothing about the angel, mentioned in the same source, who appears in order to strengthen Christ's resolve.

I am not finding fault with Ignatius here, so much as pointing once more to the tendency of his book to set out a framework that still needs elaboration, development, elucidation, explication, intellectual and spiritual completion. These important supplementary tasks are carried out with great patience and zeal by the Spanish Jesuit Thomas de Villa-castin in *A Manuall of Devout Meditations and Exercises* (1618), a book made available to English readers in a translation by Henry More, also a Jesuit, and the great-grandson of Sir Thomas More. Villa-castin devotes two substantial chapters (Book 2, Meditations 23 and 24) to the agony in the garden. He provides Christ with motives that are completely absent in Ignatius. The big motive, of course, and the one he never loses sight of, is his "great desire ... to suffer for our sake,"[5] but this overriding mission is complicated by the human aspects of his character. Jesus knows that Judas is likely to look for him in the garden, so that is exactly where he goes, "to shew that of his owne freewill he offered himselfe" (P3). While he prays, Villa-castin's Jesus feels isolated; his disciples fall asleep, his Father doesn't answer him, and "his most holy Mother was also absent" (P4ᵛ). But Jesus persists, going back to pray a second time, and then a third. Villa-castin draws a number of inferences from this pattern of deferral and repetition. The reason God delays his answer is evidently to emphasize the magnitude of the occasion: a quick response wouldn't feel sufficiently momentous. And the individual Christian can, as always, benefit from watching Christ's behaviour: "Learne, not to complaine, nor to be weary when thou prayest, if God do not heare thee: for certainely he heareth thee." If Christ had to wait for an answer, we can surely expect to do the same. And waiting will be good for us in the long run, of course, because God is all along teaching us the value of "patience and perseverance" (P5).

So far I have restricted my description of Villa-castin's account of the agony to the first of the two chapters dedicated to this occasion. Were I to describe the second one, I would be obliged to notice the angel who now appears "to comfort and strengthen" (P5ᵛ) Jesus, and of course his anticipation of the "torments" he will soon have to endure, which cause "a bloody sweat to fall downe from his face, neck, breast & shoulders, leaving him wholly bathed and embrued in his owne bloud" (P7). But it is perhaps not essential to follow Villa-castin's phenomenology of meditation step by step, now that his strategies of amplification have been suggested. Like Wallace Stevens, Villa-castin can always think of at least thirteen ways of looking at a blackbird, and that makes him a congenial guide on a spiritual journey that might otherwise seem far more austere.

Robert Southwell, also a member of the Society of Jesus and famous in part for having been executed at Tyburn on 21 February 1595/6, wrote at least three poems representing the agony in the garden. I will concentrate here on the second of the three, "Christs Bloody Sweat," even though doing so will marginalize its companion pieces, "Sinnes

5 *A Manual of Devout Meditations and Exercises, Instructing how to Pray Mentally: Drawne for the Most Part, out of the Spirituall Exercises of B.F. Ignatius*, trans. [Henry More] ([St Omer]: English College Press, 1618), P3.

Heavie Loade" (in which Christ's gesture of prostration is at issue) and "Christ's Sleeping Friends" (in which the disciples are rebuked for complacency). The second phase of this three-part meditation in verse runs as follows:

Christs Bloody Sweat

Fat soile, full spring, sweete olive, grape of blisse,
That yeelds, that streams, that pours, that dost distil,
Untild, undrawne, unstampt, untoucht of presse,
Deare fruit, cleare brookes, faire oile, sweete wine at will:
Thus Christ unforst prevents in shedding blood
The whips, the thornes, the nailes, the speare, and roode.

He Pelicans, he Phenix fate doth prove,
Whom flames consume, whom streames enforce to die,
How burneth bloud, how bleedeth burning love?
Can one in flame and streame both bathe and frie?
How could he joine a Phenix fiery paines
In fainting Pelicans still bleeding vaines?

Elias once to prove gods soveraigne powre
By praire procur'd a fier of wondrous force
That blood and wood and water did devoure,
Yea stones and dust, beyonde all natures course:
Such fire is love that fedd with gory bloode
Doth burne no lesse then in the dryest woode.

O sacred Fire come shewe thy force one me
That sacrifice to Christe I may retorne,
If withered wood for fuell fittest bee,
If stones and dust, yf fleshe and blood will burne,
I withered am and stonye to all good,
A sacke of dust, a masse of fleshe and bloode.[6]

6 *The Poems of Robert Southwell, SJ*, ed. James H. McDonald and Nancy Pollard Brown (Oxford: Clarendon, 1967), 18–19.

Unlike Villa-castin, Southwell does not ponder the psychological pressures of the scene; his interest is rather in its layering of symbolic meanings. So the first stanza sees in Christ's liquid gift a fertility of significance, in that he spontaneously anticipates (the old meaning of "prevents") what the various instruments of torture will soon be taking by force.

But the complications really begin in stanza 2, where Christ, by sweating blood, is said to "prove" (i.e., experience) the fates of two radically different birds: the pelican and the phoenix. The first of this pair is doubtless the pious pelican referred to in the hymn "Adore te devote," often attributed to St Thomas Aquinas: "Pie pellicane, Jesu Domine."[7] The mythological properties which make the pelican pious are its shedding of blood and its willingness to nourish its own offspring with this precious liquid.[8] The phoenix doesn't bleed, but it burns (as Christ does with divine love). The "phoenix riddle," made famous through Donne's use of this phrase in "The Canonization,"[9] is the paradox whereby this bird ends its life in flames (having carefully manufactured a nest of twigs and ignited it) only to be reborn from its own ashes. In their different ways, both birds are Christlike: the pelican in its act of self-sacrifice, and the phoenix in its miraculous resurrection. Christ is therefore the means by which we as Christians can "both bathe and frie" in the blood and fire of his love.

The image of fire had an almost mesmerizing hold on Southwell's imagination. His most frequently anthologized poem, "The Burning Babe" (15–16), introduces the scorching heat of Christ's love into the Christmas story. In "Christs Bloody Sweat," once fire has been introduced (by the phoenix) it will continue to rage (though not quite out of control) for the rest of the poem. Stanza 3 refers to the Old Testament story in which Elijah by himself enlists the help of God to gain a striking moral victory over 450 prophets of Baal. Following Elijah's instructions, the false prophets slaughter a bullock, place its flesh and plenty of fuel upon their altar, and then pray to their unresponsive god to send fire to consume

7 See no. 82 in *The Catholic Hymnal*, ed. William L. O'Farrell (Cambridge: Office of the University Journal, 1926), where the Latin text is quoted and translated as "Pelican of mercy, Jesu, Lord and God."

8 See Isidore of Seville, *Étymologies* 12, ed. and trans. Jacques André (Paris: Les Belles Lettres, 1986), 244: "Le pélican est un oiseau d'Égypte qui habite les régions désertes du Nil ... On raconte, si cela est vrai, qu'il tue ses petits, les pleure pendant trois jours, puis se fait une blessure et ressuscite ses petits en les aspergeant de son sang."

9 *Complete English Poems*, ed. A.J. Smith (Harmondsworth: Penguin, 1971), 47.

their offering. Elijah likewise slaughters a bullock and prepares an offering; but before calling on God he has his servants drench the altar three times with large quantities of water. Elijah's prayer is quite spectacularly answered: "Then the fire of the Lord fell and consumed the burnt-sacrifice, and the wood, and the stones, and the dust, and licked up the water that was in the trench" (1 Kings 18:38). Southwell alludes very precisely to these details, and then moves rather surprisingly to the inference, "Such fire is love." The end of the story of Elijah and the prophets doesn't seem like love at all; having been publicly vindicated, Elijah is able to seize the opportunity to execute all 450 of his opponents. But for Southwell this is nonetheless evidence of God's love for his true prophet, and in that sense it looks forward to Christ's love for humankind.

As he watches Christ suffering in preparation for the ultimate sacrifice, Southwell's speaker longs for an opportunity to "retorne" a sacrifice of his own. So he imagines himself made of the very materials consumed by fire in the Elijah story: "withered wood" but also stones, dust, flesh, and blood. His desire to be consumed by flames is a metaphor of extreme piety: he wants to be annihilated by divine love. And in Southwell's case it is impossible to declare this death wish inauthentic. He felt called by God to a life of service that he knew to be filled with peril and likely to lead, as indeed it did, to an early death.

As I remarked at the outset of this chapter, and as the case of Robert Southwell makes only too clear, the great confrontations of the early modern period left behind highly public markers of the divisions between Catholic and Protestant Christianity. But it still makes sense to ask whether the same division holds true in private. When they entered their prayer closets to communicate with God, were English Protestants doing anything strikingly different from what their Catholic counterparts and predecessors had been practising? I will address this question systematically in due course, but only after reviewing two texts of Protestant piety, one a meditation in prose, the other a poem from a collection of devotional verse, and both of them concerned in very different ways with interpreting the agony of Christ in the garden.

The prose writer I have chosen is Samuel Rutherford, better known for his many public contributions to Scottish Presbyterianism,[10] but important

10 See John Coffey, "Rutherford, Samuel (c. 1600–1661), Church of Scotland minister and political theorist," *Oxford Dictionary of National Biography* (2009).

here as the author of *Christ Dying and Drawing Sinners to Himselfe* (1647), a book which might be described as a sustained meditation on the relationship between the Christian soul and Christ, interrupted at intervals to allow Rutherford to score debating points against his doctrinal and political enemies (from Arminians to Anabaptists), all of it originating as a series of sermons Rutherford preached on the gospel of John. He declares and quotes his text at the outset, namely, this cryptic utterance of Jesus Christ's: "Now is my soule troubled: and what shall I say? Father, save me from this houre: But for this cause came I unto this houre. Father, glorifie thy name" (John 12:27–8).[11]

Like a skilful interpreter of drama, Rutherford draws attention to the internal conflict his protagonist has to work his way through. He's not sure that his text is representing the same situation that the other gospels narrate as happening "when his soule was troubled in the *garden*, in his *agonie*." But even if the situation is less precisely described in John (as will always be the case in this most metaphysical of gospels), the words are "of the same matter" (B1). They show Christ wanting to resist, however tentatively and temporarily, the long-term assignment that God has given him. This resistance, though of course it is and must be overcome in the end, is exactly what interests Rutherford about Christ's state of mind, about his "Soule-trouble" as Rutherford memorably calls it. In this case internal conflict cannot be fully understood without reference to Christ's dual nature. Insofar as he is divine, "*Christ* loved us, not according to what wee were, but to what *Grace* and *Love* was to make us; and that was faire and spotlesse" (T1^{v}). This divine love then, the ultimate motive for his gift of death, was absolute, and about it there can be no wavering. But Christ inhabited a human nature too, and "In this there is offered to us a question, Whether or no there be in this Prayer any repugnancy in the humane will of *Christ* to the will of *God*?" (T1^{v}). The answer is, yes, there is a repugnancy, but it's not sinful in any way, because Jesus is in the act of subordinating his will to the will of the Father.

And in the way he handles internal conflict, Christ sets an example that we may follow. First, we notice that he imagines the cost of his role in the redemption story – the pain and suffering he will have to endure –

11 *Christ Dying and Drawing Sinners to Himselfe, Or a Survey of our Saviour in His Soule-Suffering, His Lonelynesse in His Death, and the Efficacie Thereof* (London: Andrew Crooke, 1647), B1.

before the actual event. This, Rutherford tells us, is a good thing for a Christian to do: "it were good, ere the crosse come, to act it in our mind, and take an essay and a lift of *Christs* crosse, ere we beare it, to try how handsomely wee would set back and shoulders under the *Lords* crosse" (B1[v]). Such planning in advance will help the Christian to prepare for the moment when he or she is required to subordinate his or her human will to the divine will: "The Law of *God* is so spirituall, straight and holy, that it requireth not onely a conformity to it, and our will, actions, words and purposes; but also in all our affections, desires, first motions, and inclinations of our heart, that no unperfect and halfe-formed lustings arise in us, even before the compleat consent of the will, that may thwart or crosse the known Law and command of *God*" (T1[v]). This is a very demanding system indeed, because it looks so deeply into the hidden recesses of human motivation. But Rutherford is in fact more permissive (or perhaps I should say that his God is) than the above quotation suggests. He recalls the Old Testament story in which Abraham is ordered to sacrifice his son Isaac, which he agrees to do, while of course retaining paternal feelings for his son. Abraham's desire for his son to escape the death penalty is not sinful, even if it is contrary to the express command of God. Why? Because "A conditionall and submissive desire, though not agreeable to a positive Law and Commandment of *God*, is no sinne" (T2[v]). It all depends on the way in which the negotiation between our natural desires and God's will is conducted. If we are always seeking to submit our wills to God's, and acknowledging the absolute authority of his commandments over us, then we will organize our internal conflicts, as Jesus did, without committing sin or incurring the wrath of God in the process.

If Rutherford's book includes the most persuasive account of the ethical ambiguity inherent in Christ's "soule-trouble," the most suggestive treatment of the symbolism inherent in the garden scene is George Herbert's "The Agonie." Like Rutherford, and unlike the Catholic writers cited earlier, Herbert gives us very little descriptive comment on the scene itself; indeed, only the second stanza of his poem is explicitly located in the garden, and we know that only by way of the invitation to find Jesus on Mount Olivet, where the Garden of Gethsemane was presumably located. But if there's only a glimpse of Christ in the garden in Herbert's poem, there is a great deal else, including an epistemological opening and a eucharistic ending, both of which will require further comment. It is a short poem, and deserves to be quoted in full:

The Agonie

Philosophers have measur'd mountains,
Fathom'd the depths of seas, of states, and kings,
Walk'd with a staffe to heav'n, and traced fountains:
But there are two vast, spacious things,
The which to measure it doth more behove:
Yet few there are that sound them; Sinne and Love.

Who would know Sinne, let him repair
Unto Mount Olivet; there shall he see
A man so wrung with pains, that all his hair,
His skinne, his garments bloudie be.
Sinne is that presse and vice, which forceth pain
To hunt his cruell food through ev'ry vein.

Who knows not Love, let him assay
And taste that juice, which on the crosse a pike
Did set again abroach; then let him say
If ever he did taste the like.
Love is that liquor sweet and most divine,
Which my God feels as bloude; but I, as wine.[12]

The last three words of the first stanza, "Sinne and Love," are an interesting surprise, but a fully justified surprise that announces the subjects of the two remaining stanzas. To "know Sinne" we need to watch Jesus bearing its unimaginable weight as he prays to his Father in the garden. It is the weight of the sin of all humankind that bears down upon him (like a "presse") and squeezes him (like a "vice") until "his hair,/His skinne, his garments" are drenched with what might be sweat but seems more like blood. What Herbert is able to capture here is a vicarious sense of the pain that Jesus endures as he takes on the burden of our collective sinfulness. This idea is rendered quite specifically in two metaphors: one in which pains (plural) cause contortions ("wrung with pains"), the other in which pain (singular) is a ravenous eater of the nourishment to be found in "ev'ry vein" of Christ's body. What we see is the contortions and the

12 *The English Poems of George Herbert*, ed. C.A. Patrides (London: Dent, 1974), 58.

bloody sweat, but what we come away with is a deep understanding of sin as the source of Christ's agony in the garden.

To understand love, however, we need to look ahead, to see Christ "on the crosse," as the final stanza invites us to do. We need to remember the soldier who pierced his side, so as to release a stream of water mixed with blood: the "juice" that will represent Christ's love to us. In the sacrament of the eucharist he will continue to say to us: "Take and drinke ye all of this: doo thys in remembraunce of me."[13] And at this moment another mysterious substitution of one liquid for another will occur. What Jesus himself "feels" as his blood, shed on account of his love for humankind, feels like nourishing and thirst-quenching "wine" by the time it touches the speaker's lips. And at this moment, only a backward glance is needed to remind us that the mingling of liquids (the fluidity of fluids, so to speak) has been rhetorically present throughout the poem. Even in stanza 1, the fluidity of "seas" and "fountains" is what makes them difficult to measure. But it is not until we get to stanza 2 that we see a liquid that is held to be two liquids (blood and sweat), a pattern repeated twice in the final stanza, implicitly with the liquid gushing from Christ's side (water and blood), explicitly through the allusion to the eucharist (blood and wine).

The relationship between the opening stanza and the rest of the poem, though still a puzzle, should now be capable of resolution. It is clear from every example the speaker proposes in stanza 1 that he is interested in epistemology. Moreover, he is interested in a particular epistemological problem: the problem of magnitude. How can we know the size of something (a mountain, for example) so much larger than we are that it escapes our usual frame of reference? The answer of course is that we need to invent a system of measurement appropriate to the object in question: a system that will compare mountains with other mountains, seas with other seas, kings with other kings, and so forth. The speaker assumes that such systems are the work of philosophers: natural philosophers where the objects are mountains and seas; moral philosophers where the objects are kings. The image of the philosopher stepping off the heavens by means of his staff is there to remind us that quantification can also, given an inappropriate set of instruments, lead to absurd results. But now the rules have been set in place to guide the rest of this

13 *The Booke of Common Praier, and Administration of the Sacramentes, and Other Rites and Ceremonies in the Churche of Englande* (London: Richard Jugge and John Cawood, 1559), M5–5ᵛ.

exercise, which will be an effort to find out the magnitude of those "two vast spacious things," sin and love. The magnitude of sin comes to be measured in terms of the weight it presses down upon Christ's body. But the magnitude of love, as expressed in Christ's willingness to shed his blood, is simply incommensurable. That is why, in stanza 3, we feel we are being taken to the edge of the infinite.

After having listened carefully to individual voices on both sides of the divide between Catholic and Protestant piety, I propose returning to the larger question of whether there are significant differences between the devotions of the one and the other. Basing my judgment only in part on the sample of writers cited so far, I would say that the principal differences strike me as polemical, semiological, and iconographical.

Protestant piety differs from Catholic in the first instance because Protestants never tire of saying they're not Catholics and are happy not to be. This would be the best reason for Daniel Featley's decision, in 1626, to dedicate the first edition of *Ancilla Pietatis: Or, the Hand-Maid to Private Devotion* to Katherine Villiers, duchess of Buckingham, whom he has recently come to admire: "since your happy departure from the *Romish Synagogue*, and repairing to our true reformed Church, we may say … *we have gained a most precious Jewell to the Church*."[14] The conversion reported here took place in 1620, as part of the preparation for the marriage of Katherine Manners, then just seventeen, to the most glamorous bachelor in the realm.[15] Featley may not have known that, after the assassination of Buckingham in 1628, the duchess reverted to Catholicism; in any case, the editions of his book published in 1630 and 1633 reprint the dedicatory epistle to her. When the duchess married an Irish Catholic, Randal MacDonnell, Lord Dunluce, in 1635, her allegiances were blatantly visible to all, and the 1639 edition of *Ancilla Pietatis* came out with a brand new dedication, this time to Buckingham's sister, Susan Feilding (née Villiers), countess of Denbigh. Featley had no way of foreseeing that by 1652 this lady too would become a Catholic, the addressee of a poem by Richard Crashaw, "To the Noblest & Best of Ladyes, the

14 *Ancilla Pietatis: Or, the Hand-Maid to Private Devotion: Presenting a Manuell to Furnish Her with Instructions, Hymnes and Prayers Fitted to the Christian Feasts and Fasts, the Weeks of the Yeere, the Daies of the Weeke*, 2nd ed. (London: Nicholas Bourne, 1626), A2^{v}.

15 See Jane Ohlmeyer, "MacDonnell [née Manners; other married name Villiers], Katherine, duchess of Buckingham and marchioness of Antrim (1603?–1649), noblewoman," *Oxford Dictionary of National Biography* (2008).

Countesse of Denbigh: Perswading her to Resolution in Religion, & to Render her Selfe without Further Delay into the Communion of the Catholick Church," and the dedicatee of his posthumously published book of poems, *Carmen Deo Nostro* (1652).[16] By this time Featley was gone too; he died in 1645, and the subsequent reprintings of his still popular book (in 1647, 1656, and 1675) appeared with no dedication at all, other than "The Preface to the Reader" printed in all editions. In retrospect the polemical efforts to mark off one set of beliefs from another can have an almost comical appearance, but for the partisans on both sides the differences were momentous. Only in extreme cases would human lives be lost, but in all cases, according to believers on both sides of the great divide, the kind and quality of life after death were at issue.

Semiologically, one striking difference between Protestant piety and Catholic has to do with biblical citation. Featley's manual is demonstrably and principally a gathering of relevant biblical texts; at least two-thirds of the book consists of quotation or close paraphrase from the Bible. And because book, chapter, and verse references are given in the margins, it means that the appearance of the book includes a pretty messy pepper spray of citation both to the left and the right of the principal visual field. This is a good thing, from a Protestant point of view, because the messy annotations are calling us back, again and again, to the word of God.[17] Nor is Featley at all unusual in this practice; every work of Protestant piety I have consulted is dotted with numerous and precise biblical references, usually in the margins, often at the headings of chapters, and sometimes within the text itself. The Bible is important for Catholic writers too, and it is frequently quoted or paraphrased. But exact references are not supplied. The accuracy of the quotation, and the interpretation being given to it, are meant to be taken on trust by the reader, and that trust is based on the authority of the writer. Villa-castin's *Manuall* tells us that Christ prayed in the garden "with great love and confidence" and

16 See Richard Crashaw, *The Poems: English, Latin and Greek*, ed. L.C. Martin, 2nd ed. (Oxford: Clarendon, 1957), 236, 231. Heather Wolfe gives 1651 as the date of Lady Denbigh's conversion; see "Elizabeth (Tanfield) Cary, Vicountess Falkland, to Susan (Villiers) Fielding, Countess of Denbigh (c. December 1626)," in *Early Modern Women: An Anthology of Texts in Manuscript and Print, 1550–1700*, ed. Helen Ostovich and Elizabeth Sauer (London: Routledge, 2004), 214.

17 This observation is consistent with the overall thesis of Barbara Kiefer Lewalski's *Protestant Poetics and the Seventeenth-Century Religious Lyric* (Princeton, NJ: Princeton University Press, 1979), 8.

gives us his exact words too: "Father if thou wilt, transfer this Chalice from me: But yet not my will, but thyne be done" (P4^{v}–5). These words, however, are not set off from the rest of Villa-castin's text by quotation marks or italics, nor is a reference of any kind made to any of the four gospels. Instead, we have the word of Reverend Father Thomas Villa-castin, avowedly based on *The Spiritual Exercises* of the Blessed Father Ignatius, and translated for us by "a Father of the same Society" (title page). When three members of the Society of Jesus are telling us how Jesus prayed, we don't need to check the reference for ourselves.

The iconographical difference I want to notice here is the spectacular and inescapable demotion of the Virgin Mary in Protestant piety. She is still the Virgin Mary, of course, and the mother of Jesus. But she no longer mediates between us and God, because only Jesus is authorized to do this job.[18] And the celebrations of her Assumption and Coronation disappear from the Christian calendar, Protestant style, because there is no warrant for them in scripture. But there are much smaller ways in which Mary's role is further reduced. She seems to be always present, even if absent, in Villa-castin's meditations. Recall that, in describing Christ's isolation in the garden, Villa-castin mentions his mother's absence as a contributing factor. And whenever he can, Villa-castin brings her onstage, in a primary supporting role. When Villa-castin's Jesus decides, at age thirty, that he ought to be baptized, the first thing he does is ask his mother's permission. After all, he's been living with her for thirty years, and she's now a "poore widdow," so it's easy to imagine her, at his departure, "with teares trickling fast down her cheeks" (L4^{v}). And when he rises from the dead, whom does Jesus visit first? "The first visit, & apparition which Christ Jesus our Lord made, is thought to have been to the most Blessed Virgin his mother" (T10^{v}). Ever the loyal son, Jesus wants to relieve his mother's distress (over his crucifixion) at the first available opportunity. Never mind that the Bible tells us no such thing; Villa-castin protects himself here with the phrase "is thought to have been," a proviso which lets him add Roman Catholic teaching and tradition to the authority of scripture. Elsewhere he achieves the very same purpose with a similar formula, "it is credible, that" (H2^{v}). Perhaps, but not to Protestants, who want to know that "It is written" (Matthew 4:4).

18 "For there is one God and one mediator between God and men, the man Christ Jesus" (1 Timothy 2:5).

I am not trying to applaud the relegation of the Virgin Mary by Protestantism; I am merely drawing attention to it in the hope of suggesting that it mattered. It would be possible to argue that Reformation Christianity took a great many steps that had the overall effect of repudiating much of the female imagery available to Catholics. Not only did the Blessed Virgin lose prestige – a prestige upheld in part by beautiful likenesses of her in places of Catholic worship – but a long roll-call of female saints (from Matilda of Saxony to Teresa of Avila) was simply swept away, as were the opportunities for spiritual and intellectual development within female monastic orders. In return for all of these losses, the Reformation held out to female worshippers the prospect of marriage to a clergyman: a step that would certainly confine any woman to an explicitly domestic role. There is more that needs to be said about female devotions, both Catholic and Protestant, but I suspend the question for now, knowing that it will arise again (and urgently so) when Jesus is figured as a spouse yearning for his bride.

But before leaving the question of the Protestant/Catholic divide, let me say that, despite the differences I have outlined, when early modern Christians engaged in private devotions, their experience seems to have been coloured by a longing for inwardness regardless of where they stood on the spectrum of sectarian affiliation. The "grape of blisse" which yields "sweet wine" at the beginning of Southwell's poem is after all not so different from the "liquor sweet and most divine" which leads to the end of Herbert's. The isolation that Jesus feels in Villa-castin's account is after all not so different from the "soule-trouble" he confronts in Rutherford's text. And the experience of the individual Christian engaged in meditation will be an exercise which depends on and develops interiority. This much was true, I believe, for Christians of all denominations.

The Chamber within Us

Describing the soul as the bride of Christ has a venerable place in the traditions of Christian piety, partly because of St Bernard's great esteem for this metaphor and his joy in explicating it in his sermons on the Song of Solomon.[19] The metaphor, and even St Bernard's commentary

19 *Cantica Canticorum: Eighty-Six Sermons on the Song of Solomon*, trans. Samuel J. Eales (London: Elliot Stock, 1895), 33: "*Let Him kiss me with the kisses of His Mouth.* Who is it speaks these words? It is the Bride. Who is the Bride? It is the Soul thirsting for God."

on it, seem to have been readily available to Catholics and Protestants alike. Thus Villa-castin recommends that his reader "consider that our Lord is the Spouse of thy soule, in whom in most perfect manner is found all that can be desired in a good Spouse" (2A1–1^{v}). These attributes include beauty, nobility of birth, discretion, wealth, and love for his bride, which he expresses by "observing towards her the cerimonies of true love, and taking pleasure to see and discourse with her dayly" (2A1^{v}). The Protestant writer Joseph Hall has recourse to the conjugal metaphor when he recommends that the soul should be "solitairie and silent" when preparing to communicate with her true spouse: "It was a wittie and Divine speach of *Bernard*, that the spouse of the soule, Christ Jesus, is bashfull, neither willingly comes to his bride in the presence of a multitude."[20] What is being valued here is an intimate relationship with the divine, and the bride of Christ is the vehicle by which we are encouraged to imagine such intimacy.

Because the bride of Christ is common property to both Catholics and Protestants, I will at this point abandon the practice of highlighting this polarity, and will make room instead for a rather more diversified chorus of voices, most of which could probably be included within a very comprehensive definition of Protestantism, and some of which will call to mind the recognition, made earlier, that devotional life in early modern culture was the work of both genders. Religious affiliation is still a question that I will draw attention to and comment upon, whenever necessary, but only as one item among several.

The Mysticall Marriage by Francis Rous is an explication of the metaphor in question so detailed as to border, at times, on the absurd. Even the dedicatory address, "To the Bride the Lambes Wife," shows Rous working rather too hard to extend the metaphor: "There is a chamber within us," he writes, "and a bed of love in that chamber, wherein Christ meets and rests with the soule."[21] The "chamber" by itself is fine as a way of suggesting interiority, the place where the soul lives. But as soon as the chamber is provided with furniture that makes it a bedroom ("a bed of love" is the item in question), the vehicle of the metaphor gets uncomfortably specific. It doesn't help matters much to say, euphemistically,

---

20 *The Arte of Divine Meditation: Profitable for All Christians to Knowe and Practise; Exemplified with a Large Meditation of Eternal Life* (London: Samuel Macham and Mathew Cooke, 1606), B10^{v}.

21 *The Mysticall Marriage: Or, Experientall Discoveries of the Heavenly Marriage betweene a Soule and Her Saviour*, 2nd ed. (London: Jasper Emery, 1635), A3.

that Christ "meets and rests with" his bride on that bed. We all know what beds of love are for, and this isn't it.

But Rous is undeterred by the canons of good taste, and he is enraptured by the prospect of mystical intimacy. So he advises the soul, in seeking her true spiritual husband, to use exactly the tactics that would be roundly condemned in the physical realm: "Looke on him so, that thou maist lust after him, for here it is a sinne, not to looke that thou mayst lust, and not to lust having looked. For the spirit hath his lust also; it lusteth against things contrary to it, and lusteth for things connatural to it. Accordingly it lusteth against the flesh; but it lusteth after spirituall objects; whereof Christ Jesus is the chiefest" (A11). The big distinction here is between carnal lust, which has to be hedged about (after the fall) with all of the well-known prohibitions, and spiritual lust, which seems to be, for Rous at least, completely uninhibited. That's why the soul, once married to Christ, can and indeed ought to use all of the strategies of the spiritual seductress: the "face" of the soul, as the bridegroom approaches her, should "shine brightly in his eyes, being annoynted with fresh oyle" (M5); every gesture should imply her eager receptivity; "And if hee come not yet into thee, stirre up thy spirituall concupiscence, and therewith let the soule lust mightily for him, and let her lusts and desires ascend up to him in strong cryes and invocations, & then by his spirit he will descend unto thee" (M8v). The soul doesn't have to be passive in her erotic dealing with this bridegroom; she is advised to "Touch him hard with thy faith, sucke him strongly with thy love, that more vertue may come out of him" (N4). It's as if Rous now knows that he has some explaining to do. The spiritual sucking he recommends is, he argues, comparable to the action of a tree branch sucking sap and nourishment from the trunk. This should be the soul's model: "And that thou maist thus grow, let not swelling, but growth be the end of thy sucking," he advises; "Grow thou in the reall excellency of a divine Nature, and not in the empty swellings of a fleshly pride" (N5v–6). I can't imagine a clearer statement of reassurance to the effect that the bride of Christ is not giving oral sex to her bridegroom. But then, it's the erotic language of the text itself that has created the need for this denial.[22]

22 Here, and throughout this chapter, I follow Richard Rambuss's lead in wanting to confront, without embarrassment or censorship, the perversity that characterizes much early modern devotional writing. Where I do not follow Rambuss, however, is in assuming, as I think he does, that late twentieth-century queer theory is the

Although mystical marriage holds out the promise of ecstatic rapture, it is neither easy nor unproblematic. Its origin is a very messy love triangle, in which the soul has married a husband unworthy of her, and must now give consent to a murder plot: "Her old husband was concupiscence, to whom she was married in carnall generation, and this husband must bee slaine, and put off by death, if Christ Jesus the new and true husband of the soule shall be put on in regeneration" (B2). Although the bride here is moving in the opposite direction to Gertrude's journey in *Hamlet*, Rous sounds a little like Hamlet himself advising his mother to "Look here upon this picture, and on this,/The counterfeit presentment of two brothers" (3.4.51–2). But even after the murder plot has been successfully carried out, the bride's new husband will frequently be away from home, and she will have to learn to live with the anxiety that accompanies these "desertions." Rous itemizes six separate arguments to support the view that the bride's "estate," while deserted, "though seemingly miserable, is indeed profitable" (E5). I will not list all six of these, because the direction they take can be clearly implied by citing two examples. Desertions are strategically beneficial because they "trie the truth of our love" (F12); the bride who remains faithful during her spouse's absence gives him, by indirection, the gift of exclusive love. And the desertions are furthermore "advantageable to the soule" because they help her to focus not on "this place," where joys are subject to interruption, but on "the place of incessant and everlasting joyes" (H1^{v}). That new place, on any Christian reading that I am aware of, would be the one Jesus says he will prepare for us to inhabit in the life after death.

Still, for the soul engaged in that second and mystical marriage, life need not be just a vale of tears. The description Rous gives of the happiness of the soul is positively rapturous: "God being tasted, overfloweth, and steepeth, and drencheth the soule with overcomming and inebriating sweetnesse. For a high, and large, and mightie joy, poured into a low, and measured, and weake spirit, overcommeth her with quantity, and

normative position from which all perversities should be evaluated. I prefer a method of analysis that gives authority to the perversities embedded within early modern culture itself, and that is why my analysis includes the notion of sin, the distinction between Catholic and Protestant, and the desire to transcend the body: three essential ideas that seem to me almost completely absent from his book; for a brief but inadequate comment on the Catholic/Protestant distinction, see *Closet Devotions*, 158–9n4.

quality, and so carries her away into extasie and ravishment: she is too narrow and feeble to containe and beare a joy that is too large and strong for her; and therefore having filled her to the utmost capacity, it goes beyond and runnes over" (C3v–4). The rhetoric of excess is so pronounced here as to recall the baroque style in visual art and poetry, including the story of St Teresa of Avila, ravished by the angel who appeared to her in a vision. Here the experience of ecstasy is represented by fire instead of water, but the notion of excess remains the same. "I did see an angel," St Teresa declares in what purports to be an autobiographical text; "I did see in his hand a long darte of gold, and at the end of the yron head it seemed to have a litle fyre, this he seemed to passe thorough my heart sometimes, and that it pierced to my entrayles, which me thoght he drew from mee, when he pulled it out agayne, & he left me wholy enflamed in great love of God, the payne was so great that it made me complayne greevously, & the sweetnesse was so excessive, which this exceeding great payne causeth, that I could not desire to have it taken away."[23] There are differences between these two accounts of ecstatic joy, to be sure. St Teresa claims explicitly that the angel appeared to her "in corporall forme," an assertion that Rous certainly doesn't make about the bridegroom, whose conjugal relations with the soul he imagines to happen on an exclusively spiritual plane. But in their reliance on a rhetoric of excess, everywhere encoded as the rhetoric of sexual excess, these two writers are in such powerful agreement as to appear almost competitors.

Which indeed they are. By the time he published *The Mysticall Marriage* Rous was a Member of Parliament with a growing reputation for supporting and sponsoring radical Puritan measures. He described the Roman Catholic church as "the mother of spiritual fornications,"[24] and the Church of England also drew his contempt. His support for Parliament and later for Cromwell would lead eventually to appointments as provost of Eton College (1644) and speaker of the House of Commons (1653). This public profile might not have led us to expect the luxurious erotic

23 *The Lyf of the Mother Teresa of Jesus, Foundresse of the Monasteries of the Descalced or Barefooted Carmelite Nunnes and Fryers of the First Rule: Written by Her Self, at the Commandment of Her Ghostly Father, and Now Translated into English, out of Spanish*, trans. W.M. (Antwerp: Henry Jaye, 1611), 2F4v.

24 Quoted in Colin Burrow, "Rous, Francis (1580/81–1659), religious writer and politician," *Oxford Dictionary of National Biography* (2008). This article is also the source for the biographical details about Rous given here.

coloration of his inner devotional life, but it is still possible, I think, to delight in his excesses. If he was a little too eager to condemn the excesses of others, that is a shortcoming he shared with contemporaries on every wavelength of the cultural spectrum.

The Female Soul

Female authors of devotional verse and prose are often drawn to the metaphor of the bride of Christ, but (contrary to what we might expect) not easily, naturally, or unproblematically. In *Salve Deus Rex Judaeorum* Aemelia Lanyer seeks to renegotiate the relationship between some of the principal events of the Christian narrative and a group of female readers, including her distinguished female patrons, and of course herself. This work has attracted ample commentary in recent years, so I will restrict my account of it to the stanzas in which Lanyer, according to her own marginal note, seeks to offer "*A briefe description of his beautie upon the Canticles.*"[25] Christ has just risen from the dead,

> And now those pretious oyntments he desires
> Are brought unto him, by his faithfull Wife
> The holy Church. (1290–2)

Far from joining her own soul to Christ in spiritual ecstasy, Lanyer chooses another allegorical interpretation, also authorized by St Bernard and by long tradition, in which the bride is a collective entity, the church.[26] But Christ is still very much the bridegroom, and that is why, after his wounds have been attended to, his beauty becomes the source of veneration:

> This is that Bridegroome that appeares so faire,
> So sweet, so lovely in his Spouses sight,

25 *The Poems of Aemilia Lanyer: "Salve Deus Rex Judaeorum,"* ed. Suzanne Woods (New York: Oxford University Press, 1993), 107. Subsequent references are to this edition, and are made with line references only.

26 See *Cantica Canticorum,* 281: "Let us now inquire what is the spiritual significance of all these things. First, it refers to the Church. And I consider that the 'bed' upon which rest is taken means the monasteries and cloisters in which a quiet and peaceable life is passed, exempt from the cares and inquietudes of the world."

That unto Snowe we may his face compare,
His cheekes like skarlet, and his eyes so bright
As purest Doves that in the rivers are,
Washed with milke, to give the more delight;
His head is likened to the finest gold,
His curled lockes so beauteous to behold. (1305–12)

What strikes me most forcefully about this passage is how completely unlike the Song of Songs it is. The bridegroom isn't "leaping upon the mountains" like "a young hart" (Song of Solomon 2:8–9); he is not cradling the bride's head with his left hand, nor embracing her with his right; he is not speaking to her at all, let alone calling for her to arise, make haste, and come with him. Instead, the bridegroom Lanyer gives us is as motionless, speechless, and curiously distant as the lady in Petrarchan poetry.[27] He has some of the same physical features too: the white and red of his complexion, his golden curls, and so on. This much might be implied in previous comments about the representation of Christ in this poem as feminized or even androgynous.[28] But to make matters worse, this apparently beautiful icon has to be "Washed with milke" to make him even more desirable. The allusion of course is to a well-known Jacobean cosmetic treatment: namely, what Vindici refers to in *The Revenger's Tragedy* as "sinful baths of milk."[29] Lanyer certainly didn't mean to attribute anything sinful to her Jesus, but I'm not sure that she managed her rhetorical task with sufficient skill when she decided to describe his beauty. Earlier, in addressing the Countess of Cumberland, she disparaged "outward Beautie" as vulnerable to time, and declared it to be "not the subject I will write upon" (185–6). I can respect the ambiguity she feels about physical beauty, all the more so since I imagine her own beauty to have been her ticket to a glamorous life at the Elizabethan court. But I don't think she purged the ambiguities, or even guarded against them in any way, before she assigned this attribute to Christ.

---

27 See Lyn Bennett, *Women Writing of Divinest Things: Rhetoric and the Poetry of Pembroke, Wroth and Lanyer* (Pittsburgh, PA: Duquesne University Press, 2004), 237–8.

28 See Randall Martin, ed., *Women Writers in Renaissance England* (London: Longman, 1997), 364.

29 See *The Revenger's Tragedy*, ed. R.A. Foakes, Revels Student Editions (Manchester: Manchester University Press, 1996), 3.5.86.

Indeed, I think the idea of posing as the bride of Christ makes Lanyer feel uncomfortable. She's far better at imagining intimacy with Jesus when she writes about Christ's mother, whom she describes in the following lines as she is just after receiving the news from the angel Gabriel:

> Thus being crown'd with glory from above,
> Grace and Perfection resting in thy breast,
> Thy humble answer doth aproove thy Love,
> And all these sayings in thy heart doe rest:
> Thy Child a Lambe, and thou a Turtle dove,
> Above all other women highly blest. (1089–94)

Here is a female role with which Lanyer can identify, not in the sense that she thinks she *is* the blessed Virgin, but rather in the sense that this is a role she would love to play. Perhaps the Italian half of her heritage (her father, Baptist Bassano, was Venetian by birth) kept alive for her a veneration of the Virgin Mary that included identification of this kind.

The bride of Christ may have been a more attractive role for women members of dissenting sects and communities; Eliza, the devotional poet who will feature prominently in chapter 5, would be an example of this pattern if indeed she came from a dissenting background. Sarah Davy (née Roane), certainly a dissenter, seems to have developed an interest in the metaphor as a schoolgirl. Her mother having died when Sarah was eleven, she was sent away to school, but returned home to find Mr Pierce, a new minister, in charge of family worship: "the first Sermon I heard from him did much take upon my affections and raise up my desires unto the ways of God," she writes; the text was Canticles 7:8, "wherein he opened the beauty of a Soul in Christ."[30] If Mr Pierce was quoting the King James Bible on this occasion, then his auditors would be aware that the bridegroom has just likened the bride to a "palm tree," and her "breasts to clusters of grapes." Then comes the text in question: "I said, I will go up to the palm tree, I will take hold of the boughs thereof: now also thy breasts shall be as clusters of the vine, and the smell of thy nose like apples" (Song of Solomon 7:7–8). We don't get Sarah Davy's commentary on the text or her summary of the sermon, but we do know that,

30 *Heaven Realiz'd: Or the Holy Pleasure of Daily Intimate Communion with God, Exemplified in a Blessed Soul (Now in Heaven)* ([London]: A.P., 1670), B6.

years later, she remembered (or thought she remembered) the powerful emotional impact of the occasion.

The best clue to Davy's religious affiliation comes in her account of meeting a special friend with whom she can share aspects of her spiritual life: "she was of a society of the *Congregational way* called *Independants*" (C5). If we assume, as I think we should, that the events being narrated are happening about mid-century, then the orientation here would be quite similar to that of Cromwell himself. We are given a little help with such historical conjectures when, roughly halfway through the book, a second title page announces that what follows is work done "before her Marriage" by Sarah Roane and records the date "December 1660" (D8). Since the original title page, dated 1670, claims that Sarah Davy died "about the 32 Year of her Age," we must assume she was twenty-two when she married.

About her terrestrial marriage we can recover nothing from this text. But A.P., who identifies himself by initials alone, tells us in the address "To All Sort of Readers" that Sarah Davy was "sick of Love to blessed Jesus Christ, whom she had chosen her *Saviour, Bridegroom*[,] *Lord*, and *King*; whose *love, beauty*, and *glory* ravished her heart" (A3). Was A.P. the Mr Pierce who preached that memorable sermon on the Song of Songs? He has enough insider knowledge to affirm that she was a member of the "*Congregation of Christ*" (B1[v]), and that "Praying, Reading, Meditation" were "her Morning and Evening exercise" (B1) until she "*fell asleep in Jesus*" because "she could hardly bear the absence from her dear Lord any longer" (A8[v]).

This image of the pious female Christian is supported in extenso by the meditations collected under her maiden name, Sarah Roane. These include a conventional piece, "Meditations of Death" (G7[v]–8[v]), and a somewhat more imaginative remake of the same subject, "My Further Meditations on Death" (K6–7[v]). "Death is a Jaylor who unlocks the prison doors of *a gratious soul*," she announces; thus released, the soul can enter heaven, "there to be imbraced in the arms of a loving Saviour" (K6). The point here is that, for Sarah Davy, life as the bride of Christ begins after death. And that is why, in her untitled treatment of this theme, being ready for death is crucial:

That when my Bridegroom comes
I may be drest,
With him to go unto that
Marriage Feast. (I7[v])

The concern for proper garments is perhaps a domestication of the mystical marriage, but the poem does strike the rhapsodic note as well:

Inflame my heart Lord
with more heavenly fire,
And fill my heart with love
more to aspire,
Through grace dear Lord
thou hast made love to me,
More sweet and pleasant
then all Wines can be. (I8)

The phrase "made love" deserves attention. It is just possible that "love" is a noun, and that the Lord has transformed ("made") love into something sweet and pleasant for the speaker. But I take it that, in its primary sense, "made love" is a compound verb which expresses something the bridegroom has already done to the bride. If that is the case, then it must be understood as Jane Austen would have understood it: the bridegroom has *courted* the bride by offering her grace. Ravishment has been deferred, but is certainly anticipated here; the rhetoric of wine tasting calls back the sensory appeal of the Song of Solomon: "How fair is thy love, my sister, my spouse! how much better is thy love than wine!" (4:10). Sarah Roane is ready, but will have to wait for ten years to be the bride of Christ.

To help situate the practices of female piety, both materially and socially, I draw attention now to the diary of Lady Margaret Hoby, itself a document created by pious exercise. Born Margaret Dakins in 1571, as a young woman she was an heiress who attracted the attention of three successive younger sons, all of them from the social elite, and married each of them in turn. Her first husband, Walter Devereux, younger brother of the famous earl of Essex, died in military combat after about two years of marriage; her second husband, Thomas Sidney, youngest brother of the famous poet, died after about three and a half years of marriage. Sir Thomas Posthumous Hoby, son of Castiglione's English translator, became her third husband in 1596. He seems to have been by far the least attractive of the three, utterly lacking in *sprezzatura*, for example; but he was the husband who lasted, and in fact outlasted his wife by seven years (she died in 1633, he in 1640). The diary as it has come down to us includes only entries from the relatively early years (1599–1605) of this long marriage.

The earliest entries begin with a virtual formula, "After I was redie I betooke my selfe to privat praier."[31] To be "redie" in Elizabethan English is to be fully dressed, and to engage in "privat" prayer is to perform a devotional exercise alone, quite apart from whatever acts of worship will be performed collectively by the household as a whole. Sometimes Lady Hoby specifies that she prays "privatly in my Closett" (13 September 1599), a reminder that Hackness Hall and the surrounding estate, in which she lived during all three of her marriages, was a property sufficiently grand to afford her privacy if she wanted it. The diary suggests that she practised her devotions with great regularity, morning and evening; that she often attended church on weekdays and almost always (twice) on Sundays; that meals were preceded or followed by public acts of piety, such as prayer and reading from scripture; and that many of Lady Hoby's discretionary hours were spent in further meditation, reading, or other religious exercise. The most recent editor of the diary, Joanna Moody, believes that "more than half" (xxxvii) of Lady Hoby's waking hours were spent in explicitly religious activity. Nobody has claimed that this is the norm in Elizabethan culture; in view of the many markers of strong Puritan orientation in the Hoby household, I think we should assume otherwise. But even when such allowances are made, the diary reminds us that we are dealing with a culture in which piety, both public and private, mattered a great deal.

Some of the particularities of the diary, both those which I have been underscoring here and others as well, can be observed in this emotionally complex entry:

September 1599, 1 _Saterday_

After praier in the morninge, I, beinge not well, did heare Mr Rhodes read of Gyffard upon the songe of Sallemon: sone after I went to breakfast, and so walked allmost tell dinner time: then I Came in, and praied, and so to dinner: after which I walked about the house, barne, and feeldes, and, when I Came home, I praied privat with Mr Rhodes, wherein I had more comfort then ever I received in my Life before, I praise god: then I went to take my Beesse, and, after that, I returned to privat praier my selfe and

31 *The Private Life of an Elizabethan Lady: The Diary of Lady Margaret Hoby, 1599–1605*, ed. Joanna Moody (Thrupp, Stroud, Gloucestershire: Sutton, 1998), 3 (entry for 10 August 1599). Subsequent references are to this edition and are made by date entry alone.

examination: then I went to se my Honnie ordered, and so to supper: after which I went to lector, and soone after to bed.

Not feeling well is no reason whatsoever for skipping the devotions that precede breakfast. Perhaps Lady Hoby's physical indisposition is the reason she relies on Richard Rhodes, her chaplain, to read to her rather than reading by herself. In any case, Rhodes reads to her from a book that comments, at length, on the metaphor of the bride of Christ.[32] The author of this book, George Gifford, was a clergyman whose Puritan leanings had from time to time provoked his superiors in the church hierarchy;[33] still, he took the line that the primary allegorical meaning of the bride in the Song of Solomon is the true church, though he allowed for a second interpretation (as the individual Christian soul) that would complement rather than contradict the first. We cannot know which passages of Gifford's book were read out by Mr Rhodes, nor whether they elicited any comments. But I think we can be certain that the metaphor of the bride of Christ once again called up a strong response.

So much is required, I believe, as preparation for the devotional event of the afternoon: "I praied privat with Mr Rhodes, wherein I had more comfort then ever I received in my Life before, I praise god." Lady Hoby very seldom makes admissions about her emotional reactions, so this moment stands out loud and clear. She very seldom shares her "privat" space with anyone, so Mr Rhodes must be aware that this is a special occasion. And, having identified this man only as Lady Hoby's chaplain, I should add that his name appears more frequently in the diary than anyone else's, with the possible exception of Mr Hoby's. And "Mr Hoby," referred to in that formal way in virtually all of his appearances, never provokes an emotional response as powerful as the one recorded here. There are of course a lot of quotidian activities in the entry I'm concerned with here that I've said nothing about so far. For someone who began the day feeling ill, Lady Hoby does a prodigious amount of walking: enough to fill up nearly the whole interval between breakfast and noon, and then to take her around the property again in the afternoon. Somehow she has energy left over for collecting honey from her bees,

32 George Gifford, *Fifteene Sermons upon the Song of Salomon* (London: Felix Kingston for Thomas Man, 1598).

33 See Brett Usher, "Gifford, George (1547/8–1600), Church of England clergyman and author," *Oxford Dictionary of National Biography* (2004).

and for giving directions for its use, presumably to her cooks and other household servants. But I don't think the walking or the sudden attention to the ordinary are able to diminish the emotional effect that I am reading into the central passage of this entry. If anything, the emotional impact is heightened by what appears to be, on Lady Hoby's part, an almost blissful escape into the routines of her life as the manager of a large domestic economy.

For anyone seeking a full disclosure of Lady Hoby's private self, this diary will be a source of frustration. Although married three times, Lady Hoby had no children. Was she devastated by what she must have perceived as her own infertility? In her numerous comments about her own husband, she treats him always with the respect one might reserve for a partner, but never with the fondness or playfulness that might suggest intimacy. Did she find him a disappointment, by comparison with her previous husbands in particular? Conversely, did she feel attracted to Mr Rhodes? Did she have to bite her lip when, not so long after the death of his first wife, Mr Rhodes courted and married her most recently appointed maidservant, Mercie Hunter? All of these are questions that we could answer only if we knew the contents of the exercise which Lady Hoby designates, repeatedly, as "privatt praier and examenation" (see 7, 13, 14, and 15 January 1601). The "examenation" here is the searching of one's conscience for sins, of commission or omission, that have not yet been confessed to God. Habitual practice of this exercise will help the Christian to become aware of, and hence better able to resist, temptations that may lie ahead.

The practice of piety as recorded by early modern women differs from that of their male counterparts in at least one important respect: it is altogether less prescriptive, less dogmatic, and more confessional. No doubt this difference comes about in part because almost all of the male writers are clergymen of one kind or another; the only exception to this rule among the male writers cited here would be Francis Rous who, if not ordained, was nonetheless a religious educator and spokesperson. But the difference remains a difference. Male devotional writers, on the whole, are willing to advise their readers to take the following steps to prepare for devotions, to approach God with language of a particular kind, to make these gestures rather than those while engaged in prayer. The texts of female piety cited here contain no overt instructions of this kind. Lanyer's *Salve Deus Rex Judaeorum*, even if it has the educative mission of revisiting the place of woman in the Christian narrative, tends to proceed by indirections rather than by positive assertion. The writers of female piety, far from claiming clerical authority for themselves, are more likely to seek out the support of a male clergyman who can serve as a mentor. Hence the role of Mr Pierce in the early life of Sarah Davy (née Roane), and of Mr Rhodes in the spiritual struggles of Lady Margaret Hoby. The bride of Christ could expect a great many blessings, but gender equality was not among them.

Sacred Lust

I will end this chapter with some reflections on the private devotions of John Saltmarsh, a figure who calls for attention precisely because he doesn't fit into most of the categories that seventeenth-century piety would construct for him. His own beliefs and the destabilizing events of the 1640s drew Saltmarsh into polemical writing for which he has been justly admired as a man of principle and an advocate of religious toleration well ahead of his time.[34] In response to the highly restrictive Calvinism which had dominated Protestant theology for a century, Saltmarsh articulated a doctrine of free grace, in which salvation is available to all human beings: "Thus *God* in *free-grace* had *mercy* on us, and gave *Christ* for us; and in him we are made capable of the *love* of *God*."[35] In response to the eagerness of the Presbyterians to exercise control over forms of worship, Saltmarsh proposed the unanswerable question: "Why was it such a crime to count any *Schismaticks* and *factious*, under *Prelacy*? and why is it now under Presbytery matter of just report against others?"[36] In response to Cromwell's willingness to purge the New Model Army of troublesome dissidents after the Putney debates, Saltmarsh is said to have arisen from his sickbed in order to ride from Ilford to London, where he confronted Fairfax and Cromwell, without removing his hat, and renounced their strategy as contrary to Christian principles.[37] This courageous action by a former chaplain of the New Model Army was

34 See W.K. Jordan, "Sectarian Thought and Its Relation to the Development of Religious Toleration, 1640–1660," *Huntington Library Quarterly* 3 (1939–40): 307–8.

35 *Free-Grace: Or the Flowings of Christs Blood Freely to Sinners* (London: Giles Calvert, 1645), F9^v.

36 *Groanes for Liberty* (London: Giles Calvert, 1646), C3^v.

37 See A.L. Morton, *The World of the Ranters: Religious Radicalism in the English Revolution* (London: Lawrence and Wishart, 1970), 66–7; and Roger Pooley, "Saltmarsh, John (d. 1647), preacher and religious controversialist," *Oxford Dictionary of National Biography* (2004).

given something close to mythic status when it was discovered that, four days later, attended by only his wife Mary, "he dyed very peaceably and quietly."[38] For these and other reasons, Saltmarsh remains an interesting if obscure public figure whose actions during a time of rapid social change were admired, with good reason, as exemplary.

But the Saltmarsh who interests me here is an altogether more private person. He was a young clergyman in the Church of England, the Rector of Heslerton in his native Yorkshire, when in 1640 he published *Holy Discoveries and Flames*, a highly idiosyncratic book of meditations. Two engraved emblems (and only two) are printed again and again as iconic signifiers of two different kinds of meditation. An upward-looking eye signifies that what follows will be a discovery of spiritual "knowledge."[39] This is what happens in "The Mountain," a meditation which begins with a biblical quotation: "And seeing the multitude, hee went up into a Mountain" (Matthew 5:1). For Saltmarsh, Christ's action here implies that "it is good not to be always too publike and popular" but to allow times for "retirement" as well (B9–9^{v}). By contrast, the icon of a heart engulfed by flames signifies an emotional experience, a meditation designed to promote "affection" (A7), an example of which will follow in due course.

As an even younger man, while engaged in studies at Magdalen College, Cambridge, that would lead to degrees of BA (1633) and MA (1636), Saltmarsh wrote devotional verse. He collected his poems and published them, with dedications to some of his tutors and mentors, perhaps as a way of marking his departure from the university and acknowledging its influence upon his intellectual and spiritual life. These poems are not uniformly brilliant, but they deserve much more than the cursory mention they are (infrequently) given. "Meditation 6: The Emblemes of the Resurrection" is an interesting case of a young poet finding his own voice. After an opening stanza in which the bodies of Christians are said to be asleep underground, and before the final two stanzas in which the eventual reunion of body and soul is celebrated, the young Saltmarsh gives us a series of metaphysical conceits:

38 *Wonderfull Predictions Declared in a Message, as from the Lord, to His Excellency S[i]r Thomas Fairfax and the Councell of His Army* (London: Robert Ibbitson, 1648), A4^{v}. The title of this brief pamphlet attributes its contents to Saltmarsh himself, a claim which cannot hold for the passage just quoted.

39 *Holy Discoveries and Flames* (London: Phillip Nevill, 1640), A7.

We are Gods tapers, this dark world's his night:
Death his extinguisher puts out our light:
Our bodies fall like snuffe; yet will he deigne
At his great fire to light us up again.

We see the Eastern bird, whose ashy nest
Is a rare embleme of our latest rest:
We see the flying serpent shift his slough
To frolick in a fresher: 'tis enough.[40]

The indebtedness to Donne is perhaps a bit obvious; Donne's poems had been published just three years earlier, and for a young apprentice in the profession of divinity, his influence may have been irresistible. So Donne's conceit of the lovers as "tapers" who "at our own cost die"[41] becomes an extended metaphor in which all Christians are "Gods tapers." The change in emphasis allows for a distinction between the transitory body, visualized here as "snuffe" (the residue, the used-up part of the taper), and the immortal soul, capable of reanimation at God's behest. If this counts as a significant reorientation of Donne's conceit, and I think it does, we might still find it striking that the next stanza opens with an image borrowed from the very same poem by Donne, namely the "Eastern bird" (or phoenix), already cited in connection with Southwell's imagery, as a harbinger of the resurrection. Still, to fault a young poet of 1636 for indebtedness to Donne is at best ungenerous; and my claim is not that Saltmarsh has found his own voice in *Poemata Sacra*, but that he is in the process of finding it.

In order to locate Saltmarsh more precisely in relation to the rhetoric of private devotions, I will cite some of his redesignings of the metaphor of the soul as the bride of Christ, both in prose and in verse. In *Holy Discoveries and Flames*, the meditation titled "The Bride-chamber" is among the flames, and therefore by definition it should evoke an emotional response. As we would expect, the tone of this devotion is created in part by quotations from the Song of Solomon, and sustained by the rhetoric of pleasure: "Here is no weeping, no teares, for God is here, and shall *wipe away all teares*; here is nothing but revellings and divine espousals, here is

40 *Poemata Sacra, Latinè & Anglicè Scripta* (Cambridge: Thomas Buck and Roger Daniel, 1636), C5.

41 "The Canonization," *Poems*, ed. Smith, 47.

the *Bride-chamber*, here is the sweet celebration of the spirituall marriage, here are the holy embraces of Christ and the soule, the blessed recumbencies and reposings, the interchange of sacred courtship" (B4[v]). The adjectives "spirituall," "holy," "blessed," and "sacred" remind us that all of this is happening at a level that transcends the sensory, and we must therefore guard against getting the wrong idea about this rapturous experience. But it remains true nonetheless that spiritual joy is represented in sexual language, and the Song of Solomon is taken as justification, if any were needed, for this rhetorical strategy.

The strategy itself is the subject of one of Saltmarsh's most interesting poems, "A Meditation upon the Song of Songs, or, a Request to Solomon" (*Poemata Sacra*, C8–D1). Solomon is addressed in the opening line as "blessed Poet," and the speaker asks him a series of questions about his art: where does he get his inspiration, does he have muses, does he have a mountain similar to Parnassus, or a stream like Aganippe, and so on. These questions matter only because the speaker admires the emotional power of Solomon's poetry. Compared with his own "fainter flames," he says, "I see thee ravisht with a holy lust." Once again the key adjective, "holy," is called upon to ensure that the sexual metaphor will be read as referring to a spiritual occurrence. And this holds true for the poem as a whole, in which the speaker questions Solomon in detail about his representation of Christ as the amorous bridegroom:

> Blest Poet to the Deitie, I'le ask
> One question, and I pray thou would'st unmask;
> How is my Saviour such a lover turn'd?
> Is he grown wanton, amorous, that mourn'd?
> Is he recover'd of his wounds, and fit
> To court and woo a beauty? can he sit
> And use such blessed dalliance?

These are of course rhetorical questions, even though the poem will eventually provide an explicit answer. But before the anticipated "yes" is uttered, we are asked to consider Christ's role here as anomalous:

> Can his complexion suit a Ladies room
> Who hath but lately peept out of his tombe?
> Whose hair & breath's still powderd with the dust,
> Perfumed with a grave, can he breathe lust,
> Lust holy like himselfe?

Here is the second occurrence of the word "lust," and this time the experience is attributed to Christ himself. Perhaps the poet feels that he's treading on dangerous ground here, because he immediately repeats the key term, this time with the qualification "holy," the same adjective he had used before. Here in particular the qualification sounds like a protective manoeuvre, because it leads to the otherwise ungainly repetition of "lust" as the final word of one line and the first word of the next.

With the qualification securely in place, the poem can now propel its readers forward, towards an ecstatic conclusion. The asterisks in the lines quoted below signal references to three passages from the Song of Solomon: "My beloved is like a roe or a young hart" (2:9); "My beloved is gone down into his garden, to the beds of spices, to feed in the gardens, and to gather lilies" (6:2); and "I am my beloved's, and my beloved is mine: he feedeth among the lilies" (6:3). With these words of scripture authorizing his ecstatic mission, Saltmarsh concludes his version of the mystical marriage:

Say, can he love this beautie, call her dear,
Who for an arrow's wounded with a spear?
Can he glide * like a Roe, so brisk, so light,
Upon whose feet hung such an iron weight?
* Will he to th'garden usher her, (O blisse!)
And there was first betrayed with a kisse?
* Can he trip through the lilies as he goes,
And thus with wounds crimson'd into a rose?
O yes, he's now, now in a glorious plight;
Now his *hypostasis* sheds stronger light,
To be ador'd, admir'd: see Lady, see;
You never saw lover so bright as he.
Myriads of sp'rits, of naked souls a rout
Whose old bare liverie bodies are worn out,
Now clad in richer excellence, do wait
About this sacred lover. O rare state!
Who would not be thy spouse? O let me be
But a poore page O Lord to wait on thee.

The tensions which have hitherto rendered this relationship paradoxical, as in the oxymoron "holy lust," are still visible near the beginning of this passage. An invitation to enter the garden is a promise of "blisse," but also a reminder of that other garden (Gethsemane) where the bridegroom was "betrayed with a kisse." But when all the rhetorical questions are answered at last with the long-awaited "O yes," we enter the final phase of the poem, where the paradoxical tensions implicit in the whole relationship are at last resolved through the sheer brilliance of Christ's own person. The "*hypostasis*" is the spiritual essence of (in this case) the second person of the trinity. And it shines with such fierce brightness that every Christian soul will want to acknowledge this being as her spouse.

This last idea raises the interesting question of the relationship between the body and the soul in this poem and in Saltmarsh's thinking as a whole. I will offer some tentative observations on this matter here, in the hope that they may lead to a retrospective reappraisal of the body/soul problem in devotional literature as a whole. For Saltmarsh, it is clearly the soul alone (and not the body) that enters the nuptial garden. In its life on earth, the soul was clothed in flesh, but the "liverie" of the body is now "worn out," as is the case for the many other "naked souls" waiting to be admitted to the bridegroom's garden. The wait is worth it, of course, because each soul is given a better body ("richer excellence") than anything it had before. And in this new, improved state of being, the soul can be united with her "sacred lover" at last.

It would not be much of a stretch to say that the body is the cause of a certain kind of spiritual revulsion in Saltmarsh. Among the *Holy Discoveries and Flames* is a meditation on the teaching of Jesus whereby the disciples are told that, "if thy right eye offend thee, pluck it out, and cast it from thee" (Matthew 5:29), the same holding also for the right hand, except that you "cut it off" (Matthew 5:30). For most of us, such vigorous self-mutilation would be out of the question, especially when directed against body parts that we rely on every day. But Saltmarsh gets over the self-preservation instinct very quickly (though he does acknowledge it), and repudiates the body: "yet this flesh that I thus dismember and disavow, is none of my flesh; these members were made *the members of unrighteousness*, these parts were alienated and divorced from me, I had put them away for their spirituall adultery, and fornication, and rebellion; there was *a law in* these *members which warred against the law of my minde*" (E7^{v}). The casting out of these rebellious body parts is therefore an unambiguous victory of the spiritual over the physical, and that, for Saltmarsh, is simply a good thing.

A similar point is made, less grotesquely to be sure, by a pair of poems near the end of *Poemata Sacra*. Saltmarsh is here interested in the claim that "God created man in his own image" (Genesis 1:27), and he writes a series of six poems (which he designates chapters) that comment on some of the interpretive puzzles that arise from this idea. The two items of direct relevance here are chapter 5: "Gods Picture Not in the Bodie of Man" and chapter 6: "Gods Picture in the Soul, and What it is." The titles by themselves give the game away. If you think that God has ears and eyes and "back parts" because "Moses saw them," well, Saltmarsh is going to form a dim view of your intelligence: "Is there a soul yet so concrete with sense,/So stupid with a bodies influence?" (D5ᵛ). A man would make such a blunder only because "he knows no spirits nakednesse": that is, he has never encountered spiritual phenomena directly, without the mediation of the physical. The "essence" of God, however, far from being "corporeal," is the "eternall figure of his minde" (D6). So it follows that the image he transmits to man is not a physical substance but a spiritual essence: "The image is the Soul, a spirit made/Fit to present a Deitie, who's said/To be a spirit too" (D6). These are the opening lines of the second of the paired poems. In the remaining forty lines Saltmarsh gives us some interesting metaphors to express what I take to be pretty conventional ideas: that the soul was perfect as God created it, that the fall spoiled everything, but that all can be repaired by applying the sacred "juice" (D6ᵛ) that flowed from the side of our Saviour. Here Saltmarsh is using the very same word that he could have read in Herbert's "The Agonie." Clearly there are many lines of linkage and filiation – both theological and stylistic – between Saltmarsh and other writers engaged in private devotions. But one way in which he stands out is in his desire to transcend the physical entirely: to cast off the garment of the flesh as if it were really not his own.

In the Presence of God

While Saltmarsh was creating his *Holy Discoveries and Flames*, a French resident of North Holland was writing a Latin text, *Meditationes de prima philosophia*, that curiously and famously raises some of the same issues. Like Saltmarsh, Descartes is keenly interested in the relationship between the soul (or mind) and the body. The mind certainly has logical priority over the body in Descartes; indeed, the mind ("a thinking thing")[42] is the only part of the self, or of the world for that matter, that can't be removed from reality, even provisionally, by the strategy of maximum doubt.

42 *Meditations on First Philosophy*, in René Descartes, *Selected Philosophical Writings*, trans. John Cottingham, Robert Stoothoff, and Dugald Murdoch (Cambridge: Cambridge University Press, 1988), 82.

Although Descartes will restore the body eventually, on the grounds that "I am very closely joined and, as it were, intermingled with it, so that I and the body form a unit" (116), it remains clear that the "I" is really the mind and the body is something else – "a kind of machine," he will say later (119) – connected to it. The mind, because it is the real "I," is "utterly indivisible," whereas no such claim can be made for the body: "if a foot or arm or any other part of the body is cut off, nothing has thereby been taken away from the mind" (120). This last example of the precedence of mind over matter is strikingly similar to Saltmarsh's meditation on offending body parts. But I am not trying to suggest influence here; since both texts were published in 1640, influence in either direction is extremely unlikely. What I am suggesting is that both Descartes and Saltmarsh are contributing to a large cultural project that we might describe as the advancement of interiority.

The relationship between this project and the growing need for privacy may be largely self-evident, but it needs to be acknowledged. If truth is held to inhabit not the ideologies and institutions constructed in its name, but the inner recesses of the individual mind or soul, then it becomes crucial to establish conditions under which the self can meditate. This is just as clearly the case for Descartes, who carefully sets the stage at the beginning of the First Meditation by banishing anything that might interrupt his tranquil mood as he sits by the fire in his dressing gown, as it is for Edward Wetenhall, who constructs with equal care the prayer closet in which he hopes to communicate with God. The similarity is not exact in every respect (Descartes's explicit goal is the avoidance of error, not the forgiveness of sin), but a pattern can be seen emerging.

Is this a pattern that holds for all of the authors and texts quoted in this sampling of private devotions? If allowance is made for various degrees of emphasis, then it probably is. To engage in private devotions at all, and to encourage others to do so, is to recognize (at least implicitly) the value of interiority. Even if Protestant writers tend to be more overtly committed to the culture of interiority than their Catholic counterparts, and even if women writers find the ardent representation of interiority somewhat more difficult than men, the spiritual turn inward remains a moment to be valued. With these thoughts in mind it might be helpful to recall the figure of Robert Southwell, passionately filled with the fire of God's love, but obliged by law to keep secret his identity as a Jesuit missionary. For Southwell, interiority cannot be fully celebrated as valuable in itself so long as it remains a strategic postponement of the much greater value of martyrdom. Or consider the figure of Lady Margaret

Hoby, certainly dedicated to the cultivation of interiority, as the many instances of "privat praers" would attest, but unable to record (except in rare instances) anything about the quality of her meditations. If Lady Hoby's soul was able to rise above the level on which her ordinary life had to be lived, there are only sparse and indirect hints to suggest as much. This task was apparently easier for Francis Rous, the figure who resembles Saltmarsh perhaps more closely than any other writer cited here. Notice that Rous sets in motion *The Mysticall Marriage* with an explicit claim for interiority: he calls attention to the "chamber within us" that will shelter the mystical union of the soul as bride and Christ as her spouse. In the rapturous excesses of Rous's ecstasies there is a letting go of the body that is perhaps the aim of much private devotion, though it is very seldom achieved with such unambiguous joy.

And so we arrive at yet another paradox in the early modern representation of privacy. This time, the best private experience is that in which someone else (namely, God) is most fully present. To hide from God is of course impossible; all versions of Christianity give him the attribute of omniscience, and one of the emblematic signs of this attribute is the eye of Providence, often pictured as watching over some aspect of his creation. And even if we could hide from God's all-seeing eye, only a guilty sinner would want to, as the story of Adam and Eve should remind us. So private devotions are not in fact directed towards solitude, but towards partnership. The Christian who knows how to meditate is the one who can overcome the fear of being exposed in the presence of God, who can admit his own inherent sinfulness, and who can therefore delight in the raptures that lift him above the body and into a spiritual embrace.

Chapter Three

Voyeurism

Why a chapter on voyeurism in the middle of a book about privacy? There is an easy answer to this question. Anyone who gives it a moment's thought will realize that the two concepts have a symbiotic relationship: they live together and depend on one another for at least some of their significance. The voyeur couldn't be a voyeur if he didn't have privacy as the territory he likes to invade. And perhaps the private self couldn't be fully private either, or at least not fully aware of its own privacy, if it weren't making efforts to exclude intruders (like the voyeur) from gaining access to it.[1] But I think it would be a mistake to assume that voyeurism in the early modern period was no different than it is today, or that the relationship between privacy and voyeurism is unchanging. So it may be worthwhile to historicize the notion of voyeurism by observing some early modern voyeurs in action. This activity will require more than the customary frankness about the private parts, of bodies and of lives. Reader beware.

Diana and Susanna

Let me begin by narrating two stories, one classical, one biblical, both of which help us to situate voyeurism within early modern culture. First, the story of Diana and Actaeon, based on Ovid's account in the

1 On this question, and others of relevance to this chapter in particular, see Tony Doyle, "Privacy and Perfect Voyeurism," *Ethics and Information Technology* 11 (2009): 181–9.

Metamorphoses, but mediated to early modern readers and spectators by Arthur Golding's translation (1567) and by Titian's painting, *Diana and Actaeon*. Actaeon, after a successful morning of hunting, declares the afternoon a time of recreation. He wanders into a beautiful grove which happens to be sacred to the goddess Diana, who, after her own hunting exertions, loves to bathe in the "lively spring with crystal stream"[2] that irrigates the grove. This is exactly what Diana and her nymphs are doing, when Actaeon enters the scene. The nymphs do their best to hide Diana's nakedness, and their own, but it's not enough. Diana, furious at having been observed, throws a handful of water at Actaeon's face and says:

> Now make thy vaunt among thy mates, thou saw'st Diana bare.
> Tell if thou can; I give thee leave. Tell hardly; do not spare. (3.227–8)

Now horns begin to sprout from Actaeon's head, his neck elongates, his skin turns to speckled hide: in short he changes into a stag. His dogs recognize him not as their master but as their accustomed prey; they run him down and dismember him.

> So fierce was cruel Phoebe's wrath, it could not be allayed
> Till of his fault by bitter death the ransom he had paid. (3.303–4)

The second story is *The History of Susanna* as found in the Apocrypha, a gathering of fourteen non-canonical books printed between the Old Testament and the New in the King James Bible (1611), and found also in a surprising number of Renaissance and baroque paintings, beginning with Lorenzo Lotto's version. Joakim, a young, wealthy Babylonian, marries Susanna, the beautiful and pious daughter of Jewish parents. Two elders of the Jewish community, both of them strongly attracted to Susanna, conspire to hide themselves in Joakim's garden so as to gain access to his wife. Susanna enters the garden, sends away her maids, and prepares for her bath. The elders, overcome with lust, rush forward and demand that Susanna comply with their sexual wishes, adding that they'll accuse her of adultery if she doesn't.

2 *Ovid's Metamorphoses*, trans. Arthur Golding, ed. Madeleine Forey (Harmondsworth: Penguin, 2002), 3.188.

Figure 2 Titian, *Diana and Actaeon* (1556–9), National Galleries of Scotland, Edinburgh, and National Gallery, London, UK/Bridgeman Images

Figure 3 Lorenzo Lotto, *Susanna and the Elders* (1517), Galleria degli Uffizi, Florence, Italy/Bridgeman Images

Susanna is understandably disturbed by what she recognizes as her entrapment. But she cries out in defiance of the elders, her servants return, and the elders make their formal accusation. Susanna is found guilty and condemned to death; the sentence is about to be carried out when a young man called Daniel shouts: "I am clear from the blood of this woman."[3] When asked to explain himself, Daniel declares his belief that Susanna has been wrongly accused. He demands that the elders be separated, and then asks each of them in turn: under which tree did Susanna and her lover commit adultery while you watched this event? "Under a mastick tree," says the first elder (54); "Under a holm tree," says the second (58). The contradiction is accepted as proof that the elders are lying. Susanna is restored to the bosom of her family and the embrace of her husband. The elders are punished for false witness "according to the law of Moses" (62), which assigns to them the very sentence they had "maliciously intended" (62) to impose on their victim: that is, they are summarily put to death.

Both of these stories are subtle enough to have provoked commentary of a very high order, some of which I will be citing in the remarks that follow. But for now I want to avoid the nuances in order to stress one crude and obvious point. In both stories, the pagan myth and the biblical history, the perpetrators of voyeurism meet the same decisive end: they are killed without apparent remorse. There may be other motives, intentions, or extenuating circumstances, but the pattern is nonetheless inescapable: a male viewer, by surreptitiously looking at a naked woman, sets off a chain reaction that leads to his death. The unforgiving severity of this ethical paradigm is even more striking when we recall that the crucial scene from both stories, as represented by visual artists, is characteristically the one in which centre stage is occupied by a naked female form. As viewers of the painting, we are being invited to participate, though at a second remove, in the very act of voyeurism that, for the unlucky male gazers in the picture, will lead to annihilation.

The voyeurism embedded in both of these narratives has been remarked upon, but always in such a way as to suggest that it isn't the main point. Leonard Barkan, for example, gives a persuasive and sensitive description of the "erotic voyeurism"[4] implicit in Titian's painting,

---

3 Daniel 46 in *The Apocrypha* (Oxford: Oxford University Press, 1895).

4 "Diana and Actaeon: The Myth as Synthesis," *English Literary Renaissance* 10 (1980): 345.

but then cancels his own good work by suggesting that the "references to vision" in the picture must have a "broader meaning" (346). His article as a whole advances the claim that the myth of Diana and Actaeon is a synthesis of many cultural strands, including the always perilous relationship between human identity and knowledge of the divine. So Actaeon is in one sense desecrating a shrine, and his hounds can be (and have been) variously moralized as those forces within him which render him unworthy of access to divinity. Theresa M. Krier, writing with great subtlety about Spenser's adaptations of Ovid's story, poses the question, "How does Spenser evaluate the voyeur?"[5] Though her treatment of vision, specifically the gendered visual pattern of men gazing at naked women, is richly documented and amply developed, the idea of voyeurism seldom recurs, and the question she poses is never answered to my satisfaction. The scholar who comes closest to accepting the challenge of voyeurism in this case is Thomas Puttfarken, whose intelligent commentary on the *poesie* Titian painted for Philip II of Spain, of which *Diana and Actaeon* is one of the finest specimens, includes the warning that here "painting allows us – like sculpture – to be *voyeurs* in the round" and the claim that "in contemplating all these beautiful goddesses and nymphs we commit the same crime for which Actaeon has to pay with his life."[6] But even in Puttfarken's analysis, these are incidental moments of recognition in a project clearly headed in another direction.

Critical responses to *Susanna and the Elders* have been dominated, for at least a generation now, by feminist voices. In one sense this has been the natural result of Germaine Greer's discovery of Artemisia Gentileschi,[7] the painter who created a particularly moving and unusual version of the Susanna story. Mary D. Garrard has argued, with great conviction, that Gentileschi's painting stands apart from the exercises in "legitimized voyeurism"[8] created by her male predecessors and contemporaries. The difference lies partly in the representation of the female figure: Susanna's body includes "touches of realism that are unflattering by conventional

5 *Gazing on Secret Sights: Spenser, Classical Imitation, and the Decorums of Vision* (Ithaca, NY: Cornell University Press, 1990), 7.

6 *Titian and Tragic Painting: Aristotle's "Poetics" and the Rise of the Modern Artist* (New Haven, CT: Yale University Press, 2005), 160, 175.

7 See *The Obstacle Race: The Fortunes of Women Painters and Their Work* (1979; repr., London: Picador, 1981), 189–207.

8 "Artemisia and Susanna," in *Feminism and Art History: Questioning the Litany*, ed. Norma Broude and Mary D. Garrard (New York: Harper, 1982), 149.

Figure 4 Artemisia Gentileschi, *Susanna and the Elders* (1610), Schloss Weissenstein, Pommersfelden, Private Collection/ Bridgeman Images

standards of beauty, such as the groin wrinkle, the crow's foot wrinkles at the top of her right arm, and the lines in her neck" (157). Garrard believes that these blemishes are part of what distinguishes Susanna as a heroic figure. Gentileschi herself was raped by her tutor, Agostini Tassi, the year after she completed the painting, and for Garrard the work of art is therefore a "reflection," and a rare glimpse one might add, "of how the young woman artist felt about her own sexual vulnerability" (165).

For Griselda Pollock, writing as she does from a subsequent wave of feminist critique, these biographical readings of the painting are far too naive. Rather than offering us the endorsement of female heroism, Gentileschi's painting (on Pollock's reading) is unable to "achieve resolution."[9] There are too many things wrong with its organization. The viewer is situated "in the bathing pool" (113), the trees required by the narrative are nowhere in sight, and the elders are whispering to one another even though they're easily close enough to Susanna to be overheard. For Pollock, these "aberrant details" are signals that invite us to imagine an almost impossible quest: "how a woman artist might have found her difference through the very act of making art" (115).

My point is not that these other concerns don't matter: they certainly do, and they deserve the attention that scholars have given them. My point is rather that the question of voyeurism gets rather badly upstaged when we're urged into complicity with a Neoplatonic reading of Diana and Actaeon, or a feminist reappraisal of Susanna and the Elders.[10] Even worse, once the question of voyeurism gets sidelined, it is very likely to disappear without ever being raised again. And the implicit connection between voyeurism and capital punishment is therefore unlikely to be interrogated.

9 "The Female Hero and the Making of a Feminist Canon: Artemisia Gentileschi's Representations of Susanna and Judith," in *Differencing the Canon: Feminist Desire and the Writing of Art's Histories* (London: Routledge, 1999), 115.

10 Though I here take my distance from certain predictable kinds of feminist critique, I do not wish to imply that feminist research and thinking about these issues are beside the point. An example which proves the contrary is Sarah Toulalan's "'Private Rooms and Back Doors in Abundance': The Illusion of Privacy in Pornography in Seventeenth-Century England," *Women's History Review* 10, no. 4 (2001): 701–19. Toulalan has grasped the importance of the relationship between privacy and voyeurism, and her research shows, for example, that the early modern gaze is not exclusively male. Hers is a feminism that is willing to ask new questions and reopen some old ones.

Figure 5 Tintoretto, *Susanna Bathing* (1555–6), Kunsthistorisches Museum, Vienna, Austria/Bridgeman Images

Defining the Term

For these many reasons, therefore, I want to insist on the question of voyeurism. I want to insist, even further, that we know what we are talking about. Given the early modern examples that we now have at our beck and call, what exactly *is* voyeurism? To answer this question we might appeal to Joel Rudinow, whose excellent article on the subject makes the following points: (1) Voyeurism depends on *asymmetry*. "The voyeur seeks a spectacle," Rudinow writes, "the revelation of the object of his interest, that something or someone should be open to his inspection and contemplation; *but no reciprocal revelation or openness is conceded*, for the voyeur requires at the same time to remain hidden."[11] (2) The asymmetrical pattern depends on a paradox: "the wish both to be and not to be in the presence of the object of interest" (176). (3) The voyeur knows that he's engaged in "an act of aggression, specifically invasion" (176), and that "to treat something as a voyeuristic spectacle is to ruin it for other more fundamental human purposes: it cannot be touched, one cannot be touched by it, one cannot reveal oneself to it" (176). (4) From the desire to maintain this delicately balanced asymmetry, so as to return to it again and again, arises "the voyeur's paradoxical care for the spectacle which he would destroy" (177).

Both of the narratives I've been analysing here conform quite readily to this definition, but only up to a point: the point, namely, at which the object of voyeurism becomes aware of being watched. For this reason we might say that Tintoretto's *Susanna Bathing* is the most perfectly voyeuristic painting of this theme. We might conclude, if we follow Rudinow, that voyeurism describes an asymmetrical but very precise relationship, and that any pressure on the situation – a tug in this direction or that – is bound to destroy the truly voyeuristic setup.

But I think we should complicate matters by referring to several more images, all of them by Titian, with whose work we began. The first is the famous *Venus of Urbino*, which I reproduce here as the context for looking at *Venus with an Organist and Cupid*, a painting which would be followed in subsequent years by several treatments of the same theme, and then a dozen years later by *Venus and the Lute Player* (1562).[12] I think it would be fair to say that each of these paintings evokes a strong feeling of voyeurism, even though none of them conforms to Rudinow's definition. The female figure, in each case, would seem to be perfectly aware that her nakedness lies open to observation, but I don't think she's at all concerned about this. In the *Venus of Urbino* the woman offers her nakedness to the

11 "Representation, Voyeurism, and the Vacant Point of View," *Philosophy and Literature* 3 (1979): 176.

12 For commentary on this sequence of images, see Erwin Panofsky, *Problems in Titian, Mostly Iconographic*, Wrightson Lectures (New York: New York University Press, 1969), 122–5. Panofsky sidesteps the voyeuristic appeal of these images entirely in order to argue that they represent various stages of a contest between visual and aural beauty, between the appeal of sight (the naked goddess) and sound (the music being performed).

Figure 6 Titian, *Venus of Urbino* (before 1538), Galleria degli Uffizi, Florence, Italy/Bridgeman Images

(male) viewer, almost as a challenge; and in *Venus with an Organist and Cupid*, she throws out a different kind of challenge by feigning indifference to the musician who peers intently in her direction.

So in fact we need a more flexible theory of voyeurism – perhaps the sort of theory we could infer from Alberto Moravio's novel *The Voyeur* (1985). The narrator of this work, thirty-five-year-old Edoardo, is a professor of French literature at an Italian university. He gives a detailed account of how he met his wife Sylvia. While on vacation he returns to his seaside *pension* with the intention of taking an afternoon nap. On looking out of the window, however, he discovers that the *pension* immediately opposite has the shutters of its window open, and he sees in the room various traces ("a big Florentine straw hat, pale yellow with a black

Figure 7 Titian, *Venus with an Organist and Cupid* (1548), Prado, Madrid, Spain/ Bridgeman Images

ribbon")[13] of an absent female occupant. He decides to wait, and is at last rewarded by the entrance of a young woman who, though noticing his attention, doesn't close her shutters but instead initiates a striptease which ends with her straddling a chair, absolutely naked, strumming a few chords on her guitar, and revealing to the narrator "the white of a cotton-wool tampon" (94). The next day he arranges to be introduced to her on the beach, and a year later they are married.

Edoardo believes that his "voyeurism" has called into being Sylvia's "exhibitionism" (95); he therefore comes very close to enacting the position outlined by Christian Metz in "Story/Discourse (A Note on Two Kinds of Voyeurism)." Metz's two kinds are in fact exhibitionism, which

13 *The Voyeur*, trans. Tim Parks (1985; repr., London: Abacus, 1991), 92.

he associates with classical theatre, and voyeurism proper, which he associates with the cinema. Exhibitionism is "always bilateral, in the exchange of phantasies if not in its concrete actions."[14] This kind of exchange seems to me close to what is happening in the story of Edoardo and Sylvia, and in the Titian paintings of Venus and the players of various instruments. Cinematic voyeurism, on the other hand, "involves a different regime, that of the primal scene and the keyhole" (95). Metz argues that "cinema manages to be both exhibitionist and secretive" (95) by means of a process he calls a "double denial" (97): the actor behaves as if unaware that he's being observed, and the voyeur is unaware of his voyeurism.

Moravia's novel seeks not only to represent voyeurism, but to theorize it as well. Edoardo is developing a theory which holds that voyeurism is an essential quality "of a great deal of fiction writing" (28); it is not a static image that calls voyeurism into being, he argues, but narrative movement. Among the examples he uses is a poem by Mallarmé, "A Negress Possessed by the Devil," which describes a sexual encounter (in "the erotic position usually known as the sixty-nine") between an adult black woman and a white girl. Edoardo invents a plausible set of circumstances that might surround this encounter, including the happenstance that "the son of the master of the house, a boy without sexual experience, but curious" (32) is able to witness it surreptitiously. The first thing the boy sees is the image which concludes the poem: "the palate of that strange mouth,/Pale and pink as a seashell" (30). The boy is a voyeur because he has seen what is forbidden. "In other words," and I now follow Edoardo's ruminations for a moment, "voyeurism implies a need to discover the unknown. And all at once it comes to me that there's an obscure, but unquestionable relationship between the way voyeurism discovers things and the way science does" (33). If it appears that we've now left early modern voyeurism far behind, perhaps I should remind you of the story of Galileo, peering at sunspots through his telescope in the quest for knowledge he would soon be forbidden to teach or publish. I shall be returning to Galileo, albeit briefly, in chapter 7. For now, what matters is the symbolic parallelism between his position and that adopted by Petrarch's speaker at the end of *Canzoniere* 23. Petrarch's "I," after

14 "Story/Discourse (A Note on Two Kinds of Voyeurism)," trans. Celia Britton and Annwyl Williams, in *The Imaginary Signifier: Psychoanalysis and the Cinema*, trans. Celia Britton, Annwyl Williams, Ben Brewster, and Alfred Guzzentti (Bloomington: Indiana University Press, 1982), 93.

a number of Ovidian transformations, finds himself in Actaeon's pose: "I stood and watched while shame took over her body," he says; and after the "arc of water" strikes his face, he feels his own metamorphosis and knows the consequences: "I can hear the dogs while I write this."[15] Both Galileo and Petrarch are aware that they are entering grounds marked off as forbidden, and both of them find the forbidden secret impossible to resist.

My working definition of voyeurism is therefore as follows. It is a mode of observation that transgresses an acknowledged boundary. For the voyeur, the pleasure and value of the experience derive in part from its transgressive character. The object of the voyeur's gaze may or may not be aware of being watched, and the voyeur's experience will certainly be altered by any such awareness. The voyeuristic experience is by definition paradoxical, in part because it includes both a yearning for intimacy and a desire to remain distant on the part of the voyeur. And with this definition in mind, I propose to bring into play a few telling instances of voyeurism in early modern poetry and theatre.

The Striptease Aesthetic

The practice of voyeurism in literature differs from what visual culture might lead us to expect in at least one important respect: in literature it's generally the voyeur, not the object of the gaze, who commands centre stage. This principle holds true, perhaps surprisingly, for the many descriptions of the woman's person circulated in the various branches of the Petrarchan tradition. Sir Philip Sidney's "What Tongue Can Her Perfections Tell" would be a spectacular English example. The speaker lavishes praise on the golden hair, white forehead, perfectly arched eyebrows, and black eyes of the woman. By now we know what's next: the red and white of her cheeks, lips, and neck; "the lovely clusters of her brests"; her alabaster belly; and then the "chiefe resort" of Cupid, the body part that can't be named.[16] Clearly this is not a poem about or for a real woman, even an elevated female goddess like Astrophil's Stella. This is a description of the female body meant to be circulated among men only, for masculine endorsement and gratification, and it therefore

15 Francis Petrarch, *Songs and Sonnets from Laura's Lifetime*, trans. Nicholas Kilmer (San Francisco: North Point Press, 1981), 27.

16 *The Poems of Sir Philip Sidney*, ed. William A Ringler, Jr (Oxford: Clarendon, 1962), 87–8.

represents the male gaze as unproblematic. Everybody follows the speaker's guided tour of the female body parts, and the woman doesn't object, because she's clearly a fabricated sex toy rather than a person with a mind of her own.

The setup gets more complicated (and more interesting) in the erotic poetry of John Donne, for example. The voyeuristic potential of Donne's verse is the subject of an excellent article by William Shullenberger, "Love as a Spectator Sport in John Donne's Poetry."[17] Shullenberger begins by noticing "a strong voyeuristic component" (47) in what appear to be Donne's most private love poems. This quality comes into being through the repeated representation of "a third party" (47), that is, someone other than the lovers themselves, who is variously reviled for interrupting the lovers (as in "The Sun Rising") or castigated for disapproving of their intimacy (as in "The Canonization") or called upon to witness their transcendent union (as in "The Ecstasy"). This voyeuristic pattern is certainly striking enough to demand explanation, and I think Shullenberger has made a valuable survey of the problem. From a social point of view, he argues, the difficulty of securing private space in the culture of Donne's day is a realistic motivator of these intrusive scenarios, and "Donne's love poems, then, may be taken as early steps in the formation of a modern concept of privacy" (49). From a psychological (or at least psychoanalytic) point of view, the third party is the disapproving father, who threatens the security the speaker hopes to find in the maternal embrace. And from an aesthetic point of view, the third party is the reader, who is being taken into the world of the poem and therefore becomes complicit in its "voyeuristic pleasure" (61). Because I find Shullenberger's discussion largely convincing, especially in its social and aesthetic dimensions, I turn to another poet whose voyeuristic practice is if anything more persistent and enigmatic than Donne's.

The poet I am referring to is Robert Herrick (1591–1674), the author of a single volume of poetry published in two parts, *Hesperides* (the secular poems) and *His Noble Numbers: or, His Pious Pieces* (1648). He was born into a family of London goldsmiths, who, after he served an apprenticeship, sent him to St John's College, Cambridge, where he prepared himself for a career in the church. He was ordained (1623) and sent on the expedition to the Isle of Rhé (1627) as chaplain to the Duke of Buckingham, a position that must have required an exceptionally flexible conscience. He

17 In *Renaissance Discourses of Desire*, ed. Claude J. Summers and Ted-Larry Pebworth (Columbia: University of Missouri Press, 1993), 46–62.

succeeded to the vicarage of Dean Prior in Devonshire (1630), a post he would hold for seventeen years (until his ejection by Parliament in 1647) and then for another fourteen (1660–74) after the Restoration.

He appears to have hated Devonshire, to judge from the poems he wrote about his "discontents" while resident there. During his unauthorized sojourns in London, he may have become the father of an illegitimate child borne by Thomasine Parsons, daughter of John Parsons, organist of Westminster Abbey.[18] But he never married, and the numerous mistresses he addresses in *Hesperides* cannot be identified with real people. He was a poet for whom voyeurism was an art that needed both to rise above and to confirm its indebtedness to nature.

The particular quality I am identifying as characteristic of Herrick has been noticed by other readers. Achsah Guibbory, for example, begins her persuasive account of Herrick's aesthetic principles by observing that "the speaker in Herrick's poetry often seems something of a voyeur."[19] For Guibbory this is an opening gambit in a discussion of creativity. The poems are Herrick's true mistresses, "the actual objects of his love" (80), and it is towards them that his gaze is directed. Not so for Moira P. Baker, who concludes her attack on Herrick's erotic strategies with a principled denunciation: "The gaze enacts the voyeur's desire for power, in which the object of the gaze is cast as its passive, masochistic, feminine victim."[20] In their different ways, both of these readers want to get rid of the voyeurism in Herrick's verse. Guibbory wants to allegorize it, so that what appears to be sexually motivated watching can be resituated as artistic perception; Baker wants to expose it for all to see as nothing more than masculine appropriation of the female body, presumably on the grounds that, when properly demystified in this way, the voyeur's power will collapse of its own rhetorical emptiness.

I propose a more systematic and less polemical reading of Herrick's voyeurism. It will be helpful to begin with a particular poem in mind, chosen (in this instance) for its brilliance and its brevity:

---

18 *The Poetical Works of Robert Herrick*, ed. L.C. Martin (Oxford: Clarendon, 1956), xvi. References to the poems are from this edition.

19 "'No Lust There's Like to Poetry': Herrick's Passion for Poetry," in *"Trust to Good Verses": Herrick Tercentenary Essays*, ed. Roger B. Rollin and J. Max Patrick (Pittsburgh: University of Pittsburgh Press, 1978), 79.

20 "'The Uncanny Stranger on Display': The Female Body in Sixteenth- and Seventeenth-Century Love Poetry," *South Atlantic Review* 56, no. 2 (May 1991): 22; see also Lilian Schanfield, "'Tickled with Desire': A View of Eroticism in Herrick's Poetry," *Literature and Psychology* 39 (1993): 63–83.

Upon Julia's Clothes

When as in silks my *Julia* goes,
Then, then (me thinks) how sweetly flowes
That liquefaction of her clothes.

Next, when I cast mine eyes and see
That brave Vibration each way free;
O how that glittering taketh me! (261)

I think all readers agree that this is a poem about the gaze, and most would agree that it asks us to imagine a man looking at a woman. Disagreements arise, however, about the quality of that look and about the relationship between the viewer and the viewed. Is the gaze an act of homage or a sexual leer or neither (or both) of these? Do the man and the woman know one another, in the biblical as well as in the more usual sense? Is she aware that he is looking at her, and if so, does this awareness affect her behaviour? All of these questions are raised and debated in the surprisingly rich archive of critical commentary about this text, much of it appearing in the pages of *The Explicator*, a journal whose mandate made it the ideal vehicle for brief discussions of very short texts. One especially arresting contribution to this archive was Elisabeth Schneider's claim, advanced in 1955, that Herrick's male readers had been missing the obvious: "His subject, surely, is nothing more, or less, than in stanza 1, Julia dressed, in stanza 2, Julia undressed."[21] Schneider supported her position by noting that the first word of the second stanza, "Next," implies that a significant change has happened in the interval, and she located this change in the difference between "the liquid flowing movement of silk" and "the rhythmical motion back and forth, 'each way free,' of her unencumbered naked limbs."

Male response to Schneider's disrobing of Julia was surprisingly frosty. Nat Henry was the first to attempt a rebuttal, which he claimed to achieve by arguing that Julia presents "a front view" of herself in the first stanza and "a rear view" in the second, a change of perspective which motivates "Next" even if she remains fully clothed.[22] William O. Harris asserted that the difference is one of sensation: the speaker merely *hears* Julia (i.e., the rustling of her silks) in stanza 1, and then turns to see

21 "Herrick's 'Upon Julia's Clothes,'" *The Explicator* 13, no. 5 (March 1955): item 30.
22 "Herrick's 'Upon Julia's Clothes,'" *The Explicator* 14, no. 3 (December 1955): item 15.

her in stanza 2.[23] Richard J. Ross rather ungenerously didn't mention Schneider at all, though he cited a great many male critics in an article, "Herrick's Julia in Silks,"[24] which seems to have been written for the express purpose of getting Julia properly clothed again. "It is quite sufficient that Julia is only being 'mentally undressed,'" says Ross rather petulantly (172). He's right at least in the sense that all actions within a poem are mental actions. And he has conceded more than he realizes, I believe. Both Ross's formulation and Schneider's point to a pattern that is central to the erotic watching that goes on in Herrick's poetry: a pattern that I will call the striptease aesthetic.

I adopt this term as a way of resituating a discussion often referred to as the art-above-nature topos. Many of Herrick's most perceptive readers have singled out "The Lilly in a Christal" as the virtual embodiment of Herrick's aesthetic and erotic theory.[25] The poem begins by offering a series of examples of natural objects visually enhanced by artificial (or at least artful) presentation. A rose is more beautiful when viewed through a semi-transparent film of lawn; a lily is more beautiful when encased in crystal; and further examples amplify the principle, namely that natural objects don't reach their full attractiveness

> Without some Scean cast over,
> To juggle with the sense. (76)

In the last two stanzas the same principle is applied to erotic behaviour. The speaker advises women that simple "nakednesse" might be too "glaring" to achieve a full erotic effect, and that "Lawns & Silks" can enhance female beauty by placing "Into a doubtful Twi-light" the otherwise dazzling whiteness of the naked body.

If this is as close as Herrick comes to writing an *ars poetica* (or an *ars amatoria*), it would be false nonetheless to attribute to him a fixed preference for the artful over the merely natural. A striptease is not a static pose, and that is why I find it a useful way of denoting Herrick's voyeuristic strategies. If "The Lilly in a Christal" seems to arrest and transfix the beautiful effect, there are moments when the opposite is true, as in this evocation of nakedness:

23 "Herrick's 'Upon Julia's Clothes,'" *The Explicator* 21, no. 4 (December 1962): item 29.

24 *Essays in Criticism* 15 (1965): 171–80.

25 See Ann Baynes Coiro, *Robert Herrick's "Hesperides" and the Epigram Book Tradition* (Baltimore: Johns Hopkins University Press, 1988), 163–4.

Display thy breasts, my *Julia*, there let me
Behold that circummortal purity:
Between whose glories; there my lips Ile lay,
Ravisht, in that faire *Via Lactea.* (96)

This poem, aptly titled "Upon Julia's Breasts," calls attention to the other part of the striptease: the moment when the lawn or curtain (the "Scean" as he has called it) is removed so as to reveal unembellished nature. The same is true of "Clothes Do But Cheat and Cousen Us," where the speaker again celebrates woman "Drest in her nak't simplicities" (154) after all the fashionable fabrics have been tossed aside. But it would also be short-sighted to attribute to Herrick a simple preference for nature over art. The striptease requires both; there is pleasure in watching the revelation of what was masked or hidden, but such pleasure depends upon the prior existence of the covering which serves its whole purpose in the act of being removed.

The striptease in Herrick is in general an event complete in itself: a plot with its own beginning, middle, and end. That is because the pleasures it offers are known to be visual pleasures and are not expected to lead to something else. But there are examples of voyeurism that results in frustration rather than satisfaction, though perhaps my wording here obscures the degree to which deferred gratification is a satisfaction too. Something of this kind is apparently going on in "Julia's Petticoat," where the blue garment worn by Julia does what sounds and looks like a very sexual dance ("Sometimes 'twou'd pant, and sigh, and heave") that explicitly engages with her body ("Then to thy thighs so closely cling"). The speaker is able to reach not gratification but something closer to confusion through the process of watching; he feels "Drown'd in Delights; but co'd not die" (66–7). Two historical glosses are perhaps in order here. The petticoat, though technically an undergarment in the early modern period (because it was worn underneath the gown and kirtle), was nonetheless meant to be visible when a woman was walking or dancing.[26] True enough, but in this poem its proximity to Julia's "thighs" gives it a spectacular metonymic advantage; it is able to stand for the parts of the body which it touches. Second, it's worth remarking that

26 See M. Channing Linthicum, *Costume in the Drama of Shakespeare and His Contemporaries* (Oxford: Clarendon, 1936), 187.

in Herrick's day (or Shakespeare's for that matter) "to die" was a euphemism for sexual orgasm, just as "to come" is today.[27] Herrick's speaker appears to have been anticipating a climax that did not occur.

It will be obvious that voyeurism, in Herrick and elsewhere, tends to transgress or at least challenge a taboo: the requirement that private space be secure from observation, at very least, or the ban on exposure of the private parts. With this principle in mind it becomes possible to discover voyeurism not only in Herrick's erotic verse, but in his epigrams and his religious poetry too. One brief example of each will have to suffice. The epigrams are the least admired of Herrick's poems, because of their calculated tastelessness, as in this example, "Upon Sudds a Laundresse":

> Sudds Launders Bands in pisse; and starches them
> Both with her Husband's, and her own tough fleame. (98)

Perhaps there's not much to be said about this, except that it's disgusting and is meant to be.[28] I'm not so sure that the same holds for "To His Saviour: The New Yeers Gift":

> That little prettie bleeding part
> Of Foreskin send to me:
> And Ile returne a bleeding Heart,
> For New-yeers gift to thee. (376)

I am aware that New Year's Day is for Herrick the feast of the circumcision, though it should be added that the Puritan establishment that had expelled him from the priesthood the year before these poems were published had declared feast days to be idolatrous and would have found in Herrick's way of celebrating it evidence for his unreconstructed popery.[29]

27 See the entry for this word in Eric Partridge, *Shakespeare's Bawdy: A Literary and Psychological Essay and a Comprehensive Glossary*, 2nd ed. (London: Routledge, 1955).

28 See Michael C. Schoenfeldt, "The Art of Disgust: Civility and the Social Body in *Hesperides*," *George Herbert Journal* 14 (1990): 127–54. Schoenfeld wants to argue that disgust serves an ideological purpose: "The lack of bodily control in the figures whom Herrick foregrounds functions to justify their abjection, and to sustain the fiction of his own superiority" (128).

29 See Achsah Guibbory, *Ceremony and Community from Herbert to Milton: Literature, Religion, and Cultural Conflict in Seventeenth-Century England* (Cambridge: Cambridge University Press, 1998), 84.

I am further aware of the scholarly arguments advanced by Leo Steinberg about the reasons for the visibility of Christ's sexual organ in Renaissance visual art.[30] Even so, I find the gift of the divine foreskin a bit disconcerting and I can't help wondering how it's going to be "sent" to the speaker. However legitimate its religious objectives, this poem may strike readers as grotesque because it threatens to violate a particularly sacred boundary: the one which guarantees the sanctity of Christ's person in the flesh.[31]

It's a different boundary that Herrick is challenging in "The Vine," a poem which clearly announces itself as a sexual fantasy:

> I dream'd this mortal part of mine
> Was Metamorphoz'd to a Vine. (16)

The extensions of the vine are able to enclose and embrace the sexual parts of Lucia's body: "Her Belly, Buttocks, and her Waste." All of this sexual touching leads at last to an awakening, the moment of truth in every dream, where the speaker finds

> this flesh of mine
> More like a *Stock*, then like a *Vine*.

The joke here is on the reader,[32] who has been expecting something less obvious than an allusion to the speaker's erection. The challenge of a taboo in this case is almost too glaring to require comment.[33]

What then should we conclude about voyeurism in Herrick's poetry? First, we should agree that it happens everywhere in his text, and that the many variations of it only highlight its ubiquitous influence on his aesthetic and erotic practice. Second, we should admit, I think, that there's something attractive about the voyeurism in Herrick's poetry. It's

30 See *The Sexuality of Christ in Renaissance Art and in Modern Oblivion* (New York: Pantheon, 1983): "to profess that God once embodied himself in a human nature is to confess that the eternal, there and then, became mortal and sexual. Thus understood, the evidence of Christ's sexual member serves as a pledge of God's humanation" (13).

31 For a more sanguine interpretation of this poem, see Pamela Hammons, "Robert Herrick's Gift Trouble: Male Subjects 'Trans-Shifting' into Objects," *Criticism* 47 (2005): 50–2.

32 See Roger B. Rollin, "Robert Herrick and the Erotics of Criticism," in *Renaissance Discourses of Desire*, ed. Claude J. Summers and Ted-Larry Pebworth (Columbia: University of Missouri Press, 1993), 140.

33 Though very capable critics have nonetheless ventured: see William Kerrigan, "Kiss Francies in Robert Herrick," *George Herbert Journal* 14 (1990): 164–8.

too easy to condemn the striptease aesthetic in advance, and I think in Herrick's case there's something of real value that is lost when we allow ourselves to do so. Finally, the case of Herrick would suggest to me that voyeurism does not occupy an ethically stable position: just as it is impossible to condemn every act of voyeurism because it resembles what happens in the story of Susanna and the Elders, so it is impossible to exonerate every voyeur because he's simply taking a second look at Julia's clothes. It is therefore of great importance, as always in sexually inflected matters, to be able to distinguish between the playfully outrageous and the downright dangerous. The subsequent discussions of *Much Ado about Nothing* and *The Duchess of Malfi* will underscore this imperative.

Not[h]ing in Messina

The world of Shakespeare's comedies is filled with highly artificial behaviour that somehow begins to seem natural once the spectators let their guard down. *Much Ado about Nothing* stands out, even in this context, as more strictly artificial than most. Perhaps this effect of heightened artificiality comes about because of the ways in which the characters are motivated. Nobody in Shakespeare's Messina acts spontaneously, or even on impulse; everyone looks around and hopes to be prompted into action by some signal from the social environment. Under such circumstances, love doesn't seem so much a reckless personal encounter as a carefully designed cultural achievement. So much would follow from Don Pedro's boast, made good when he and his allies bring Beatrice and Benedick into accord, that "Cupid is no longer an archer ... for we are the only love-gods."[34]

The artfulness of human behaviour in this play, the sense that human actions both great and small are contrivances, is supported by the social authority given to noting (in the sense of observing, marking, or watching) by everyone from Don Pedro to Dogberry. This idea has been present in the archive of Shakespeare interpretation for about 150 years, ever since Richard Grant White advanced the claim that the word *Nothing* in the title would have been pronounced *noting* in Shakespeare's day, and that noting the conversations of their friends and servants (in the

34 William Shakespeare, *Much Ado about Nothing*, ed. Sheldon P. Zitner, Oxford Shakesspeare (Oxford: Oxford University Press, 1993), 2.2.381–2. Subsequent references are to this edition.

parallel overhearing scenes) is exactly what leads Benedick and Beatrice to banish reluctance and declare themselves ready for love.[35] Dorothy C. Hockey, though not entirely convinced about the pun in the title, would nonetheless go on to argue that noting (in the sense of seeing, hearing, and judging) is at the thematic centre of the play. "*Much Ado* is a comedy of *mis*-noting," she declared; "nobody's eyes or ears are to be trusted – certainly not those of a lover."[36] Hockey's is a persuasive account of the play, because it is able to enrich our understanding of Beatrice and Benedick, to be sure, but also of Claudio, Leonato, Friar Francis, the Watch (including Dogberry), and even Don John. For all of these reasons, and because it appeared in a leading Shakespeare journal more than fifty years ago, Hockey's article has entered what we might call the public domain of Shakespeare criticism: her thesis shows up in a great deal of subsequent commentary even though her article is rarely cited.[37]

The category of noting is broad enough to include both seeing and hearing, and hence gives rise to what Hockey calls "the eye-ear refrain" (355). As she sets the trap for Beatrice, Hero wants to make sure that Beatrice will listen: "that her ear lose nothing/Of the false-sweet bait that we lay for it" (3.1.32–3). And after she has noted the charade, Beatrice responds just as Hero would have wished: "What fire is in mine ears?" she says; "Can this be true?" (3.1.107). But if Margaret is right about Beatrice, then visual noting matters too: "methinks you look with your eyes, as other women do" (3.4.87–8). Here we could say that eyes and ears are working in collaboration, but elsewhere they contradict or correct one another. At the masked ball, for instance, the disguises worn by Beatrice and Benedick do nothing to retard their verbal competition. In a play where the spoken language is the object of both "distrust and delight" for virtually all of the characters, as Camille Wells Slights argued,[38] the ear is in general given more authority than the eye. Still, both

35 See the Introduction to *Much Ado* in *The Works of William Shakespeare*, ed. Richard Grant White (Boston: Little Brown, 1859–65), 3:226.

36 "Notes Notes, Forsooth ...," *Shakespeare Quarterly* 8 (1957): 354, 356.

37 See, for example, Barbara Everett, "*Much Ado about Nothing*: The Unsociable Comedy," in *English Comedy*, ed. Michael Cordner, Peter Holland, and John Kerrigan (Cambridge: Cambridge University Press, 1994), 75, and Zitner's introduction to the edition cited (14–15).

38 See "The Unauthorized Language of *Much Ado about Nothing*," *Shakespeare's Comic Commonwealths* (Toronto: University of Toronto Press, 1993), 173.

can be deceptive, especially in isolation; intelligent noting would require that visual and verbal observations be able to corroborate one another.

The one striking exception to the pattern I have been describing is the character of Claudio. He would seem to be a person for whom visual impressions carry the day. His courtship of Hero begins and comes to a successful conclusion without the help of a single conversation between them. There has been plenty of visual "checking out," however, at least from his point of view. "Benedick, didst thou note the daughter of Signor Leonato?" he asks (1.1.157–8); and when his friend implies that Hero is nothing special, Claudio disagrees: "In mine eye she is the sweetest lady that ever I looked on" (1.1.182–3). Don Pedro now offers to manage the entire courtship by proxy, and before long he's able to announce that everything has been decided: Hero has agreed to the marriage, and Leonato has given his consent. All of this without the exchange of a single word between the lovers themselves. Indeed, this couple might never break out of their inarticulate daze were it not for their loquacious friends. Leonato makes a formal offer of his daughter to Claudio, and Beatrice has to nudge him: "Speak, Count, 'tis your cue" (2.1.302). Claudio now comes up with three sentences of stilted prose, beginning with "Silence is the perfectest herald of joy" (2.1.302). Even if this is defensible as a general principle, it's not something you should say to the woman you are about to marry. Hero says nothing in reply, even when Beatrice urges her to; perhaps she takes the alternate course: "if you cannot, stop his mouth with a kiss" (2.1.306–7).

The point I wish to make here, implicitly and indirectly, is that Claudio's position from the beginning of *Much Ado* is very much like that of the paradigmatic voyeur. He has been looking at Hero with an erotically admiring gaze, but he hasn't declared his position. In the absence of any such declaration, Hero can of course feel no loyalty to him. So when Leonato reports to her the rumour that Don Pedro may be interested in marrying her, there's nothing to stop her from considering such a proposal, and nothing to stop Claudio from thinking that she's receptive to a proposal from Don Pedro as soon as he forms the view (prompted by Don John) that "the Prince woos for himself" (2.1.175). And the prospect that the Prince might win her now infuriates Claudio, as the possessive rage of this outburst implies:

> Let every eye negotiate for itself,
> And trust no agent; for beauty is a witch
> Against whose charms faith melteth into blood. (2.1.179–81)

In one sense Claudio is at least willing to learn from what he thinks is a bad experience: he would be better off if he could find the courage to do the wooing himself. But in another sense he remains in the paralysed position of the voyeur: both enraptured with the object of his gaze, and unwilling to have the desired object step outside the frame within which he pictures her. If she acts in any unexpected way, she becomes a "witch" bent on destroying even the sacred bonds of fidelity between friends.

Such a superstitious view of female behaviour is possible only for someone who has resolutely withdrawn from interactions with women. Benedick, by contrast, might fear that Beatrice is a formidable opponent or a talkative shrew, but he would never call her a witch. And it is precisely the underdeveloped relationship between Claudio and Hero that leaves them both so perilously vulnerable on the eve of their marriage. Here I am not trying to excuse or extenuate Claudio's fault, only to understand it.

It is not in fact Claudio's observation of Margaret (in Hero's gown) flirting with Borachio that shakes his confidence in Hero's fidelity; it is rather the proleptic account (by Don John) of what he is going to see. "Go but with me tonight, you shall see her chamber window entered, even the night before her wedding day" (3.2.106–8). With these words Don John opens in Claudio's mind the fear of being disgraced. From now on he will occupy a position very much like that of the stereotypical cuckold, as described by Katharine Eisaman Maus: "Unlike an ordinary voyeur, moreover, he has a proprietary claim upon the sexual scene acted out before him; he *ought* to be able to interfere, and has every reason to do so. But he is pointedly excluded, unable at least for the moment to affect the outcome of events or to announce his presence."[39] Don John continues the confidence game: "If you dare not trust that you see," he says with palpable contempt, "confess not that you know" (3.2.113–14). Under pretext of exhorting Claudio to trust his own eyesight, Don John is in fact telling him what to see and how to interpret the evidence. Before he has seen anything, Claudio knows how to respond: "If I see anything tonight why I should not marry her, tomorrow, in the congregation where I should wed, there will I shame her" (3.2.117–19). After this it is a foregone conclusion. Shakespeare doesn't show us (and doesn't

39 See "Horns of Dilemma: Jealousy, Gender, and Spectatorship in English Renaissance Drama," *ELH: A Journal of English Literary History* 54 (1987): 570.

need to show us) the scene of Margaret impersonating Hero (though he will ensure that it is described many more times from many points of view),[40] because we know already what the outcome will be. Claudio will come to the altar, as if to marry Hero, and when asked about his intentions he will answer "No" (4.1.6). Soon he will denounce her as a "rotten orange" (4.1.32) and he'll resolve that, on account of her, he'll never let beauty bewitch him again:

> For thee I'll lock up all the gates of love
> And on my eyelids shall conjecture hang
> To turn all beauty into thoughts of harm,
> And never shall it more be gracious. (4.1.104–7)

Stepping out of the voyeur's protected, undisclosed location has been a task too difficult for Claudio. He wants to retreat to a world where he doesn't have to take any sexual risks. And while he eagerly seeks to protect himself, he seems oblivious to the damage done to Hero. When Hero faints, Claudio will promptly leave the scene without another word, once again following the suggestion of Don John.

The most controversial utterance in the entire play is of course spoken by Beatrice, to Benedick, only minutes after everyone else has left the stage. To Benedick's offer to do anything for her, she says: "Kill Claudio" (4.1.289). No matter how this line is spoken, or how it is interpreted by Benedick, it is an expression of outrage. To claim that she wants Benedick to execute his friend without a second thought is perhaps too literal a way of reading her words. When Benedick accepts his assignment, he does so in terms that translate it into another idiom: "Enough, I am engaged; I will challenge him" (4.1.331). But the chivalric rereading of her injunction is his, not hers. Beatrice has pronounced something closer to a death sentence than to the opening move in a game. As Beatrice knows only too well, Hero's life has been irreparably damaged by Claudio's cruel accusation, and she wants him to pay for what he has done. The logic here is surprisingly similar to that which calls for the death penalty in the story of Susanna and the Elders. In both cases the voyeurs bear false witness, and it is therefore not the act of looking, by itself, that calls for

40 On this point see Nova Myhill, "Spectatorship in/of *Much Ado about Nothing*," *Studies in English Literature, 1500–1900* 39 (1999): 301.

punishment. Even so, the symbolic pattern is remarkably constant in its insistence that the man who gazes must be put to death.

This being a comedy, both Hero and Claudio can be rescued from the grave: she by the revelation that the news of her death was in fact a rumour, he by a conspiracy of forgiveness and a second chance to marry her. This too is a controversial moment which divides readers into those who will never forgive Claudio and those who go to great lengths to invent reasons for doing so.[41] On almost any reading (including Claudio's own: "Yet sinned I not/But in mistaking" [5.1.268–9]), Claudio gets off rather easily, perhaps too easily. But he doesn't escape the rod of chastisement entirely. Having been told that he must marry Hero's cousin, Claudio agrees, and Antonio brings in "*the ladies masked*" (5.4.51.2). Claudio wonders which of the ladies is to be his bride, Antonio identifies her, and Claudio says, "Why then, she's mine. Sweet, let me see your face" (5.4.55). But now Leonato steps in, having at last decided that he owes his daughter some paternal care: "No, that you shall not till you take her hand/Before this Friar and swear to marry her" (5.4.56–7). Claudio's voyeuristic gaze has caused no end of trouble already, Leonato seems to be suggesting. He wants to reach closure before Claudio has another chance to begin noting this or that about Hero. So Claudio swears and Hero unmasks, in a gesture that surely gives Claudio all he could ask for and more than he deserves.

Spectatorship in Malfi

The idea of noting, in all of the Shakespearean senses and perhaps others, is at least as important in *The Duchess of Malfi* as it was in *Much Ado*. Indeed, to call Webster's play a *tragedy* of mis-noting would capture something of great interest about it. The Duchess herself is constantly being looked at, by her steward Antonio, for instance, who notices that she returns his gaze:

Whilst she speaks,
She throws upon a man so sweet a look

41 See Michael D. Friedman, who poses the question, "Why do editors, directors, and critics go to such lengths to induce readers and spectators to pardon Claudio?" The essay from which this quotation is taken, "The Editorial Recuperation of Claudio," *Comparative Drama* 25 (1991–2): 369–86, is an extended treatment of the question.

> That it were able raise one to a galliard
> That lay in a dead palsy, and to dote
> On that sweet countenance.[42]

Of course Antonio rules out any "lascivious" (1.1.200) intention on her part, and on his, because the difference in birth between the two of them compels him to. But he is wrong in this fastidious interpretation of her come-hither look, as she will explain to him, slowly and with great gentleness, in the courtship scene that brings Act 1 to a beautiful conclusion with their secret and surreptitious marriage. Antonio therefore cannot occupy the voyeur's position, because his gaze is quickly made legitimate. Look at me as much as you like, the Duchess says in effect; she teases him by suggesting that the real thing will be more to his liking than a simulacrum:

> This is flesh and blood, sir;
> 'Tis not the figure cut in alabaster
> Kneels at my husband's tomb. (1.1.453–5)

The love story reaches its offstage consummation in the "marriage bed" (1.1.496) that awaits these newlyweds.

The wedding has to be secret and the relationship surreptitious because the Duchess is under constant surveillance. Her twin brother Ferdinand is always watching, and lets her know that he is. Together with their younger brother, the Cardinal, Ferdinand stages an interrogation which lets the Duchess know that his real interest is in her sex life: "You are a widow," he begins: "You know already what man is" (1.1.293–4). He warns her not to indulge in the pleasures that widows are said to be unable to resist: "Your darkest actions – nay, your privat'st thoughts –/ Will come to light" (1.1.315–16). At this point Ferdinand does not yet situate himself as the voyeur; rather he lets the Duchess know that she is always subject to his vigilance, perhaps because he really thinks he can control her actions. The voyeur's role he assigns to a creature of his, Daniel de Bosola, the intellectual turned malcontent who seems

42 John Webster, *The Duchess of Malfi*, ed. John Russell Brown, Revels Student Editions (Manchester: Manchester University Press, 1997), 1.1.194–7. Subsequent references are to this edition.

ready to perform any service provided that the price is right. Ferdinand gives gold to Bosola so that he will "live i'th' court here, and observe the Duchess" (1.1.252–3). And the kind of observation he wants Bosola to make is always sexually inflected: "She's a young widow –/I would not have her marry again" (1.1.255–6). How Bosola carries out his assignment is a matter of great interest, and a question to which I shall shortly return. But there's more to be said about Ferdinand first, as I have already implied. He does not take the position of voyeur at the outset, but he soon comes to occupy it nonetheless.

Nominally Ferdinand can assign the task of watching the Duchess to someone else, but he certainly can't keep her out of his mind. After Ferdinand has been informed that his sister has given birth to a child, his brain threatens to spin out of control. "Methinks I see her laughing," he says to the Cardinal; "Talk to me somewhat, quickly,/Or my imagination will carry me/To see her in the shameful act of sin" (2.5.38–41). Even when he's not literally watching her, Ferdinand is daydreaming about his sister. And the Cardinal's next line – "With whom?" (2.5.41) – is hardly calculated to disrupt his brother's reverie, which continues to accelerate:

> Happily with some strong-thighed bargeman,
> Or one o'th' woodyard that can quoit the sledge
> Or toss the bar, or else some lovely squire
> That carries coals up to her privy lodgings. (2.5.42–5)

Such obsessive concern with the Duchess' presumed sexual partners, along with the need to debase them by using the markers of class and occupation against them, is perfectly in accord with the way in which sexual jealousy was played in the theatre of Webster's day. And if a man is held in the powerful grip of a sexual jealousy over his sister, then it follows that his attachment to her is an incestuous fantasy. That, indeed, is how actors, at least since John Gielgud's performance in 1945, have been inclined to interpret it.[43]

43 For comment on this production (at the Haymarket, London), see Edmund Wilson, *Europe without Baedeker: Sketches among the Ruins of Italy, Greece and England* (Garden City, NY: Doubleday, 1947), 11–12. In the Cheek by Jowl production (1996), Scott Handy played Ferdinand with "a hint ... of greedy adolescent incest"; see John Peter, "Keep It in the Family," *Sunday Times*, 7 January 1996, 10.19.

The next time we encounter Ferdinand he is securing from Bosola "a false key/Into her bed-chamber" (3.1.80–1), a device he promptly uses to put himself into the voyeur's position at last. In a brilliantly handled scene of intimacy (3.2.), the Duchess combs her hair as part of her bed-time ritual, and exchanges light-hearted banter, some of it sexually suggestive, with Antonio and her maid Cariola. The poignancy of this scene depends in part on its precarious placement: as spectators we either know or at least suspect (depending on production technique) that Ferdinand is watching everything. But he cannot maintain the voyeur's undeclared position. No sooner have Antonio and Cariola left the Duchess to herself, as part of a frivolous game, than the stage direction "*Enter* FERDINAND" (3.2.62.1) brings the charade to a decisive and premature end. When the Duchess turns to confront Ferdinand, perhaps after spotting his image in her looking glass, he "*gives her a poniard*" (3.2.71.1) but does not molest her any further. To her words of self-defence – that she's married and hasn't done anything unsanctioned by custom – he turns a deaf ear. He seems far more interested now in his rival, the man who has enjoyed his sister. He calls out to this unknown enemy, forbidding him ever to reveal his name:

> Enjoy thy lust still, and a wretched life,
> On that condition. (3.2.98–9)

Now he turns to his sister, tells her a moralistic fable designed to convince her that she's ruined her reputation, and leaves with a threat that might also be read as a promise: "I will never see thee more" (3.2.141). For the moment it is not clear what Ferdinand means. Is he expecting her to commit suicide in response to the not-so-subtle hints he has offered? Is he now determined to go back into the protected space of the voyeur, this time permanently? Or is he announcing the intention to have her killed? With someone as radically disturbed as Ferdinand shows himself to be, it's difficult to be sure.

Of course he does see her more. His sickness is that he can't stop himself from seeing her, again and again and again. His next two encounters with the Duchess give us the most ghoulish moment of the play and one of its most poetical. The first of these is the famous scene of the dead man's hand. He comes to her in the dark, so as to nominally keep his pledge not to see her. But the effect of this precaution, of course, is that she can't see him; nor can she see that the hand extended for her to kiss is not her brother's but a fragment taken from some unidentified corpse. Now she calls for lights, and Ferdinand goes out, while he gives the cruelly sardonic order, "Let her have lights enough" (4.1.53). The lights come up or, more properly on the Jacobean stage, are brought in, to reveal "*the artificial figures of* ANTONIO *and his* children *appearing as if they were dead*" (4.1.55.2–3). As Ferdinand will explain later, these are not "real" bodies, but waxwork dummies, created precisely to make the Duchess cringe. Bosola helps things along now, by observing that the Antonio corpse is missing the very hand that the Duchess has so recently kissed and recoiled from. (Need I add that, in the theatre, the "real" actors will be enlisted to impersonate the wax dummies of themselves, and that Antonio's hand will be disguised by a trick of costume?) Webster is asking us, the spectators of this scene, to engage in a metatheatrical perception puzzle while the Duchess is being forced into abjection. And where is Ferdinand while this is going on? Is he living up to his pledge never to see her more, or is he spying on her from an undisclosed off-stage location? The second position is the likely one, to judge by his first words, spoken to Bosola, when he re-enters: "Excellent, as I would wish; she's plagued in art" (4.1.111).[44] Ferdinand's position is not only disturbing and loathsome; it is downright contradictory. He wants to be the voyeur, but he also wants to be in control of the scene he pretends to be merely watching. Yes, he is able to violate his sister's privacy: to destroy its satisfactions and to annihilate any chance of its recovery. But he accomplishes these dubious ends not simply through the disciplined watching of the voyeur, but also through the theatre of cruelty.

At last she lies dead before him, strangled without pity by his hired executioners. Two of her children lie dead at her side. It is at this moment that Ferdinand's investment in watching her is most blatantly declared. Bosola helps him declare it by pointing to the body (or bodies) and saying, "Fix your eye here" (4.2.259). This Ferdinand will do, we do not know for how long, but at least he will look at her "Constantly" (4.2.259) during the next few lines of dialogue. And then he will speak his mysterious poetical tribute to her: "Cover her face; mine eyes dazzle; she died

44 My reading of Ferdinand's line is in agreement with that advanced by Anat Feinberg in "Observation and Theatricality in Webster's *The Duchess of Malfi*," *Theatre Research International* 6 (1980–1): 39. My overall view of the play, however, runs directly counter to Feinberg's thesis: "*The Duchess of Malfi* is notable for the diversity of instances in which observation leads to understanding and knowlege" (37). My reading would suggest that the more likely results are pain and terror.

young" (4.2.263). Perhaps this line is so memorable because of its cryptic understatement. A character given to violent and abusive outbursts has at last found value in a softer form of speech. But I think it is memorable too because Ferdinand must now renounce his whole voyeuristic project. His eyes "dazzle" for the last time, because he has killed the object of his gaze. He has deprived her not only of privacy, but of life itself.

The professional voyeur in *The Duchess of Malfi* is not Ferdinand, however, but Bosola. At the outset he is, on Ferdinand's commendation, made provisor of the Duchess' horse, a position that will allow him "To note all the particulars of her haviour" (1.1.253) and eventually "gain/ Access to private lodgings" (1.1.280–1). So it is that Bosola studies the Duchess' personal habits and the shape of her body:

> I observe our Duchess
> Is sick o' days, she pukes, her stomach seethes,
> The fins of her eyelids look most teeming blue,
> She wanes i'th' cheek, and waxes fat i'th' flank,
> And (contrary to our Italian fashion)
> Wears a loose-bodied gown. (2.1.66–71)

By now every spectator will have joined Bosola in conjecturing that the Duchess is pregnant. When he offers her "Apricocks" (2.1.134) a few minutes later and watches her devour them, all the more greedily after she learns they were ripened "in horse dung" (2.1.144), Bosola is sure he has discovered something. And a few scenes later, when Antonio drops a piece of paper – on which someone has calculated the horoscope of the Duchess' newborn infant – he has his confirmation. "If one could find the father now!" Bosola muses (2.3.71), and it's here that his powers of observation fail him. Indeed, one is tempted to ask, if Bosola is as clever as everyone takes him to be, and if he has privileged access to the household of the Duchess, why does his espionage uncover so little and why does it take so long?[45] The Duchess will bear two more children before

45 Frances E. Dolan argues, in "'Can this be Certain?': The Duchess of Malfi's Secrets," in *The Duchess of Malfi: A Critical Guide*, ed. Christina Luckyj (London: Continuum, 2011), that "the play depicts its characters trying, and failing, to confide their own secrets ... as well as trying, and failing, to grasp what others hold inside them" (129). This is a perceptive observation, but Bosola's failure to interpret the evidence is nonetheless unusually obtuse.

Bosola learns the identity of the father, and even then she has to virtually force him to draw the conclusion he should long have suspected. He has been praising Antonio, perhaps testing her as he does so, when she says at last, "This good one that you speak of is my husband" (3.2.278), foolishly placing her safety into his hands. To her he now sings further praises for her brilliant choice, but as soon as he's alone on stage we learn his true intentions: "What rests but I reveal/All to my lord?" (3.2.329–30). Unlike Ferdinand, Bosola knows how to keep his cover, how to remain unobserved while observing.

After the waxworks scene, Bosola has seen enough of the Duchess' torment. "Must I see her again?" he asks Ferdinand (4.1.132). And when Ferdinand insists, overriding Bosola's refusal, the response is equivocal, as of course Bosola's whole part has been: "Never in mine own shape;/ That's forfeited by my intelligence/And this last cruel lie" (4.1.134–6). The cruel lie is the implicit claim that her husband and children are dead. Bosola's "intelligence" is the direct access he's had to the Duchess' suffering by coming to her openly as Ferdinand's agent. He has briefly come out of camouflage to declare his allegiance, and this has been profoundly painful not only for her, but for him too.

So, when he returns to the Duchess, Bosola is disguised as "*an old man*" (4.2.112.2) and identifies himself as "a tomb-maker" (4.2.146–7). Although her final scene is a stunning duet with Bosola as her partner, she makes no sign of recognizing him, except insofar as she seems to have an intuitive grasp of exactly what to say to each of his melancholy cues. "Didst thou ever see a lark in a cage?" he asks; "Such is the soul in the body; this world is like her little turf of grass, and the heaven o'er our heads, like her looking-glass, only gives us a miserable knowledge of the small compass of our prison" (4.2.127–31). This fanciful metaphor, which, when challenged, he will continue to explicate as the cause of her broken sleep patterns, calls up at last the moving response: "I am Duchess of Malfi still" (4.2.141). Now Bosola has the voyeur's most difficult and most degrading task: from behind the protection of his disguise, and under strict orders from his superior, he can watch her die.

This he does with great ceremony: slowly he prepares her for the cord that will strangle her and introduces her to the Executioners who will do the job. He allows her to listen to a beautiful dirge, and waits patiently while she speaks. This she does at some length, exhibiting in her speech a profound capacity for love, undiminished even in the face of death, and a command of metaphor that rivals Bosola's own. The last sentence she speaks to her maid is a request that her little boy be given his cough syrup and that her daughter be reminded to say her prayers (4.2.202–4). As for her own predicament, she faces it with dignity:

> I know death hath ten thousand several doors
> For men to take their exits; and 'tis found
> They go on such strange geometrical hinges,
> You may open them both ways. (4.2.218–21)

These are not yet her last words, though they already have the ring of finality, the sonority of closure. In fact the last words of the Duchess will be rather curiously dispersed through the rest of the play, if we include the echo heard by Antonio and Delio when they visit "*the* Duchess' *grave*" (5.3.0.2). Her last complete sentence is a command: "Go tell my brothers, when I am laid out/They then may feed in quiet" (4.2.234–5). Now the stage direction, "*They strangle her,*" requires her silence. But, after her corpse has been shown to Ferdinand, and after Bosola learns that his only reward will be immunity from prosecution for murder, she revives for long enough to speak two more words: "Antonio!" and "Mercy!" (4.2.349, 352). Bosola, the sole witness to this momentary reprieve, is wild with excitement and ready for a miraculous recovery. But all he gets is a second chance to watch her die, and the implicit obligation to dispose of her body with respect.

In the curious and difficult fifth act of this play, Bosola tries to reinvent himself as the Duchess of Malfi's champion. This new departure only adds to his record as a serial killer: he dispatches Antonio (by accident if you believe his own account), an unnamed Servant, the Cardinal, and Ferdinand: that's four more corpses in a performance time of perhaps ten minutes. Still Bosola wants to evade responsibility, describing himself as

> an actor in the main of all
> Much 'gainst mine own good nature, yet i'th' end
> Neglected. (5.5.85–7)

Yes, he has been betrayed by his employers, but in employment of this kind, should he be surprised? As he approaches his end, Bosola calls upon "worthy minds" to face death without flinching, but then utters a fragment: "Mine is another voyage" (5.5.105). These are his last words, and they seem to call for an emotional, ethical, or even a physical shrug.

In a previous discussion of this play I raised the question of the special authority given to Bosola by readers and spectators alike. The first printed text of the play (Q1, 1623) includes a cast list, in which "Bosola, *J. Lowin*" stands first, an emphasis that overturns the custom of printing characters' names in descending order of rank, men's roles first, then women's. Not only does John Lowin (the original Bosola) stand at the top of the list, but he supplants his far more famous contemporary, Richard Burbage (the original Ferdinand). What is it, I asked, that confers (now as in Webster's own day) special authority on this character? The answer I gave, and stand by still, is that, in his curious way, he's in love with the Duchess from the beginning of the play to the end.[46]

But I now think that Bosola's authority has more to do with strategies of spectatorship – that is, with voyeurism – than my earlier formulation suggested. That Webster had a particular interest in spectatorship has been suggested by several readers.[47] Dena Goldberg has argued, with respect to *The White Devil*, that Webster deliberately puts his audience into a voyeuristic position. To counter by observing that all theatrical spectatorship is intrinsically voyeuristic does not refute Goldberg's position; what she has discovered is a more specific and more subtle dramaturgical design which "causes the audience to identify its own spectator role with the spectator role played by the actors on the stage."[48] In *The White Devil* such identification produces a highly unstable effect, because the observing character changes from scene to scene: Flamineo, Zanche, Cornelia, Montecelso, and Bracciano all play the spectator role at various times. In *The Duchess of Malfi* we are given fewer alternatives and we are therefore in a position where we are far more likely to choose a particular allegiance. Like the prominent male characters in the play, we are most interested in watching the Duchess. But we can't see her through Antonio's eyes, not after Act 1 in any case, because the moment he marries her he becomes part of what we're watching. Nor can we see her through Ferdinand's eyes, because Ferdinand does everything we need

46 See *The Performance of Pleasure in English Renaissance Drama* (Houndmills, Basingstoke: Palgrave Macmillan, 2003), 115–16, 121.

47 See, for example, Feinberg, "Observation and Theatricality in Webster's *The Duchess of Malfi*," 36–44; Andrea Henderson, "Death on the Stage, Death of the Stage: The Antitheatricality of *The Duchess of Malfi*," *Theatre Journal* 42 (1990): 194–207; and Marcus Nordlund, *The Dark Lantern: A Historical Study of Sight in Shakespeare, Webster, and Middleton*, Gothenberg Studies in English 77 (Göteborg, Sweden: Acta Universitatis Gothonburgensis, 1999), 355–435.

48 "'By Report': The Spectator as Voyeur in Webster's *The White Devil*," *English Literary Renaissance* 17 (1987): 72.

to discredit his own viewpoint as insane. Can we see her through Bosola's eyes? Yes, I think we can, and do. Not that we idealize his viewpoint. He is a man with a criminal record and a troubled conscience; he enters into an arrangement of doubtful morality, and hasn't got the courage to escape from the consequences. He bears a heavy burden of guilt for having presided over the murder of the Duchess without protest. But then we have been watching too, and, far from protesting, we have enjoyed the tragic spectacle.[49] To say that Bosola is in love with the Duchess from the beginning of the play to the end is one way of declaring his kinship with the necessarily voyeuristic spectator of the drama.

Voyeurism and Privacy

What then do the representations of voyeurism contribute to our understanding of early modern privacy? First, and this point is implicit in my whole treatment of *The Duchess of Malfi*, anyone's claim to privacy in early modern culture was precarious. Catherine Belsey long ago identified *The Duchess of Malfi* as "a perfect fable of emergent liberalism," by which she meant, among other things, that the play treats the nuclear family "as a private realm of warmth and fruitfulness separate from the turbulent world of politics, though vulnerable to it."[50] These are carefully chosen words, and they point to some of the play's most striking aesthetic qualities. Take the scene in which the Duchess prepares for bed in the company of Antonio and Cariola, praised by many critics, including Belsey, for its representation of intimacy. While playing her part in an extended and light-hearted conversation, the Duchess interrupts herself by remarking, "I prithee,/When were we so merry? – My hair tangles" (3.2.52–3). The verisimilitude here is unprecedented in English drama; no stage Duchess had ever mentioned her hair until now, certainly not in this casual and quotidian way. So there's a real sense in which Webster is able to give us glimpses of an emergent privacy, of a set of expectations about the private life that is gradually but decisively gaining ground in

49 Here I am raising, if only for a moment, the question which A.D. Nuttall answers with great subtlety and patience in *Why Does Tragedy Give Pleasure?* (Oxford: Oxford University Press, 1997).

50 *The Subject of Tragedy: Identity and Difference in Renaissance Drama* (London: Methuen, 1985), 197, 198.

the cultural imagination. But as spectators we are never allowed to forget that Ferdinand is lurking somewhere, just offstage. The few private moments that the Duchess can claim become all the more precious when we know that they are always threatened by the predations of surveillance.

Does it follow, then, that voyeurism is by definition destructive, and characteristically antagonistic to the emergence of the private self in early modern culture? Most of the textual material I have been citing here would support such a view. The verbal and visual accounts of Susanna and the Elders tell the story of a young woman's domestic arrangements being placed into extreme peril by monitors who represent (albeit maliciously) the values of her community. The same pattern is repeated in *Much Ado*, where Hero's prospective happiness is shattered, for the moment, as a result of surveillance devised, not by the true prince, but by his bastard brother, Don John. The gaze in every one of these cases is male, and the object of the gaze is an exposed female who is, characteristically, unaware of the voyeur's presence. And since the exposed woman's life is about to be destroyed by the indirect results of surveillance, it is understandable that we are asked, in effect, to sign on for capital punishment. Daniel calls us back to the seat of judgment so that we will give our assent to the stoning of the wicked elders, and Beatrice calls upon Benedick not to challenge but to "Kill Claudio." These are unforgiving judgments but, if the failure to make them will bring on the Duchess of Malfi's story, then extreme vigilance is in order.

But surely there are occasions on which voyeurism is a victimless crime or, as that phrase always implies, not a crime at all. The striptease fantasies of Herrick's poetry do not put anyone at risk, so far as I can tell, and they are completed within a framework that celebrates, sometimes with laughter, sometimes with awe, but always with joy. We might think of the striptease as occupying one end of the continuum of benign voyeuristic activities: the one in which voyeurism merges with exhibitionism. At the other end of the scale would be socially motivated but benevolent observation of the kind we get in the Beatrice/Benedick plot of *Much Ado.* At this end of the continuum voyeurism tends to merge with gossip, and the kind of noting that goes on will have at least as much to do with the ear as with the eye: the parallel overhearing scenes in *Much Ado* require, above all, that Benedick and Beatrice hear the conversations invented for their benefit. We can of course imagine cases where misleading gossip of this kind would not be so benign, but we'd be inclined to think of its perpetrators as meddlesome rather than dangerous.

Finally, there is a sense in which voyeurism is a precondition for any representation of privacy to begin with. Here I am of course thinking of voyeurism as an aesthetic (not an ethical) practice. The significant long-term changes in attitudes towards privacy which I have been mapping in much of this book would be invisible if we were unable (or unwilling) to be voyeurs ourselves. The position from which we find out about Hamlet's interest in Gertrude's sex life, or Susanna's vulnerability to the gaze of the Elders, or Herrick's fascination with women's clothing is in many senses a voyeuristic one. This does not deny the value of intellectual curiosity, but it allows for a less abstract motivation too: a desire to pry into what was once forbidden, to see what has always been hidden, to discover the private voices of the people who made privacy matter.

Chapter Four

The Commonplace Book and the Private Self

The evidence I have been using to construct various images of early modern privacy has been drawn, up to this point, from published work. And published documents, of course, even if they purport to reveal the most intimate truths about their authors' hearts and minds, have always been made ready, in one way or another, for the public domain. This thought prompted me, while already engaged in research on early modern privacy, to wonder what I might find if I were to consult works still in manuscript. Would I be able to get at least a glimpse of what went on behind that curtain drawn by the printed text between the reader's eye and the naked truth? With this question in mind I set myself the task of burrowing into, not always to the same depth, some 120 manuscript books held at the British Library, the Bodleian Library, the Cambridge University Library, several Oxbridge college libraries, the University of Newcastle Library, the Folger Shakespeare Library, and the Rosenbach Library in Philadelphia.

I began by selecting manuscripts that I had some reason to believe would contain erotica. Acting on the principle that, if a manuscript contains one erotic poem it is likely to contain other specimens of erotica, I used the standard reference guide to help me draw up two lists: one of manuscripts known to contain one version or another of Donne's "Elegy 19: To His Mistress Going to Bed" (64 items); the other of those containing Carew's "A Rapture" (29 items).[1] Once I had begun exploring

1 See Peter Beal et al., *Index of English Literary Manuscripts* (London: Mansell, 1980–97), 1.1:493–8 and 2.1:83–5.

these texts, many items were added for reasons that would be difficult to explain in advance, but that everyone who does research will appreciate. When Anne Vavasour and Walton Poole caught my attention, for example, I soon expanded my manuscript sample to include all items in which their names or their work were known to appear.

Almost all of the manuscripts I studied belong to the very baggy continuum of objects known as poetical miscellanies and commonplace books. The distinction between the two extremes on this scale might be drawn as follows. Poetical miscellanies are more or less systematic collections of poetry: usually anthologies of work by several authors who interest the compiler, but sometimes selections from the works of just a few poets, or even a single poet. Commonplace books, on the other hand, are collections of *aperçus* (which might very well be poems) gathered under a series of explicit or implicit topics: the places of rhetoric and memory. An example of the first position would be Trinity College Cambridge MS R 3.12, which, for the first 237 of its 250 pages, is a John Donne manuscript, and a very fine one at that, produced in a regular, beautiful, and easy-to-read hand, perhaps the hand of E. Puckering, who identifies himself thus on the opening page. The last twelve pages of this manuscript contain poems by other authors (Thomas Randolph, Henry Rainolds, Henry King) and in other hands, but on the whole this compendium will be of far more interest to the editor of Donne's poems than to the researcher on the track of privacy. At the other extreme is a book like BL MS Sloane 104, a true commonplace book in which thoughts and citations are listed under abstract headings like, for example, *Lust.* The compiler informs us, under this heading, that "Cyrene invented 22 wayes to delight the senses" and that "Aretine found out 42 which he calls his postures" (fol. 64). But most of the manuscripts I consulted fall between these two extremes, and that (for me) is a very good thing. The less systematic the manuscript, the more likely it is that something about private life will be perceptible in it.

One highly unsystematic document is CUL Add 4138, a work of bricolage that includes an assortment of textual materials. This manuscript begins with a series of poems about royal visits to Cambridge University (fols. 1–12), some of them quite funny, all of them characterized by a distinctive undergraduate brio. After parts 1 and 2 of a satiric poem, "The distracted puritane" (14–16), the compiler sets up the headline, "Of London Phisicons" (16^v). Here we are given versified attacks on the sexual vices of a long series of doctors, Simon Forman among them (17^v). Then comes a collection of more serious poems, including Henry King's

"A meditation of Death" (23) and Carew's "A Rapture" (30–2). There's also quite an effective satiric poem on the Overbury scandal (50–50^{v}), and a beautiful three-part suite of "virses upon severall pictures in the gallerie at yorke-house" (54–54^{v}), here attributed to Thomas Browne. The compiler of this manuscript, if indeed it was a single individual, seems to have had a taste for satire; for this reason, in part, there are many vulgar phrases in the collection as a whole. One instance, a couplet "Of Mr John Chidley, and S^{r} Ch: Blunt," has been crossed out in pen as if for deletion and, of course, inadvertently highlighted as a result. It reads:

> Here lyes John Chidley, and Sr Charles Blunt.
> The one lov'd a horse, the other a C:/ (48^{v})

This of course is not the usual verbal register for manuscript writers, but it is an example of the liberties they were prepared to take.

We are lucky that, in this instance, the prudishness of an early reader was unable to obliterate what appears to have been a pretty tasteless joke about a Jacobean sex scandal, and we should resist the tendency to dismiss the joke now as just another instance of misogyny. I am recommending that we look for evidence, in the manuscript sources, of how early modern people thought about their private selves. Yes, the evidence will be marked by gender bias, since most of the manuscript books were compiled by men. And what we are likely to find will not in any sense be unmediated recordings of privacy. Commonplace books were often shared, in the sense that they were read, appreciated, and probably contributed to by groups of men – perhaps the men who attended a particular Oxbridge college, or one of the Inns of Court. Still, what makes these manuscripts valuable for my study is the sign of limited access that hangs over these works. When people know that they are writing for a limited audience of like-minded individuals, they are far more likely to be indiscreet than when they're in the public eye.

Most of the manuscripts I have studied include poems by such writers as Ben Jonson, Robert Herrick, Thomas Randolph, Katherine Philips, and (with surprising frequency) Richard Corbett and William Strode. They also tend to include a great many anonymous or at least unattributed poems. Some of these collections include material not strictly poetical: a series of Latin exercises, for example (BL Sloane 542, fols. 1–10), a report of King James's position on the Frances Howard divorce case (Bod Rawl poet 117, fol. 36), a list of remedies for various illnesses (CUL Add 5778, fols. 86–128^{v}), a beer-making recipe attributed to Sir Robert Tabor

(129). The diversity of this material may in part be the result of ownership changes: a manuscript book that began life as a young gentlemen's poetry collection may have become, by means of inheritance perhaps, a country doctor's table book. The first page of BL Add 30982 records four (or perhaps five) ownership claims: "Ismal Seare his booke," "A Croke," "Anthony Evans his booke" (fol. 1), "Daniell Playe his booke. witness William Strode," and "Alexander Croke his Book" (1^{v}).

My approach to the commonplace book is decidedly unlike that taken by Ann Moss in *Printed Common-Place Books and the Structure of Renaissance Thought.*[2] Moss is explicitly interested in the specimens of the genre that were printed and therefore treated as exemplary models; she does little with the vast archive of manuscript sources, beyond mentioning its existence. Furthermore, she is interested in the organization of thought in these documents especially insofar as it plays a role in the decidedly public agenda of humanist education. She recovers a theory of commonplaces from the educational writings of Erasmus, Melancthon, Vives, and others, and she values individual members of the genre insofar as they demonstrate, contribute to, or modify this theory. Given these assumptions about the nature of the genre, it is easy to see why Moss believes the seventeenth century to have seen its decline into something akin to chaos, where "Every private commonplace-book is strictly personal to its owner-author" (276). Given my interests, however, and the subject of the book I am writing, manuscript books are valuable precisely when and if they do what Moss doesn't want them to do.

Because of the unsystematic character of the manuscript material, it would be clearly impossible to give a comprehensive account of it. I have therefore decided to be very selective and to focus attention on two manuscripts which, in my judgment, offer glimpses of privacy that aren't available in other sources, on one charismatic figure who makes brief and tantalizing appearances in many different manuscript sources, and on one poem that recurs with surprising frequency in many of the manuscripts I have consulted. The two manuscripts are Bodleian MS Rawl poet 148 and Rosenbach MS 1083/17, the charismatic figure is Anne Vavasour, and the poem is "To his M^{ris} in despaire because her eyes and haire were blacke."

2 Oxford: Clarendon, 1996.

The Private Life of John Lilliat

Bodleian MS Rawl poet 148 is the work of a single compiler, John Lilliat, who also contributed a generous sampling of his own original poetry to the volume. This manuscript has been edited with great scholarly care by Edward Doughtie and published as *Liber Lilliati*;[3] as a result, readers have the advantage of ready access to a great deal of valuable information about Lilliat himself and about the contents of his book. I will be relying on this material (citing it parenthetically as *LL*) in the following discussion; citations to the manuscript itself, however, are from the original volume as preserved in the Bodleian Library.

Doughtie has established that John Lilliat was a singer: a boy chorister at Christ Church College, Oxford, in 1565, and then a vicar choral first at Wells Cathedral (beginning in 1583) and then at Chichester Cathedral (from 1591 and for at least the next thirty-one years). His lifelong interest in music is reflected in numerous ways in the manuscript book he assembled in the 1590s when, if he was born as Doughtie conjectures in 1555 (*LL* 24), he would have been in his late thirties and early forties (*LL* 16). By this time he was a married man with a family to support. He and his wife Mary were the parents of at least five children: Priscilla (1597–1616), Mary, Edward, Elizabeth, and Martha (*LL* 29–30). The details of his domestic life might seem to be of little interest today, except that they do inflect the meaning and tone of some of his original poems, as I will soon demonstrate.

But first I want to acknowledge the genuinely miscellaneous character of this collection. It includes the printed text of Thomas Watson's *Hecatompathia* (fols. 5–60) bound together with five folios preceding and fifty-four following the printed text. Some of the poems gathered in the manuscript are by clergymen – Richard Eedes, John Langworth, and Richard Latewar – whom Lilliat must have met in the course of his professional life. Others are by poets ranging from the famous (Sidney, Marlowe) to the now obscure (Sir Edward Dyer, Sir Henry Lee) to the unidentified. The topics addressed are as various as this list of names would imply, and can be suggested by recording some of the titles or first lines: "The solace of the soule" by Richard Eedes (71), "Of a sealed

3 *Liber Lilliati: Elizabethan Verse and Song (Bodleian MS Rawlinson Poetry 148)*, ed. Edward Doughtie (Newark: University of Delaware Press, 1985).

dove" by Sidney (86), "The lowest trees have topps" by Dyer (103), "Come live with me and be my Love" by Marlowe together with "Her answer" by Ralegh (96[v]), and "Adam his fall" by John Langworth (105[v]). Although this book is the work of an English Protestant, with contributions from several other English Protestants, it includes two substantial poems written in celebration of Edmund Campion, SJ, executed for treason on 1 December 1581 and declared a martyr by the tributes to him copied here (79[v]–83[v]). Lilliat situates the first of these by calling it "A good verse, upon a badd Matter" (79[v]).

There is plenty of variety here, but Lilliat's book is perhaps not as baggy as its successors would be in the seventeenth century. He was after all a man with a serious vocation and, as Doughtie points out, he was when he began his collection already "beyond that age at which amateurs traditionally indulged in poetry" (*LL* 18). And I think Lilliat's training in music gives to his collection a kind of coherence it would otherwise lack. Some of the manuscript entries are accompanied by musical notation suggesting how they should be sung; these instances are faithfully gathered in Doughtie's Musical Appendix (*LL* 209–15). But there are many other instances of poems having traditional musical settings, others that were clearly meant to be sung, and still others that take up music either as a topic for reflection or as a metaphorical pattern.

It is within this verbal universe, hovering always on the brink of music, that Lilliat seeks to make his mark as a poet. I agree with Doughtie that his mourning poems are among his worst, though I think there is something admirable (if overdone) about "A ditie upon the death of *Dulcebell Porter*, my scholler: whose Mother died the .20. of November, being Munday 1598, and this her daughter Januarii .20. 1598" (93[v]). The long title itself is a significant act of mourning, which the poem almost lives up to: "Sweet *Dulcebell*, for thee I playne./whose tender years cropt in the bud:/shewes, for the world thou was too good" (93[v]).

The closer Lilliat comes to writing about his private self, the better he is as a poet. In my view he is at his best when he's being enigmatic, as in this entry: "The authore heere, commendeth above all:/His bosome birde, in verse Heroicall" (76[v]–77). The first two stanzas enumerate the admirable qualities of various real birds: the nightingale, who greets "the morninge gray" with "Madrigalls"; the "Thristlecock" who could hold his own in "the quier of a Queene," and so on. But in stanza three the speaker introduces the bird capable of striking the others mute: "My bird I meane which in my bosome lies:/Feeds on my fist, and never from me flies." This imagery is perhaps sufficiently conventional to assure us that the bird is the speaker's female companion, but it is too mysterious to be just that. The final stanza makes the bosom bird into a transcendent presence which, even if it is metaphorically the speaker's lover, is also metonymically his consciousness itself, his very soul:

> Her feathers fram'd, of heavenly Angells winges,
> Her voyce of force, to charme *Ulixes* powre:
> She chirpps, she chauntes, all day she sweetly singes,
> When night draws on, my bosome ys her bowre.
> So that of birds (boone sooth) both great & small:
> My bony bird, lo she surpasseth all.

If "His bosome birde" is in fact a poem about Lilliat's wife Mary, then it does not stand alone. Two other poems are explicitly about her, but I will mention them only after a brief detour to acknowledge this couple's daughter, Priscilla. "A Ditie, upon his beloved Daughter *Priscilla*: of th'age of .2. yeers and a quarter. 1599" (103^{v}–4) is the only poem in the collection about any of the Lilliat children. It is the work of a proud parent who promises that both father and mother will continue to thank God for "this blessinge" in song. Whatever joy Priscilla brought to her parents was cut regrettably short by her death at age eighteen and her burial on 14 June 1616 (*LL* 192).

Marriage was not a uniformly gratifying experience for Lilliat, to judge by "Of a weyward wife, wedded to her will" (102^{v}–3). In the opening stanza the speaker claims that he regrets having chosen as he did and, if he could do it again, "to wive I would refuse." His reason clearly has something to do with "tauntes" uttered by what he regards as his wife's "poisoned tongue." This could be just a temporary spat, of the kind that anyone who has ever been married knows about. But it was important enough for Lilliat to write down his exasperation and record it in his manuscript book. To be fair I should note that, in the final lines of this text, he hopes for an "end" to "the Cumbats jarr."

Perhaps the most moving (and most unusual) poem in the collection is "To his lovinge Wife, a welcome home: in Verse, DECASYLLABICAL" (107–7^{v}). Here the speaker begins by drawing a distinction between "*Venus Love*" and "*Vestas Love*, the *Love* twixt Man & Wife." To suggest the special value of the second kind of love, he alludes to the relationship between David and Jonathan, which (if we are to believe its partisans), "all womens *Love* exceeded." A superior valuation of the homosocial bond cannot, however, be sustained in the final stanzas. The speaker asks us to "looke on her, sweet *Loves* allpleasinge object"; he will celebrate the joy of their union, "Vaunting thie *Love*, my heart stringes sweet delight." I am not claiming that this is a great poem, but I do think it is a highly unusual one. Northrop Frye suggested long ago that the pleasures of married life had no adequate representations in literary art. Lilliat's poems come perilously close to being the exception to this otherwise unimpeachable rule.

In the attempt to capture something of interest and value about Lilliat's private self, I have perhaps made him out to be more boring than in fact he was. He does have a sense of humour, and he is capable of irony, though I have given him very little credit here for either of these virtues. Without a sense of humour he wouldn't have bothered with "The old Lord Marques (being Lord Thesaurer of th'age of .94.) his sayinge":

> Late eatinge and drinckinge I doe forbeare,
> Both wyne & women I doe forsweare:
> My neck and feete I keepe from colde,
> Why mervayle you though I be olde?

And certainly not with "The Answer":

> The first line made thy bodie stronge,
> The second, made thy witt last longe:
> The third, did help both theis to thrive,
> I mervayle th'art not now a live. (110)

Without a well-developed appreciation for irony he would not have been attracted to "Of lingeringe Love" (62^{v}), or to the song, "Change thy mynd since she doth change" (67–7^{v}), attributed to the earl of Essex. These are qualities which merely link Lilliat's sensibility to his time and place. Still, my whole enterprise here has been not to separate him from Elizabethan culture, but rather to discover how he found a private place within it.

Erotic Fantasy

In Rosenbach MS 1083/17, by contrast, the perspective of a single individual is not what matters. The poetry, however, certainly does. At the beginning of the collection and at the end there are gatherings of poems about death: "An Elegy upon ye death of ffran: Beamont" (pp. 1–3),[4] "Upon Prince Henry being in a slumber a little before his death" (11), "An Epitaph on Will. Shakesphear" (6–7) by William Basse, "Upon ye death of Lady Haddington who dyed of ye small Pox" (8–10) by Richard Corbett, "Upon ye Countess of Pembrook" (164^{v}) by William Browne, "Upon the death of an expert Phisitian" (164^{v}–5^{v}), "Upon the death of y^{t} famous Actor R. Burbadge" (165^{v}–7), and so on. Many of the persons being mourned were famous, and most of them had been dead for years by the time this compilation was made (ca 1638). The tribute to the countess of Pembroke is the one which begins "underneath this sable Herse/lyes ye subject of all verse/Sidneys sister Pembroks mother ..." (164^{v}). In the margin a seventeenth-century reader (with handwriting slightly different from that of the compiler) has written the word "printed." And he's right, of course: the poem about the countess of Pembroke had been published in Camden's *Remaines* (1623).[5] But this reader seems to be pointing out an exception; his reaction would suggest that, on the whole, poetry would not circulate in manuscript once it had appeared in print.

After the opening sequence of elegies the Rosenbach manuscript gathers a large number of poems by Thomas Carew: "Lipps and Eyes" (19), "Song: A Bewtifull Mistress" (20), "A Cruell Mistress" (21), "Song: Murdering Bewtie" (22), "My M^{rs} com[m]andinge me to returne her letters" (22–5), "Mediocritie in love rejected" (28–9), "A Rapture" (49^{v}–53), and many, many more. None of these poems is signed by or attributed to Carew in the manuscript, but they would all find their way into Carew's *Poems* (1640) in a few years' time.

From Carew it's a pretty effortless transition to a sequence of poems about female appearance. These include, for example, Edmund Waller's defence of the maligned Saccarissa in "Of ye misreport of her being painted" (84^{v}–5). There is also an amazingly ghoulish treatment of female beauty in a poem here called "To a M^{rs}" (85^{v}–6), though in another manuscript it is titled "To Mrs Katharine Bacon" and attributed to Nicolas Oldisworth.[6] The speaker of this poem alleges that the woman's beauty

4 After four preliminary folios (i–iv), this manuscript is paginated in pages (1–34) and then in folios (35–168). My own references will follow this (inconsistent) practice.

5 See *Remaines, Concerning Britaine: But Especially England, and the Inhabitants Thereof*, 2nd ed. (London: Nicholas Okes for Simon Waterson, 1623), Y6^{v}.

6 See Margaret Crum, ed., *First-Line Index of English Poetry 1500–1800 in Manuscripts of the Bodleian Library Oxford* (Oxford: Clarendon, 1969), Y249.

is far in excess of what any man could deserve, so she's right to remain single and disdainful. Still, if "some new trick" could be found whereby her excellent parts might be distributed:

> if wee could sever you wthout yor harme
> and give this Prince a leg y^{t} Duke an arme
> ...
> then might you be unvirgin'd and then wee
> quite rounde ye world should happie husbands be. (86)

In our generation we've developed subtle critical tools for arguing that the blazon of the Petrarchan tradition is implicitly a kind of dismemberment.[7] Poor Nicolas Oldisworth, a poet on whom such subtleties would be wasted. And poor Katharine Bacon, who, if she ever read this tribute to her "parts" (85^{v}), must have sensed that something creepy was going on.

I take this admittedly extreme example as a way of suggesting that the poetry in this manuscript (and others like it) is full of erotic fantasy, and that such fantasy is almost always represented exclusively from the male point of view. But Rosenbach 1083/17 interests me precisely because it contains some remarkable exceptions to this nonetheless reliable rule. Someone involved with the creation of this manuscript, especially the second half of it, had begun to wonder what the woman is thinking while all these acts of courtship, seduction, adultery, harassment, voyeurism, and so on are unfolding around her. The immediate provocation for this thought seems to have been a long series of aggressive poems spoken in the voice of the male lover/seducer. Beaumont's "A Charme" (90–90^{v}), for example, gives the lover's incantation the power to ensure that the husband will continue to snore while Corinna steals away to be with him. "A Privat discourse wth a M^{rs}" (91–1^{v}) gives us a speaker with less cunning and more alacrity: "Come Ladie come yor leggs display/And lett me clime ye milkie way" (91). Jonson comes next, though he's not named, and his poem is rather curtly called "Another": "Come sweet M^{rs}

7 Nancy J. Vickers has been at the forefront of this enterprise; see, for example, her claim that "within the context of Petrarch's extended poetic sequence, the lady is corporeally scattered," in "Diana Described: Scattered Woman and Scattered Rhyme," *Critical Enquiry* 8, no. 2 (Winter 1981): 274.

lett us prove/Whilst wee can ye Sports of love" (91^{v}). If we substitute "my Celia" for "sweet M^{rs}" we can of course hear Volpone in these lines as he struts his stuff for Corvino's beautiful wife. The compiler of Rosenbach 1083/17 heard all these voices, and then said to himself (because I reluctantly infer that he was himself a man),[8] the woman has got to have a voice of her own. And if she does, what would it sound like?

To the great credit of this compiler, he soon found evidence that different women would have different things to say. I will deal with the first three female voices very quickly, because the fourth one deserves special attention. The speaker of "Bewtyes Invitation," which follows Jonson's poem immediately, is clearly female:

> Tast all my sweets come here & freely sipp
> divinest Nectar from my melting lippe. (92)

Not only is she female, but she's willing to take the initiative. She invites her reticent lover to "Twine" his "long fingers" through her "flaxen haire" and, if he likes, "Play with my teats y^{t} swell to have impression" (92). Maybe this is not a real woman speaking, so much as a man ventriloquizing a female voice he would like to hear. But that at least is a start.

Two poems purport to give us the voices of (unhappily) married women. "A Gentlewomans complaint upon a second match to an old rich man" (102^{v}) is an undistinguished poem. The title says it all. The first husband was young and virile, but she didn't know how lucky she was until he died. Now she's eager for it, but the old husband who's given her economic security isn't up to the mark. This is a less desperate position

8 The marks that would identify a female compiler are simply absent from this manuscript. Such marks might be, for example, a woman's name recorded on a signature page; see for example BL Add 44,963, which contains the signature "Anthony Scattergood" at the beginning (4) and the words "Elizabeth Scattergood her Boke 1667/8" near the end (132^{v}). By contrast Rosenbach 1083/17 contains at least five male signatures (Thomas Arding, William Harrington, Horatio Carey, John Anthelhope, and Clement Poxall) and no female identification marks. Furthermore, the entire manuscript is in Elizabethan secretary hand – a system of writing that was not taught to women. Rosenbach MS 240/7, by contrast, is written in at least three different hands: a round italic hand (19, 53–4 and elsewhere), a large secretary hand, and a small secretary hand. The first of these is the one that seventeenth-century women were likely to use.

than that of the "Wretched" speaker of "A maryed womans complainte" (94v–5). She's got a young husband who seems to be "Of great performance" but nothing comes of it: specifically, the speaker has no children, and believes that her female friends "bragg and scoff" at her while "giving sucke" to their own infants. The speaker ends her complaint by arguing that women should "try/Befor they wedd" so as to forestall the disappointments she is obliged to endure.

But in my judgment the most surprising text in Rosenbach 1083/17 is the poem which follows in full below (142v–3v):

A Ladyes dreame

ffly Paper fly to his beloved hands
Soone lett him know I am at his com[m]ands
I have not patience longer, Ile not try
Who first shall make it knowne, or he or I.
Wee love, heare dumbe delay, I will say this
he happily may be mine I must be his
Tell him in his dead shadow is more blisse
Then in the substance of anothers kisse
A meere Imaginary Act with him
More then the wanton shiveringe of a limbe
In Venus sport, witness my last Nights dreame
me thought wee floated one a chrystall streame
bottomless and boundless, yet dreadless wee,
Encourag'd by that God who cannot see
I was the Barke ye ballast was my love
wee rose and fell just as the waves did move
Neither for port nor Haven were we bound
Wee charmed were wthin the watry rounde
A Couch wee had more soft then downey freeze
yt dwells upon the backe of humble Bees
And one the couch a Coverlett in hew
like to ye sunshine and the morning dew
so rare so fine yt with the greatest streyne
it tore and of it self dearn'd up againe.
Our Canopy as wide as heaven and spred
with sun and moone and stars embroydered
so Naturall yt my meane Philosophy
knew not wch mov'd or couch or canopy

I sence had only of o^{r} proper motion
And seem'd to active for the brickle Ocean
As two young Jennetts shackled in a roome
but now broke from their hardly usinge Groome
skudes to & fro as if the spatious Plaines
could not conteyne their prickt up tailes & maines
Such was our courage heated with such fire
The watry world enflam'd not quencht desire
Insatiate Lust such pleasure never try'd
we were unwearyed not unsatisfy'd
Our joynts so supple made the world appeare
A race to short for only our Careere
A shoale of Dolphins like a liveing floure
Road under us, one of them proudly bore
Amphyon one his backe, who playd & sunge
A thousand Lullabies, ye scaly thronge
Danc'd, y^{t} they made us dance, as jacks doe make
In virginalls the strings above to quake
Now suddenly a silent calme began
When thus discour'st our moyst musitian
Mighty Imaginac[i]on thou art stronge
Substance growes feeble & lyes all alonge
Action is an unthrift & it self doth spend
Imaginac[i]ons vigor hath noe end
Action must borrow and conceit must lend
Love is effectless wthout such a freind
What I have sayd these lovers apprehend
And will not spare their power to com[m]end
Whereat I yawned & had scarcely time
befor I wakned to compose this rime.

The erotic content of the dream is framed by the speaker's admission that she's prepared to be indiscreet to declare her love, because "A meere Imaginary Act" with the man she desires is worth more than real sex with anyone else. As proof of this claim she gives an account of "last Nights dreame." Some of the imagery here is quite conventional. To imagine herself as "the Barke" and her lover as "ye ballast" is not an original turn, and comparing sexual motion to "waves" is almost inevitable. Perhaps the couch, the coverlet, and the "embroydered" canopy are a little *précieuse*. But there is a real energy in this dream – an energy that takes off when the lovers are compared to "two young Jennets" breaking out of their confined space, and that builds into beautiful motion when the "shoal of Dolphins" induces the lovers to dance, "as jacks doe make/In virginals the strings above to quake." There's room to argue about whether this is an accurate or powerful or suggestive representation of female erotic fantasy. But I am sure that it's *not* the standard fare of the male-centred position: there's no enumeration of the parts of the woman's body, no appeal to possession or conquest, no replication of the Petrarchan (or anti-Petrarchan) conventions. Has this author been able to capture female erotic fantasy in his poem? Well, at least he was interested in the question, and probably curious about what women had to say about it.

Anne Vavasour

Some years ago, while rummaging through the manuscript books at the Bodleian Library, I became aware of the name Anne Vavasour for the first time. Perhaps it was Bodleian MS Rawlinson poetical 85 that especially aroused my curiosity, with the heading "Verses made by the earle of Oxforde/and Mrs Ann Vavesor" (fol. 11). The stroke which apparently cancelled the second half of this attribution wasn't enough to quench my curiosity, especially when I read "Though I seeme straunge" (fol. 17).

Before quoting this poem in full, I want to sketch in a little of the context. Anne Vavasour, according to the entry under her name in the *Oxford Dictionary of National Biography*, was maid of honour to Queen Elizabeth I, and the mistress of Edward de Vere (seventeenth earl of Oxford). On 23 March 1580/1 she gave birth to a son, Edward Vere, who would go on to a successful military career and a knighthood in 1607. His parents, however, were both sent to the Tower (briefly) to remind them of how naughty they had been.[9]

The version of the poem I reproduce here isn't the one I found at the Bodleian, nor is it the one I had encountered earlier at the British Library (Harley 6910, fol. 145–45^{v}), where it is subscribed "La B to N."

9 See Stephen W. May, "Vavasour [*married names* Finch, Richardson], Anne (fl. 1580–1621), lady of the royal household," *Oxford Dictionary of National Biography* (2004).

Rather, I quote the poem from Folger MS V a 89, a manuscript book owned by Anne Cornwallis, later countess of Argyll, and assembled by someone who seems to have known more than most people about the affair between Oxford and Vavasour.

Thoughe I seeme straunge sweete frynd be thou not soe
doe not annoye thy selfe with sullen will
my hearte hathe vowed although my tonge sayes no
to rest thyne owne in fryndlye liking still

Thou seest we live amongste the lynxes eyes
that pryes & spyes eache pryvye thought of mynd
thou knowest ryghte well what sorrowes may aryse
yf once they chance my setled lookes to fynde

Contente thy selfe y^{t} once I made an othe
to shielde my selfe in shrowde of honest shame
and when thow liste make tryall of my trothe
soe y^{t} thou save the honor of my name

And let me seme althoughe I be not coye
to cloke my sad conceipts wth smyling cheare
lett not my gestures showe wherein I Joye
nor by my lookes let not my love appeare

We sillye dames y^{t} false suspecte doe feare
and lyve wthin the mouth of envyes lak
must in our heartes a secrete meaninge beare
farre from the show y^{t} outwardlye we make

Goe where I like I list not vaunte my love
wher I desire ther must I fayne debate
one hath my hand another hath my glove
but he my hearte whom most I seme to hate

Thus farewell fryndе I will contynue straunge
thou shalte not heare by worde or writinge oughte
lett it suffice my vowe shall never chaunge
as for the rest I leave it to thy thought
finis vavaser (8–9)

The speaker of this poem is clearly female ("We sillye dames"), and I think she has a powerfully developed sense of how gender must affect her behaviour. Being female makes her vulnerable in ways that her sweet friend isn't, and one mark of her vulnerability is the constant surveillance she believes she's subjected to. Not even a "pryvye thought" feels safe when you've come to believe that you "live amongste the lynxes eyes." So the speaker maps out a plan for dealing with her precarious lot: a plan which calls upon her to exercise permanent restraint (she will "contynue straunge") and upon her friend to trust that nonetheless she is absolutely devoted to him, as her "vowe" establishes beyond doubt.

In one sense the speaker is taking a hypocritical stance. She wants to have things her way, without any of the messy consequences. She wants to "seme ... coy" in order to mislead those who suspect her, and then indulge herself in secret pleasures nonetheless. But even in making this description of her duplicity, I am still aware that what she wants to create and maintain at all costs is a quintessentially romantic relationship. The "secrete meaninge" which the lovers bear in their hearts is too precious to risk in the uncertain world of social negotiation. Like the love of Tristan and Isolde, or of Romeo and Juliet, this is a love that represents itself not as contingent but as absolute.

I am not certain that Anne Vavasour is the author of "Though I seeme straunge," but her name is repeatedly linked with copies of the poem that circulate in the manuscript culture. If she did not write the poem, she seems to have called it into being nonetheless, since it encapsulates something that appears to grow out of her experience, or someone else's understanding of her experience. And a similar claim may be made about a second specimen, also from Folger V a 89, an echo poem of which I offer only a brief excerpt.

Sittinge alone upon my thought in melancholye moode
in sight of sea & at my backe an auncyent horye woode
I sawe a fayre yonge ladye come her secreate teares to wayle
clad all in colour of a vowe and covered with a vayle
...
from sighes & sheadinge amber teares into swete songe she brake
and thus the eccho answered her to every worde she spake.

O heavenes quothe she who was the firste y[t] bred in me this fever   vere
who was the firste that gave the wound whose scarre I wear forever   vere
...

what makes him not regarde good will wth some remorse or ruthe youth
what makes him shewe besides his birthe suche pride & such untruthe youth
vavaser (13)

To me this seems a much less distinguished poem, but perhaps that's because I've never believed that the echo is the amazing poetic device that its many users want it to be. Once you've seen couplet A produce the echo effect, you won't be all that surprised when it happens again in couplet B. And I find the "amber tears" of the "fayre yonge ladye" more predictable than the conflicted emotions of "Though I seeme straunge." If Anne Vavasour wrote the echo poem, as she may have done, she was no longer able to keep her secret.

"Many desier but few or none deserve" has long been recognized (and rightly so) as a poem by the young Sir Walter Ralegh. It belongs to Anne Vavasour not by virtue of authorship, but by virtue of a different kind of linkage for which, so far as I know, there is no precise critical term. "Patronage" isn't quite right here, since I doubt very much that any young woman (let alone someone as obsessed with secrecy as Vavasour) would reward a young man for trespassing on her private life in the way this poem does. To say that she is his muse isn't quite right either, since he's clearly more interested in controlling her than in being controlled by her. Perhaps we need to invent a new term that will imply the dependence of a text on a person who is not its author but who, as the unique object of the poem's attention, is nonetheless a constitutive part in its making. This time I quote from Bodleian MS Rawl poet 85, though the poem appears in many other manuscript sources and in editions of Ralegh's poetry too:

Many desier but fewe or none deserve
To felle the forte of thy most constant will.
Wherefore take heede lett fancye never swarve
But unto him that will defende the still.
For this be suer the forte of fame once wonne
Farwell the rest thie happie dayes be donne

Many desier but fewe or none deserve
To plucke the branch & lett this flower fall
Wherefor take heede let fancye never swarve
But unto him that will take leaves and all
For this be sewer the flower once pluckt awaye
Farwell the rest the branch will sone decaye

Many desier but fewe or none deserve
To cutt the grafte not subject to the syckle
Wherfor take hede lett fancye never swarve
But constant stand for mowers myndes be tyckle
And this be sewer the crop beinge ounce attayned
Farwell the rest the soyle wilbe disdayned
Finis written to M^rs A V. (fol. 116)

If Ralegh was indeed warning Anne Vavasour of the dire consequences that would follow the surrender of her virtue (without the prospect of a stable marriage in sight), then he can be faulted on two counts. First, Vavasour proved herself far more resilient than he predicted. Second, a decade later he would himself earn the queen's displeasure, and a temporary stay in the Tower, by his clandestine but indiscreet marriage to another of her majesty's maids of honour, Elizabeth Throckmorton.

Before things got better, however, they got a great deal worse. De Vere was of course not in a position to offer Anne Vavasour what she deserved, because of his (unhappy) marriage to Lord Burghley's eldest daughter, Anne, not to mention his infatuation with a Venetian choirboy, Orazio Cogno, whom he kept in his London lodgings.[10] Anne Vavasour's extended family were not impressed. Her uncle, Sir Thomas Knyvet, fought a duel with Oxford in 1582, an event which settled nothing, although it led to further name calling of the kind available in the excerpt I am about to quote from British Library MS Lansdowne 99. The conventional wisdom here is that Thomas Vavasour, who signs his name to the challenge, is Anne's brother.[11] Here is a little of what he had to say:

> If thy body had bene as deformed as thy mind is dishonorable my house had bene yet unspotted and thy self remayned wth thy cowardise unkowne. I speake this that I feare thow art so much wedded to that shadow of thine y^t nothing canne have force to awake thy base and sleapye spyrytes. Is not the reveng already taken of thy vilanes sufficient but wylt thou yet use unworthy instrumentes to provoke my unwylling mind? … yf ther be yet left any sparke of honour in the, or jott of regard of thy decayed reputation, use

10 See Alan H. Nelson, "Vere, Edward de, seventeenth earl of Oxford (1550–1604), courtier and poet," *Oxford Dictionary of National Biography* (2004).

11 See E.K. Chambers, *Sir Henry Lee: An Elizabethan Portrait* (Oxford: Clarendon, 1936), 158.

> not thy byrth for an excuse for I am a gentleman but meete me thy self alone and thy lacky to hould thy horse for the weapons I leave them to thy choyse for y[t] I chalendge, and the place to be apoynted by us both at o[u]r meeting w[ch] I think may convenyently be at Nuington or els where thy self shalt send me word by this bearer. by whom I expect an answere, Tho: Vavasor (fol. 252)

If the Vavasour family was willing to confront Oxford in this way, they were doubtless putting plenty of pressure on Anne, too. In any case she married someone called John Finch, about whom nothing more than his name has been discovered.

But she was a court groupie by temperament and practice. She became the mistress of Sir Henry Lee, the queen's champion at tilt. By now (ca 1590) Anne Vavasour was less concerned with secrecy; after the death of Lee's wife, Vavasour lived openly with him in his Oxfordshire manor (Ditchley) and bore him an illegitimate son, Thomas Vavasour, alias Freeman. Something of the quality of this relationship is captured in the anecdote (from British Library Lansdowne 777) about Lee's supervision of their funeral monument.

> S[r] Henry Ley kept Mistris Vavasour and caused his Tombe to be made dureinge his life, he lyeing and she kneeling by him. And coming into the church suddainely wrote this:
>
> Heere lyes the good old knight S[r] Harry
> That long time lov'd but would not marry.
> Whilst that he liv'd, & had his feeling
> She did lye and he was kneeling,
> Now he is dead & cannot feele,
> He doth lye & she doth kneele. (fol. 67)

When old Sir Harry died in 1611, Anne received a jointure of £700: not enough, apparently, to prevent her from marrying a certain John Richardson. She may not have known that her first husband was still alive, but somebody did, so Lee's legitimate children sued her for bigamy in the court of high commission and won a settlement of £2,000.

The manuscript sources I have just been citing have only one thing in common: all of them were called into being by the curious and flamboyant life of Anne Vavasour. These texts have been quoted or printed by other scholars, but always in a context that makes Anne Vavasour a shadowy figure on the margins. That's how she comes across in E.K.

Chambers's biography of Sir Henry Lee, for example, or even in Arthur F. Marotti's detailed study of Folger MS V a 89.[12] What hasn't been done before is to bring these texts together, so as to make Anne Vavasour the protagonist of her own story.

What then has been accomplished by this act of gathering? Perhaps nothing. As the putative author of a couple of poems, Anne Vavasour is unlikely to achieve immortality. And there's not even a coherent image that emerges from these widely scattered messages, so it's difficult to reconstruct a single point of view, or subject position, or sensibility that would account for all of them.

But I think the textual traces left behind by Anne Vavasour give us something more beguiling than evidence of a coherent subject position. They give us something closer to the elements of an Elizabethan or Jacobean play: a script in which our heroine is called upon to play many parts. At first she seems as vulnerable as Ophelia: desperately in love with a famous courtier who has many more important things to do than care about her. Ralegh sees her in just this way. But Vavasour doesn't go mad or drown herself. In her determination to fend for her children and make her own erotic choices, whether her family approves or not, she exhibits some of the rashness and some of the strength of the Duchess of Malfi. The petulance with which her brother seeks to defend her has analogues in revenge tragedy too, though the overblown rhetoric might remind us of the words in which Benedick challenges Claudio in *Much Ado about Nothing*. And in her role as Sir Henry Lee's common-law partner, Vavasour escapes tragedy entirely and begins to develop entrepreneurial and sexual talents that recall the women of Middleton's city comedies (think of Mistress Allwit in *A Chaste Maid in Cheapside*), though of course she occupies a position much higher up the social scale than they do. None of these parts is exactly her, of course, but in the aggregate they give us a whole that, if not greater than, is at least different from the sum of its parts. If "All the world's" indeed "a stage,/And all the men and women merely players" (*As You Like It* 2.7.139–40), then it should be possible to supplement the series of male roles which Jaques goes on to list with a different but equally resonant set of female performances, like those played out here under Anne Vavasour's name. Perhaps the manuscripts give us no direct access to this flamboyant woman's private life, but they certainly offer us glimpses that tempt us into wanting more.

---

12 "The Cultural and Textual Importance of Folger MS V.a.89," *English Manuscript Studies 1100–1700* (2002): 70–92.

The Indiscretions of Walton Poole

Manuscript materials tended to circulate, sometimes as separates, among self-selecting groups of like-minded readers.[13] For this reason it should not be surprising to find the same item recurring several or even many times in the manuscripts under review. But there is one poem, "To his M[ris] in despaire because her eyes and haire were blacke," which appears (with variations, of course) in thirty-five manuscripts, or nearly a third of my research sample.[14] Very few items appear as frequently as this, and if they do, they are likely to be well known today; Donne's "Elegy 19: To His Mistress Going to Bed" would be a conspicuous case in point. But the poem which follows is virtually unknown today, though I think it deserves a better fate.

To his M[ris] in despaire because her eyes and haire were blacke

If shaddowes be your pictures excellence
And make them seeme more lively to y[e] sence
If starres in y[e] bright day be less in sight
And shine more glorious in y[e] maske of night
Why should you thinke faire creature y[t] you lacke

13 See Harold Love, *Scribal Publication in Seventeenth-Century England* (Oxford: Clarendon, 1993), 79–83. In general I have tried to adopt terminology consistent with Love's intelligent and useful overview of the seventeenth-century manuscript phenomenon. But, contrary to his practice and recommendation, I have preferred to refer throughout to the "circulation" of manuscripts rather than their "publication." The term "circulation," on the one hand, preserves a distinction between the dissemination of manuscripts among like-minded individuals, and the distribution of printed text to any interested buyer; and, on the other hand, it notices the difference between medieval manuscript distribution and interpretation (which was indeed a form of publication) and early modern practice.

14 BL Add 21433, BL Add 25707, BL Egerton 2421, BL Harley 6057, BL Harley 6931 (the version I have chosen to quote), BL Lansdowne 777, BL Sloane 542, BL Sloane 1446, BL Sloane 1792, BL Stowe 962, Bod Ashmole 38, Bod Eng poet c 50, Bod Eng poet e 97, Bod Eng poet f 10, Bod Eng poet f 25, Bod Eng poet f 27, Bod Rawl poet 117, Bod Rawl poet 199, Newcastle Bell-White 25, Folger V a 97, Folger V a 103, Folger V a 124, Folger V a 125, Folger V a 245, Folger V a 319, Folger V a 322, Folger V a 345, Folger V b 43, Rosenbach 239/18, Rosenbach 239/22, Rosenbach 239/27, Rosenbach 240/7, Rosenbach 243/4.2, Rosenbach 1083/16, and Rosenbach 1083/17.

Perfection cause your eyes and haire are blacke
Or that your beauty which so farre exceeds
The new sprung lillies in their maidenheads,
That cherry colour of your cheekes and lippes
Should by their darkenesse suffer an eclipse?
It is not fit that nature should have made
So bright a sunne to shine without a shade
It seemes that nature when shee first did fancy
Thy rare composure studdyed Necromancy:
And when to thee those gifts shee did impart
She studied altogether ye blacke art
Shee drew ye magicke circle of thine eyes
And made thine haire a chaine wherein shee tyes
Rebellious harts; those blew vaines wch appeare
Turnd in Meander like to either spheare
Misterious figures are, and when you list
Your voyce com*m*andeth like an exorcist.
Or if in Magicke you have skill so farre
Vouchsafe to make me your familiar.
Nor hath kinde nature her blacke art reveald
On outward parts alone, some ly conceald
For as by ye spring head a man may know
The nature of ye streame y^{t} runnes below;
So thy blacke eyes and haire doe give direction
To judge the rest to bee of like perfection,
The rest where all rest lyes that blesseth man
The Indian mine, the straights of Magellan,
The worlds dividing gulfe, which who so venters
With swelling sayles, and ravisht senses enters
Into a world of blisse. Pardon I pray
If my rude muse now chance for to display
Secrets unknowne, or hath his bounds o'repast
In praising sweetness wch I shall nere tast
Starvd men know there is food, & blind men may
Though hid from them know if there is a day.
The rover in ye marke his arrow stickes,
Sometimes as well as hee y^{t} shootes at prickes;
But if I might my shaft direct aright
The blacke marke would I hitt, & not ye white.

Walton Poole (BL Harley 6931, fols. 8^{v}–9^{v})

This poem strikes me as remarkable for at least three different reasons: (1) the cleverness of the metaphorical process whereby the dark, the shadowed, the obscure are given precedence over the bright and apparent; (2) the boldness of the speaker's approach to the hidden parts of the woman's body; (3) the precariously maintained dignity of the speaker's tone of voice. Let me comment further on each of these three attributes in turn.

The speaker begins by invoking the principle of aesthetic contrast in language reminiscent of the chiarascuro technique as practised by Caravaggio or even, in a context closer to home for the readers of this poem, by such portrait painters as Isaac Oliver and Anthony van Dyck. The point here is the simple but important recognition that the beauty of a painted face, let us say, is enhanced by shadowing – the technique whereby spatial depth and hence personal interiority can be suggested even on a perfectly flat surface. The principle which holds for artificial constructions of beauty is said to hold true for natural objects as well: "starres," for example, emerge as "more glorious" against the dark background of the night sky. So the woman of the poem needs to reinterpret her own black eyes and hair; far from being aesthetic disadvantages (whereby her other beauties might "suffer an eclipse"), the woman's dark parts have special value because they enhance her beauty as a whole. The speaker now brings together the natural and the artificial in the figure of magic: nature herself was obliged to study "Necromancy" or "ye blacke art" when she produced this paragon.

So far the speaker has been concerned with the magical power of the woman's "outward parts," but now he turns to those that "ly conceald": what is true of her visible parts will no doubt be true also of "the rest." And it is at this point that the speaker's rhetoric soars to the level of the rhapsodic. What can he possibly be referring to when he invokes "The rest where all rest lyes that blesseth man"? Or when he alludes to "The Indian mine, the straights of Magellan"? In one sense the answer is so obvious as to resist spelling out. The mine is a concealed source of value, as it is in Donne's "mine of precious stones" or "both th'Indias of spice and mine."[15] The Straits of Magellan consist of a narrow passage between two land masses: mainland South America and Tierra del Fuego. The

15 From (respectively) "Elegy 19: To His Mistress Going to Bed" and "The Sun Rising" in *The Complete Poems*, ed. A.J. Smith (Harmondsworth: Penguin, 1971), 125, 80.

concealed value of the woman is clearly her sexual value, and the narrow passage is the one between her thighs. No other reading accommodates the imagery of the last fifteen lines of the poem, including the metaphor from archery at its close. The "rover" is a long-distance shooter, who (like the speaker) would have to be very lucky to hit the "marke" – much luckier than the archer engaged in close-range target practice (shooting at pricks). In any case, the speaker adds, it's the black target he would like his "shaft" to hit: that is, because he believes that the woman's hidden parts take their "direction" from her black hair and eyes, the speaker thinks he has established the blackness of her pubic hair, and declares himself especially attracted by this feature.

If I am right about the meaning of this poem, then it follows that the speaker is engaged in an act of quite spectacular indiscretion. It would be easy for the rhetorical strategy undertaken here to descend into simple prurience, and an unsympathetic reading might indeed advance the claim that this is what occurs. But I think the speaker disarms exactly this objection in the clause which begins, "Pardon I pray." The dignity of his tone of voice is earned precisely through the recognition that he is treading on dangerous ground. He has been revealing what he doesn't really know to be true; he has transgressed the "bounds" of propriety in making his assumptions about the woman's sexual being; he acknowledges that the pleasure he imagines is a "sweetnesse wch I shall nere tast." In this very acknowledgment one can locate a certain reticence even in the midst of indiscretion: a reticence based on awareness of the woman's otherness and respect for her privacy. The speaker's verbal poise allows him to resist the temptation to say anything demeaning or damaging about the woman; by recognizing the ambiguity of his own situation, he is able to recast his impropriety as poetry.

The quality of sexual indiscretion which I locate at the centre of this poem has always, I believe, been the secret of its attractiveness to readers, though it has never been identified before. Previous commentators have been sufficiently distracted by the search for factual information *about* the poem, so as to leave the question of any qualities *within* it virtually untouched. One of the factual issues has been the identity of the poem's author, a question which seems to have been resolved in favour of Walton Poole. It is a legitimate question, however, and an open one for the poem's first readers: the gentlemen who participated in the circulation of this text from one manuscript volume to another. Of the manuscripts I examined, twenty-six make no claims about authorship, five assign it to Walton Poole, three to Richard Corbett, and two to Ben

Jonson.[16] The latter claim has no backing from Jonson himself (who of course decided what ought to be included in his *Workes* [1616]), nor from Herford and Simpson, nor from subsequent editors of Jonson's poems.[17] At least one manuscript I haven't seen assigns the poem to John Donne, an event which led E.K. Chambers to include it under "Appendix A: Doubtful Poems" in his edition of Donne, and Grierson to print it in Appendix C, a collection of poems sometimes attributed to Donne but, in Grierson's opinion, very unlikely to be by him.[18] Since neither Jonson nor Donne is a serious candidate, Walton Poole and Richard Corbett appear to emerge as the most likely authors; but Corbett's modern editors are as dismissive as Jonson's and Donne's.[19] The reasons in favour of Poole's candidacy are explored in detail by the poem's most scholarly reader, Edwin Wolf 2nd.[20]

Aside from the appearance of Walton Poole's name in selected manuscripts, the most important piece of evidence in support of his claim of authorship has to do with the identity of the woman being addressed by the speaker of the poem. Her identity is left indefinite in most manuscript copies of the poem, as in the title quoted earlier, "To his M^{ris} in despaire." But sometimes the title is more revealing: "Upon M^{s} Poole whose haire & eyes wher blacke" (BL Sloane 1792); "On Mrs Beata Poole with blacke eyes" (Bod Rawl poet 199); or "To Mrs Poole ye L^{d} of Shandois Sister, who had black haire & black Eies" (Bod Eng poet e 97). Historically and genealogically the woman identified here was Beatrice Brydges, daughter of William, 4th Baron Chandos of Sudeley, Gloucestershire, and sister of Grey, 5th Baron Chandos. Beatrice Brydges became Beatrice (or Beata) Poole when, "some time before 1616 she married Sir Henry

16 For Walton Poole see BL Harley 6931, BL Lansdowne 777 (signed "W:P"), BL Sloane 1446, Folger V a 97, and Folger V b 4; for Richard Corbett see Bod Eng poet f 10, Folger V a 345, and Rosenbach 239/27; for Ben Jonson see BL Add 21433 and for Ben Johnson BL Harley 6507.

17 See *Ben Jonson*, ed. C.H. Herford, Percy Simpson, and Evelyn Simpson (Oxford: Clarendon, 1925–52).

18 See *Poems of John Donne*, ed. E.K. Chambers (London: Lawrence and Bullen, 1886), 2:267–8; and *The Poems of John Donne*, ed. Herbert J.C. Grierson (London: Oxford University Press, 1912), 1:460–1.

19 See *The Poems of Richard Corbett*, ed. J.A.W. Bennett and H.R. Trevor-Roper (Oxford: Clarendon, 1955), 178: "The ascription to Corbett is as unconvincing as that to Ben Jonson or to Donne, who are credited with it in other MSS."

20 "'If Shadows be a Picture's Excellence': An Experiment in Critical Bibliography," *PMLA* 63 (1948): 831–57.

Poole, of Saperton, co. Gloucester."[21] We have now arrived at the surname Poole, but not yet at the putative author's family. First we must distinguish between the Pooles of Saperton (Gloucestershire) and the Pooles of Wiltshire. Only among the Wiltshire Pooles does the Christian name Walton occur. The reason for this phenomenon can be traced back to the mid-sixteenth century when Edward Poole married Margaret Walton, a union which resulted in six children: Henry, Walton, a third son, Katheryn, Margaret, and Elinor.[22] For our purposes, only the first two sons, Henry and Walton, need be of concern. The original Walton Poole is a generation too old to be the author of our poem, but his name will recur. Henry Poole, the original Walton's elder brother, made a will dated 7 March 1630/1 which names his son Sir Nevill Poole sole executor, and which reserves a rent of £60 on the manor of Yewen "for son Walton Poole."[23] This Walton Poole, doubtless so named in honour of his uncle, would have been born at some time in the 1590s, making him exactly the right age to be the author whose name is attached to the manuscript poem.

However, we still have no link between Beata Poole, married to Sir Henry Poole of Gloucestershire, and Walton Poole, the putative author and resident of Wiltshire. The missing link is a marriage between Sir Henry Poole's sister Frances and Walton Poole's older brother, Sir Nevill Poole. Our putative author is therefore connected by marriage to the person to whom his poem is addressed, but he is also kept at several removes from her by the same kinship network. She is the daughter of a baron who marries a knight. The knight has a sister who marries another knight, Walton Poole's elder brother. But Walton Poole himself, as a younger brother, is entitled neither to the family property, nor to a coat of arms, nor to the attentions of a dark haired beauty who had been taught to expect that marriage would secure her future wealth and prestige. Here I am indulging in speculation, of course, but speculation perfectly in keeping with the conventions of early modern society, and with the text of a poem which encodes the woman's sexual attractiveness as a "sweetnesse wch I shall nere tast." Indeed, the biographical information

21 Ibid. 835.

22 M, "Wiltshire Members of the Long Parliament," *Wiltshire Notes and Queries* 1 (1893–5): 329–32.

23 Ibid., 332.

about Beata Poole and Walton Poole, sparse and unrevealing though it may be, makes it even more likely that this poem was read in the seventeenth century as an act of sexual indiscretion.

Walton Poole's poem is unusual in part because it works, even for readers in the twenty-first century, both as an artistic object and as a social document. The cleverness of its verbal configurations and the subtlety of its tonal register belong to its artistic dimension; it is these qualities that prompt readers into treating the text as a poem in the first place. The adroitness with which the text negotiates kinship networks, the assumptions it makes about permissible behaviour among early modern upper gentry, and the strategies by means of which it reinforces normative gender assignments belong to its social dimension. It is these qualities that tend to be enhanced by research into one or other of the contexts occupied by the text: the culture of gentlemen readers and writers of manuscripts; the Poole families of Gloucestershire and Wiltshire; the marital expectations of younger sons, and so on.

Glimpses of Privacy

Two manuscripts, then: one in which a cathedral musician has gathered poems by others and contributed poems by himself, another in which a Caroline gentleman has troubled his mind about female erotic fantasy; a striking female figure who brings a field of manuscript writing into being; and a single poem which circulates in dozens of manuscripts. But what does any of this have to do with privacy? I think there are two ways of meeting this challenge. First, I should point out again that privacy is always and by definition a receding objective. Just when you think you've exposed the private, you realize that you've exposed it: it's now in the public domain. I'm just the latest in a long line of scholars to have recognized this phenomenon as the paradox of privacy. But the other answer is important too, and it would go something like this. When you're engaged in reading a large number of seventeenth-century manuscripts, much of what you read will have little or nothing at all to do with privacy. Much of what you read may be identical with what is already available in the public domain. Some of what you read will have been private matter for its first readers, though destined (like Carew's poems in the Rosenbach manuscript) to become public very shortly afterwards. The private material, in manuscript culture as elsewhere, is very often what falls into the cracks. So the poetry of John Lilliat goes unnoticed because he isn't one of the conspicuous trendsetters of Elizabethan culture. And

"A Ladyes dreame" goes unnoticed because it doesn't have a bearing on how we read (or edit) the poetry of Carew or Jonson or even William Strode. Anne Vavasour goes largely unnoticed too because she spends her life in the (private) shadow cast by male figures a great deal more prominent (at least in public) than she. And Walton Poole's remarkable poem fades from literary memory because it's not by Donne or Jonson or even Richard Corbett. But falling into the cracks is in one sense a good thing, because the very elusiveness of these materials preserves their connection with a privacy we can no longer fully recover. In manuscript sources we can still find texts in a relatively naked state, not subjected to the pruderies of other times or our own. A poem which alludes to the colour of Beatrice Poole's pubic hair probably couldn't have been printed during her lifetime. But in manuscript the poem survives, escaping both the moral disapprobation that it might have provoked in an earlier generation, and the ideological vigilance more characteristic of ours. So I think that, in their different ways, John Lilliat, the author of "A Ladyes dreame," Anne Vavasour, and the still-neglected Walton Poole can open windows onto the experience of early modern privacy. The manuscript culture which they inhabit occupies a liminal position between the public and the private, and it therefore offers us glimpses of a private world it would be very difficult to visit in any other way. Manuscripts like the ones I have been citing here don't give us a complete picture, but they help us to imagine possibilities we hadn't seen before.

Chapter Five

Privacy and Gender

The question I propose to address is this: In early modern culture, did women and men experience privacy in much the same way? The short answer is of course no, for a variety of intuitively sound reasons. Think of the relationship between the male speaker and the female listener in Donne's "A Valediction: Forbidding Mourning." Wonderful and mutual and interdependent though their love may be, they can create the perfect circle at the end of the poem only if they stick to their specifically gendered patterns of behaviour: she's the "fixed foot" of the compass who remains at home while he roams far into the outside world and eventually returns to her. The woman, in short, never moves outside the private domain, because there is no need for her to do so. The man's life includes public responsibilities which insist on his departure ("Though I must go")[1] but allow for his return to the private realm with renewed appreciation of its comforts. To put it crudely though not inaccurately, privacy is a cage for the woman, a refuge for the man.

The terms in which I have cast the distinction would certainly not be acceptable to William Gouge, Puritan divine, authority on privacy, and author of the conduct book for married couples, *Of Domesticall Duties*. Gouge is clearly seeking to valorize the private sphere throughout this text, and especially in a chapter entitled "Of the lawfulnesse of private functions in a familie."[2] He offers both reassurance and exhortation to those "weake consciences," as he terms them, "who thinke that if they have no publike calling, they have no calling at all." If this line

1 *The Complete English Poems*, ed. A.J. Smith (Harmondsworth: Penguin, 1971), 84.

2 *Of Domesticall Duties* (London: John Haviland for William Bladen, 1622), C1–2^{v}.

of reasoning were valid, Gouge argues, "what comfort in spending their time should most women have, who are not admitted to any publike function in Church or common-wealth?" (C1[v]). The diligent performance of domestic tasks is just as pleasing to God as the exercise of public functions. Indeed, the virtuous private life can in itself be a sufficient calling: "If a master of a family be also an husband of a wife, and a father of children, he shall finde worke enough: as by those particular duties, which we shall afterwards shew to belong unto masters, husbands, and parents, may easily be proved." This principle, moreover, has the appearance of applying equally to both genders: "So a wife likwise, if she also be a mother and a mistris, and faithfully endevour to doe what by vertue of those callings she is bound to doe, shall finde enough to doe" (C2). This may look like fair play, but it is certainly not (and isn't intended to be) equality. Gouge is forthright in promoting the view that the wife's first duty to her husband is "subjection" (S6–7); indeed, one of the common sources of disharmony in the home is the "fond conceit" of some women "that husband and wife are equall" (S8). So, even if a man and a woman both find sufficient employment in the private sphere, the man's duties will include the exercise of authority (though not of course tyranny) over his wife, and the woman's will include submission (though not of course enslavement) to her husband's will.

Nobody is free to neglect the private sphere entirely, Gouge argues, not even those with pressing public responsibilities. "Though a man be a magistrate or a minister, yet if he be an husband, or a father, or a master, he may not neglect his wife, children, and servants" (C2[v]). The person with both public and private callings is of course male; Gouge does not ask us to imagine the same problem arising for the other gender ("Though a woman be a doctor or a lawyer ..."), because it simply can't happen in his society. The distinctively female problem, to judge by Gouge's endlessly benevolent advice, is how to be happy while remaining exclusively within the private world. The male problem, by contrast, is how to move responsibly from private to public and back again.

The difference I have outlined is a point of departure only; I am using it here as a first step in a more complicated exploration of privacy as represented in some especially revealing textual materials from the seventeenth century: two diaries (by Lady Anne Clifford and John Ramsey), two autobiographical narrations (by Lucy Hutchinson and Sir Simonds D'Ewes), and two poems (by the poet known only as Eliza and by Henry Vaughan). In choosing these texts I have been guided throughout by the desire to find sources that would offer interesting ways of imagining and in some senses reconstructing the experience of privacy in seventeenth-century culture. But since my focus here is explicitly on gender differences, I have adopted wherever possible the Noah's ark principle: one female and one male in each pair. This rigid rule is applied only to written texts, where the sheer amount of material is now quite plentiful, thanks to the recovery or the revaluation of early modern women writers in the last three decades. With visual materials I have not been able to live up to the same standard of equity. The works of visual art I refer to were all created by men; but I cite them nonetheless, because of what they suggest about the experience of privacy, by women and by men. If there was a female Vermeer in the seventeenth century, her work has yet to be recovered.

The Loneliness of Anne Clifford

Privacy did not come naturally to Lady Anne Clifford. She was twice married, but in neither case was wedded life the source of deep or lasting satisfaction. Looking back on her earlier self from the vantage point of her mid-sixties, Clifford herself admits that both marriages were filled with tension: "those two lords of mine, to whom I was afterwards by the Divine providence marryed, were in their several kinds worthy noblemen as any then were in this kingdom; yet was it my misfortune to have contradictions and crosses with them both."[3] For perfectly understandable reasons in both cases, Clifford refused to be the submissive wife in either of her marriages. When she married her first husband, Richard Sackville, earl of Dorset (in 1609), she was already fighting legal battles to ensure that the vast Clifford lands of Westmorland would be hers (as the only surviving child of her father, George Clifford, earl of Cumberland) and not added to the property of her uncle and his male heirs, if any (as specified in her father's will). Sackville, instead of standing by her side as an ally, urged her to accept a financial settlement in exchange for her putative rights to the land. His ambition was to cut a very considerable figure at the court of James I, and therefore he was always in urgent need of spending money. When, after six years of widowhood, Clifford married

3 *A Summary of the Records and a True Memorial of the Life of Me the Lady Anne Clifford*, in *Lives of Lady Anne Clifford Countess of Dorset, Pembroke and Montgomery (1590–1676) and of Her Parents*, ed. J.P. Gilson (London: Roxburghe Club, 1916), 39. Hereafter cited as the *Life of Me.*

Philip Herbert, earl of Pembroke and Montgomery (in 1630), she believed that at last she had found someone mean and influential enough to ensure "the crossing and disappointing [of] the envy, malice and sinister practices of [her] enemies" (*Life of Me*, 49). But she was wrong again, in the sense that Herbert's loyalty quickly faded when he couldn't get what he wanted: a marriage between one of his sons and Clifford's younger daughter, Isabella. The consequences of standing up for her land in the one case, and for her daughter in the other, were protracted alienation from her first husband, decisive separation from the second. For a person of her temperament and social position, Clifford alleges, tranquil domesticity simply wasn't an option:

> from my childhood, by the bringing up of my said dear mother, I did, as it were, even suck the milk of goodness, which made my mind grow strong against the storms of fortune, which few avoid that are greatly born and matched, if they attain to any number of years; unless they betake themselves to a private retiredness, which I could never do till after the death of both my two husbands. (*Life of Me*, 35–6)

I have quoted Clifford at length here in order to show that she herself was aware that for her "a private retiredness" was a vain, elusive wish. But I would also like to notice the rhetoric in which Clifford's judgment is articulated: she begins with the quintessentially maternal image of breastfeeding, and makes this into the source of strength which enables her to resist. Donne is reported to have said of Clifford "that she knew well how to discourse of all things, from Predestination, to Slea-silk."[4] Her mental world included both domesticity and metaphysics, a combination that Donne would have found especially attractive. But if Clifford's intellect could attract the admiration of a famous poet and wit, it might also seem exasperating or threatening to a husband less enraptured with cleverness and more accustomed to obedience. That, at least, is the impression created by the records Clifford kept during three exceedingly difficult years of her first marriage.

4 Attributed to Donne by Edward Rainbow, bishop of Carlisle, in his funeral sermon for Clifford; see *A Sermon Preached at the Funeral of the Right Honorable Anne Countess of Pembroke, Dorset, and Montgomery* (London: R. Royston and H. Broom, 1677), E3^v.

The events Clifford recorded in her *Diary* for 1616, 1617, and 1619 (there are no surviving entries for 1618) are usually retold as the story of heroic resistance[5] leading at last to a happy conclusion: the vast Clifford lands became hers in law and in fact after the deaths of her uncle (in 1640) and his only male heir (in 1643). It is true of course that Clifford did resist, and it is impossible not to admire her resistance. When her husband applied direct pressure to exchange land for money, she was able to stand firm. But this only led to a build-up of indirect pressures of various kinds. In February 1615/16 Sackville summoned her to London for the purpose of discussing the land/money problem. On 16 February she was visited by a Lady Grantham, who urged her "very earnestly to agree to this business"[6] and who mentioned that the Archbishop of Canterbury would be calling on her the following day. On 17 February Archbishop Abbot arrived, and with him a number of Sackville relatives, all male, plus "a great company of men of note." Abbot "took me aside & talked with me privately one hour & a half" (41), hoping to get her to sign an agreement proposed by her husband. Still she said no, arguing that her mother would have to be involved in any decision. Within days she was travelling north to consult with her mother, and within a couple of months she had returned to the great Sackville country house, Knole in Kent, where she got "but a cold welcome from my Lord" (44). On 1 May Sackville sent her a message, indicating that she would have to leave Knole if she didn't sign. Two days later he wrote her from London, requiring that she send up to him their only child, Margaret, not yet two years old. Through all of this harassment Clifford yielded in small things and in some large ones too – she did send him the child, and "wept bitterly" as she did so (46) – but she stood firm on the one point that she had declared untouchable. There would be no settlement involving the land.

---

5 See, for example, George C. Williamson, *Lady Anne Clifford, Countess of Dorset, Pembroke and Montgomery: 1590–1676* (Kendal: Tits Wilson, 1922) 114–21; Martin Holmes, *Proud Northern Lady: Lady Anne Clifford, 1590–1676* (Chichester: Phillimore, 1975) 41–55, 76–86; Barbara K. Lewalski, "Re-writing Patriarchy and Patronage: Margaret Clifford, Anne Clifford, and Aemilia Lanyer," *Yearbook of English Studies* 21 (1991): 93–7; and Helen Wilcox, "Private Writing and Public Function: Autobiographical Texts by Renaissance Englishwomen," in *Gloriana's Face: Women, Public and Private, in the English Renaissance*, ed. S.P. Cerasano and Marion Wynne-Davies (Hemel Hempstead: Harvester Wheatsheaf, 1992), 51–3.

6 *The Diary of Anne Clifford, 1616–1619*, ed. Katherine O. Acheson (New York: Garland, 1995), 40. Subsequent references are to this edition.

Before long King James began showing an active interest in the dispute between Sackville and Clifford, and on 18 January 1616/17 they appeared together before the king. First of course they had to pass "through my Lord Buckingham's Chamber who brought us into the King being in the drawing Chamber" (66). While husband and wife "kneeled by his chair," the king told them he would settle their disagreement, and they could put the matter "wholly into his hands." Sackville eagerly consented, "but," says Clifford, "I beseech'd His Majesty to pardon me for that I wou'd never part with Westmorland while I lived upon any Condition Whatsoever" (66). The king wasn't pleased with this bold retort, and two days later both Clifford and Sackville were back in the king's drawing chamber, this time accompanied by Clifford's uncle and cousin (the legal heirs of the Westmorland property), three noblemen, and at least five lawyers. When asked whether they would "submit to [the king's] judgement in this case," all of the interested parties said yes; all except Clifford, that is, who said again that she "wou'd never agree to it without Westmorland" (67). On the previous occasion King James had "used fair means & perswasions, & sometimes fowle means" (66) in the effort to gain her submission; this time, with even less subtlety, he "grew into a great Chaffe" (67). To lower the pressure Sackville led his wife out of the room, and before long she was informed that "if I wou'd not come to an agreement, there should be an agreement made without me" (68). This indeed happened, and the Westmorland estates became incontestably the property of her uncle. Nominally, Clifford had been defeated. But she had shown herself capable of amazing courage, and it is easy to believe (as she herself did) that her virtue was at last rewarded when the lands reverted to her (on the failure of her uncle's male line) in 1643.

Moving and edifying though this narrative of heroic resistance may be, it's not the whole story. The counter-narrative I am about to construct takes as its centre of attention not Clifford's highly visible confrontations with authority, but her intimate life, her private self, insofar as she discloses this in her *Diary*.[7]

---

7 I do not claim to be alone in sensing that the narrative of resistance rewarded is not the whole story. Mary Ellen Lamb, in "The Agency of the Split Subject: Lady Anne Clifford and the Uses of Reading," *English Literary Renaissance* 22 (1992): 347–68, seems to me especially sensitive to the ironies inherent in Clifford's situation. And Mary O'Connor, in "Representations of Intimacy in the Life-Writing of Anne Clifford and Anne Dormer," in *Representations of the Self from the Renaissance to Romanticism*, ed. Patrick Coleman, Jayne Lewis, and Jill Kowalik (Cambridge: Cambridge University Press, 2000) 79–96, is interested in the gestures by which Clifford reaches toward intimacy.

In April 1617 Clifford wrote the following entry: "Upon the 7th my Lord lay in my Chamber" (78). This may seem an unremarkable event in the life of a married couple. Clifford nonetheless chose to remark upon it, so I'm tempted to ask why. The answer, I believe, is that intimacy with her husband, including sexual intimacy, was a rare occurrence in her life; indeed, the entry I've just quoted stands almost alone, and is surrounded by many others which suggest that Sackville was at best a reluctant husband. A few days after sleeping with his wife Sackville turned "very ill" (78), and as a result Clifford changed her sleeping arrangements: first she moved to a "pallet" so as to be near his bedside, and then to another room, "Judith's chamber where I mean to continue until my Lord be better" (78). As Sackville recovered, Clifford grew ill, but soon both were in good enough health to continue their long-standing dispute. On 23 April Clifford wrote, "this night my Lord shou'd have layen with me in my Chamber, but he & I fell out about Mathew" (80). The third party here is Mathew Caldicott, identified as "my lord's favourite" in the "Catalogue of the Household and Family" which survives from this period of the marriage.[8] The bond between Sackville and his favourite may well have been sexual.[9] If so, that would help to account for some of the arrangements designed to ensure their privacy. In December 1617, for example, Sackville left for Buckhurst, taking many of his servants with him, for the purpose of enjoying the country pleasures of hunting and feasting. After 13 December he dismissed his entourage, and "from this day to the 20th my Lord lived privately at Buckhurst having no Company with him but only Mathew" (95). If indeed this was a sexual relationship, then Clifford's suspicion of and hostility to Mathew would be based on her perception of him as a genuinely threatening rival. When she's urged by the chaplain, Mr Ran, to settle her grievances against Mathew, she's unable to do so: "I told him that I had received so many injurys from him that I cou'd hardly forget them" (90). Earlier she had been provoked to the point of writing "a letter to the Bishop of London against Mathew" (85), but whatever the contents of this complaint, it doesn't seem to have inhibited the behaviour of her husband or his favourite.

8 See Williamson, *Lady Anne Clifford*, 477.

9 Lewalski, among others, does read the evidence in this way; Clifford, she says, "intimates a homosexual relationship" between her husband and "a gentleman-servant" ("Re-writing Patriarchy," 96). See also Acheson, "Introduction," 10.

Nor was Mathew her only rival in Sackville's affections. Aubrey claims that Sackville "was extremely enamoured of" Lady Venetia Stanley, who bore him either one or two illegitimate children before settling down as wife to Sir Kenelm Digby. Aubrey also says that Elizabeth Broughton was his mistress: "whether before or after Venetia I know not, but I guess before."[10] Clifford's *Diary* implies that in the summer of 1619 Sackville was amorously involved with Lady Penniston, wife of Sir Thomas Penniston. Both of the Pennistons visited Knole on 25 August, staying all day and all night, and leaving on the following day. Clifford doesn't record her own judgment of this event, except insofar as it coincides with public opinion, which she does cite in a marginal note: "This coming hither of my Lady Pennistons was much talked of abroad in the world & my Lo[rd] was much Condemn'd for it" (116).

Privacy does not appear to have been, on the whole, an experience that Clifford and Sackville were capable of sharing. Even the private joy of reading, for which Clifford had a considerable appetite, she was able to lavish on herself only in the absence of her husband. Following the death of her mother, Clifford spent several months in the north, mostly at Brougham Castle, her mother's last residence. By October 1616 Clifford was bored, and she wrote to her husband telling him she would like to return to London. Soon a messenger from Sackville arrived, informing her that she "could not goe to London all this winter" (59). Now, for the first time in the *Diary*, she mentions her reading: "this month I spent in working & Reading. Mr Dumbell read a great part of the History of the Netherlands" (59). As this last entry implies, Clifford's reading wasn't necessarily silent and solitary; someone of her social rank could depend on having servants capable of oral reading, and could therefore listen to a book being read while doing another task, such as needlework.[11] Thus the entry for 9 November 1616: "I sat at my work & heard Rivers & Marsh read Montaignes Essays which book they have read almost this fortnight" (59). Elsewhere she records reading Chaucer, Spenser's *Faerie Queene*,

10 John Aubrey, *Brief Lives*, ed. Oliver Lawson Dick (1949; repr., Harmondsworth: Penguin, 1972), 260, 201.

11 And, if Aaron Kunin is right, then the same principle applies to the act of writing the diary as well. "In this household, writing, like reading, always takes place through the intervention of someone else," Kunin alleges; "the many scenes of reading and writing included in the diary are populated by servants who perform manual and interpretive labors under the direction of their employer." See "From the Desk of Anne Clifford," *ELH: A Journal of English Literary History* 71 (2004): 603–4.

Sidney's *Arcadia*, Ovid's *Metamorphoses*, Augustine's *City of God*, and the entire Bible between 1 February and 20 March 1618/19 (102). In almost all of these cases there's explicit mention of Sackville's absence during or departure just before the period in which reading takes place. On one occasion Sackville arrives home with a bit of a cough, spends the night in a separate chamber, and then gets out of the wrong side of bed: "my L[or]d found me reading with Mr Ran, & told me that it wou'd hinder his Study very much so as I must leave off reading the Old Testament till I can get somebody to read it with me" (76). Doubtless it was nothing more than irritability that caused Sackville to object. But object he did, to a practice that his wife normally carried on discreetly, or on the frequent occasions when he was away from home.

On 8 January 1616/17 Clifford and Sackville had one of their many inconclusive arguments about the northern lands. The next day both of them chose isolation: "Upon the 9th I went up to see the things in the Closet & began to have Mr Sandys his Book read to me about the Government of the Turks, my Lord sitting the most part of the day reading in his closet" (65). The overt parallelism shouldn't be allowed to hide the many asymmetrical features of this quotation and the situation to which it refers. The husband's closet is *his* closet, as if ownership is secure and specific; the wife's is *the* closet, assigned to her as if by accident or convenience, but not really belonging to her. Other evidence from the early modern period would suggest that, if a husband's closet were furnished with resources needed to master the world (books, maps, and scientific instruments), his wife's would be likely to contain materials of household management (baskets, bottles, and cooking utensils).[12] While Sackville sits in his closet reading (in silence, I presume), Clifford is read to in hers (by a household servant, no doubt). This difference may be one of temperament, but it probably suggests greater fluency in silent reading on the part of the husband; he had after all been educated at Oxford, while she was privately tutored at home, most notably by the poet Samuel Daniel. The difference certainly ensures that the woman's reading will be subject to scrutiny by at least one other person, and therefore perhaps to censorship as well, even if this is indirect or self-imposed.

12 See the discussion by Alan Stewart in "The Early Modern Closet Discovered," *Representations* 50 (Spring 1995): 82–3, and the inventory of the contents of husband/wife closets in John Evans, "Extracts from the Private Account Book of Sir William More, of Loseley," *Archaeologia* 30 (1855): 290–3.

The contrast between two spouses, both sitting resolutely in their respective closets, is but a momentary image in Clifford's *Diary*. More typical is the contrast between a man who moves from place to place at will, and a woman who follows his movements only in her mind. On 12 May 1616 Clifford pauses to reflect on the emotional cost of the situation I've just described:

> All this time my Lord was at London where he had infinite & great resorte coming to him. he went much abroad to Cocking, to bowling Alleys, to Plays & Horseraces, & [was] Commended by all the World. I stay'd in the Country having many times a sorrowfull & heavy heart, and being condemn'd by most folks because I would not consent to the agreements, so as I may truly say I am like an owl in the Desert. (48)

Like her husband, Clifford was a relentlessly social person. Also like him, she was brought up to believe in herself as the natural centre of attention. Her talent for society simply didn't have much scope for development at Knole, especially since her husband preferred conducting his social life elsewhere. As Élisabeth Bourcier points out,[13] solitude was the real source of her suffering at Knole. Though surrounded by elegant luxury, though catered to by many servants, though always within reach of her infant daughter, Lady Anne Clifford as a young woman still in her twenties had more privacy than she would have wanted. Or perhaps she had the wrong kind of privacy: not the pleasure of precious minutes stolen from a busy routine, but the loneliness of having many uncommitted (because unwanted) hours. To be an owl in the desert is to suffer alone, unregarded, unheard. That seems to me the primary resonance of the metaphor in the biblical source from which Clifford borrowed it (Psalms 102:6–7), and that indeed is how she felt her situation, though the act of recording it has given her a voice that can still be heard.

The Restlessness of John Ramsey

The male diarist I have chosen as a counterpart to Clifford is John Ramsey, born in London on 22 March 1578/9, and the compiler of a

13 Élisabeth Bourcier, *Les journaux privés en Angleterre de 1600 à 1660* (Paris: Publications de la Sorbonne, 1976), 403.

manuscript book now held in the Bodleian Library (Douce 280). The usual generic designation for this manuscript would be to call it a commonplace book, and it might therefore have made an appearance in chapter 4. But I have placed it here because it includes a series of entries that ask us to read them as we would a diary. This notion would be inescapable to any reader of the manuscript, as the following description of it will show.[14]

The early pages of Douce 280 indicate a developing interest in mathematics and astronomy: "Propositions of the caelestiall globe" (fol. 1^{v}) are subdivided into observations on the "Circles of the Globe" (2^{v}) including "the greate circle" and "the lesser circles" (2^{v}–4^{v}). But these explorations seem to be preliminary to the desired goal of "Cantabrigia" (4^{v}), the destination that Ramsey would eventually reach when he was admitted to Peterhouse, Cambridge, in 1601. Ramsey gives an outline of the Cambridge curriculum as it stood in 1601 (5^{v}), and he provides details about admission standards and costs, among other things (6). But these notes about student life are badly upstaged by the "Narratio de mea Progressione Vitae" which occupies almost all the space still available on folios 5–8 on the several occasions between 1601 and 1633 when Ramsey decided to compose episodes of his biographical account.

Ramsey points out that in "ye 24th daye after my birth" (5) in 1579 he was farmed out to a wet nurse in Kent ("my lovinge Nurse," as he calls her) for three years, after which he "was brought home" for a period of six essentially wasted years in his "fathers house." He was grateful to be sent away to Wolverhampton, "to be instructed in good literature by my most kinde & lovinge Tutor Mr Maddox, $M^{[aste]r}$ of y^{e} free School there." This happy time came to a close only because of "y^{e} misfortunate request of my Mother," at whose insistence young Ramsey wasted another "4 compleat yeares" living at home and not learning a thing. Only after being sent away again, to be tutored by Mr Leede of Essex "in his private house" (5) for another four years did Ramsey manage to gain admission, at the advanced age of twenty-two, to "ye most famous Universitye of Cambridge" (5).

14 My account builds on, but differs in some essentials from, that of Edward Doughtie, "John Ramsey's Manuscript as a Personal and Family Document," in *New Ways of Looking at Old Texts: Papers of the Renaissance English Text Society, 1985–1991*, ed. W. Speed Hill (Binghamton, NY: Renaissance English Text Society, 1993), 281–8.

The next event Ramsey reports is the death of his "Most deare, lovinge & naturally ... affected Father" (6[v]) in 1605. The qualities mentioned distance the father from "y[e] villanous & wicked enterprises" of those now "nearest to me," a group that presumably includes Ramsey's mother, and that prevented him from inheriting the family home: "our Mannor was unjustlye extorted from me," Ramsey claims. Still, he does get "the pleasant Mannor of ... Whitesgreene with all y[e] royaltyes appertaininge" plus a farm plus lands in Wales: the whole package being sufficient motivation to withdraw from "y[e] Courte" where he had evidently been seeking preferment, and to begin "livinge a quiet, contented, private life" (6[v]).

The problem with this commitment to the private life is that the country gentlemen Ramsey met turned out to be "very insufficient" in the conduct of "publique meetinges" of any sort. So Ramsey went off to study law at the Middle Temple in 1606, nominally because he wanted "to doe my Neighbours & Cuntrye Good" (6[v]–7). What he hadn't reckoned on was a "Burninge Feaver" which he suffered with for the next six years, after which he went to Heidelberg (and from there to Italy, Cyprus, Jerusalem, Greece, France, and Spain) in the entourage of the Prince Palatine and "his royal Spouse" Elizabeth, daughter of James I. On returning home he did a tour of England and Scotland, and later in life (at age 55) he set out on "a noble voyage" (8) to the new world.

It begins to appear that, like many members of his class, John Ramsey had little talent for privacy. Whatever lip service he might pay to the idea of private life, his actions show him strongly preferring and then assiduously seeking a place away from home: with his tutors in Wolverhampton and Essex, at his college in Cambridge, at the Inns of Court, in the entourage of the Queen of Bohemia, on a voyage to the Americas. It would appear that the private life is in a symbolic way at least inflicted upon John Ramsey. He begins his account of 1618 by apologizing for his handwriting. He has "loste y[e] use of [his] right hande" (7[v]) by taking "an unhappye blowe" in a duel, so now he has to write with his left. However, there have been compensations: "to recompense soe greate a losse my good god blest me wth a most happye hopefull spouse, y[e] joye of my life, & comfort of my dayes, La Bella mia dolce cuore" (7[v]). Although her name is never mentioned, we learn that she is the daughter of Sir Edmond Bell of Beau-prey-hall in Norfolk, and that she becomes in due course the mother of eight little Ramsey children during a span of thirteen years. Only one of these eight is singled out, in exactly the way we might have predicted: "It pleased my most mercifull god y[e] 24th of October 1622 to sende me my first borne sonne & heyre whoe was borne att my house in greate St Bartlemewes London, Christened, John" (8). Did his marriage and the arrival of his children offer a sufficient incentive to attach John Ramsey to the private life? Here's his account:

> my life being all waies active & not havinge employm[en]t to my desire I was even torne awaie as it weare from my most deare Spouse (ye Joye of my life) for her worth & goodness not to be paralelde, & soe went [on] a noble voyage to Guiana in ye Maine continent of America ye 10th of October. 1633. (8)

There's a great deal more to this manuscript than I have offered in this description. There are geographical observations (9–12^{v}), a catechism (13–21^{v}), medical cures (61–1^{v}), a list of "offices in Englande" (64^{v}–5^{v}), a Ramsey genealogy (72–6), and Ramsey's advice to his son (92–3^{v}). There's poetry too: Spenser's "Prosopopoeia" (22–34^{v}) and "The teares of the muses" (36–43), along with "Songs & Ditties to ye Lute & Viol de gambo" (67–9). The poems attributed to "Sheephearde Montanus" appear to be original compositions by John Ramsey.[15] But perhaps "original" is the wrong word. "A Sonnet" (35) written "By him y^{t} must love/ or not live. Poore JR" (35) turns out to be largely stolen from Spenser's *Amoretti* 64. What little we can learn about John Ramsey's private self comes not from the poetry he wrote or from the poems he collected, but from the fragmentary prose narrative which he added to his book from time to time.

And even here there is not enough quotidian detail to allow us to form a three-dimensional picture of the diarist. Isolated events are kept in isolation, so we are unable to infer the connections between two possibly related occurrences. And when Ramsey himself forges a link between cause and effect, the explanation is as likely to generate suspicion as to inspire confidence. I've already mentioned his belief that God gave him a beautiful spouse to compensate for the injury to his right hand. Similarly, he attributes his six-year fever to the death of his father: "O ye losse of my dearest Father! brought such a greveous sicknesse upon me (being taken wth a Burninge Feaver) y^{t} there was wanting but a stepp betwixt me & death" (7). To the questions we might be most curious

15 See Arthur F. Marotti, *Manuscript, Print, and the English Renaissance Lyric* (Ithaca, NY: Cornell University Press, 1995), 189–94.

about (How did he meet the young woman who married him? Did he ever recover the use of his right hand? How did he get introduced to the Prince Palatine and the Winter Queen?) he gives us no hint of an answer.

But he shows us enough to suggest that, for an eldest son and a landowner, privacy is always and at best supplementary to something that matters more. The man who has his life in order will enjoy the private life, but without any sense of being contained by it. For such a man, there is always a world elsewhere.

Life Writing by Lucy Hutchinson and Sir Simonds D'Ewes

Lucy Hutchinson and Sir Simonds D'Ewes were both, broadly speaking, Puritans, though neither of them felt comfortable with this label. In *The Life of Mrs Lucy Hutchinson, Written by Herself*, a brief document prefixed to the much longer biographical account of her husband, Hutchinson points out that as a young woman her mother lived for a time with a French minister and his wife in one of the Channel Islands, where "she was instructed in their Geneva discipline, which she liked so much better then our more superstitious service."[16] Hutchinson seems to have been strongly influenced by her mother's teaching, and at times she moved even further into the radical wing of non-conformity. While living in Nottingham Castle (as the wife of the governor), Hutchinson came across a set of notes attacking the practice of infant baptism left behind after "a private meeting in the cannoneer's chamber" (2:103). This question was of special interest to Hutchinson, since she was in the advanced stages of one of her many pregnancies. After diligently comparing the arguments set forward with the scriptures, after consulting at length with her husband, and after seeking (though in the end not taking) the advice of local clergy, Hutchinson simply decided that her newborn infant would not be baptized. Still, she didn't like being called a fanatic and an Anabaptist (as she was on this occasion) any more than she liked the term "Puritan" as a general indicator of religious orientation. In a

16 *Memoirs of the Life of Colonel Hutchinson*, ed. Julius Hutchinson, 3rd ed. (London: Longman, 1810), 1:17. The autobiographical sketch occupies the first twenty-eight pages of volume 1; the colonel's life fills some further 700 pages. All citations, whether from the autobiographical *Life* or from the biographical *Memoirs*, are taken from this edition. For clarity I use the unmodified surname "Hutchinson" only to refer to Lucy Hutchinson; her husband I will designate as "Colonel Hutchinson" or simply as "the colonel."

digression on the history of the English Reformation Hutchinson comments at some length on the rhetorical use of the word "Puritan" by her ideological enemies. In response to the debaucheries of the Jacobean court and the consequent moral decline throughout England, she alleges, God's chosen prophets did manage to bring some people back to the straight and narrow path, "but at court these were hated, disgrac'd, and revil'd, and in scorn had the name of Puritane fix'd upon them" (1:119). Anyone expressing grief at oppressive government would be stigmatized as a Puritan in the pulpit, on the stage, and in the table talk of the Jacobean establishment. To be called a Puritan under these circumstances was in one sense a mark of distinction, but not an honour Hutchinson would have chosen for herself.

Sir Simonds D'Ewes, though he speaks with great pride of being "knighted by King Charles at Whitehall"[17] in 1626, and though he came to occupy a socially central and even prominent position as high sheriff for Suffolk and as an MP in the Long Parliament, was a Puritan in both the ethical and the political senses. Even as a young man at St John's College Cambridge he was appalled by the "swearing, drinking, rioting, and hatred of all piety and virtue" which he saw around him; indeed, "the very sin of lust began to be known and practised" among the students, "so as I was fain to live almost a recluse's life, conversing chiefly in our own College with some of the honester fellows thereof" (1:141–2). As a mature man in his mid-twenties he avoided "any controversial sins" such as "usury, carding, dicing, mixed dancing, and the like" (1:354). He developed a growing hostility to "those prelates" who "increase the multitude and burden of the ceremonies and intermixtures in the Church"; he saw in this drift towards Rome a strategy to "oppress the consciences or ruin the estates of many godly Christians, falsely by them nick-named Puritans" (2:113). Small wonder, he remarks, that large numbers of English Christians are emigrating to the New World to preserve the integrity of their faith. For D'Ewes, as for Hutchinson, the principles and practices of Puritanism were in fact the right ones; only the name "Puritan" was unacceptable because of its manipulation by the adversaries of true piety and morality.

---

17 *The Autobiography and Correspondence of Sir Simonds D'Ewes, Bart., During the Reigns of James I and Charles I*, ed. James Orchard Halliwell (London: Richard Bentley, 1845), 1:325. Subsequent references are to this edition.

How much room did the Puritan household, subject as it was to the constant surveillance of the providential gaze, manage to create for the pursuit of private pleasures? This is a larger question than I can fully address in the present context, but I offer the experiences of two Puritan sensibilities as a point of reference. Both Hutchinson and D'Ewes learned to escape from the incessant demands of a good home into the secluded practice of reading. Hutchinson remembers being a bookworm from an early age. As a four-year-old she could read English "perfectly" (1:25), but her precocious gifts were already in the public domain. Because of her excellent memory, she would be "carried to sermons" (1:25) so as to learn them by heart and repeat them to members of the household. Her parents hired many tutors to cope with her educational needs; she remembers having eight tutors at age seven, to provide instruction in "languages, musick, dancing, writing, and needlework." Much of this effort seems to have been wasted on a pupil who was "quite averse from all but my booke" (1:25); she wouldn't practise her lute or harpsichord lessons because she didn't enjoy them, "and for my needle I absolutely hated it" (1:26). But she soon outshone her older brothers in Latin, and she developed a passionate fondness for reading: "After dinner and supper I still had an hower allow'd me to play, and then I would steale into some hole or other to read." Never mind that her mother thought excessive reading to be bad for the child's health; "this rather animated me then kept me back, and every moment I could steale from my play I would employ in any booke I could find, when my own were lockt up from me" (1:26). The private "hole" into which this child escaped was a refuge from parental authority, from social convention, from the inanity of childhood games, from the endless inhibition connected with being female in the seventeenth century.

D'Ewes too loved to escape into reading. While a student at Cambridge he began buying books, a habit he never relinquished. By the time of his death in 1650 he was the owner of about 1,000 printed books – roughly the same number as the holdings of the Cambridge University Library at this date.[18] During his residence in the Middle Temple he began reading manuscripts at the Tower of London, and soon he was both transcribing and purchasing large quantities of manuscript material. He met Sir Robert Cotton, whom he credits with having inspired and encouraged

18 See Andrew G. Watson, *The Library of Sir Simonds D'Ewes* (London: British Museum, 1966), 40.

his antiquarian interests. He projected using his vast scholarly resources in various useful ways – to write a properly documented history of Great Britain, for example, or to compile an Old English dictionary – but he never completed any of these ambitious works. That he loved his library, however, and devoted himself to it, of this there can be little doubt.

In 1626 D'Ewes was enmeshed in a very complicated set of negotiations which would soon lead to his marriage to Anne Clopton. He was impatient to reach closure in this matter, for a variety of reasons: he was afraid that the girl's guardian (her maternal grandmother, Lady Barnardiston) might come across a more attractive offer; he was afraid that his father might withdraw his tacit and financial support; and he wanted to get away from the pressures of courtship so as to return to his library. "Besides," to quote D'Ewes's own words about the courtship ritual, "it took my whole time and thoughts; and I desired again some freedom for my studies" (1:319). Fortunately the delay was not a long one: D'Ewes married Anne Clopton on 24 October 1626. Since his bride was not yet fourteen years old, D'Ewes indicated in advance that he was prepared to wait for her to mature before requiring the performance of her sexual duties. And wait he did, for at least eight months, until the summer of 1627. In the meantime, however, Anne Clopton was already a source of great pleasure and satisfaction to her husband: she was a very considerable heiress who had greatly augmented her husband's wealth; and she brought with her a pedigree of some distinction which D'Ewes believed he could trace back through at least 500 years of the history of Suffolk. Thus marriage, for D'Ewes as a twenty-four-year-old newlywed, brought with it a special gratification: "my very study of records grew more delightful and plesant unto me than ever before; because I often met with several particulars of moment which concerned some of those families to which she was heir, both of their bloods and coat-armours" (1:325). It was a marriage made, if not quite in heaven, then at least in the next best place: the library of rare and antiquarian books and manuscripts.

Indeed, both Hutchinson and D'Ewes seem to have been lucky in marriage: both write about their spouses in ways that suggest long-term attraction and admiration. In Hutchinson's text the story of her love is told by indirections and in ways that conform to patriarchal standards, but it is a love story all the same. The autobiographical prelude to her text contains no reference to her husband; it may at one time have included accounts of previous suitors in the missing leaves, which, according to her editor, have left "a great chasm" (1:28n) in the manuscript.

Once she turns to her subject proper, the life of *Colonel* Hutchinson, there's no longer an independent position for Hutchinson to occupy; indeed, she abruptly stops using the first-person singular pronoun and makes her further appearances as "the governor's wife" (1:266), as "his wife" (2:230), as "Mrs Hutchinson" (2:262), or as "she." This rhetorical strategy doesn't prevent her, however, from giving a brief account of her courtship, albeit an account that purports to be told from the male point of view.

As a young man, recently graduated from Peterhouse, Cambridge, John Hutchinson met by chance his future wife's younger sister. This enterprising child brought him back to her mother's house while her mother and sister were away from home. He was able to achieve a kind of intimacy with his future wife before having so much as met her: "one day when he was there, looking upon an odde byshelf, in her sister's closett, he found a few Latine bookes." He enquired about the owner of these volumes, was told that they belonged to the "reserv'd and studious" elder sister who in any case was out with her mother shopping for a husband in Wiltshire. But the young man was not to be denied; the various tokens of Lucy Apsley's (as she was then called) had "so much inflam'd Mr Hutchinson's desire of seeing her" (1:86) that he found himself unable to resist when the great moment did arrive: "She was not ugly, in a carelesse riding-habitt, she had a melancholly negligence both of herselfe and others, as if she neither affected to please others, nor tooke notice of anie thing before her" (1:91). But now, at the moment of their first meeting, Hutchinson is unable to sustain the pretence that this is not her own story: despite "all her indifferency," Hutchinson writes of herself, "she was surpriz'd with some unusuall liking in her soule, when she saw this gentleman, who had haire, eies, shape, and countenance enough to begett love in any one" (1:92). And as her love awakened, so did his; indeed, the transcendent nobility of his love for her now becomes the rhapsodic theme of Hutchinson's account: "never was there a passion more ardent and lesse idolatrous; he lov'd her better then his life, with inexpressable tendernesse and kindnesse" (1:95). Even her faults melt away under the benign influence of his love, and she becomes "a very faithfull mirror, reflecting truly, though but dimmely, his owne glories upon him" (1:95–6). Elsewhere she calls herself, without irony or resentment, "his shadow"; she claims that her value and her beauty were dependent on his approving gaze: she believes she "was nothing before his inspection gave her a faire figure" (1:96). They were married on 3 July 1638, but just before this event they were given a further proof of the sanctity of their love. This came in the form of a severe case of smallpox which briefly threatened the bride's life and then disfigured her face for a considerably longer period. The betrothed husband showed his true character by marrying her anyway, spots and all, on the appointed day; and God did his part too, rewarding the bridegroom's "justice and constancy, by restoring her, though she was longer then ordinary before she recover'd, as well as before" (1:97). This episode worked out perfectly, then, because it gave Hutchinson virtual proof that her husband valued her not for her outside but for the beauty of her soul.

As Colonel Hutchinson played his conspicuous part on the stage of public affairs, his wife was indeed little more than a shadow. He was appointed governor of Nottingham Castle and given the task of holding the castle and city for Parliament against the aggressive incursions of royalist forces under the earl of Newcastle. After successfully driving the royalist soldiers out of town, the colonel returned to the castle bringing with him a number of prisoners and a number of casualties: one dead man and five more with injuries. The wounded "were brought to the governor's wife, and she having some excellent balsoms and plaisters in her closett, with the assistance of a gentleman that had some skill, drest all their wounds" (1:274). Hutchinson seems content with her supplementary role in a passage such as this one; her husband's military achievements are what she celebrates, his anxieties are what she alleviates, his failures are what she extenuates. Her own part is to assist, whether as a mirror, a shadow, or in this case as a healer.

Colonel Hutchinson's career seems to have peaked in 1649 when he was appointed to the first Council of State of the Commonwealth. After that date his influence declined, perhaps because he neither liked nor trusted Cromwell, and by 1653 he had been "reduc'd into an absolute private condition" (2:207). If enforced early retirement was discouraging for him, it wasn't nearly as bad as what was soon to come. The Restoration was disturbing news for him, because he had been a member of the court which tried Charles I and sentenced him to death in 1648/9. He was therefore expelled from Parliament as a regicide in 1660 and virtually went into hiding to await the results of further deliberations that might have cost him his property or indeed his life. Lucy Hutchinson now perceived that her husband "was ambitious of being a publick sacrifice, and therefore, herein only in her whole life, resolv'd to disobey him" (2:262). It was, of course, a disobedience which proved her undying love, because it was directed towards saving her husband from further pain and humiliation. She drafted a letter under the colonel's name addressed to the Speaker of the House of Commons. Though the exact words of this letter are unknown, in substance it was an act of supplication, indeed of submission. Hutchinson claims that she was told by a friend that the timing was perfect for a brief on behalf of her husband; rather than seeking his approval, which would have caused needless delay, she simply forged his signature and sent the letter along. The results of this action were quite startling. First, "the letter was very well receiv'd" (2:264) – so well, in fact, that the colonel was declared exempt from further penalty, with the exception of a perpetual ban on his holding public office. The second and more ironical result Hutchinson could not have predicted: her husband never forgave her for this one disobedient action. He couldn't bear the stigma of being let off while others, who had acted as he did, were being punished. Hutchinson seems to have been both hurt and confused by this turn of events: "His wife, who thought she had never deserv'd so well of him, as in the endeavours and labours she exercis'd to bring him of[f], never displeas'd him more in her life, and had much adoe to perswade him to be contented with his deliverance" (2:275). She had made the mistake of venturing for once outside the private world and into the public domain. She had forgotten – or almost forgotten – that her accepted role was to be a mirror, a shadow. I say she had almost forgotten because, even in her account of the act of forging her husband's signature, what she fastens on is the element of mimickry involved: she was able to do a plausible signature, she says, because she was often copying him in any case, "being us'd sometimes to write the letters he dictated, and her character not much differing from his" (2:264). Technically the word "character" here means "handwriting," but I think the ambiguity which the seventeenth-century ear could easily have heard is very much to the point. Hutchinson presumed to speak for her husband because she believed that her agenda and his were inseparable. And indeed this assumption was sound, as long as she practised good works, such as healing the wounded, in the privacy of her closet; when she went beyond this, into the glare of the public workplace, she was by definition unable to please a man who wanted to hear not an independent voice but an echo.

The marriage between D'Ewes and Anne Clopton was of course no closer to being a relationship of equals. The serious and somewhat pompous young scholar knew, even before marriage, that he was getting someone of great value: a girl of almost fourteen who had been given the right religious upbringing, the heiress of ample estates in Suffolk, the scion of an ancient and locally distinguished family, the prospective mother of children who would bear his name and inherit his library – all this, and a beautiful young woman too, "every way so comely," D'Ewes writes, "as that alone, if all the rest had wanted, might have rendered her desirable" (1:308). In tabulating the "qualifications" (1:307) for the role of wife, which he finds so splendidly fulfilled in the person of Anne Clopton, D'Ewes is behaving as you might expect a great collector to behave. She is a particularly gratifying piece – indeed, an essential piece – of a private world which he is assembling with remarkable patience and care.

He's proud of the fact that, despite physical intimacies of various kinds, he abstained from sexual intercourse for the first eight months of marriage. Such heroic restraint he praises as "perhaps the first example that ever was of that kind; and so impossible it seemed, as others could scarcely be brought to believe it" (1:320). But by August of 1629 D'Ewes was troubled that his young wife, now sixteen, showed no signs of producing an heir: "we had now been partakers of the nuptial rites about two years, and yet had as little expectation of issue as in the first eight months of our continence next after marriage" (1:417). D'Ewes didn't know that his wife was already two months pregnant. She gave birth to a daughter on 30 April 1630, and after that she was pregnant at least six more times (including once with twins) before she died in 1641 at the age of twenty-eight.

Their first son, whom they named Clopton D'Ewes, was born on 24 June 1631 and died two weeks later. Twin boys were born in 1633, but both died in infancy. Another son, again named Clopton, was born on 18 July 1634. He was a sickly boy from the beginning and developed his first "convulsion fit" (2:123) at the age of nine months. D'Ewes had several healthy daughters, but his dynastic ambitions were being borne by this frail little boy. D'Ewes searched desperately for the best medical advice then available, but it wasn't enough. In early May of 1636 D'Ewes alone was in charge of the household at Stow Hall, his wife having gone to London on a family visit. The little boy had a series of fits much more severe than on previous occasions: "I was near him all the time," D'Ewes writes, "bestowing my heavy tears, deep sighs, and humble prayers, upon him" (2:144). But these efforts made no difference; the little boy died that afternoon, at the age of one year and nine months, leaving D'Ewes "the most sad and disconsolate father that could possibly be" (2:145).

The autobiography ends here, "with the decease of my sweet and only son" (2:147), as D'Ewes pointedly observes. A good deal more can be inferred about his domestic life from the letters he wrote to his wife, his family, and members of his household while serving in Parliament after his election in 1640. During one of his absences from home, D'Ewes learned that his wife had contracted smallpox. He hurried back to Stow Hall at once, and finding that she was already well on her way to recovery, he stayed for only three days and returned to London. The next report he received was the news of her death.

Accustomed though he was to accepting personal disaster as part of a providential plan, D'Ewes found this last blow a difficult one to absorb. He wrote letters to his stepmother and to his servant James in which he searches in vain for ways in which his wife's death might have been prevented. He seems to demand from his correspondents the reassurance that every possible precaution had been taken, and at the same time he seems to be blaming them for doing less than they might have. The letter to his servant James, dated 2 August 1641, is especially revealing: "James, I doe now write to you concerning some matters of privacie," it begins (2:275). What follows is a series of demands, itemized into eight separate categories. For example, he expects James to write a detailed account of his wife's last days of life, "especiallie of that which happened those two dreadfull dayes after my departure" (2:276). Clearly, D'Ewes is overcome with guilt whenever he thinks of this subject. Over and over again he tells himself (and others) that he was only acting reasonably when he left for London, that he was right to rejoice in her recovery with "noe other trouble but the losse of her naturall beautie." But at the same time he wonders whether he betrayed her, whether he wasn't motivated in part by the thought – the perfectly reasonable and prudent thought, of course – that he "might take infection [him]selfe" (2:277). In his heart of hearts he believed that he should have risked his own life to be at her side, but he was unable to do so. This thought, with its sense of the betrayal of a private trust, and of the disappearance of an opportunity never to be had again, was the real bitterness in his bereavement. But even the bitterness is proof, if any more were needed, of the value he placed on the person he had lost.

In stressing the connections between Hutchinson and D'Ewes – their Puritan orientation, their love of reading, their marital devotion – I have obscured the real differences which separate them. Hutchinson was a modest and self-effacing person, or at least she became so after she married a man who would of course be her superior. D'Ewes was arrogant and full of himself, obsessed with recording and improving upon the prestige of his pedigree. So reading, for example, wasn't the same experience for them at all. Hutchinson crept into a "hole" with whatever book she might be able to hide from her mother's disapproving eyes; D'Ewes gathered around him a magnificent collection of books and manuscripts which he read in part to seek public approval for his erudition. Nor, given the conventions of the time, could the experience of marriage have been similar for the two of them. For Hutchinson, marriage was clearly a vocation of servitude, as it would still be for Jane Eyre 200 years later. It was a servitude she accepted with joy and found it impossible to relinquish (after the death of her husband she continued to serve him by writing his biography), but a servitude nonetheless. For D'Ewes, on the other hand, marriage was an essential step on the road to becoming the master of Stow Hall – a position in which he expected to be served, not only by his wife, but by a small army of servants and domestic officers.

What I am pointing out is that, despite all of the similarities in ideology and culture, privacy was not the same thing for Hutchinson as for D'Ewes. This is an inference I will return to later, but for now it may be enough to observe that for her privacy is furtive and surreptitious, while for him it is simply his due, and is therefore supported and guaranteed by the members of his household. After she effaces herself in order to be the colonel's mirror and shadow, does Lucy Hutchinson continue her practice of voracious, unauthorized reading?[19] If so, she doesn't mention it, and in any case it wouldn't be worth mentioning, because the story she tells is now not hers but her husband's. D'Ewes feels no obligation to be apologetic about his reading practices, no matter how eccentric they may be; indeed, he often remarks that he's spent an entire month reading Anglo-Saxon charters, for instance, as if there were nothing unusual in this. When Hutchinson says that her husband, after the Restoration, "lay very private in the towne" (2:268), she implies that the hidden space of the private isn't really good enough for someone of the colonel's integrity, though it may be a necessary retreat at the moment. When D'Ewes, in the pain of bereavement, writes to his servant about "some matters of privacie" (2:275), he is if anything augmenting the importance of his words by invoking the private. These will be matters too profound for public display, and he therefore asks for confidentiality with complete conviction that his wishes will be respected. Privacy may still be privacy, for both of them, but they engage with it in strikingly different ways; where she always finds a rabbit, he can see only a duck. And this

---

19 She certainly did continue her literary pursuits; for example, she translated Lucretius into English verse. See David Norbrook, "Hutchinson [*née* Apsley], Lucy (1620–1681), poet and biographer," *Oxford Dictionary of National Biography* (2008).

divergence is caused, not by misunderstanding on either part, but by the gendering of experience in early modern culture.

The Darling of Heaven's Prince: Eliza

Nothing is known of the poet Eliza beyond what can be inferred from her single publication, *Eliza's Babes: or The Virgin's Offering* (1652), a book of lyric poetry, most of it religious, followed by a sequence of prose meditations. Eliza's religious orientation was definitely towards Puritanism, though not in the highly sectarian senses of the word. In her youth, she says, she would have been ready for martyrdom: "if the contrary Religion (which then too much abounded) had prevail'd, I then might have offered up my life in flames."[20] The "contrary Religion" must be Roman Catholicism, always considered a threat by early modern Protestants, but especially so in the years after Queen Henrietta Maria in effect gave the Catholic faith a new prestige in England, and its adherents a new source of protection. "But now thou hast turn'd the tide," Eliza continues (115), attributing the victory of Puritan culture not to human agency but to divine will. The somewhat nervous endorsement she gives to the Puritan cause may be deduced from a comparison of two political poems, "To the King: writ, 1644" and "To Generall Cromwell." The first of these is a plea for Charles I to adopt a conciliatory stance in his dealings with Parliament, based on the logic that this would be the Christian thing to do: "My Prince by yeelding won the field,/Be not too rigid, dear King yeeld" (76–7). The poem on Cromwell is offered in support of the Puritan enterprise, but embedded in this text is considerable fear of Cromwell's ambition. Eliza calls Cromwell the "rod" which God has chosen to scourge her with, and she tries to be "a good child" whose role it is to "kiss the Rod, and honour thee."[21] But having assigned herself this humble part, she goes on to instruct the patriarch in his task: "And if thou'rt vertuous as 'tis sed,/Thou'lt have the glory when thou'rt dead" (101). She is alarmed, as were many of her contemporaries, at the

---

20 *Eliza's Babes: or The Virgin's Offering (1652): A Critical Edition*, ed. L.E. Semler (Madison, NJ: Fairleigh Dickinson University Press, 2001), 115.

21 This line is the source of the title of the anti-patriarchal text *Kissing the Rod: An Anthology of Seventeenth-Century Women's Verse*, ed. Germaine Greer, Susan Hastings, Jeslyn Medoff, and Melinda Sansone (London: Virago, 1988), in which Eliza's work is briefly discussed (141–2) and five of her poems are printed (142–7).

prospect of Cromwell claiming glory for himself, now, and being unable to wait for the hereafter. Eliza's religious convictions and political allegiances are secure enough,[22] but on the character of particular individuals she wisely reserves judgment.

In her personal life, Eliza seems to have made a strong early commitment to celibacy. She imagines herself as the bride of Christ, and implies in numerous ways that a lesser love wouldn't be worth having; indeed, she virtually says this in "The Life," a poem which opens with an urgent claiming of transcendence: "If as men say, we live not, where we are,/ But where we love,/I live above" (67–8). The erotic possibilities of union with Christ are a special attraction for a female poet, and Eliza takes full advantage of this opportunity in such poems as "The Dart," "The Lover," and "The Bride." In the last of these she rhymes "slavish life" and "wife" (83) in such a way as to imply withering contempt for quotidian marriage. So it comes as a bit of a shock to discover (in "On Marriage") that Eliza herself is contemplating such a step, or to put the matter in language closer to hers, that she's willing to submit to marriage if God has "ordain'd" it so (91). The man she marries certainly has to be content to play second fiddle; he is told that his wife is just on loan from her real spouse: "He lent me but awhile to you,/And now I must bid you adieu" (94). The point is made even in the unusually long title of the poem from which this last quotation is taken: "Not a Husband, Though Never So Excelling in Goodness to Us, Must Detaine our Desires from Heaven." In "My Second Part" Eliza confronts the difficulties she's experienced in adjusting to a way of life she had earlier renounced. She claims to have lived apart from the vanities of the world in her "best age" and to have become a wife only at the behest of God and against

22 Though other scholars might be more inclined to debate this question. Semler wants to locate Eliza "firmly within the reformed protestant tradition"; see "The Creed of *Eliza's Babes* (1652): Nakedness, Adam, and Divinity," *Albion* 33 (2001): 197. More specifically, he wants to claim that she shares George Wither's orientation and that she may have been Wither's wife Elizabeth [Emerson]; see "Who Is the Mother of Eliza's Babes (1652)? 'Eliza,' George Wither, and Elizabeth Emerson," *Journal of English and Germanic Philology* 99 (2000): 519–29. Erica Longfellow argues, on the other hand, that Eliza's religious and political positions are easily compatible with Anglican orthodoxy, and that "in seventeenth-century terms, Eliza is in fact no radical"; see "*Eliza's Babes:* Poetry 'Proceeding from Divinity' in Seventeenth-Century England," *Gender and History* 14 (2002): 261.

her own inclination. But she is learning, because God has discovered "a means to turne [her] heart" (99). She can be content in an ordinary life, so long as she remains ultimately dependent upon God. So she reassures herself: "Heavens Prince will never thee forsake,/But still his darling will thee make" (99). There is no indication that the earthly marriage produced any children, though of course the heavenly one was fertile: thus the "Babes" of her title are not literal children, but the poems begotten upon her by her spiritual spouse.

In her prefatory address "To the Reader" Eliza claims that the reason she has chosen to enter the public domain at all is because privacy simply isn't enough. She presents this as an argument not about personal gratification but about Christian witness. At first she shunned the very idea of publication, but at length she concluded "that those desires were not given me, to be kept in private, to my self, but for the good of others" (57). To keep them hidden would be an act of shame, and therefore unworthy of a God who was willing to make a public spectacle of himself: "shall I be ashamed to returne him publique thankes, for such infinite and publ[i]que favours?" (58). While this argument makes perfect sense, if taken on its own terms, I don't think it tells Eliza's whole story. At times her rhetoric suggests that she cares more about personal gratification than she wants to let on. "I cannot be content, to be happy alone," she says with a frankness that asks the reader to become her partner in blessedness, "nor can I smother up those great and infinite blessings, that I have received from him, with private thankes" (57). No, privacy is not enough for Eliza, and in holding this position she bravely parts company both with the many women writers who claimed to be publishing only under protest or at the insistence of male patrons, and with the many others who didn't publish their work at all.

What happens to privacy in the poems is a rather more complicated question, because they are after all poems that valorize a private relationship between the soul and God. In "The Invocation," for example, Eliza calls upon her "Sacred Muse" to find shelter "Within the closet of my brest" (59). Here the metaphor of enclosure would imply an equation between inwardness and value: the place to harbour sacred thoughts is deep within the self. But there are other possibilities, some of them less reassuring, as in the following poem, "To a Friend for Her Naked Breasts":

> Madam I praise you, 'cause you'r free,
> And you doe not conceal from me

What hidden in your heart doth lye,
If I can it through your breasts spy.

Some Ladies will not show their breasts,
For feare men think they are undrest,
Or by't their hearts they should discover,
They do't to tempt some wanton Lover.

They are afraid tempters to be,
Because a Curse impos'd they see,
Upon the tempter that was first,
By an all-seeing God that's just.

But though I praise you have a care
Of that al-seeing eye, and feare,
Lest he through your bare brests see sin,
And punish you for what's within. (102–3)

It was of course an age of décolletage. As a young woman, perhaps in her late teens, Frances Jennings had herself painted in miniature by Samuel Cooper; she wears a dress that straddles the almost imperceptible line between high fashion and bad taste – a dress that reveals not quite everything, but is always on the verge of doing so. The dating of this portrait (ca 1665) places it after the Restoration, and therefore some dozen years after *Eliza's Babes* was published (1652). But plunging necklines were certainly all the rage in the 1630s when Van Dyck and his numerous imitators painted Henrietta Maria and her numerous imitators. During the Commonwealth there was pressure to adopt a more modest standard of dress, as Eliza's poem would attest. But fashion was still fashion, at least in the more privileged levels of society; Cromwell's favourite daughter Elizabeth, to judge by John Michael Wright's depiction of her in the National Portrait Gallery, is only slightly less amply displayed than were the wives and daughters of the Cavaliers.

So the occasion for this poem is the observation by a modest and, I think, a mature woman that her younger female friend is wearing clothes that reveal rather a lot of voluptuous flesh. I posit the difference in age because of the didactic quality in the speaker's tone of voice, especially at the beginning of the final stanza: "But though I praise you have a care." I think this tonality has been there from the beginning, though submerged under demonstrations of overt approval. If, in the first line,

Figure 8 Samuel Cooper, *Frances Jennings, Duchess of Tyrconnel* (1665), The National Portrait Gallery, London

the emphasis falls on *praise* ("Madam, I *praise* you, 'cause you'r free"), then rhetorically the speaker may be pointing out that her reaction (praise) is the surprising one, as opposed to other more expected reactions ("Madam, I suspect you," or "I condemn you," or "I just don't know about you") that could easily have arisen, especially in a Puritan context. To say that the praise is insincere from the outset, however, is being too hard on the speaker. She is trying to see her younger and more daring friend in the best possible light, and it occurs to her that the unveiling of the body signifies the absence of deceit. The younger woman doesn't "conceal," and thus brings into being the conditions for real intimacy. The speaker thinks it may be possible to look "through your breasts" and into her friend's heart, to discover what is "hidden" there. If the speaker is right, and if she is getting privileged access to the contents of her friend's heart, then the whole display has been perfectly innocent: there's nothing to worry about, because nobody is hiding anything.

So far the poem has proceeded on the assumption that breasts are women's business, and that conversations about breasts simply happen between friends. In the second stanza all this changes because of the introduction of "men" and what men "think." What men do think is of course always the same thing: that a woman who exposes her breasts is trying to attract male (sexual) attention. This horrifying notion, the speaker says, has led "Some Ladies" to desist from showing their breasts altogether. It was fine when practised innocently, between women, but heterosexual lust poisons the environment and women are obliged to cover up. The third stanza, by far the weakest in the poem, continues to develop the idea of female fear, this time by comparing sexual temptation to the original temptation. This is hardly a novel idea, especially in the seventeenth century, and the poem doesn't seem to me to do much with it. But the first temptation leads to the thought of the "all-seeing God" who dispenses justice to tempter and tempted alike. This idea carries forward into the final stanza and motivates the change in tone which I've already remarked upon.

The speaker wags her finger at the friend to remind her that not every fashion statement is innocent, and that God's "al-seeing eye" will discover the "sin," if any, that's hidden in her heart. God has (as usual) a difficult part to play: he is both the court of last appeal and the cosmic voyeur. In the first of these functions he has to be severe and unrelenting; if he finds "sin," he has to "punish." He is therefore unlike the speaker, who can afford to be far more generous, who can indeed make the presumption of innocence and therefore "praise" her friend. In his role as voyeur, God is of course infinitely alert, and therefore far more disturbing than the men of stanza 2. "Some Ladies" rather cautiously drew back for fear of what men might say, though this hasn't bothered the friend heretofore. But she can't risk being indifferent at the thought of what God will say. Will she then cover up to protect herself from God's "al-seeing eye"? Perhaps, but if she does her modesty will be gestural only, because God will continue to see … well, everything. Indeed, God sees right "through" the friend's "bare brests"; unlike the men who see only the surface and guess at motivation, God has access to "what's within." And this privilege he shares, curiously, with the speaker, who can also see what is "hidden," or at least thinks she may be able to see it, by looking "through" the friend's breasts. God has the power to see through flesh and find guilt; the speaker has the gift of seeing through flesh to find presumed innocence.

So what does this poem have to do with privacy? Rather a lot, I would suggest, if the female breast is taken as a particularly potent sign of the liminal zone between the private and the public. Indeed, when the word is used in the singular, it immediately suggests interiority, as in "the closet of my breast" (from "The Invocation") as a haven of intimacy. This meaning is not the primary one in "To a Friend for Her Naked Breasts." How could it be, when the "breast" has become "breasts," and the act of exposing them at least enough to justify the adjective "naked" has brought them into the public domain? The sense of interiority is still present, of course, in the references to the "hidden," the "what's within" that lies underneath the surface. In short, this poem is concerned in its every nuance with the dialectic between hiding and showing, concealing and exposing, covering up and undressing. That's why it is in a curious way such an erotic poem. And there's a further though unacknowledged way in which this poem might be an exploration of the private. In the speaker's preoccupation with her friend's body, in her possessive solicitude, and in her celebration of nakedness there must surely be an element of same-sex erotic attraction. This reading of the relationship would doubtless have shocked Eliza, or she might have considered it ludicrous and sent it back to the realm of the unthinkable. As a seventeenth-century Puritan, Eliza may well have experienced private pleasures that she couldn't acknowledge. Her special gift was one of hiding and showing; concealing the erotic quality of her friendship, even from herself, and then writing about it anyway.

The Sweet Self-Privacy of Henry Vaughan

Henry Vaughan has a long-standing reputation as a poet of privacy. Some of his most memorable poems are explorations of bereavement, loss, and loneliness:

> They are all gone into the world of light!
> And I alone sit lingring here.[23]

A number of sad events in Vaughan's life may have played their part in releasing the last-remnant feeling which this poem, first printed in the second edition of *Silex Scintillans* (1655), captures so beautifully. His younger brother William died in 1648, a loss which Vaughan alludes to in several poems.[24] His first wife Catherine Wise, who bore him four children, died about 1653; if the lines I've quoted were written after this and before Vaughan married Elizabeth Wise, his first wife's younger sister, then indeed they might include the anxiety of the single parent. It was also an event in Vaughan's life (though not in his alone) when the king whom he had revered and served as a soldier was put on trial and executed in January 1648/9. Indirectly it was a sad event in Vaughan's life when the Act for Better Propagation and Preaching the Gospel in Wales was passed by Parliament in 1650, because it swiftly led to the eviction of his twin brother, Thomas Vaughan, from the rectorship of St Bride's Church. These were indeed great personal losses: more than enough to motivate a melancholy poem, however fine. But the condition represented in the poem is not just the versified equivalent of his lived experience. The speaker says, for instance, that his "days ... are at best but dull and hoary,/Meer glimering and decays" (484). The tonality here is remarkable when you consider that their author could not have been more than thirty-three when he wrote these words, and that he would go on glimmering and decaying for another forty years before his death in 1695. The feeling of isolation which Vaughan creates in the poem is not the remainder left behind when all his personal losses have been subtracted. It is, rather, a curiously positive feeling, despite all the gloom.

---

23 *The Works of Henry Vaughan*, ed. L.C. Martin, 2nd ed. (Oxford: Clarendon, 1957), 483. Subsequent references are to this edition.

24 Namely, these untitled elegies from *Silex Scintillans* (1650): "Thou that knows't for whom I mourne" (416–18), "Come, come, what doe I here?" (420), "Silence, and stealth of dayes" (425–6), and "I walkt the other day" (478–9).

Stevie Davies, in a thoughtful biographical study of Vaughan, has identified a state of mental being very close to what I have in mind. "Nostalgia is the compulsive force which drives his poems," she writes; "it is the strongest passion he knows, and the source of his most moving effects."[25] I would add only that it is the nostalgia of a solitary figure who has lost his appetite for the joys of the present and who therefore waits, with longing, for union with God.

Although he has a splendid talent for making art out of loneliness, Vaughan is by no means an apolitical writer; the assumption that he is, according to Chris Fitter, has been the besetting sin of Vaughan criticism.[26] But in "The King Disguis'd" he refers to Charles I as "Royal Saint" (625), and in "Religion" he argues that the refreshing waters of the true church have been polluted until only the "tainted sink" (405) of the Puritans is left. In the wake of the victory of Parliament over the king, the Anglican Church as Vaughan knew it had in effect been destroyed in Wales.[27] His twin brother was only one of many clergy to suffer expulsion, and the vacancies created by this policy were filled, if at all, by itinerant Puritan preachers. Under these circumstances Vaughan became a conservative activist; he set to work on a treatise called *The Mount of Olives: Or Solitary Devotions* (1652) in which he outlines in some detail prayers, meditations, and other forms of worship that an Anglican might practise in daily life. This work includes "A Prayer in Time of Persecution and Heresie," in which the rhetorical energies of the worshipper will be directed both towards God and against a readily identifiable target: "Thou seest, O God, how furious and Implacable mine Enemies are, they have not only rob'd me of that portion and provision which thou hadst graciously given me, but they have also washed their hands in the blood of my friends, my dearest and nearest relatives" (167). This prayer goes on to ask God to help the speaker rise above the need for vengeance and to find the charity to extend forgiveness. But before doing so it establishes a context in which the Puritans are the aggressors, and Anglicans the persecuted victims. In his prefatory address "To the Peaceful, Humble,

25 *Henry Vaughan*, Border Lines Series (Bridgend, Mid Glamorgan, Wales: Seren, 1995), 28.

26 See "Henry Vaughan's Landscapes of Military Occupation," *Essays in Criticism* 42 (1992): 123–47.

27 See Louis L. Martz, *The Paradise Within: Studies in Vaughan, Traherne, and Milton* (New Haven, CT: Yale University Press, 1964), 13.

and Pious Reader" Vaughan asks his fellow Anglicans not to feel isolated: "Think not that thou art alone upon this Hill, there is an innumerable company both before and behinde thee" (141). But the fact remains that, as the subtitle claims, these are *solitary* devotions; Christ retired to the Mount of Olives to be alone with God, and the title of this work asks Anglican believers to do the same. Ironically, Vaughan is here appropriating on behalf of Anglicanism a kind of private piety which the Puritans were fond of claiming as their own.[28] The private devotional exercises of the individual Christian, sometimes written down as in Vaughan's case either in prose or in verse, became acts of resistance in a long and public battle for authority over the practice of religion.

As a Christian, as a member of the body politic, and certainly as a poet, Vaughan needed privacy and seems to have gathered certain kinds of strength from it. For him the journey inward is a crucial step in the direction of a destination he always desires: union with God. The process I am describing is articulated with special clarity and considerable power in "Vanity of Spirit":

> Quite spent with thoughts I left my Cell, and lay
> Where a shrill spring tun'd to the early day.
> I beg'd here long, and gron'd to know
> Who gave the Clouds so brave a bow,
> Who bent the spheres, and circled in
> Corruption with this glorious Ring,
> What is his name, and how I might
> Descry some part of his great light.
> I summon'd nature: peirc'd through all her store,
> Broke up some seales, which none had touch'd before,
> Her wombe, her bosome, and her head
> Where all her secrets lay a bed
> I rifled quite, and having past
> Through all the Creatures, came at last
> To search my selfe, where I did find
> Traces, and sounds of a strange kind.

28 See Davies, *Henry Vaughan*, 20. See also Janet E. Halley, who develops this point in interesting ways in "Versions of the Self and the Politics of Privacy in *Silex Scintillans*," *George Herbert Journal* 7 (1983–4): 61–6.

Here of this mighty spring, I found some drills,
With Ecchoes beaten from th' eternall hills;
Weake beames, and fires flash'd to my sight,
Like a young East, or Moone-shine night,
Which shew'd me in a nook cast by
A peece of much antiquity,
With Hyerogliphicks quite dismembred,
And broken letters scarce remembred.
I tooke them up, and (much Joy'd,) went about
T' unite those peeces, hoping to find out
The mystery; but this neer done,
That little light I had was gone:
It griev'd me much. At last, said I,
Since in these veyls my Ecclips'd Eye
May not approach thee, (for at night
Who can have commerce with the light?)
I'le disapparell, and to buy
But one half glaunce, most gladly dye. (418–19)

The speaker who emerges from his "Cell" in the opening line must be thinking of himself as a hermit; certainly he has been engaged in deep contemplation already, because he is tired of mental work and ready to look to nature for refreshment and rejuvenation. While he takes in the beauty and splendour of the natural world, he formulates a desire to know the Creator of these marvels. This is no idle wish, but a passionate need; he begs and groans for an answer, but receives none. Then, in the second stanza, he brings to the interpretation of nature a more active strategy. In a frenzy that resembles the panic of the mad-scientist caricature, he summons, pierces, breaks, and rifles. Nature is here personified as a woman, and the speaker's violence is directed quite specifically at her sexual parts ("Her wombe, her bosome") and also at her intelligence ("her head"). This explosion of violence may not have seemed as distasteful to Vaughan's first readers as it does today, but even then it would have been recognized for what it is: a rape. The speaker's violent need to know is driving him beyond restraint, but it is bringing him no nearer to the truth he seeks.

Now he turns his gaze inward, and begins to search him "selfe." Until this point his quest has been thwarted by the indifference or the resistance of nature to his desires, and his own responses have been characterized by frustration. But now, upon turning inward, he begins to discover at least something: “Traces, and sounds of a strange kind.” Evidence of God’s being is not directly available to the seeker after truth, but there is indirect evidence (“Traces”) within the mind of the self. These traces are now further defined by the use of a series of metaphorical strategies. First, if God is the “mighty spring,” the source of the flowing water of the created world, then within the mind there are “drills,” that is, rivulets or small streams (see *OED* drill *n*^{1}. 2). If God is considered in his aural aspect, as the infinite voice, then there are “Ecchoes” of his sonority within the self. Or, to use Vaughan’s favourite poetic medium of light, darkness, and shade, the internal trace of God is perceived as a dim glowing of “Weake beames” or as the intermittent flashing of fire. Such intermediate glimmerings of divine light are enough to bring into view the new and surprising metaphor of the not-quite-legible hieroglyph. Sir Thomas Browne, between whom and Vaughan there are many affinities of spirit and language, believed that God has contrived a series of “common Hieroglyphicks” to enable us “to suck Divinity from the flowers of nature.”[29] In Vaughan’s poem it is human nature that bears the imprint of the divine author. But it is not a transparently readable imprint; even if it were perfectly preserved the hieroglyph would still need to be deciphered, decoded, interpreted. In the fallen condition of humankind the divine imprint is not only cryptic but broken into fragments. The speaker says he has almost succeeded in uniting the fragments, which presumably would lead to his interpretation of the sign, when the “little light” by which he has been working fades and he is unable to complete the task.

Is this then a text in which knowledge of God is shown to be impossible? In a sense it is: perfect, unmediated knowledge of God is impossible so long as we are in our mortal state. Indeed, it is vanity of spirit, as the title implies, to think that perfect knowledge could be had. So the speaker longs, in the last five lines, for the day when the “*veyls*” will be removed from his “*Ecclips’d Eye*” and he will be able to experience God directly. Such a happy, unmediated view of God is possible, but only in the life after death, as Vaughan well knew from any number of biblical texts, including this special favourite: “For now we see through a glass, darkly; but then face to face” (1 Cor. 13:12). To achieve this longed-for

29 *Religio Medici* 1.16, in *The Works of Sir Thomas Browne*, ed. Geoffrey Keynes, 2nd ed. (London: Faber, 1964), 1:25.

result, the speaker says he will "*disapparell*" – that is, he will cast aside the vestments of human flesh in which his divine soul has been enclosed, in order to achieve union with God in the afterlife. He will achieve his long-deferred goal by being naked with God at last. This is perhaps a mischievous way of glossing the image of disrobing, but one that preserves something of the yearning for intimacy which is entirely characteristic of Vaughan.

The remedy for loneliness in this strange poet is not a social readjustment but a metaphysical transfiguration. At the end of "They are all gone into the world of light" the speaker feels the disorientation that comes from living in a world of blurred vision, and he calls on God to provide redress in one of two specific ways:

> Either disperse these mists, which blot and fill
> My perspective (still) as they pass,
> Or else remove me hence unto that hill,
> Where I shall need no glass. (484)

The first alternative might well refer in part to a reordering of the social world: to the resumption of Anglican forms of worship, for example, and the removal of obstacles preventing it. Even so, the weight of emphasis falls on the second alternative: removal from this life, and translation into a higher plane of being. To be in a world where "no glass" is needed is to be in the presence of God.

The privacy which Vaughan celebrates in his poetry is therefore something altogether removed from domesticity. Vaughan was the father of eight children, four from his first marriage, four from his second. But these family matters have left no mark upon his poetry or even, so far as I am aware, on his prose. The privacy which interests him is the blessed loneliness of walking with God. In "Rules and Lessons," one of his most didactic and least accomplished poems, he advises his reader to "Seek not the same steps with the *Crowd*; stick thou/To thy sure trot." The solitary jogger will get his reward in the end, because "A sweet *self-privacy* in a right soul/Out-runs the Earth, and lines the utmost pole" (437). The sense of being out of step with the majority is far more beautifully captured in "The Retreate," the text in which Vaughan anticipates Wordsworth by seeking traces of the divine imprint in the spiritual integration of childhood, the state of "Angell-infancy." Because the speaker is convinced that he once had intuitive access to the divine, he wishes he could "travell back" (419) to recapture the light he has lost:

Some men a forward motion love,
But I by backward steps would move,
And when this dust falls to the urn
In that state I came return. (420)

Here walking with God has become a sacred paradox in which progress is made by means of regress and, in a quintessential Christian oxymoron, life is achieved in death. All of this is, of course, doctrinally sound and unexceptional. But the image of the speaker as the odd man out, as the one backward walker in a world of people busily trying to get ahead, this is Vaughan at his best. Within a fairly narrow range he had a gift for understanding a certain kind of privacy, and a genius for being out of step with the world at large.

His Privacy and (Provisionally) Hers

To judge by the written evidence created by six people, three from each gender, it would appear that men in early modern culture felt more secure about the experience of privacy than did women. This conclusion may seem counter-intuitive, and I freely admit that it is not the view I held when I started this investigation. I would have been far more likely to believe, given the pervasiveness of early modern teachings about the private sphere as the natural place for women, that women writers would eagerly claim the space of privacy as their own. Instead, there would appear to be a deep-seated ambivalence about privacy in women's writing.[30] Eliza's insistence that privacy is not enough is an articulation of a restlessness and a need for public endorsement that can also be traced, though less directly, in the writing of Lady Anne Clifford and Lucy Hutchinson. The male writers, by contrast, recognizing that privacy is only one aspect of a busy life, are free to celebrate it. I am not claiming that the valorization of privacy in Ramsey, D'Ewes, and Vaughan is unproblematic;

30 So it should not be surprising to find this ambivalence reflected in feminist thinking about early modern women's writing; for a lucid and coherent account of the tensions created by the notion of privacy within feminist critique itself and within feminist writing about early modern women, see Joanne H. Wright, "Reading the Private in Margaret Cavendish: Conversations in Political Thought," in *British Political Thought in History, Literature and Theory, 1500–1800*, ed. David Armitage (Cambridge: Cambridge University Press, 2006), 212–19.

indeed it may seem at times to be mostly compensation (for lost public status) or nostalgic longing (for an impossible wholeness). But the male writers do value privacy, and they return to it again and again as to a place of security and rest.

It is true, of course, that the gender difference I'm suggesting depends on my selection of writers, and that the particulars of my argument wouldn't be the same if my diarists had been Lady Margaret Hoby and Ralph Josselin, my autobiographers Alice Thornton and Lord Herbert of Cherbury, my poets Katherine Philips and Andrew Marvell. But I doubt that my first conclusion, though I wish to hold it tentatively and provisionally, would be seriously challenged. Indeed, I suspect that exploration of other writers would qualify in interesting ways but ultimately support the view I am proposing. My reasons for this belief lie in the structure of early modern culture itself, and in the inequalities that it not only practised but supported with vast ideological and material resources. The early modern men whom I have been citing all went to Oxford or Cambridge; none of the women did, nor could they have done so. And this was only the finishing touch on a process of educational streaming that put Latin classics into the heads of boys, needlework into the hands of girls. Under the circumstances it was a very unusual woman who put pen to paper at all: either a woman of immense privilege, or of relentless determination, or of exceptional intelligence, or of some combination of all three. Such women are very unlikely to raise an unambiguous chorus in praise of a privacy they have only just managed to subvert or escape. They are much less likely, than male writers, who have been taught that the borderline between public and private is theirs to cross at will, to experience privacy as a socially sanctioned and temporary retreat. A woman who succumbs to the view that privacy is her lot in life will never be heard from again. A man who retires to the privacy of his library, as Montaigne did at the age of thirty-eight, may be embarking on the very enterprise that will ensure his visibility and fame.

Of the six writers to whom I've given special attention, the men have far more to say about children and childhood than do the women. This is an even more surprising development, and one which I would not wish to advance as a general conclusion. If the selection of writers were revised in the way I suggested earlier, then the women's comments on childbearing and child rearing would be far more forthcoming, and men's attention to children considerably diminished. Still, for these six writers it is true that women are comparatively less concerned with childhood than men. Lady Anne Clifford does mention her daughter fairly frequently in the *Diary*, referring to her rather stiffly as "the Child" and sometimes finding her company "very tedious" (82). But she does record events in her daughter's life, such as illnesses, the wearing of new clothing, or the cutting of two "great teeth" (73). Lucy Hutchinson, who bore eight children between 1639 and 1662, gives them only the most fleeting attention in her writing, as she hurries from one of her husband's achievements or disappointments to the next. Eliza too is the mother of many "Babes," though these are in fact her fantasy children and therefore don't provide her with the usual pleasures or anxieties of parenting. These indeed are far more luminously captured in D'Ewes's moving account of the death of his only remaining boy than in any of the texts by women which I've cited here. Ramsey does count his eight children among his blessings, though he takes patriarchal satisfaction only in the eldest son who, fittingly, bears his father's name. Even Vaughan, though he doesn't allude to his children in any specific way, is keenly interested in childhood (albeit, childhood idealized by retrospection) as an integrated state of being. It may of course be true that female authors from a privileged fraction of society didn't have nearly the hands-on involvement in the details of childcare that ordinary women did, and it may also be true that the male authors I selected, largely for their interests in privacy and related questions, are far more child-centred than a random selection of authors would be. But even when these adjustments and allowances have been made, the male/female imbalance on the subject of children remains a remarkable surprise.

Finally, the evidence I have been able to assemble would suggest that men are free to interrupt women's privacy virtually at will, but that the converse does not apply. Just what is at stake here can be more clearly demonstrated in the visual culture of the seventeenth century. In Vermeer's *Young Woman Seated at a Virginal* the atmosphere of female privacy is evoked with astonishing subtlety. The seated figure seems absolutely composed, perfectly at home in a room filled with artistic pleasures and performances. Her hands are touching the keys with a lightness that makes her own art seem natural. She does not need to refer to the score as she plays, because she has internalized the music, made it her own. What then is missing from this picture of wonderful composure? Only one thing: a man. There are three indications within the picture that this is so. One is the framed canvas just above the young woman, identified by art historians as *The Procuress* by Dirck van Baburen. The lighting obscures the precise content of this painting within the painting, but a discerning viewer might notice that its two commodities are music

Figure 9 Johannes Vermeer, *A Young Woman Seated at a Virginal* (ca 1670), National Gallery, London, UK/Bridgeman Images

and sex, both apparently being offered by the bold woman on the left. Second, the viola da gamba in the left foreground seems to be waiting for a practised hand to take it up, and from the size of the instrument as well as its pitch, I would assume that this would be a man's hand. Third, the turn of the young woman's head and the enigmatic smile on her lips would suggest that she has just noticed the approach of a new presence, perhaps the very male presence required to man the gamba and to turn her solo into a duet. The fact that she also looks in the direction of the painter and spectator doesn't change the equation, at least not for the male spectator, who feels drawn in by the look of calm expectation. All of these devices create a "feeling of male absence"[31] within the painting, a feeling of absence that appears to be on the verge of being relieved by the arrival of a man.[32]

What happens after the man arrives is brilliantly suggested by Gabriel Metsu's *A Man and a Woman Seated at a Virginal.* First, she has stopped playing and her attention is now focused entirely upon him. She rests her left hand on top of the instrument, and with her right hand extends the sheet of music for his perusal. He points in the direction of the score with the index finger of his left hand, and in his right hand he holds a tall, half-filled wine glass. The flagon placed on the floor near the man's left foot would imply that there's more wine to be had when the glass has been emptied. Svetlana Alpers assumes that the man is offering the woman a drink, but she argues that in other respects the relationship between the two figures is "unstated": "Does she want it? Should she? Should he offer it? The painting hardly seems to consider these questions."[33] This is well observed, but there is one element of their relationship that deserves further notice: her deference to his presumed authority. The wine glass is certainly a wine glass, but he holds it as if it were a baton. Indeed, he may very well be beating time to the music with his feet, demonstrating some nuance of interpretation with his voice, and conducting this whole

31 This phrase is from Edward A. Snow, who uses it in connection with another Vermeer painting, *Girl Asleep at a Table*; see *A Study of Vermeer* (Berkeley: University of California Press, 1979), 54.

32 See also the excellent discussion of this painting by H. Perry Chapman in "Inside Vermeer's Women," a contribution to Marjorie F. Wieseman, *Vermeer's Women: Secrets and Silence* (Cambridge: Fitzwilliam Museum, 2011), 104–6.

33 *The Art of Describing: Dutch Art in the Seventeenth Century* (Chicago: University of Chicago Press, 1983), 186.

Figure 10 Gabriel Metsu, *A Man and a Woman Seated by a Virginal* (ca 1665), National Gallery, London, UK/Bridgeman Images

ensemble with his wine glass/baton. Her body language does not provide any clues about her receptivity, either to his musical performance, or to his offer of wine, or to the implicit erotic appeal made both by the man and by their situation. In this sense she is like Vermeer's young lady: she remains a model of quiet and dignified composure.

Taken together these two images, one of a woman about to be interrupted by a man, the other of a woman patiently deferring to a man's interruptions, virtually define the always provisional character of female privacy in the early modern period. There is something surreptitious about the woman's recourse to privacy because she knows she can be interrupted at any moment. Thus Lady Anne Clifford goes on vast binges of reading when her husband is away, but when Sackville returns and discovers her at it, he can stop her at once with an irritable prohibition. Thus Eliza, even while she celebrates the bond of intimate trust between herself and her female friend, knows that such privacy is subject to invasion perhaps by disruptive male expectations and certainly by divine voyeurism. Would the converse ever be the case? Would Richard Sackville abandon his program of reading if his wife were to object to it? The answer of course is that the situation wouldn't arise; men are not called upon to defer to the authority of women in this way. Would Sir Simonds D'Ewes expect to be interrupted, in his dedicated study of Anglo-Saxon charters, by the female shadow of Anne Clopton across his ancient page? This is a more plausible kind of interruption, and I would not rule it out, even though no event of quite this kind is recorded in the texts under review. Women certainly did send messages, to the Houses of Parliament, for example, which interrupted the public pursuits of their menfolk by asserting the urgency of domestic concerns. And I'm sure that in any household where goodwill prevailed, women interrupted male privacy as well. But I doubt that such interruptions were routine, and I imagine that they were accompanied by various signs of womanly deference. In short, I am convinced that private life in the early modern period, however companionate, was at all times inflected by the semiology of male privilege. In a world where one gender was expected to govern and the other expected to obey, it could not have been otherwise.

Chapter Six

Privacy in Paradise

When early modern thinkers and writers tried to imagine the perfect world, what role did they assign to privacy within it? English literary culture is particularly rich in what have become known as utopian fictions: rich not only in the number of such constructions (only a few of which I will be able to analyse in detail here), but also in the range and variety embedded in these thought experiments. I will begin with two radically divergent texts, both of which have earned their canonical stature by casting large and lasting shadows (or, if you prefer, enduring brightness) over the work of many subsequent writers. They are historically divergent texts in the sense that the first of them, Sir Thomas More's *Utopia* (1516), is situated very near the beginning of the English Renaissance, and the second, Milton's *Paradise Lost* (1667), is often thought of as marking its end. Once I have outlined the assumptions about privacy in More's perfect commonwealth, and in Milton's prelapsarian Garden of Eden, I will complicate matters by introducing two further texts – Francis Bacon's *The New Atlantis* (ca 1624), and Margaret Cavendish's *The Convent of Pleasure* (1668) – which conform neither to More's model nor to Milton's. This will not be in any sense an exhaustive survey of utopian writing,[1] but it will be a sufficiently diversified sampling to allow some valuable inferences about privacy to emerge.

---

1 An exercise which has often been undertaken, sometimes with great scholarly erudition and critical acumen. See, for example, J.C. Davis, *Utopia and the Ideal Society: A Study of English Utopian Writing, 1516–1700* (Cambridge: Cambridge University Press, 1981), and Amy Boesky, *Founding Fictions: Utopias in Early Modern England* (Athens, GA: University of Georgia Press, 1996).

Full Disclosure in Utopia

It is easy to identify the particular attitude towards privacy framed by Sir Thomas More in the process of constructing his *Utopia.* It would be reckless indeed to claim that More endorsed this attitude as his own position; the fragments I'm about to quote are at least twice removed from More's immediate authority, first by fiction and second by translation. The utopian viewpoint is narrated by the persona More invented for the purpose of telling the tale: Raphael Hythloday, mariner, adventurer, follower of Amerigo Vespucci, incurable optimist, diligent observer, and astonishingly tireless talker. The Latin text of *Utopia* was first published in 1516, within months of More's completion of a draft good enough to send to his friend Erasmus. It was first translated into English by Ralph Robinson in 1551; the second edition of Robinson's homespun though at times effusive text (1556) is the source of the quotations which follow.

While he is still setting out the ground rules for his description, Raphael Hythloday makes it clear that private property is simply inadmissible among the Utopians: "where possessions be private, where money bearethe all the stroke, it is harde and almoste impossible that there the weale publique maye justelye be governed, and prosperouslye floryshe."[2] In a sense More is here following Plato while anticipating Marx and Engels. But there are nuances which give Utopian society its own coloration, such as the universal practice, even in the capital city of Amaurote, of never locking or bolting residential doors. Why would anyone bother? "Whoso will, may go in," Hythloday explains, "for there is nothinge within the houses that is private, or anie mans owne" (H4). Robbery has been ruled out of existence by removing its various incentives, such as starvation and covetousness. The abolition of private property, it would appear from the example of the unlocked doors, is going to have an impact on other kinds of privacy as well. Even in the streets of Amaurote there is no escape from the uniformly clear lighting which accompanies rational social planning: "There be neither winetavernes, nor alehouses, nor stewes, nor anye occasion of vice or wickednes, no

2 *A Frutefull Pleasaunt, and Wittie Worke, of the Beste State of a Publique Weale, and of the Newe Yle, Called Utopia,* trans. Ralph Robinson, 2nd ed. (London: Abraham Vele, [1556]), G1.

lurkinge corners, no places of wicked counsels or unlawfull assembl[i]es. But they be in the present sighte, and under the eies of every man" (K4[v]). There is a price to be paid for achieving a society without vice, namely, submission to a comprehensive, unrelenting network of surveillance. To be constantly open to inspection, "under the eies of every man," seems to me even worse than being followed incessantly by the ever watchful eye of Providence, as sixteenth-century Christians were. For More and his contemporaries there were comforts to be drawn from the thought of the providential eye, but such reassurances don't easily survive the transfer to the idea of collective surveillance. Hythloday's praise of a city with "no lurkinge corners" may sound reassuring until you try to place yourself into this landscape; if there are no taverns in the city, nor even any "lurkinge corners," then how could anyone begin to explore it? The answer is clear: only by means of the officially guided tour, subject at all times to full collective surveillance.

Under the glare of this constant searchlight, can there be sex in Utopia? Yes there can be, but within such strict limits as to be an embarrassment even to Raphael Hythloday. There's only one custom of the Utopians that provokes Hythloday into outright laughter, and it has to do with the selection of marriage partners. In order to forestall post-nuptial disappointment, Utopian couples undergo a comprehensive and rationally monitored inspection: "a sad and an honest matrone sheweth the woman, be she mayde or widdowe, naked to the wo[o]er. And lykewyse a sage and discrete man exhibyteth the wo[o]er naked to the woman" (N5[v]). Europeans may find this practice risible, but the Utopians reply that the real folly rests with other cultures, where the choice of a lifelong mate is recklessly undertaken without full disclosure. This line of argument may justify the act of disrobing, but why should the display of bodies require the assistance of the "honest matrone" and the "discrete man"? Clearly sex in Utopia is not only and not even principally a private interaction between consenting adults. In a world of perpetually unlocked doors, sex, like everything else, becomes the subject of responsible public planning.

So it looks at first blush as if the commonwealth of Utopia is a world from which privacy has been erased. People are simply prepared to share everything, and they don't engage in frivolous competitive practices: there are no sartorial rivalries, since everyone wears the same brown uniform; there are no social rivalries, since aristocratic titles don't exist; there are no rivalries of ostentation, since houses are assigned to families by lot and exchanged every ten years. But in curious ways privacy is allowed to sneak back into the edges of this picture.

The gardens of Utopia are of special interest in this respect. "On the backe side of the houses through the whole length of the streete, lye large gardens inclosed rounde aboute wyth the backe part of the streetes" (H3[v]). According to Hythloday, the Utopians "set great store by their gardeins." He reports that he has never seen gardens more flourishing or better tended in all his travels. And he speculates about the reasons for this excellence: "Their studie and diligence herin commeth no[t] onely of pleasure, but also of a certen strife and contention that is betwene strete and strete, concerning the trimming, husbanding, and furnishing of their gardens: everye man for his owne parte" (H4). It's as if the striving for private gain, having been ruled out of existence by the design of the front door, remains nonetheless part of human nature, even if it can be revealed only in the back garden. And here competition is downright helpful; rather than conducting wasteful rivalries of conspicuous consumption, the Utopians compete in the conspicuous production of the "fruite, herbes, and flowres" (H4) that everyone will enjoy.

It would appear that moral competition is possible too, at least for the particular segment of Utopian society which dedicates itself to good works. "Some therefore of them," says Hythloday, "attende upon the sicke, some ... clense ditches, repaire bridges, digge turfes, gravell, and stones" (Q6[v]), and all of this is done for no personal gain: "They neither reprove other mens lives, nor glorie in theire owne. These men the more serviceable they behave themselves, the more they be honoured of all men" (Q7). As in the case of gardens, the cultivation of good works may have its origins in personal striving, but its results are benefits for the commonwealth as a whole.

Should we be hearing in this cultivation of virtue with no expectation of rewards a proleptic echo of Richard III's famous line, "I thank my God for my humility" (2.1.71)? At very least we should be reminding ourselves that More is an ironist: that he is fond of taking away with one hand what he appears to be offering with the other. Thus, when an absence of "glorie" in a virtuous man's motivation leads him to be "honoured of all men," I think we can be sure that More is aware of the irony. The character in *Utopia* to whom he gives his own name remains a sceptic to the end; after Hythloday finishes his long narration, More finds that he "can not agree and consent to all thinges that he saide" (S3[v]). And of course Hythloday has been marked by irony from the outset, in the sense that his name (in Greek) means, roughly, purveyor of nonsense, just as Utopia is in fact nowhere. That's why it's funny when More, in his letter to Peter Giles, claims that he regrets not asking Hythloday exactly where in the New World Utopia could be found. It's not a real place, to be sure, but it does offer More a way of commenting on some real problems, including, as he sees it, abuses that remain hidden behind the cloak of privacy.

The Blissful Bower in Eden

When Milton created paradise, one of his objectives was to come up with something radically different from the world in which he lived. So much would be implied, I think, in his treatment of Adam and Eve's unembarrassed prelapsarian nakedness. To deny them clothing is of course not an innovation: it is consistent with the Genesis account[3] and with the practice of many generations of visual artists in the tradition of Albrecht Dürer and Lucas Cranach the Elder. But Milton doesn't simply take the nakedness of Adam and Eve for granted; he insists on it in ways that go well beyond the needs of the narrative. Our first glimpse of the primal couple includes a celebration of their nakedness:

> Two of far nobler shape erect and tall,
> Godlike erect, with native honor clad
> In naked majesty seemed lords of all. (4.288–90)[4]

These lines are followed by a notoriously gendered description of the first human pair: Adam is all strength and authority and appears to have regular haircuts; Eve's curves and tendrils might seem unruly but in fact they yield to the control of Adam's gentle hand.[5] And Milton's long

---

3 "And they were both naked, the man and his wife, and were not ashamed" (Genesis 2:25), authorized version.

4 John Milton, *The Complete Poetry and Essential Prose*, ed. William Kerrigan, John Rumrich, and Stephen M. Fallon (New York: Modern Library, 2007), 394. Subsequent Milton references are to this edition.

5 For comment on the gendering of experience in these descriptions, see William Shullenberger, "Wrestling with the Angel: *Paradise Lost* and Feminist Criticism," *Milton Quarterly* 20 (1986): 275–8; Catherine Belsey, *John Milton: Language, Gender, Power* (Oxford: Blackwell, 1988), 64–6; Anne Ferry, "Milton's Creation of Eve," *Studies in English Literature, 1500–1900* 28 (1988): 116–17; and Elspeth Graham, "'Vain Desire,' 'Perverseness' and 'Love's Proper Hue': Gender, Sexuality and Feminist Interest in *Paradise Lost*," *Critical Survey* 4 (1992): 133–4.

Figure 11 Lucas Cranach the Elder, *Adam and Eve* (1526), © Samuel Courtauld Trust, The Courtauld Gallery, London, UK/Bridgeman Images

description is explicitly not censored: "Nor those mysterious parts were then concealed,/Then was not guilty shame" (4.312–13). In his beautiful and frequently reproduced painting *Adam and Eve*, Cranach may choose to depict his couple at precisely the angle at which a luxuriant vine is masking Adam's crotch and (strange coincidence) a leafy branch is reaching up to conceal Eve's. But for Milton such strategies of disguise would imply compromise with the values of the fallen world; he rejects the protective fig leaf because Adam and Eve have done nothing to hide: "So passed they naked on, nor shunned the sight/Of God or angel, for they thought no ill" (4.319–20).[6]

When they have sex – and Milton makes it his business to assure us that they do[7] – Adam and Eve don't have to bother to get undressed; they are "eased," says Milton's narrator, "the putting off/These troublesome disguises which we wear" (4.739–40). The striptease would be completely impossible in paradise, or (in language more congenial to Milton's assumptions about sex) it would be completely unnecessary: sex between Adam and Eve is already perfect, and it couldn't be improved by inflecting it with the anxieties, prohibitions, distortions, and artifice of the fallen world.

For Adam and Eve as sexual partners, nakedness turns out to be not only natural but downright convenient; perhaps more surprising, it's no disadvantage for them when they're entertaining. The moment Adam notices the approach of Raphael he puts Eve in charge of making lunch and goes out himself to meet the angel:

> without more train
> Accompanied than with his own complete
> Perfections, in himself was all his state. (5.351–3)

6 On this point, see Roland Mushat Frye, *Milton's Imagery and the Visual Arts: Iconographic Tradition in the Epic Poems* (Princeton, NJ: Princeton University Press, 1978), who discusses at some length the "strategies of concealment" adopted by visual artists in their depictions of Adam and Eve, and draws the inference that "Milton's repudiation of this conception could not have been more complete, or more explicit" (266).

7 For detailed commentary on Milton's commitment to the view that Adam and Eve were sexual partners before the fall, see James Grantham Turner, *One Flesh: Paradisal Marriage and Sexual Relations in the Age of Milton* (Oxford: Clarendon, 1987), 232–87.

The primary sense here is that Adam proceeds alone, without equipage or entourage, but by now we have seen enough of Adam's "complete/ Perfections" to ensure that only a hint is needed to remind us that, as he walks out to meet Raphael, Adam is (naturally, unproblematically) naked. When Eve's turn comes to meet the angel we get more than a hint: she is "Undecked, save with herself" (5.380); she is lovelier than the three "naked" (5.382) goddesses in the judgment of Paris story; but she needs "no veil" (5.383) because innocence has nothing to hide. Adam and Raphael sit down to enjoy a splendid vegetarian lunch followed by copious, leisurely conversation (2,679 lines of it, to be precise). Under these circumstances Eve does exactly what Milton expects the perfect wife to do:

> Meanwhile at table Eve
> Ministered naked, and their flowing cups
> With pleasant liquors crowned. (5.443–5)

The narrator acknowledges at once that what he's just described is a very sexy scene: he alludes to the story in Genesis in which the "sons of God" are sexually enraptured by the "daughters of men" (Genesis 6:2); he implies that on this occasion it would have been understandable had Raphael fallen in love with Eve. But of course no such thing happens because paradise is paradise: there's no jealousy here, the narrator assures us, because there can be no infidelity. So Eve's nakedness is again returned to the realm of the unproblematic, though only after a number of potential problems have been posited if only to be disposed of.

My point is that Milton goes to great lengths to distinguish between life in the seventeenth century and life in paradise; between the civilized need for clothing on the one hand, the escape into nakedness on the other. But there's one interesting respect in which Milton does not liberate Adam and Eve from the conventions of civilized life, and that is their need for privacy.

When they retire for the night, Adam and Eve enter an enclosure most often identified as their "bower," and referred to when first introduced as "their blissful bower" (4.690). This is a structure created, like everything else in paradise, by God, and specifically "Chos'n" by him for "man's delightful use" (4.691–2). Its principal characteristics are designed so as to ensure comfort, pleasure, and above all seclusion. Its roof is the "thickest covert" of interwoven "Laurel and myrtle" (4.693–4). Its walls are made of shrubs "Fenced up" (4.697) so as to prevent intrusion.

The floor of the bower is a "Mosaic" (4.700) of beautiful and odoriferous flowers. Such careful attention to the borders surrounding and containing the *locus amoenus* is completely absent from Milton's prototype, the "Bower of Bliss" (2.12.69.4) in *The Faerie Queene.* The approach to Spenser's bower is made through an enticing labyrinth of "covert groves and thickets close" (2.12.76.6),[8] but there is no definite boundary and hence no sense of seclusion.

The centrepiece of Milton's bower is the "nuptial bed" (4.710) decorated by Eve "With flowers, garlands, and sweet-smelling herbs" (4.709). When Adam and Eve enter the bower they are entitled to the pleasures of intimacy; indeed they are guaranteed the pleasures of intimacy by the exclusion of other forms of curious life:

other creature here
Beast, bird, insect, or worm durst enter none;
Such was their awe of man. (4.703–5)

The question that arises from this arrangement is the obvious one: why? Why is it that Milton, after going to such lengths to insist on the innocence of prelapsarian sexuality, after exhibiting the human couple in their resplendent nakedness, now goes to the trouble of guaranteeing their privacy, of sheltering them even from the curious eyes of insects and of worms?

The short answer to this question might be that privacy is simply an inherent good to Milton, and that he is therefore obliged to include it in paradise, where all things beneficial to humankind will of necessity be represented. Privacy would then occupy a place in the social setup of paradise roughly parallel to that of modesty in the moral setup. There is of course no shame in paradise, because nothing to be ashamed about. But is there modesty? When Adam tells the story of the creation of Eve, he points out that when she's first presented to him, Eve turns away and retreats from him because she sets a high value on her "virgin modesty" (8.501),

8 Edmund Spenser, *Books I and II of "The Faerie Queene," the "Mutability Cantos," and Selections from the Minor Poetry*, ed. Robert Kellogg and Oliver Steele (New York: Odyssey Press, 1965), 394–6.

> That would be wooed, and not unsought be won,
> Not obvious, not obtrusive, but retired,
> The more desirable. (8.503–5)

We might imagine Milton's construction of Eve's modesty to run roughly parallel to St Anselm's argument for the existence of God. Think of a female being infinitely desirable in every respect, the being (as God says to Adam) "exactly to thy heart's desire" (8.451). Now think of another being who includes within herself all of the attributes of the former, *plus* modesty. Which of these two women is the more desirable? The second, of course, and therefore she must be Eve. Modesty only makes her all the more desirable by enhancing the value of her other attributes. Of course Adam quickly overcomes Eve's reticence, because she is given the virtue of submission. "To the nuptial bow'r," says Adam, "I led her blushing like the morn" (8.510–11). To those austere Puritans who object that there ought to be no blushing in paradise, Milton would have a ready answer: blushing is an act which enhances the beauty of woman and enriches the pleasure of sexual conversation. Since these are good because ordained by God, blushing must be good too, and therefore part of paradise.

Milton doesn't use the word "privacy" in *Paradise Lost*, but he establishes the concept most clearly in his creation of the bower, and he alludes to it by means of a variety of synonyms. The bower itself is described as a "sacred and sequestered" (4.706) place: sacred in the sense that it is the locus of the "rites/Mysterious of connubial love" (4.742–3) and sequestered in the sense that all beings other than Adam and Eve are denied entrance. When God looks down on his newly created human pair he sees them enfolded in "Uninterrupted joy, unrivaled love/In blissful solitude" (3.68–9). Clearly this is the shared solitude of being alone together, a paradoxical state of unity in doubleness which is inflected though not fundamentally altered by the rest of the poem. In the final lines Adam and Eve must leave the enclosure of paradise forever, and with it the enclosure within the enclosure represented by the bower; but as they take "their solitary way" into the future they are still walking "hand in hand" (12.648–9). They have become public figures in the great story of the fall, but their relationship to one another still includes the notion of a shared privacy that can be observed from the outside but not really penetrated from within.

Among the most interesting of Milton's synonyms for privacy is the idea of the "close recess." In this phrase "close" retains its early modern connotation of secrecy,[9] and its kinship with the closet, a room designed to harbour and protect the intimate treasures of aristocratic and upwardly mobile middle-class men and women.[10] "Recess" has both its modern sense of a spatial indentation, and its earlier meaning of withdrawal from public activity into private retirement. When Milton's narrator takes us inside the bower for the first time he tells us that we are entering a secret place: "Here in close recess," he says, as if to warn us that we should respect the intimacy of the scene, "Espousèd Eve decked first her nuptial bed" (4.708–10). Secrecy is here given a completely honourable coloration, as I have already implied, because it inhabits the very centre of the structure of paradise. So it is oddly disconcerting to find the very same phrase used in connection with Satan's political activities. Part of Satan's appeal in the early books of *Paradise Lost* is his charisma as a great public leader; he gathers the rebel angels at will and dominates them with his rhetoric. But then, after reducing his numerous followers to miniature size, Satan withdraws for consultation: "far within/And in their own dimensions" the principal demons gather "In close recess and secret conclave" (1.792–5). There can be no doubt that this is the kind of event that has given the phrase "private and confidential" such a bad reputation; the secrecy of inner-cabinet consultation is here a ruse to disguise political manipulation.[11] Much later the two morally opposite meanings of "recess" are conflated. After Eve leaves Adam's side to do her own gardening, she is discovered by Satan tending a little plot of flowerbeds:

> Such pleasure took the serpent to behold
> This flow'ry plat, the sweet recess of Eve
> Thus early, thus alone ... (9.455–7)

9 See Hotspur's description of Kate as "for secrecy/No lady closer" (*1 Henry IV*, 2.3.105–6).

10 See Georgiana Ziegler, "'My Lady's Chamber': Female Space, Female Chastity in Shakespeare," *Textual Practice* 4 (1990): 73–7, and Alan Stewart, "The Early Modern Closet Discovered," *Representations* 50 (Spring 1995): 76–87.

11 The "secret conclave" is evidence in support of James Dougall Fleming's thesis, in *Milton's Secrecy: And Philosophical Hermeneutics* (Aldershot: Ashgate, 2008), that "when not applied to God in the poem, 'secret' is simply *the* Miltonic keyword of Satanic sin" (10). It follows that only God is allowed to be secret or secretive, though Fleming does acknowledge that the bower has a special status in which human secrecy is sanctioned by God (8).

Here "close recess" has become "sweet recess"; the privacy of Eve is no longer protected by the sacred enclosure; and unprotected privacy is subject to invasion.

Although the word "privacy" is absent from *Paradise Lost*, the adjectival form "private" does occur, but only once. The occasion is Adam's interpretation of Eve's disturbing dream in Book 5. He begins with a few remarks about the construction of the soul, its division into many faculties, their subordination to reason, and the important work of fancy in forming images out of the material supplied by the senses. But at night, Adam says, fancy "retires/Into her private cell when nature rests" (5.108–9). That's why "mimic Fancy" (5.110) has her chance, during sleep, to create the misshapen material of dreams. Here the idea of privacy is quite strikingly connected to a sense of interiority – of an inner space within the self in which momentous decisions can be made. The sense of interiority has been achieved in part by a system of concentric layering. Paradise itself is surrounded by a "verdurous wall" (4.143) from the top of which Adam can view the surrounding plain of Eden. Within paradise is the bower, protected again with walls and now roofed in as well. When Adam and Eve retire for the night they enter "their inmost bow'r" (4.738), presumably the location of the much-decorated nuptial bed. On the morning of Eve's dream Adam is afraid that, while they were asleep, some aspect of evil has approached them, though of course he cannot yet have knowledge of evil. "Yet evil whence?" he says to Eve; "In thee can harbor none,/Created pure" (5.99–100). What does harbour inside Eve is the soul, still pure because Eve has not assented to whatever suggestions of evil may have invaded her sleep. And "in the soul" (5.100), Adam explains, are the various faculties: reason, fancy, mimic fancy, and so on. Even deeper within the soul, very near the centre of this vast concentric system, it would appear, is the "private cell" to which fancy withdraws during sleep. Interiority is represented here as the centre of consciousness itself. Milton's metaphysics is indeed a metaphysics of presence; privacy is among the devices he uses to fill and replenish the self.

Like Eve, Adam has an internal "cell" to which fancy retreats while dormant. You would expect this to happen while God is creating Eve out of Adam's rib, because God takes the precaution of giving Adam a transcendental anaesthetic before he performs the operation. But surprisingly, Adam's fancy remains active during this procedure:

> Mine eyes he closed, but open left the cell
> Of fancy my internal sight. (8.460–1)

This is handy, in terms of narrative technique, because it allows Adam to recall exactly all of the steps in the formation of his helpmate. But there is a further sense in which this account of Adam's interior subjectivity is especially moving. Notice that in Adam's case the cell of fancy is equated with "internal sight." At first glance this notion simply runs directly parallel to the image-making property assigned to fancy in the interpretation of Eve's dream. But the phrase "internal sight" must have held peculiar resonance for a poet who had been blind for some twenty years by the time he began the composition of *Paradise Lost.* If privacy is understood as interiority, then there is a biographical reason why it would be especially meaningful to Milton. As in the case of Adam, God had closed Milton's eyes too, but left intact the "internal sight" by which he could create his poem.

Privacy in all of its forms – spatial, sexual, and psychological – is available to both Adam and Eve, but it does not follow that privacy in paradise is a gender-neutral term. In fact Eve is associated far more closely with the values of the private than her husband.[12] So much could already be inferred from the description of the bower as a "close recess" and its linkage to the "sweet recess of Eve," or from the division of responsibilities implied in the lines which describe Eve decorating "*her* nuptial bed" (my emphasis). Adam is given various public functions that Eve would rather avoid. When Raphael arrives, Adam greets him at the threshold of the bower while Eve is busy "within" (5.303), preparing lunch. This pattern remains constant after the fall, when Michael pays a visit to instruct the fallen pair on their new relationship to God's will. Adam senses that their new guest will expect compliance to a gendered code of behaviour: "whom not to offend," he explains to Eve, "With reverence I must meet, and thou retire" (11.236–7). On learning that they will have to leave paradise, Adam laments the prospect of "Departure from this happy place, our sweet/Recess" (11.303–4). Eve's concerns are far more specifically motivated by attachment to the plants she has tended and to the "nuptial bower, by me adorned" (11.280). In giving Adam the public voice of the first family and Eve the responsibility for domestic arrangements, Milton

12 For some interesting parallel findings, see Mary Nyquist, "The Genesis of Gendered Subjectivity in the Divorce Tracts and in *Paradise* Lost," in *Re-Membering Milton: Essays on the Texts and* Traditions, ed. Mary Nyquist and Margaret W. Ferguson (London: Methuen, 1987), 120–2, and Mary Beth Long, "Contextualizing Eve's and Milton's Solitudes in Book 9 of *Paradise Lost,*" *Milton Quarterly* 37 (2003): 100–15.

is of course doing nothing surprising for his time and place. Morally speaking, the gendering of privacy may be unfair to Eve: the balance is tilted so that her interiority is receptive to Satan's dream, so that her inwardness is analogous to Satan's secrecy, so that her decision to venture out alone leaves her unprepared and vulnerable to temptation. But in artistic terms it is Eve who gains from this unfair division: it is she who dreams and sallies forth and makes the fatal error of trusting her own inner resources when she ought to have simply obeyed. When Michael tells Adam that his loss will be replaced by "A paradise within thee, happier far" (12.587), the announcement is in one sense an endorsement of privacy and of Eve's part in nurturing the private self.

I return now to the question which has brought these reflections into being: Why does Milton ensure that Adam and Eve will have privacy, even in paradise? The long answer to this question is implicit in all of the separate observations offered so far. For Milton, the perfect state of being has to include perfect sexual interaction. That's why, even if he's risking inconsistency, he gives Eve the characteristics (such as modest reluctance) which he finds sexually attractive. That's also why privacy has to be established and maintained, even in paradise. Without privacy, human sexuality would be less than perfect: it would be subject to voyeurism, at very least, and therefore tarnished by association. This kind of devaluation is on the verge of happening when Satan observes the conjugal attraction of our first parents and turns aside with envy. But Milton rescues his human pair by giving them a blissful bower in which their sexual desires are in every way pleasing, both to themselves and to God. Paradise without sex? For Milton that would have been unthinkable. Sex without privacy? That would have been unbearable. So paradise is designed to ensure that Adam and Eve will have plenty of both.

But Milton was also a child of the English Reformation, and it is in his deep religious allegiances that we can find the reasons for the persistence of privacy during and beyond the fall. Jürgen Habermas has historicized the value of privacy in early modern culture in ways that Milton might have found congenial: "The status of the Church changed as a result of the Reformation; the anchoring in divine authority that it represented – that is, religion – became a private matter. The so-called freedom of religion historically secured the first sphere of private autonomy."[13] In

13 *The Structural Transformation of the Public Sphere: An Inquiry into a Category of Bourgeois Society*, trans. Thomas Burger and Frederick Lawrence (Cambridge, MA: MIT Press, 1989), 11.

Paradise Lost, and indeed in much of his thinking and writing over the years, Milton was taking an active part in the great historical change which Habermas here describes. Why was Milton, obviously a deeply religious man, so unwilling to associate himself with any established church? Because he valued the exercise of private devotions far more than public forms of worship. Why did Milton, a vigorous campaigner on behalf of Parliament, insist on attacking the policies of his own party in the *Areopagitica*? Because he valued the freedom of a private conscience above any public agenda. So also in his great epic poem, with all of its public conventions and aspirations, Milton endorsed what Habermas describes as the "sphere of private autonomy." The greatest act of Eve and Adam is to choose. The autonomy of this action is theologically guaranteed by the doctrine of free will, and it is artistically secured in the creation of the private self.

The Secret Motions of Things in Bensalem

Sir Francis Bacon (1561–1626) played such a conspicuous part on the public stage as a courtier, politician, philosopher, and advocate of empirical science that his admirers may be forgiven for treating him as if he had no private life at all. The reason for including Bacon here is his unfinished and posthumously published piece of utopian writing, *The New Atlantis* (1626). There are numerous ways in which this work depends upon and continues Bacon's ample and widely disseminated public projects, and some of these will become apparent in the discussion which follows. But there are also questions that arise in *The New Atlantis* that are bound to be misunderstood if approached in the abstract, without reference to Bacon's private self. So I begin with brief commentary on the two trouble spots in his private life: his marriage and his homosexuality.

"He that hath wife and children hath given hostages to fortune; for they are impediments to great enterprises, either of virtue or mischief," Bacon declares in one of his most memorable opening sentences from *The Essays.*[14] In his mid-thirties Bacon had considered giving hostages when he asked his friend the earl of Essex to write letters on his behalf to

14 "Of Marriage and Single Life," Francis Bacon, *The Major Works,* ed. Brian Vickers, revised ed. (Oxford: Oxford University Press, 2002), 353. Bacon quotations, unless otherwise identified, are from this collection.

a young and extremely wealthy widow, Lady Hatton.[15] When she instead married his political enemy, Sir Edward Coke, Bacon may have thought she was sending a message.

Some five years later he was introduced to another heiress, Alice Barnham, who he thought would be a suitable marriage partner. She was just eleven at the time, but she was the daughter of a wealthy London alderman who had bequeathed to her valuable lands in Moulsham and Chelmsford, County Essex. Among the incentives for Bacon was the prospect of settling his growing debts, which he seemed unable to manage on professional income alone. Eventually she did marry him, when she was just Juliet's age (almost fourteen)[16] and he was forty-five.

About the emotional texture of this relationship, very little can be inferred. When Bacon at last got his coveted appointment as Lord Chancellor and Keeper of the Great Seal in 1617, he persuaded King James to sign a document guaranteeing that Lady Bacon would now take precedence over "all ladies of what estate or degree soever" except for "the ladies or wives of the Barons."[17] Bacon was giving his wife what *he* wanted, namely rank and status in the prestige-obsessed court of Jacobean England, but not necessarily what she might have wanted, at least if her desires were anything like those she was taught that wives should have. There were no children coming from this marriage. Was there any sexual intercourse between husband and wife? Perez Zagorin thinks "it is possible that they never had sexual relations."[18]

Less than four months before his death, Bacon revised his will by adding this codicil: "Whatsoever I have given, granted, confirmed, or appointed to my wife, in the former part of this my will, I do now, for just and great causes, utterly revoke and make void, and leave her to her right only."[19] The marriage had fallen apart, and was beyond repair. Eleven days after Bacon died (on 9 April 1626), his thirty-three-year-old widow married John Underhill, formerly Bacon's gentleman usher and soon

15 See Lisa Jardine and Alan Stewart, *Hostage to Fortune: The Troubled Life of Francis Bacon* (London: Victor Gollancz, 1998), 190.

16 This point is made by G.R. Hibbard, whose account of Bacon's marriage is the first one I ever read; see "Love, Marriage and Money in Shakespeare's Theatre and Shakespeare's England," *Elizabethan Theatre* 6 (1975): 136–8.

17 Bacon, *The Letters and the Life*, ed. James Spedding (London: Longmans, 1874), 6:153–4.

18 *Francis Bacon* (Princeton, NJ: Princeton University Press, 1998), 14.

19 *The Letters and the Life*, ed. Spedding, 7:545.

to become Sir John Underhill when Charles I knighted him on 12 July 1626. Even scholars devoted to the facts will find interpretation irresistible here. Jardine and Stewart suggest that Lady Bacon may have been "overcompensating for twenty years of her husband's desertion of her in favour of a string of smooth-faced male servants,"[20] and then they quote Aubrey's claim that she caused her new husband to go "deafe and blinde with too much of Venus."[21] I think we can safely assume that her first marriage was not an entirely gratifying experience for Lady Bacon, and that her husband was made aware of her dissatisfaction in ways that he found distasteful.

Bacon's erotic preferences were for members of his own sex, to judge by evidence that is mostly gossip but, in its cumulative weight, sounds as if it's based on truth. Sir Simonds D'Ewes, in a passage of commentary dated 1621 and triggered by Bacon's political disgrace, writes at some length about "His most abominable and darling sinne"; after Bacon's public humiliation, D'Ewes claims, "yet would hee not relinquish the practice of his most horrible & secret sinne of sodomie, keeping still one Godrick a verie effeminate faced youth to bee his catamite & bedfellow."[22] Whatever D'Ewes's own faults may have been, bearing false witness was not one of them; even without corroboration, his remarks have the kind of specificity that makes them sound authentic. Aubrey described Bacon as a pederast, a word he represented in Greek orthography; and in plain English he added, "His Ganimeds and Favourites tooke Bribes."[23] In a letter to Sir Dudley Carleton John Chamberlain reported that Isaac Singleton, canon of St Paul's, preached a sermon on May Day 1619 in which he "declaimed bitterly against his [i.e., Bacon's] court, and glaunced (they say) somwhat scandalously at him and his Catamites as he called them."[24] Some fairly crude verses about Bacon's sexual conduct

20 *Hostage to Fortune*, 512.

21 *Brief Lives*, ed. Oliver Lawson Dick (1949; repr., Harmondsworth: Penguin, 1972), 174.

22 BL Harley MS 646, fol 59. I quote the manuscript here because James Orchard Halliwell, whose edition of D'Ewes I cited in chapter 5, deletes this passage and justifies doing so as follows: "D'Ewes here specifically charges Bacon with an abominable offence, in language too gross for publication" (*The Autobiography and Correspondence of Sir Simonds D'Ewes, Bart., During the Reigns of James I and Charles I*, ed. James Orchard Halliwell [London: Richard Bentley, 1845], 1:192n).

23 *Brief Lives*, 173.

24 *The Letters of John Chamberlain*, ed. Norman Egbert McClure (Philadelphia: American Philosophical Society, 1939), 2:243.

circulated in the manuscript culture of the time;[25] these are not reliable witnesses of his actual behaviour, but they are another measure of his reputation. I do not wish to blame Bacon, either for the way in which his marriage turned out, or for his sexual orientation. Rather, I would like to suggest that these two troubles of his must have inflected what he thought about the question of privacy, and therefore how he represented privacy in his utopian fiction.

Bacon's *New Atlantis*, composed not long before his death and in fact never completed, is in many respects an answer to More's *Utopia*. Bacon's narrator, unlike Raphael Hythloday, begins by recalling a sea voyage which starts from a particular place (Peru) and heads for a real destination (China and Japan), and is therefore a westward journey across the Pacific Ocean. Strong winds carry the mariners northward, and they are already preparing for the worst when they encounter the island of Bensalem, where official documents are produced in four languages (Hebrew, Greek, Latin, and Spanish) and where the inhabitants are explicitly Christian. Unlike the Utopians, whose natural religion allows them to adapt to Christianity if they wish, the Bensalemites were the recipients of a miracle in the early Christian era which left them with "all the canonical books of the Old and New Testament" (465) and a letter from St Bartholomew.

Whereas the commonwealth of Utopia is set up to ensure stability and must therefore rule out innovation, Bensalem has a far more adventuresome intellectual culture. Among its institutions is Salomon's House, referred to also as a "college" by the narrator and praised as "the very eye of this kingdom" (464). When the narrator has the good luck to be chosen as the single European to have a "private conference" (479) with the Father of Salomon's House, he is told that the institution is built on first principles that sound very Baconian indeed: "The End of our Foundation is the knowledge of Causes, and secret motions of things; and the enlarging of the bounds of Human Empire, to the effecting of all things possible" (480). This admirable and progressive agenda is supported by Preparations and Instruments which would later come to be called laboratories, experiments, and clinical trials. "We have also parks and inclosures of all sorts of beasts and birds," says the Head of Salomon's House, "which we use not only for view or rareness, but likewise for dissections

25 See Arthur F. Marotti, *Manuscript, Print, and the English Renaissance Lyric* (Ithaca, NY: Cornell University Press, 1995), 105n66.

and trials; that thereby we may take light what may be wrought upon the body of man" (482). The pursuit of knowledge is here the first step in a process that will enhance the possibilities of human life.

The narrator gets much of his information about the culture of Bensalem from a merchant named Joabin, whom he identifies as "a Jew, and circumcised" (475), and who claims to have read More's *Utopia*: "I have read in a book of one of your men," as Joabin puts it, "of a Feigned Commonwealth, where the married couple are permitted, before they contract, to see one another naked" (478). The Bensalemites disapprove of this custom, on the grounds that a negative decision following the inspection would invariably be taken as an insult. So they have designed "a more civil way" of achieving the same result: "they have near every town a couple of pools, (which they call 'Adam and Eve's pools'), where it is permitted to one of the friends of the man, and another of the friends of the woman, to see them severally bathe naked" (478). I'm by no means sure that the putative goal of the exercise (i.e., identifying physical defects) will be achieved in this revised scenario. Still, I think the changes are considerable, and they have the result of making the inspection into an erotically charged event. A prospective bridegroom would need to choose his friend very carefully before sending him off to Eve's pool to do the observation. And the friend would have to be careful to show just the right amount of enthusiasm, and no more, especially in the debriefing.

But perhaps I am manufacturing difficulties where none exist. The people of Bensalem, as Joabin explains, have agreed upon "many wise and excellent laws touching marriage" (478). Polygamy is forbidden, an interval of at least a month is required between first meeting and wedding ceremony, and parental consent is not absolutely mandatory. It's Europeans who get it all wrong, Joabin claims. Because European men have sexual opportunities outside of marriage ("a remedy more agreeable to their corrupt will"), many choose not to marry at all, many others marry late in life, and marriage becomes no more than a "bargain; wherein is sought alliance, or portion, or reputation, with some desire (almost indifferent) of issue" (477). If Bacon is allowing himself to reflect upon the failure of his own marriage here, then he is sounding a sad note indeed. And of course he is working matters out in a different way in the perfect world, where marriage is "the faithful nuptial union of man and wife" (477).

The high positive value assigned to marriage and its consequences are demonstrated in the Feast of the Family. This is a celebration that happens whenever a man has produced thirty offspring (counting children, grandchildren, and so on) of three years old or more. Because population is considered the most important resource of Bensalem, the state pays for this event, and a local politician assists the patriarch (whom they call the Tirsan) in organizing it. The Tirsan calls all of his descendants together, helps them settle any disputes, assists them in overcoming any problems, and then chooses one of his sons (not necessarily the eldest) to be called Son of the Vine. This is followed by a highly ritualistic ceremony, including a meal during which the Tirsan sits in state, is served at table by his male offspring, and eventually pronounces a blessing on each of his descendants, male and female, as they kneel before him one at a time while he "layeth his hand upon his head, or her head, and giveth the blessing" (475). The musical entertainment always sings the praises of Adam, Noah, and Abraham, "whereof the former two peopled the world, and the last was the Father of the Faithful" (475). If all of this sounds deeply patriarchal, it is, and it is meant to be. Where, we must surely be asking, is the mother of all these children? There is an answer to this question, and it includes the proviso that nobody can see her: "if there be a mother from whose body the whole lineage is descended, there is a traverse placed in a loft above on the right hand of the chair, with a privy door, and a carved window of glass, leaded with gold and blue, where she sitteth, but is not seen" (473). Even in his version of paradise Bacon can't imagine a wife being a real partner (as Milton clearly can) or even, as the Genesis account has it, "an help meet" (Genesis 2:18) for the man.

In one respect Bacon's utopian fiction is a lot like More's, and that is in its abolition of vice. Joabin reports that among the Bensalemites "there are no stews, no dissolute houses, no courtesans, nor any thing of that kind" (477). The whole island seems to be "free from all pollution or foulness" (476), a condition that comes about as a result of self-respect, or what in Bensalem is called "reverence" for the self, as in this piece of their proverbial wisdom: "the reverence of a man's self is, next religion, the chiefest bridle of all vices" (477). So the *New Atlantis* builds up a moral optimism that is at least as hopeful as anything in *Utopia.* And it adds one further stipulation: "As for masculine love, they have no touch of it" (477). This is the saddest (and for Bacon perhaps the most difficult) moment in the whole narration. Yes, Bacon seems to be saying, I can imagine a perfect world. I can do a better job of it than More did in *Utopia.* There will be plenty of room in it for all of my splendid public projects, and for a family of the kind that my father presided over. But the one thing I can't find in a perfect world, Bacon seems to suggest, is a place for people like me.

The Incloistered Self in the Convent of Pleasure

It would be an exaggeration to claim that everything written by Margaret Cavendish, duchess of Newcastle, turns out to be a utopian fiction in one disguise or another, but an exaggeration in some ways worthy of the extravagant duchess herself. The *Life* she wrote of her husband, William Cavendish, duke of Newcastle, is an interesting case in point. Today Newcastle[26] is likely to be remembered, if at all, not as a minor playwright and patron of writers, nor as a master of the French style of equestrian training (*manage*), but as the losing general in the battle of Marston Moor (1644), and therefore a major player in what would soon be the defeat of the royalist forces. Cavendish tells the story of her husband's military career in some detail, relying on information given her by Newcastle himself, or by John Rolleston, Newcastle's long-time secretary. When she is able to record a military victory, Cavendish doesn't hesitate to sing her husband's praises, but when she has to admit a setback, she invariably looks for extenuating circumstances. At length this pattern becomes so pronounced that Cavendish has to acknowledge it herself: "it is remarkable," she observes, "that in all actions and undertakings where My Lord was in Person himself, he was always Victorious, and prospered in the execution of his designs; but whatsoever was lost or succeeded ill, happen'd in his absence, and was caused either by the Treachery, or Negligence and Carelessness of his Officers."[27] Not that she should have been his shrewdest critic, of course; there were plenty of others, including the earl of Clarendon, eager to step into that role.[28]

26 To avoid confusion I will adopt the practice of referring to the duke as "Newcastle" and his wife as "Cavendish."

27 *The Life of the Thrice Noble, High and Puissant Prince William Cavendishe, Duke, Marquess, and Earl of Newcastle* (London: A. Maxwell, 1667), O1^{v}.

28 Clarendon blames Newcastle for giving up too quickly after the battle of Marston Moor, and for selling out his royalist allies by embarking the very next day for Hamburg, to begin what would become a protracted period of voluntary exile. But he nonetheless recognizes Newcastle's greatness as a soldier and a leader of men. See Edward Hyde, earl of Clarendon, *The History of the Rebellion and Civil Wars in England, Begun in the Year 1641* (Oxford: Printed at the Theater, 1702–4), 2.8:390–4.

But the strategy Cavendish adopts puts Newcastle into a kind of moral limbo: a world in which he will be praised no matter what he does, and excused from wrongdoing no matter how spectacularly he fails, and in which it would therefore be impossible to locate such a primary ethical marker as, for example, "responsibility." When the imperfections of the world we inhabit are removed in order to create an environment in which nothing can go wrong, what we are observing is the construction of a utopian fantasy.

In many other cases the signals of utopian contrivance are more obvious, and sometimes links to the tradition of utopian writing are deliberately highlighted. In *The Blazing World* (1666), for example, Cavendish uses narrative conventions that virtually allude both to More's *Utopia* and to Bacon's *New Atlantis*.[29] The heroine is abducted by a merchant and his assistants, forced into a small sailing vessel, and driven northward by an unpredictable wind. In this case, however, she is carried right to the North Pole, where the mariners die of exposure to extreme cold, but she survives to be transferred to the contiguous pole of another world, the Blazing world of the title. Here she is rescued by Bear-men, taken up by Fox-men, Geese-men, Bird-men, and so on, brought at length to the imperial city of their island kingdom, namely "*Paradise*," where she is welcomed by the Emperor, who "made her his Wife, and gave her an absolute power to rule and govern all that World as she pleased."[30] The new Empress will use her position to foreground a number of pet projects relating to early modern science, and to record the results of these enquiries she chooses "a Lady, the *Duchess of Newcastle*," who "will without question, be ready to do you all the service she can" (208). After this it will not be surprising to note an uncanny resemblance between the scientific projects of the Empress and those which Cavendish had elsewhere identified as her own. But the larger issue here is the one that connects *The Blazing World* to the *New Atlantis*, namely, the requirement

---

29 For thoughtful comment about the ways in which this text responds both to More's *Utopia* and (especially) to Bacon's *New Atlantis*, see Sarah Hutton, "Science and Satire: The Lucianic Voice of Margaret Cavendish's *Description of a New World Called the Blazing World*," in *Authorial Conquests: Essays on Genre in the Writings of Margaret Cavendish*, ed. Line Cottegnies and Nancy Weitz (Madison, NJ: Fairleigh Dickinson University Press, 2003), 165–8.

30 *Paper Bodies: A Margaret Cavendish Reader*, ed. Sylvia Bowerbank and Sara Mendelson (Peterborough, ON: Broadview, 2000), 159, 162. References to Cavendish's writing, unless otherwise specified, are to this edition.

that planning for the future of human society be based on principles grounded in natural philosophy, that is, in what would in our world be identified as the natural sciences.

If Cavendish resembles Bacon in her valorization of nature, she certainly differs from him in her treatment of gender. Whereas the setup of Bensalem makes it obvious that women's reproductivity is valued, there's not much else about women that is praised, or even noticed. In Cavendish the thirteen men who abduct the young woman, including the merchant who thinks of her as sexual prey, end up as thirteen frozen corpses, a fate consistent with "Justice" and designed "to punish their crime of stealing away a young and beauteous Lady" (251). Although the Lady enters a marriage in the new world, it's not a conventional marriage at all, in the sense that she is at once given "absolute power" and can do exactly as she pleases ever after. The agent who grants her this power is of course her new husband, the Emperor, but we are not encouraged to wonder what would happen if the Lady now used her power in ways that might irritate him. It is enough, apparently, that she has been delivered from female servitude.

The revision of gender arrangements is crucial to the utopian fictions which Cavendish invented in dramatic form, namely *The Female Academy*, *Bell in Campo*, and *The Convent of Pleasure*. It is the last of these texts that will preoccupy me in working out the problematics of privacy in Cavendish's version of utopia. But the three plays share an agenda, as Erin Lang Bonin has shown: all three "feature separatist institutions that temporarily but explicitly reject marriage and family in order to carry out their utopian projects."[31] As a way of framing what Cavendish does with this paradigm in *The Convent of Pleasure* I will comment briefly on its uses in the two earlier plays.[32]

31 "Margaret Cavendish's Dramatic Utopias and the Politics of Gender," *Studies in English Literature, 1500–1900* 40 (2000): 340.

32 Although the precise dates of composition of these plays are probably irretrievable, there is a gap of six years between the publication of *Playes* (London: John Martin, James Allestrye, and Thomas Dicas, 1662), a volume which includes *The Female Academy* and both parts of *Bell in Campo*, and the subsequent publication of *Plays, Never Before Printed* (London: A. Maxwell, 1668), in which *The Convent of Pleasure* first appears. My references to *The Female Academy* and *Bell in Campo* are taken from *Playes* (1662); my references to *The Convent of Pleasure* are from *Paper Bodies: A Margaret Cavendish Reader*.

The Female Academy offers to correct some of the well-known inequities in the distribution of educational opportunities between the genders. A group of mature women, identified in the text as Matrons, takes complete responsibility for educating the young women who attend their academy. Men are not permitted to set foot inside the building; even tasks routinely done by men in other households are here assigned to female servants. But the academy's teaching theatre has been equipped with a grate through which its activities can be observed by persons in the outside world. Needless to say, spending time at the grate quickly becomes a favourite male pastime: it is the aperture that gives men the opportunity to look at, listen to, and comment on the young women being educated.

What they are likely to observe is a Matron assigning a set topic (wit and wisdom, for example) to one of the students, who then, in the role of the Speaker or Lady Speaker, gives as persuasive an account of the topic as she can. The starting premise here is that the segregation of women is of absolute importance – that is, we wouldn't have a *female* academy without it – but there's also something laughably superficial about the procedure. Segregation only increases the likelihood that men will be talking about women, and knowledge of this phenomenon ensures that women will continue to talk about men. The Matron asks, for example, "Lady, how approve you of those Lovers that kisse the Letters, Tokens, Pledges, and the like, that are sent unto them from their Lovers? or such as wear Letters, Tokens, or Pledges in their Bosomes, and next their Heart, and take them and view them a hundred times a day?" The young woman to whom this question is addressed, the Lady Speaker, replies with scornful contempt: "Approve it say you? you mean disapprove it; but let me tell you, most Reverend Matron, that the very hearing of it makes me sick, and the seeing of it would make me die" (2.3.811). But in the act of repudiating men, this young Lady is still warbling on about their impact on members of her own gender in a way that I find obsessive. Men are the big problem for the women of *The Female Academy*, and the open grate ensures that the big problem won't go away.

The grate is decisively closed, so to speak, in order to create a more robust utopia in *Bell in Campo*, a two-part play which offers women the chance to compete with men on the military stage. The leader of the women is Lady Victoria, who has formed a convincing analysis of the subordination of women: "the Masculine Sex is of an opinion we are only fit to breed and bring forth Children, but otherwise a trouble in a Commonwealth" (*1 Bell in Campo*, 2.9.712[v]). Conforming to this passive stereotype is not good enough for Lady Victoria, who believes she has found the opportunity "to get liberty and freedome from the Female Slavery, and to make our selves equal with men" (*2 Bell in Campo*, 1.3.7P1). I do not propose to outline here the strategies used by Lady Victoria and her female army in their confrontation with the Lord General (to whom of course Lady Victoria happens to be married) and his troops. In the end the monarch of the kingdom in which the play is set declares an Act which underwrites Lady Victoria's achievements and makes them permanent in the following ways: "First, That all women shall hereafter in this Kingdome be Mistriss in their own Houses and Families. Secondly, They shall sit at the upper end of the Table above their Husbands. Thirdly, That they shall keep the purse." There are further provisions, including the guarantee that women "shall be of their Husbands Counsel" (*2 Bell in Campo*, 5.20.7V2), all of them intended to protect women from oppression in the domestic sphere. For once it would appear that the rhetoric of gender equality has been openly and vigorously deployed.

The question of privacy in general, and of female privacy in particular, is of crucial importance in *The Convent of Pleasure.* This has been noticed by other readers of Cavendish, notably but in different ways, by Julie Sanders[33] and Joanne H. Wright.[34] Sanders proposes "to challenge traditional concepts of privacy" because she believes, for example, that "the private theatricals of early modern households" are likely "to have been very public and political in their purpose" (127). She therefore sees Cavendish performing something close to a magical feat in *The Convent of Pleasure*: that is, staging Lady Happy's withdrawal from the world in such a way as to make it a visibly public event. "The paradoxes persist" (137), Sanders argues, in almost any representation of early modern privacy. Wright would doubtless agree with this judgment, though she is less inclined to believe that Cavendish is always fully in control of the ambiguities inherent in her text(s). On the one hand, Cavendish is keenly aware of the oppression of women occasioned by "the power relations within marriage" (224), and this knowledge accounts for "her darker view of

33 "'The Closet Opened': A Reconstruction of 'Private' Space in the Writings of Margaret Cavendish," in *A Princely Brave Woman: Essays on Margaret Cavendish, Duchess of Newcastle*, ed. Stephen Clucas (Aldershot, Hampshire: Ashgate, 2003), 127–40.

34 "Reading the Private in Margaret Cavendish: Conversations in Political Thought," in *British Political Thought in History, Literature and Theory, 1500–1800*, ed. David Armitage (Cambridge: Cambridge University Press, 2006), 212–34.

the private" (225). But she is also convinced that "the private is not just a space or a location, but a choice as to how to live one's life" (228); and for this reason, Wright argues, "in much of Cavendish's writing, from the autobiographical to the fictional and dramatic, her portrayal of private retirement has a celebratory tone" (230). In the analysis that follows it will become apparent that I believe Cavendish to be either unwilling or unable to reconcile these opposing senses of the private.

From the moment of her first appearance in *The Convent of Pleasure*, Lady Happy celebrates the attractions of privacy: "I intend to incloister my self from the World, to enjoy pleasure, and not to bury my self from it" (1.2.100).[35] But even though sensory pleasures of many kinds will be available in the cloister, it will be a real cloister nonetheless in the sense that men will be rigidly excluded. "Men are the only troublers of Women," says Lady Happy, because they "make the Female sex their slaves" (1.2.101). So there will be no room in the Convent for them.

What there will be room for is described in detail by Lady Happy herself. The items include visual, tactile, and olfactory blandishments (taffeta, porcelain, velvet, frangipane, cypress, juniper, and so on); a system of water running "out of small Pipes" (2.2.105) which I suspect to be indoor plumbing; a lavishly supplied art gallery; a beautifully landscaped garden; an endless supply of the finest cuisine; changes of decor and fashion with every change of season; and fabulous underwear: "our Shifts shall be of the finest and purest Linnen that can be bought or spun" (2.1.106). To enhance these joys, there will be "a great Looking-Glass in each Chamber, that we may view our selves and take pleasure in our own Beauties, whilst they are fresh and young" (2.1.105). What more could a woman want? Even the voyeuristic pleasure of the male gaze is reassigned by means of the mirror to the women themselves.

An additional thing they might want is theatrical entertainment, so one of the ladies of the Convent announces the play-within-the-play which Lady Happy and a visiting Princess (about whom I'll have more to say later) observe as "*Spectators*" (3.1.112). The only subject of the play-within-the-play, and one that is played out in a half-dozen reiterations, is the pain and grief that various women feel as a result of abusive treatment by their menfolk. The Cobler leaves his wife in the lurch when he

35 In references to *The Convent of Pleasure*, parenthetical citations identify act and scene numbers, and the page in *Paper Bodies* from which the quotation is taken.

runs off "with Goody *Mettle* the Tinker's Wife" (3.2.112). The woman who hears this account wishes that her own husband "would run away with Goody *Shred* the Botcher's wife" because he's a "drunken Rogue" who doesn't provide for his children and who "beats me all black and blew" (3.2.112). Higher up the social scale, two ladies compare notes and find that one husband has gambled away all of his own wealth and all of his wife's, while the other insists on bringing home "his Whores," as the Lady calls them, "in my house, under my roof, and they must rule as chief Mistresses" (3.2.113). Other women are shown suffering pain in childbirth, dying as a result of childbirth, being humiliated by the behaviour of their children, and so on. If this is private life when men are allowed to play their part in it, why should any woman desire it? As the Epilogue sums it up rather bluntly, "Marriage is a Curse we find,/Especially to Women kind" (3.10.117). This is indeed the darker side of privacy, the kind of privacy which Lady Happy and the other women of the Convent have chosen to repudiate. The play-within-the-play may have a kind of educational or at least motivational function: it reminds the inhabitants of the Convent why they have chosen the life they now live.

But of course there is a snake in the grass, as there always is. The Princess with whom Lady Happy has been sitting while they watch the play-within-the-play is really a man disguised as a princess. The readers of the main play needn't be aware of this, and Lady Happy evidently doesn't suspect it, not even when the Princess mentions that she has noticed members of the Convent, in their "Recreations," adopting masculine attire, and then adds this request: "I desire you will give me leave to be sometimes so accoustred and act the part of your loving Servant" (3.1.111). When the Princess dresses up as a Shepherd and proposes marriage to Lady Happy, "*drest as a Shepherdess*" (4.1.118), the tension is almost unbearable. Whether this tension can be sustained through the masque-like scenes which follow is an open question. But it is certainly dissipated at the beginning of Act 5 when Madam Mediator cries out: "O Ladies, Ladies! you're all betrayed, undone, undone; for there is a man disguised in the *Convent*, search and you'l find it" (5.1.128). This declaration leads with great quickness to the heterosexual resolution which we expect from comedy, and also (perforce) to a dissolution of the monastic order.

The masque-like scenes which I've just referred to, and which amount to perhaps the last third of the play, contain the following printed notation, "Written by my Lord Duke," at three separate locations (4.1.122, 4.1.123, 5.2.129). It may be impossible to determine precisely which lines Newcastle contributed to Cavendish's text. Perhaps his interpolations were minimal: just the twelve-line poem which follows the crowning of Lady Happy and her Princess as Queen and King of the Shepherds (4.1.122–3), the six-line poem or song to accompany the wassail (4.1.123), and a few lines only at the beginning of the penultimate scene (5.2.129–31). But it really doesn't matter. The point is that, try as she may, Cavendish never really escapes the governance of her husband. Just at the point where Lady Happy starts to worry about feeling same-sex attraction, my Lord Duke is there to ensure that the rest of the play will be moving in the direction of marriage.

Among the many paratexts which Cavendish attaches to her *Life* of Newcastle is a dedicatory letter to the duke himself. In it Cavendish speaks of "Heroick Actions," and seeks to give these exactly the kind of gendering that we might expect: "Yours were performed publickly in the Field, mine privately in my Closet" (b1). This distinction might have worked for both of them before July of 1644, when in fact Newcastle was in the field, trying against the odds to ensure that Charles I would prevail. Cavendish here pretends, doubtless with some nostalgic regret, that Newcastle's military record is simply and unalterably heroic. And she wants her own intellectual productions to be seen as heroic too, though the heroism here is performed in the private space of her closet. But what happens to the military hero who, after a stunning defeat, decides that voluntary exile is the best retreat? He will probably find himself in the closet more often than he wants to be there. His wife may find him in *her* closet more often than she might like. There's a snake in the grass, as there always is, and this time his name is William Cavendish, duke of Newcastle. Both kinds of privacy – the threatening kind and the celebratory kind – were known to Margaret Cavendish. But how to manage the transitions between the two may not have been entirely within her control.

Perfection by Negation

It is doubtless true that each utopia will offer to its citizens something unavailable in the real world: justice, redistribution of wealth, uninhibited sexuality, or any of a long list of desiderata. But the utopian structure comes into being, if I am right, not by adding something so much as by subtracting. In More the significant item to be withdrawn is private property, and as soon as it goes a number of changes will come about as corollaries, including the abolition of both hoarding and theft. In Milton's case it is original sin that is taken away, and once it goes, there's no need for clothing or for knowledge of good and evil. In Bacon's Bensalem the irrational is deducted from the human psyche, or at least from human society. That is why the Bensalemites are able to live entirely without vice, and without even a touch of masculine love, as they bend all of their progressive energies towards scientific planning for the future. In the case of Cavendish, if we take *The Convent of Pleasure* as her utopian structure, then the significant deletion, in a word, is men. We might complicate this by adding that, for Cavendish, the gender system seems to be promoting behaviours that are demeaning to women. The radical solution, therefore, is to remove the gender whose interests the system is set up to serve.

We are now in a better position to understand what happens to privacy, and why, in each of these utopian structures. In More's *Utopia*, the value assigned to privacy is exclusively negative. If privacy is also secrecy, then it is surely harbouring vice: economic greed, for example, or political favouritism, or sexual lust. These are exactly the reasons why Raphael Hythloday dismisses the notion that a wise man (like himself) should offer advice to a prince; the prince is going to ignore responsible advice and act in what he sees as his private interests rather than the public good. More could not have predicted the events that overtook him in his subsequent role as Lord Chancellor to Henry VIII, but he was certainly aware of the dangers.

I will reserve *Paradise Lost* for the end of this argument, because in it Milton takes a position diametrically opposed to More's. The valuations of privacy offered by Bacon and Cavendish seem to me different from More's, but in some ways incomplete. In *The New Atlantis*, a private meeting is not something that happens between a man and a woman. Even the suggestive bathing scenes in the Eve's pool or the Adam's pool bring into proximity not the potential marriage partners, but one partner and an agent acting for the other. The closest Bacon comes to a positive valorization of privacy is in his description of the interview between the narrator and the Father of Salomon's House as a "private conference." Here an older man is transmitting valuable knowledge to a junior male admirer. This can't become an erotic relationship, of course, because Bacon has ruled irrationality out of existence. But it is a valuable kind of privacy nonetheless.

Margaret Cavendish seems to me quite painfully divided in her attitude towards men: on the one hand, she seems to desire almost incessantly the attention and admiration of men, and on the other hand she doesn't like what this pursuit of male attraction does to her. This conflicted attitude can be inferred from her writings in various ways, and it can also be supported by some biographical traces that have survived. I am thinking here of Cavendish's widely reported appearance at the Royal Society (May 1667), an event at which she is said by Samuel Pepys to have been "full of admiration, all admiration"[36] – this in spite of her satiric portrait a year earlier of Lice-men "weighing air" (188) in *The Blazing World.* I do not wish to place more weight on this conflict than it will bear, but I do think it helps to account for the curious doubleness of privacy in Cavendish's writing. Yes, privacy would indeed be worth celebrating, Cavendish seems to suggest, if only women really had control of it. But so long as men are around, that is a difficult (and perhaps impossible) wish.

So the strongest endorsement of privacy in the utopian structures considered here comes from *Paradise Lost.* For Milton, privacy is essential to the nurturing of the companionate marriage, a relationship he had been thinking about for many years, and which he at last had the chance to capture and develop to perfection in the mutual society and love of Adam and Eve. But privacy was for Milton not only a secular experience; the sanctity of marriage itself was emblematic of the sacred and private relationship between the Christian soul and God. In short, privacy was, for Milton, the matrix in which the Christian quest could come closest to reaching its long-awaited end.

36 *The Diary of Samuel Pepys,* ed. Robert Latham and William Matthews (London: G. Bell, 1970–83), 8:243.

Chapter Seven

Privacy and Dissidence

In early modern culture, did privacy protect the heterodox? A backward glance at the treatment of religious dissent would suggest that the answer is no. Within English culture by itself it is distressingly easy to recover the names of people who were put to death for religious reasons. John Foxe's *Acts and Monuments* was popularly known, at least among Protestants, as the Book of Martyrs because it recorded the stories of hundreds of God-fearing Christians who had been allegedly persecuted by the Roman Catholic Church since the year 1000. The list contains many contemporaries of Foxe, such as Anne Askew, burned at the stake for resisting the doctrine of transubstantiation at a time (1546) when Henry VIII was seeking to reassert it; Lady Jane Grey, beheaded at age sixteen because of the threat her very existence and Protestant allegiance posed to the newly crowned Mary Tudor (1554); and Hugh Latimer, the brilliant and controversial Protestant preacher, burned at the stake in the following year (1555) for spreading what the new regime described as heresy.[1]

1 See John Foxe, *Ecclesiastical Historie: Containing the Acts and Monuments of Martyrs* (London: John Daye, 1583); see also Diane Watt, "Askew [married name Kyme], Anne (c. 1521–1546), writer and protestant martyr," *Oxford Dictionary of National Biography* (2004); Alison Plowden, "Grey [married name Dudley], Lady Jane (1537–1554), noblewoman and claimant to the English throne," *Oxford Dictionary of National Biography* (2008); and Susan Wabuda, "Latimer, Hugh (c. 1485–1555), bishop of Worcester, preacher, and protestant martyr," *Oxford Dictionary of National Biography* (2009).

The list of English Catholics who died as a result of the Reformation is also very long, reflecting as it does the degree of pressure felt by the governments of successive monarchs (especially Elizabeth I and James I) to prove that no return to the old religion could be possible, desirable, or even thinkable. In 1970 Pope Paul VI selected a top forty from the much longer list, and canonized each of his selections. They include Margaret Clitherow, sometimes known as the pearl of York, who was pressed to death in 1586 for the crime of harbouring Catholic priests in her home; Robert Southwell, SJ, whose poetry made a brief appearance in chapter 2, and who was hanged, drawn, and quartered in 1595 for the treason of proselytizing; and Nicholas Owen, sometimes known as Little John, the carpenter and lay Jesuit responsible for designing secret priest holes in the houses of Catholic gentry all over England, who was tortured to death in 1606 after having been starved out of a secret place that he himself had devised.[2]

An unorthodox religious commitment could clearly lead its adherent into danger and to death. But all of the examples just cited, of Protestant and Catholic martyrs alike, are of people who in one way or another sought to *spread* their heterodox positions, whether by evangelical preaching or by harbouring Jesuit missionaries or in some other way. In short, religious belief was not an exclusively private matter for any of these martyrs, and it would not be difficult to find evidence that they wanted to suffer for their God. It is more difficult to assess what happened to dissident Christians who were willing to hold their allegiance more passively, without challenging the established authorities in any way. Dissidents such as these, especially if they were completely successful, would have left no historical trace.

Not all heterodox thought and behaviour were religious, though the ways in which sexual, intellectual, or social non-conformity were described in early modern culture make it notoriously difficult to disentangle them from the matrix of religious teaching in which virtually everyone in Europe had been raised. To help suggest the boundaries within which

2 See Claire Walker, "Clitherow [*née* Middleton], Margaret [St Margaret Clitherow] (1552/3–1586), Roman Cathoic martyr," *Oxford Dictionary of National Biography* (2004); Nancy Pollard Brown, "Southwell, Robert [St Robert Southwell] (1561–95), writer, Jesuit, and martyr," *Oxford Dictionary of National Biography* (2008); and Michael Hodgetts, "Owen, Nicholas [St Nicholas Owen, *called* Little John, Little Michael] (d. 1606), carpenter and Jesuit lay brother," *Oxford Dictionary of National Biography* (2008).

dissidence of various kinds might occur, I will refer briefly to three iconic (though strikingly different) practitioners of heterodoxy: Christopher Marlowe, Galileo Galilei, and John Donne. These well-known figures will in this case be the background against which I plan to superimpose the stories of three English dissidents who deserve to be better known: Richard Barnfield, Elizabeth Sawyer, and Sir Henry Slingsby.

Dissidence on Display

Marlowe's reputation for heterodoxy is a subject that matters a great deal to interpreters of his plays, and that is the reason why I have written about it at some length elsewhere.[3] Here I want to make only a brief observation about one of his plays: *Edward II*. In the only history play he would write, Marlowe chose to dramatize the story of a king who makes one political mistake after another and who therefore loses the support of his barons and eventually his life. The most visible provocation of this series of disasters is Edward's infatuation with his homosexual lover, Piers Gaveston, at the expense of everything else. Early in the play it would appear that the barons might be willing to turn a blind eye to Edward's heterodox tastes. Mortimer Senior, one of the most influential noblemen, argues that the young king's love affair is tolerable as a private vice:

> Let him without controlment have his will.
> The mightiest kings have had their minions:
> Great Alexander loved Hephestion;
> The conquering Hercules for Hylas wept;
> And for Patroclus stern Achilles drooped.[4]

This isn't the majority view among the barons, but it is a position clearly marked in the text as plausible. It's a position sometimes adopted by the king himself, as in his characterization of the barons' accusations as "private libelling" (2.2.34) and in his claim that he'll be glad to give away his kingdom, "So I may have some nook or corner left/To frolic with my dearest Gaveston" (1.4.72–3). Of course privacy isn't enough for

3 See "Tobacco and Boys: Christopher Marlowe," *The Performance of Pleasure in English Renaissance Drama* (Houndmills, Basingstoke: Palgrave Macmillan, 2003), 23–45.

4 *Edward the Second*, ed. Charles R. Forker, Revels Plays (Manchester: Manchester University Press, 1994), 1.4.390–4.

Edward, and in fact it doesn't protect him against the barons' antagonism. But Marlowe has raised the possibility that it might have, and that in itself is a signal as to what was thinkable in early modern culture.

For quite different reasons, Galileo is an even more celebrated icon of the heterodox than Marlowe. In a very crude sense privacy did protect Galileo: when absolutely required to he kept his mouth shut and, unlike Giordano Bruno for example, he wasn't burned at the stake. The events of Galileo's confrontation with authority are too familiar to need retelling. But I will refer to three documents in the Galileo story as a way of suggesting what it tells us about early modern privacy.

The first of these is the minutes of a meeting of the Roman Inquisition held on 25 February 1615/16:

> The Most Illustrious Lord Cardinal Millini notified the Reverend Fathers Lord Assessor and Lord Commissary of the Holy Office that, after the reporting of the judgement by the Father Theologians against the propositions of the mathematician Galileo (to the effect that the sun stands still at the center of the world and the earth moves even with the diurnal motion), His Holiness ordered the Most Illustrious Lord Cardinal Bellarmine to call Galileo before himself and warn him to abandon these opinions; and if he should refuse to obey, the Father Commissary, in the presence of a notary and witnesses, is to issue him an injunction to abstain completely from teaching or defending this doctrine and opinion or from discussing it; and further, if he should not acquiesce, he is to be imprisoned.[5]

The most revealing stylistic feature of this document is its almost preposterous blandness. Here we are, doing our normal day's work, which happens to be preventing the spread of heresy and punishing the perpetrators thereof. And we can notice parenthetically that the particular heresy is the heliocentric model of the universe, which, by the way, has been the subject of a detailed report by the appropriate subcommittee. But what interests me even more than the complacency of this text is the space it opens up, perhaps inadvertently, between Galileo's privately held opinions and his publicly declared positions. Galileo will be warned "to abandon" his "opinions," but the officers of the Inquisition have no way of

5 *The Galileo Affair: A Documentary History*, ed. and trans. Maurice A. Finocchiaro (Berkeley: University of California Press, 1989), 147.

knowing whether he will. If he refuses to comply, they will take public sanctions: he will be forbidden to teach or defend or discuss the doctrine in question. But in this formulation one suspects a tacit admission on the part of the authorities that if Galileo continues to believe in the truth of the heliocentric model, there's not much they can do about it. So they concentrate on preventing the promulgation of heresy and otherwise leave an eccentric mathematician alone.

The space between private opinion and public declaration appears to have been closed up the very next day, in the Special Injunction of 26 February 1615/16 which instructs Galileo "to abandon completely the above-mentioned opinion that the sun stands still at the center of the world and the earth moves, and henceforth not to hold, teach, or defend it in any way whatever, either orally or in writing."[6] But if this was an attempt to police the private along with the public, in was unenforceable. During the next sixteen years Galileo desisted from open advocacy of Copernicanism and turned his public attentions to less controversial work: devising more accurate instruments for measuring longitude, following up his earlier studies in dynamics, and so on. But he couldn't just stop thinking about his really big idea, so he tried to situate his thought in a rhetorically protected way in what would be his most controversial book, the *Dialogue Concerning the Two Chief Systems of the World: Ptolemaic and Copernican* (1632). It was the appearance of this text that brought him face to face with the Inquisition a second time, that led to his condemnation for heresy, to his recantation, and to his retirement at age 70 to a villa in Arcetri, where his activities would be monitored for the rest of his life by officers of the church.

Some five years after entering this enforced retirement, Galileo wrote a letter to his friend and patron Elia Diodati which begins as follows: "Alas! reverend Sir, Galileo, your devoted friend and servant, has been for a month totally and incurably blind, so that this heaven, this earth, this universe, which, by my remarkable observations and clear demonstrations, I have enlarged a hundred, nay, a thousandfold beyond the limits universally accepted by the learned men of all previous ages, are now shrivelled up for me into that narrow compass which is occupied by my own person."[7] These are moving words: the infirmities of old age and the ironies of magnification/reduction seem to conspire in a creation

6 *The Galileo Affair*, 147.
7 Quoted in J.J. Fahie, *Galileo: His Life and Work* (London: Murray, 1903), 379.

of many-layered pathos. In the present context these words suggest a further ironic relationship, namely, the virtual equation between privacy as protection and privacy as punishment. It is of course true that the Inquisition was unable to eradicate Galileo's private thoughts, and that a private independence was offered him (tacitly if not formally) in exchange for his public gestures of submission. But privacy – considered as the withdrawal of the right to publish one's ideas, the restriction of one's movements to a single observable place, or even the reduction of one's sensory apparatus to pure interiority – privacy on these terms was a crushing blow for someone of Galileo's temperament and ambition. Did privacy protect the heterodox in Galileo's case? Yes, but at a price that he found painfully difficult to pay.

Elsewhere I have written in some detail about John Donne, drawing special attention to the many difficulties that arose for him in crossing the boundary between public and private.[8] For now I wish to raise only one question that was of particular importance to Donne: the tension between his public role as an Anglican priest and his Roman Catholic upbringing. When he entered the Anglican priesthood in 1615, Donne knew that his past could be held against him. Since he soon occupied an extremely visible position within the church, as Dean of St Paul's and as one of the outstanding preachers of his day, Donne had ample opportunity to distance himself from his Catholic heritage. And distance himself he did. In a Lincoln's Inn sermon preached around Easter 1620 Donne expresses the view that, though the Reformation has obliged the Roman church to clean up her act a bit, there's still ample ground for hostility:

> in that capacity as they were our enemies in 88. when they provoked by their *Excommunications,* dangerous invasions, and in that capacity as they were our enemies in 1605. when they bent their malice even against that place, where the Laws for the maintenance of our religion were enacted, so they are our enemies still, if we be still of the same religion. He that by God's mercy to us, leads us, is as sure that the *Pope* is *Antichrist,* now, as he was *then*; and we that are blessedly led by him, are as sure, that their doctrine is the doctrine of *Devils,* now, as we were then.[9]

8 See "'Study our Manuscripts': John Donne's Problems with Privacy," *The Seventeenth Century* 26, no. 1 (2011): 1–22.

9 *The Sermons of John Donne,* ed. Evelyn M. Simpson and George R. Potter (Berkeley: University of California Press, 1953–84), 3:124.

The general tone of this passage is about as rabidly xenophobic as anyone could wish, but I suspect that Donne has crafted it with great care so as to represent the authorized Anglican position, but not necessarily his own point of view. Notice that the belief "that the *Pope* is *Antichrist*" is explicitly attributed to King James, and while this makes it in one sense unassailable, it also says nothing about what John Donne thinks, either as an individual Christian or as a theologian. Further analysis of the rhetoric of this passage would only reveal other ingenuities by means of which Donne avoids attributing anti-Catholic hatred directly and personally to himself, though he certainly encourages the public perception of himself as a scourge of Rome.

Donne's private utterances on this question, insofar as they can be recovered, were remarkably ecumenical. In a letter to Sir Henry Goodyer, for example, he reassures his friend that a tolerant attitude towards Christians of differing professions isn't a sign of lukewarmness. Apparently Goodyer has received overtures from people seeking to convert him to Catholicism, an event which Donne now interprets as follows: "let me be bold to fear, that that sound true opinion, that in all Christian professions there is way to salvation (which I think you think) may have been so imcommodiously or intempestively sometimes uttered by you; or else your having friends equally near you of all the impressions of Religion, may have testified such an indifferency, as hath occasioned some to further such inclinations, as they have mistaken to be in you." And the charitable ecumenism which Donne attributes to his friend, he is quite willing to claim as his own. He advances the notion that the "formes, and dressings of Religion" are the product of habit and custom, and therefore culturally relative. As for Protestant and Catholic religion explicitly, "The channels of Gods mercies run through both fields; and they are sister teats of his graces, yet both diseased and infected, but not both alike."[10] Even when he's offering reassurance, as in this image of God's nurturing care, Donne is painfully aware of human imperfection – of sin, as he would say – and hence the grotesque effect when the nurturing body is declared unclean. Still, he remains even-handed: the Catholic and Protestant breasts are both "infected" because human beings and human institutions are fallen from grace.

10 *Selected Prose*, ed. Evelyn Simpson, Helen Gardner, and Timothy Healy (Oxford: Clarendon, 1967), 146–7.

When his sister Anne died, perhaps around 1616, Donne wrote a letter of condolence to his mother. The tribulations of her life, Donne tells his mother, are God's way of ensuring that she will have no leisure to stray while he's guiding her to her destination, "which is his glorious Kingdom." His mother's status as a lifelong Catholic has no bearing on Donne's assessment of where she's going, nor for that matter on how she ought to get there: "As long as the Spirit of God distills and dews his cheerfulnesse upon your heart; as long as he instructs your understanding, to interpret his mercies and his judgments aright; so long your comfort must needs be as much greater than others, as your afflictions are greater than theirs."[11] Is this just a pious formula, no different from what Donne would have addressed to any of his parishioners? Even worse, is it an insincere pious formula, addressed to a Catholic woman by an Anglican son who believes that she's destined to eternal damnation regardless of what he says? The answer to both questions is no. In the same letter Donne offers his mother material reassurance, by telling her that there will always be room in his household for her, should she require it. And indeed she lived the last years of her life, after the death of her third husband, with Donne at the Deanery. Faced with a choice between a narrow, sectarian commitment to the Church of England (which would have meant, as John Carey points out, "consigning his own family to damnation")[12] and a more liberal conviction that salvation is available through many Christian churches, Donne chose the second alternative.

This left him on insecure ground, especially at a time when wars and executions were regularly justified with sectarian rhetoric. The insecurity of his position is registered with great subtlety in his poems, as for example in Satire 3, where the person who would "Seek true religion" is told that "On a huge hill,/Cragged, and steep, Truth stands, and he that will/Reach her, about must, and about must go."[13] Although the satire, written early in his career, shows Donne already wrestling with the question of true religion, the problem is still with him when, much later on, he addresses it quite brilliantly in Holy Sonnet 18:

11 Ibid., 149.

12 *John Donne: Life, Mind and Art* (London: Faber, 1981), 29.

13 *The Complete English Poems*, ed. A.J. Smith (Harmondsworth: Penguin, 1971), 163. Further citations of Donne's poems are from this edition, and are given by page number only in parentheses.

Show me dear Christ, thy spouse, so bright and clear.
What, is it she, which on the other shore
Goes richly painted? or which robbed and tore
Laments and mourns in Germany and here?
Sleeps she a thousand, then peeps out one year?
Is she self truth and errs? now new, now outwore?
Doth she, and did she, and shall she evermore
On one, on seven, or on no hill appear?
Dwells she with us, or like adventuring knights
First travail we to seek and then make love?
Betray kind husband thy spouse to our sights,
And let mine amorous soul court thy mild dove,
Who is most true, and pleasing to thee, then
When she' is embraced and open to most men. (316)

In a sustained and artful playing out of the traditional metaphor of the church as the bride of Christ, Donne poses a series of questions which imply that the various churches of the contingent present or the historical past aren't identical with the true church, "thy spouse, so bright and clear." In figuring the Roman Catholic version as "richly painted," Donne is unavoidably calling upon the Protestant trope of the Roman church as the whore of Babylon. This would seem to settle the question, since the Reformed church, though "robbed and tore," has no comparable disgrace to live down. So you'd expect the conclusion that the true church appears not on seven hills (Rome), nor in the absence of hills (Geneva), but on the one hill, Ludgate Hill, the location of St Paul's. But the poem resists this conclusion by putting the business of hills into an unanswered question and by claiming, in the last four lines, that the true church has yet to be revealed. The anticipated revelation is implicitly an act of disrobing: Christ is asked to "Betray" his spouse by making her visible to the speaker's "amorous soul." And the nakedness of the spouse will be a good thing, because it will make her generally available, "open to most men." What looked like prostitution in the early goings is really a sign of the universal love of God as revealed in the body of the church, "most true" when most accessible.

Where does this poem stand in relation to Donne's public repudiation and private tolerance of Roman Catholicism? Somewhere between the extremes, to be sure: it is neither a sermon directed towards a large audience, nor a letter addressed to a single, especially trusted reader. But it is probably closer to the private sphere both in tone and in provenance. Like most of Donne's poems, it wasn't published during his lifetime. Unlike most of them, it appears in only one manuscript (the Westmoreland) and therefore didn't make it into the first edition of Donne's poems (1633), nor into the second edition assembled by Donne's son (1650), nor into any printed collection of his verse before Edmund Gosse's *Jacobean Poets* (1894). If Donne wanted his insecurity about religious affiliation to be a private matter, he had his way for some 274 years. Did privacy protect the heterodox in Donne's case? Yes, but only because Donne was extremely clever. Clever enough to surround his private thoughts with gestures that could be read as endorsements of a conformity he was pledged to uphold but found it impossible to venerate.

Loving a Sweet-Faced Boy

Richard Barnfield reached the pinnacle of his literary fame at the age of twenty with the publication, in quick succession, of *The Affectionate Shepheard* (1594) and *Cynthia, With Certaine Sonnets, and the Legend of Cassandra* (1595). The most striking feature of *The Affectionate Shepheard* is the relationship between a character called Daphnis (who does most of the talking) and a character called Ganimede (who has to do a lot of listening). Daphnis makes the quality of his infatuation with Ganimede both obvious and, in its way, appealing:

If it be sinne to love a sweet-fac'd Boy,
(Whose amber locks trust up in golden tramels
Dangle adowne his lovely cheekes with joy,
When pearle and flowers his faire haire enamels)
If it be sinne to love a lovely Lad;
Oh then sinne I, for whom my soule is sad.[14]

The unapologetic presentation of same-sex attraction appears to have caused Barnfield some difficulty, to judge by the awkward manoeuvres by which he tries to hedge his bets in "To the courteous Gentlemen Readers" prefixed to his next volume, *Cynthia.* He begins by acknowledging

14 Richard Barnfield, *The Complete English Poems,* ed. George Klawitter (Selinsgrove, PA: Susquehanna University Press, 1990), 79–80. Unless otherwise noted, all Barnfield citations are from this edition.

authorship of the book he had published anonymously just months ago: "the last Terme there came forth a little toy of mine, intituled, *The affectionate Shepheard.*" He then claims that some readers "did interpret" the book "otherwise then (in truth) I meant, touching the subject thereof, to wit, the love of a Shepheard to a boy; a fault, the which I will not excuse, because I never made. Onely this, I will unshaddow my conceit: being nothing else, but an imitation of *Virgill,* in the second Eglogue of *Alexis*" (115–16). Barnfield seems to be asking his readers, especially if they were shocked by the homoerotic passion expressed by Daphnis, to take his previous book as a literary exercise, and one with legitimate classical precedents at that. But readers who took him at his word might then have been surprised by the sequence of twenty sonnets (the *Certaine Sonnets* of the title) printed in the middle of *Cynthia.* In Sonnet 1 the gender of the love object is identified, in Sonnet 4 his name is given as Ganymede, and in Sonnet 6 the speaker refers to himself as Daphnis. If the pattern emerging is no more than a literary exercise, it seems to be remarkably persistent. And it is a pattern that gives rise to the creation of some remarkable poems, of which Sonnet 11 is my favourite:

> Sighing, and sadly sitting by my Love,
> He ask't the cause of my hearts sorrowing,
> Conjuring me by heavens eternall King
> To tell the cause which me so much did move.
> Compell'd: (quoth I) to thee I will confesse,
> Love is the cause; and only love it is
> That doth deprive me of my heavenly blisse.
> Love is the paine that doth my heart oppresse.
> And what is she (quoth he) whom thou do'st love?
> Looke in this glasse (quoth I) there shalt thou see
> The perfect forme of my faelicitie.
> When, thinking that it would strange Magique prove,
> He open'd it: and taking off the cover,
> He straight perceav'd himselfe to be my Lover. (127)

The word "glasse" (l. 10) appears in a context which confers upon it the primary meaning of "mirror," and that is exactly how it is glossed in Klawitter's edition (232). Ganymede takes the word in a slightly different sense, namely as referring to a "magic mirror, a crystal, etc., used in magic art" (*OED n.* 8e). So he expects the glass to reveal, by magic, the "perfect forme" (l. 11) of the woman who has captured the speaker's attention.

When the glass turns out to be a simple mirror, Ganymede suddenly learns what the reader has known all along: this is a text in which "love" describes the relationship between a man and another man. Only the reader who doesn't want to see the truth will now be taking Barnfield's prefatory disclaimer seriously. Montague Summers finds the disclaimer "singularly unconvincing and lukewarm" precisely because, for him, the love of Daphnis for Ganymede, as Barnfield represents it, "rings true in every turn, in every line."[15] I think Summers is right to claim for Barnfield a distinguished place in the long tradition of homoerotic writing, however uncomfortable such a visible position may have felt to a poet still just twenty years old.[16]

Barnfield's poetry has been in the public domain for almost as long as Shakespeare's, and it did attract some early notice: Francis Meres included Barnfield's name (along with Sidney's and Spenser's) in a list of poets who excel in the pastoral.[17] But nobody tried to write a life of Barnfield until the nineteenth century. Anthony à Wood had not made an entry for him in *Athenae Oxoniensis*, so it was left to Philip Bliss to begin the task when he undertook to revise this text in 1813; his work was then supplemented by Alexander B. Grosart and others in the later nineteenth century.[18] For Barnfield's early life these scholars were able to establish a scenario that has remained largely unchanged for well over a hundred years. He was born in June 1574 at Norbury, Staffordshire, the eldest son of Richard Barnfield, Gent., and Mary Skrymsher, both of whom came from the land-owning classes.[19] His mother died in 1581, when the poet was not yet seven, leaving behind her Richard and three

15 "Introduction," *The Poems of Richard Barnfield*, ed. Montague Summers (London: Fortune Press, [1936]), xiv, xiii.

16 For intelligent and ingeniously researched commentary on Summers's investment in Barnfield's poems, see David Theodore, "'Gay' Is the Right Word: Montague Summers and the Replevin of Richard Barnfield," in *The Affectionate Shepherd: Celebrating Richard Barnfield*, ed. Kenneth Borris and George Klawitter (Selinsgrove, PA: Susquehanna University Press, 2001) 265–79.

17 See *Palladis Tamia* (London: P. Short, 1598), 2O4. And on the very next page (2O4^{v}), Meres refers to him as "my friend master *Richard Barnfielde.*"

18 See Wood, *Athenae Oxoniensis*, ed. Philip Bliss (London: Rivington, 1813–20), 1:683–4, and *The Complete Poems of Richard Barnfield*, ed. Alexander B. Grosart (London: J.B. Nichols, 1876).

19 My account of Barnfield's life relies on Andrew Worrall's "Biographical Introduction" to *The Affectionate Shepherd: Celebrating Richard Barnfield*, 25–38.

younger siblings: Robert, John, and Dorothea. Richard matriculated at Brasenose College, Oxford, on 27 November 1589 at age fifteen, and qualified for the BA in February 1591/2. He appears to have continued working towards the MA, but was not awarded that degree. The next reliable documents are his publications, two of which I have already cited as appearing in 1594 and 1595.

If the shape of Barnfield's early life has remained stable for a century and more, the exact opposite is true for his later years, about which little is known and much has been conjectured. The will of Richard Barnfield, dated 26 February 1626/7 and held in the Lichfield Joint Record Office, used to be read as evidence that Barnfield married and settled down to a comfortable heterosexual life, and was rewarded for doing so both by inheriting his father's considerable estates and by the birth of a son (Robert) and a granddaughter (Jane), both of whom are singled out for bequests in the will. But Andrew Worrall exploded this tranquil image in 1992 when he published "Richard Barnfield: A New Biography," an article of perhaps 500 words based on research he did for his MA thesis at the University of Keele.[20] Worrall established beyond reasonable doubt that the much-cited will was not the poet's, but that of his father, also called Richard Barnfield. If this is true, then the poet's name is conspicuously absent from the will, which provides quite handsomely for his younger brother Robert. Worrall further discovered that the process of disinheriting the poet had begun in 1598. A patent roll entry from that year names Robert heir of the Barnfield lands, an arrangement confirmed by another such document in 1602. The poet Richard Barnfield may have known about his own sinking fortunes when he prepared his final book for publication, *The Encomion of Lady Pecunia: or The Praise of Money* (1598). This time Barnfield mentions Erasmus in his prefatory statement, and suggests a parallel between his master's *Praise of Folly* and his own treatment of money. But the long opening poem, "The Prayse of Lady Pecunia," shows that Barnfield doesn't have the lightness of touch required to play this game. And perhaps he has too many practical concerns, as he willingly admits in the next poem, "The Complaint of Poetrie, for the Death of Liberalitie." The weakness here is that the message is only too transparent. Barnfield writes like someone whose access

20 *Notes and Queries* 237 (1992): 370–1.

to the patronage network is being denied. Perhaps this is the splendidly public network, which had people like the earl of Southampton on the top rung (if you were William Shakespeare) or Lucy countess of Bedford (if you were John Donne). Or the problem may have arisen much closer to home, if Barnfield had been accustomed to financial support from his well-to-do father and found that he could no longer count on either money or goodwill. In either case, poetry is now in the position of "The Merchants wife," who can only hope "To see her Husband" (168) when he returns from his overseas adventure. The speaker of the poem is in a worse position: "But I, whose hope is turned to despaire,/Nere looke to see my dearest Deare againe" (168). In fact the speaker's case is like Damon's, when he "bewailed" the death of Pythias, or like Pylades mourning for Orestes. As this pattern of similes continues, it implies that real deprivation is something that happens between men:

> If *Hercules*, for *Hylas* losse were quailed;
> Or *Theseus*, for *Pyrithous* Teares did spend:
> When doe I mourne for *Bounty*, being dead:
> Who living, was my hand, my hart, my head. (168)

When Barnfield reaches for examples of profound emotion, it is once again emotion that arises from the relationship of one man to another. He may even be remembering Mortimer Senior's speech from *Edward II*, quoted at the outset of this chapter, in which Hercules is said to have "wept" for Hylas, an instance which is cited in service of the claim that "The mightiest kings have had their minions." Barnfield would certainly have had the opportunity to see *Edward II* performed, and the play's treatment of homoerotic relations would have been of great interest to him.

But I have just now been indulging in conjecture, and it is conjecture, albeit of another sort, that has led in the past to a distorted rendition of Barnfield's life story. Of course no document stands entirely on its own, not even the entry of 6 February 1620/1 in the Market Drayton parish register "which records the death of 'Richard Barnfield son of Richard Barnfield.'"[21] When he published these words in 1992, Worrall was sure that they referred to the poet, who could not have been mentioned in

21 Worrall, "A New Biography," 371.

his father's will because he had died years ago. In his later account of the poet's life, Worrall is less dogmatic, since he is now aware of an entry in the Newport parish register which records the burial of "Ricardus Barnfield" in the family tomb on 5 May 1626.[22] Clearly there were several persons called Richard Barnfield in this vicinity at this time. Still, if either of these two parish registers records the death of the poet, in neither case does he outlive his father.

Just one more document needs to be read into the record, this one pertaining to the poet's boyhood. Fred Clitheroe deserves credit for drawing attention to the following account, preserved in the Shrewsbury City Library, of the death of a woman who appears to have been the poet's mother:

> 1581. This yeare and in the moonthe of Maye one Mystress Barnefilld of Newport being xii myles from Shrewsbery kyllyd hyr sellffe the cause thereof was that not onley shee being gellows of hyr husband and also not p'fect in myde, one night being in bed w[i]th hyr sayde husband and holdinge a nackid knyffe in hyr hand wold have cutt hyr husbands throte and myssinge hys wesand pype awackid upon the same and stayed hyr furie and so callyd for helpe and locked hyr in a darcke chambere without any knyffe about hyr or any thinge ells to hurt hyr sellffe, but w[i]thin a day or twoe she aspieed a rusty broade arrowe hedd in a pryvey place and therewith cut hyr owne throate most wyckydly.[23]

If this account is in any sense accurate, then it sweeps away the passive death from complications in childbirth that was earlier taken for granted. Barnfield was only a boy of six at the time, and one hopes he was spared the details of this event, though of course he could not escape its impact.

Perhaps there is a connection between the abrupt departure of his mother and the hostility which colours almost all representations of women in Barnfield's poems. (Queen Elizabeth is the exception who, by means of her symbolic exemption from any human failing, simply helps

22 "Biographical Introduction," 36.

23 Printed in *The Life and Selected Writings of Richard Barnfield, 1574–1627*, ed. Fred Clitheroe (Newcastle: Lymes Press, 1992), 15. I quote Worrall's transcription of this document ("Biographical Introduction," 27–8), and rely on his notation of the source and location of this manuscript (37n1).

to prove the rule.) Guendolen in *The Affectionate Shepheard* is beautiful but unfaithful, prompting Daphnis to offer Ganimede this advice:

> Take not a flattring woman to thy wife,
> A shameless creature, full of wanton words,
> (Whose bad, thy good; whose lust will end thy life,
> Cutting thy hart with sharpe two edged swords:). (96)

In the narrative poem "Cassandra," which concludes *Cynthia*, Barnfield reinterprets the matter of ancient Greece so as to make the female players look like a nest of vipers. Cassandra herself extracts the gift of prophecy from Apollo in exchange for the promise of sexual favours, which she promptly denies as soon as she has her prophetic power. After this it will be no surprise to find Clytemnestra in bed with Aegistus when Agamemnon comes home, or that "this weeping Crocodile" (144) will conspire in the murder of her husband and king. The poem as a whole has a certain energy, most of it directed towards affirming its one Latin sentence: "Muliere ne credas, ne mortuae quidem" (138); never trust a woman, not even when she's dead. It is true of course that we can find copious evidence of misogyny everywhere in the culture that Barnfield inhabited, but this strikes me as anxiety of a special kind. Misogyny is a vice from which Barnfield could not escape.

Did privacy protect the heterodox in the case of Richard Barnfield? On the whole the answer is no, though we have to add the proviso that nothing of substance is known about him between 1598 and the end of his life. A second edition of his last book, this time under the title *Lady Pecunia or The Praise of Money*, did appear in 1605, with a new "Epistle-Dedicatory" (151) in heroic couplets and several added stanzas which acknowledge that "ELIZA" is no longer the "sacred Soveraigne" (157) of the land, though her "Successor" now embodies all of "her virtues" (241). But this is hardly enough to repay Richard Barnfield's admirers for his virtual disappearance from the historical record. Perhaps it would be more accurate to say that he was disciplined, punished, and silenced than that he retreated to a private haven. Or, to change the terms just slightly, we might say that publication was a step so decisive for Barnfield that he was never able to retrieve his privacy. Within the structure of his family, the eldest son was expected to be a breeder; the poet's failure to comply with this expectation led no doubt to surveillance and at length to denial of his birthright. The family that had otherwise provided for him did not foster the kind of privacy that could have protected him.

The Surveillance of Mother Sawyer

The life of Elizabeth Sawyer came to an end at Tyburn on 19 April 1621 when she was hanged for allegedly practising witchcraft. Her story has been preserved in two radically different versions: (1) a pamphlet which purports to be a documentary account of her misdeeds, confirmed by legal testimony and her own confession, all of it compiled by Henry Goodcole, who served as her chaplain while she awaited execution in Newgate prison; and (2) a theatrical reinterpretation of these events as one plot in *The Witch of Edmonton*, a play hastily but artfully put together by William Rowley, Thomas Dekker, and John Ford for performance by the Prince's men later that year. Even though the play depends on the pamphlet as part of its source material, I want to keep the two versions quite separate at the outset, and will therefore begin with an account of Goodcole's pamphlet by itself. To discover what the pamphlet has to tell us about Elizabeth Sawyer, we may have to begin by pretending that the play about her never happened at all.

The pamphlet is of course not the compilation of objective truth, but the work of a particular, fallible person. Goodcole (1586–1641) spent most of his adult life doing the work of a prison chaplain, first at Ludgate (1613–20) and then at Newgate, where he was "ordinary and visitor" (1620–35). He wrote a series of six pamphlets about London criminals, all of them purporting to offer the unvarnished truth in contrast to "what he sees as the false, popular versions of events recorded in contemporary ballads or plays."[24] Marion Gibson describes each of his crime pamphlets in sequence, and notices that over time Goodcole develops an "eye for the lurid and sentimental possibilities of print, and for the sensational (particularly sexual) detail."[25] Yes, he wants to tell the truth, but he wants to sell it to his readers too. And, as his rhetoric will suggest again and again, he very much wants to be believed.

But Goodcole is never really on his own, in the sense that his work would be impossible without the collaboration of a precisely articulated legal system on the one hand, and a deeply held set of social and moral convictions on the other. In the case of Elizabeth Sawyer's trial, the legal

24 Christopher Chapman, "Goodcole, Henry (bap. 1586, d. 1641)," *Oxford Dictionary of National Biography* (2004).

25 *Early Modern Witches: Witchcraft Cases in Contemporary Writing* (London: Routledge, 2000), 300.

system required that, as a resident of Middlesex, she be tried in the Old Bailey before a Bench (consisting of the aldermen of the City of London, the recorder, and the mayor) and a Jury. The social and moral backing for Goodcole's work came from a wide variety of sources, not all of them textual, not all of them English. Perhaps the most inescapable of these would have been King James's *Daemonologie*, published in 1587 while he was still no more than James VI of Scotland. The dialogue form in which this discourse is cast should prevent nobody from noticing that the questions posed by Philomanthes (lover of learning) are just soft lobs that allow Epistemon (Mr know-it-all) to score point after point after point. So Epistemon tells us that the devil recruits witches by approaching them when they are "solitarie" with promises of "worldly commoditie" (if they are poor) or of satisfaction "to their hartes contentment" (if they desire revenge, for example). If they consent to his temptation, he "makes them to renounce God and *Baptisme* directlie, and gives them his marke upon some secreit place of their bodie."[26] After they have been tried and found guilty, witches "ought to be put to death according to the Law of God, the civill and imperial law, and municipall law of all Christian nations" (77). When the author of these words became King of England in 1603, persons interested in stamping out witchcraft must have felt a sense of empowerment. Perhaps that is what Goodcole is referring to when he inserts the words "*Published by Authority*" on the title page of his pamphlet.[27]

As Goodcole tells the story, the deaths of "Nurse-children and Cattell" (A4) in the community of Edmonton led some of the neighbours to suspect Elizabeth Sawyer of causing these events; to confirm their suspicions "an old ridiculous custome was used, which was to plucke the Thatch of her house, and to burne it, and it being so burnd, the author of such mischiefe should presently then come" (A4–A4^{v}). Sure enough, the court was told, Sawyer would respond to such tests by showing up, uninvited, at the house of whoever had burned her thatch. They did not have to be told, though Goodcole tells his readers, that "Her face was most pale & ghoast-like," that "Her body was crooked and deformed"

26 *Daemonologie* (1597): *News from Scotland* (1591), Elizabethan and Jacobean Quartos, ed. G.B. Harrison (1922; repr., Edinburgh: Edinburgh University Press, 1966), 32–3.

27 *The Wonderfull Discoverie of Elizabeth Sawyer a Witch, Late of Edmonton, Her Conviction and Condemnation and Death: Together with the Relation of the Divels Accesse to Her, and Their Conference Together* (London: William Butler, 1621), A2.

by being excessively bent over (A4^{v}), or that one of her eyes had been "*put out*" (D1). Goodcole may have assumed that the Jury would notice, though he troubles to tell his readers, that Sawyer was "a very ignorant woman" (C1).

Once she had been arraigned, Sawyer was required to defend herself against these accusations: (1) that she used witchcraft to cause the deaths of babies and cattle; and (2) that she used witchcraft to cause the death of her neighbour, Agnes Ratcleife (B1^{v}–B2). Things went very badly indeed for her, when various neighbours testified against her and Agnes Ratcleife's husband reported that, on her deathbed, his wife asserted that "if shee did die at that time shee would verily take it on her death, that *Elizabeth Sawyer* her neighbour, whose Sowe with a washing-Beetle she had stricken, and so for that cause her malice being great, was the occasion of her death" (B2). It appears that Sawyer's pig had eaten a piece of Ratcleife's soap, which prompted the blow with the washing tool, which created the motive for murder.

But how could the jurors be certain that they were dealing here with a case of witchcraft? Arthur Robinson, Justice of the Peace at the nearby town of Tottenham, supplied "An Information" reported to him by several informants, "that this *Elizabeth Sawyer* had a private and strange marke on her body" (B3). On hearing this, the Bench created a panel of three women to examine the body of the accused. This they promptly did, despite Sawyer's resistance (she "behaved her selfe most sluttishly and loathsomely towards them" [B4]), and a mark they found, just above the accused's anus, in the form of "a thing like a Teate the bignesse of the little finger, and the length of halfe a finger, which was branched at the top like a teate, and seemed as though one had suckt it, and that the bottome thereof was blew, and the top of it was redde" (B3^{v}). This new evidence led the Jury to pronounce her "guilty, by di[a]bolicall help, of the death of *Agnes Ratcliefe*" (B3^{v}), though she was acquitted of the charges relating to nurselings and cattle.

The trial, held on 14 April 1621, would lead to Sawyer's execution five days later. But, in the meantime, Goodcole had privileged access to the condemned woman, and he made the most of it. The last half of his pamphlet uses the question-and-answer format, with Goodcole posing the questions (in italics) and Sawyer providing the answers. From the very first question it is obvious that Goodcole is conducting not an interview designed to discover the truth, but an interrogation directed at confirming guilt. "*By what meanes came you to have acquaintance with the Divell, and when was the first time that you saw him, and how did you know that it was the*

Divell?" (C1), Goodcole asks, in a risibly flagrant case of the fallacy of many questions (as in "Have you stopped beating your wife yet?"). It's only a matter of time until we learn that Sawyer first summoned the devil some eight years ago by "cursing, swearing and blaspheming" (C1–1[v]), and that he has been visiting her subsequently three times a week, on average. He came to her "Alwayes in the shape of a dogge and of two collars, sometimes of blacke and sometimes of white" (C2[v]). She called her devil Tom, and she did "*handle*" him: "Yes, I did stroake him on the backe, and then he would becke unto me, and wagge his tayle as being therewith contented" (D1). If this is sounding a little too much like an ordinary relationship between an old woman and a friendly animal, we should remind ourselves of Goodcole's question, "*In what place of your body did the Divell sucke of your blood ... ?*" and of Sawyer's answer that he would suck the "thing in the forme of a Teate" (C3–3[v]) that grows above her "fundiment" (C3) for about a quarter of an hour at a time, while she felt no pain whatsoever. She did not pull up her garments to give the devil access to her, but he "would put his head under my coates, and I did willingly suffer him to do what hee would" (C3[v]). Whatever is going on here may not sound much like witchcraft to a postmodern reader, but a Jury in 1621 had been convinced.

It is difficult to estimate the degree to which the answers were in fact Sawyer's own, because Goodcole himself is writing down every word. And it's impossible, partly for this reason, to infer how Sawyer really felt about her predicament. By the time of the interview, it was too late to escape hanging, and there may have been an element of bravado in her willingness to be seen as the devil's partner. This might be her motive for declaring that she did cause the death of her neighbours' cattle, along with the sudden addendum: "And do now further confesse, that I was the cause of those two nurse-childrens death, for the which I was now indited and acquitted, by the Jury" (C2). Still, as to the murder of Agnes Ratcleife, Sawyer accepts no responsibility: "No, I did not by my meanes procure against her the least hurt" (C2[v]). Clearly she is implying that the legal proceedings against her have been subject to error: the crime for which she has been sentenced to die is exactly the one she claims she did not commit.

Without making any attempt to address this problem, Goodcole reconfigures the interview as a "confession" (D2), which he himself reads out to the onlookers at the place of execution two days later and which Sawyer confirms ("I here doe acknowledge, to all the people that are here present, that it is all truth" [D2–2[v]]) before turning to God for forgiveness.

There are signs of scepticism in this curious document, but they are signs that the author is very eager to erase. The confirmation I have just quoted ("that it is all truth") I believe is one such sign. If the proceeding against Sawyer were as credible as Goodcole wants (and wants us) to believe, then this last act of confirmation, by the witch herself, no less, would be utterly unnecessary. The question of what would follow from her failure to cooperate at this stage doesn't even arise. Sometimes the erasure of scepticism takes the form of marginal notes, in which Goodcole explains how or why he asked a particular question. When he asks her whether she pulled up her "coates" so as to let the devil suck her, he feels called upon to defend his own motives: "This I asked of her very earnestly, and shee thus answered me, without any studying for an answer" (C3^{v}). Readers who suspect Goodcole of impropriety or Sawyer of embellishment are being disarmed by the single-minded quest for truth that motivates both partners in the dialogue.

If Goodcole allows into his text only such signs of scepticism as he thinks he can erase, that is no guarantee of the compliance of all readers. Indeed, the three readers who prepared a theatrical script, *The Witch of Edmonton,* for performance within a few months of the execution, seem to be interested in systematically creating space for doubt about the authorized version of the story. Such space is opened up in part by the very wide gap between the viewpoint taken by the citizens of Edmonton and the position articulated by the Elizabeth Sawyer character herself. When Old Banks finds that his horse has developed "the glanders," he knows at once that the problem "is long of this jadish witch, Mother Sawyer" (4.1.1–6).[28] A neighbour reports that his wife has been "bewitched" into cuckolding him, "and what witch have we about us but Mother Sawyer?" (4.1.10–12). Soon there is an outcry of hatred. One citizen does the trick of burning a handful of her thatch, and when Sawyer appears in response to this, they all cry "Out, witch! Beat her, kick her, set fire on her!" (4.1.33). What we are witnessing here is very clearly some form of mob rule, and, as I will show in due course, the playwrights are careful to situate it as such.

---

28 William Rowley, Thomas Dekker, and John Ford, *The Witch of Edmonton,* ed. Peter Corbin and Douglas Sedge, Revels Student Editions (Manchester: Manchester University Press, 1999), 95. Subsequent references are to this edition.

But first I want to draw attention to Elizabeth Sawyer's own voice, as created through theatrical mimesis. Whichever of the three playwrights wrote her part (and the consensus here would point to Dekker), he was able to give her something far more engaging (and far more terrifying in its way) than the words Goodcole ventriloquized for his witch-puppet. From the moment she appears onstage, Sawyer is eager to contest the neighbourhood's interpretation of her character:

> And why on me? Why should the envious world
> Throw all their scandalous malice upon me? (2.1.1–2)

She admits that she's "poor, deformed and ignorant,/And like a bow buckled and bent together" (2.1.3–4), but this in itself doesn't make her a witch. Indeed, if she's a witch at all, it's because her community has made her one:

> Some call me witch,
> And, being ignorant of myself, they go
> About to teach me how to be one. (2.1.8–10)

These words of resistance are spoken by Sawyer when she is alone on stage, and since they lead directly to a scene in which she is beaten and abused, they will have a powerful impact in performance. The spectators will not exonerate her of all wrongdoing, because there is too much evidence of her complicity in mischief later on. But the audience will likewise refuse to adopt the mob mentality which the citizens of Edmonton have decided to endorse. The playwrights make it virtually impossible to do so when they introduce, just at the high point of rampant anti-witch hysteria, a new character identified only as "*a* Justice" (4.1.35.1), who takes it upon himself to reprimand the mob. "How now? Forbear this violence!" (4.1.37) he warns, and he points out that suspicions are not proofs: "Come, come. Firing her thatch? Ridiculous! Take heed, sirs, what you do. Unless your proofs come better armed, instead of turning her into a witch, you'll prove yourselves stark fools" (4.1.48–51). The playwrights have gone out of their way to ensure that a sceptical voice is heard. Indeed, it is a voice very much like that of Reginald Scot, who wrote as follows in *The Discoverie of Witchcraft*: "One sort of such as are said to be witches, are women which be commonly old, lame, bleare-eied, pale, fowle, and full of wrinkles; poore, sullen, superstitious, and papists; or such as knowe no religion: in whose drousie minds the divell hath goten a fine seat; so as, what mischeefe, mischance, calamitie, or slaughter is brought to passe, they are easily persuaded the same is doone by themselves; imprinting in their minds an earnest and constant imagination hereof."[29] If this is exactly the popular stereotype embodied by Elizabeth Sawyer, according to Scot it is no more than that: "But whatsoever is reported or conceived of such maner of witchcrafts, I dare avow to be false and fabulous" (7). This may not be the unanimous conclusion which all spectators took away from the early performances of *The Witch of Edmonton* in 1621, but it was certainly a position that had been made available to them.

To the citizens of Edmonton, however, witchcraft is a threatening power which strikes at their livelihoods and their lives, and which they seek to control by retaliating against its representative, Mother Sawyer (as they call her). The damage done by her may be in dispute until Anne Ratcliffe, who (as in Goodcole's account) has angered Sawyer by striking her sow, enters "*mad*" (4.1.187.1) to Sawyer's great delight, and then, according to this report by her husband, comes to a bad end: "spite of our strengths away she brake, and nothing in her mouth being heard but 'the devil, the witch, the witch, the devil', she beat out her own brains, and so died" (4.1.223–6). The sceptical advocacy of restraint will not put to rest the agitation set in motion by events such as these.

To Elizabeth Sawyer, witchcraft looks very different indeed, but it is nonetheless real enough. For her, witchcraft is lived primarily through her relationship to the character called Dog, whom she refers to also as Tom. This can be no ordinary domestic pet, because it speaks, it offers its services to Sawyer, it laughs, and it even "*plays the morris*" on one occasion (3.4.56.1), so this is clearly a role for a gifted and versatile actor. Not that Dog's canine qualities are entirely obliterated: he does bark at times, and when Sawyer summons him "*he fawns and leaps upon her*" (2.1.251.2). The physical intimacy between them does develop an erotic dimension, not only because of the rumour that she "maintains a spirit that sucks her" (4.1.105), but also because of the language in which they converse. When Sawyer tells Dog he will have to wait for "the teat" (4.1.166), he is impatient: "Bow, wow! I'll have it now" (167). She insists that he be patient:

29 *The Discoverie of Witchcraft*, ed. Montague Summers (1930; repr., New York: Dover, 1972), 4.

I am dried up
With cursing and with madness, and have yet
No blood to moisten these sweet lips of thine.
Stand on thy hind-legs up. Kiss me, my Tommy,
And rub away some wrinkles on my brow
By making my old ribs to shrug for joy
Of thy fine tricks. What hast thou done? Let's tickle. (167–73)

There could be no better word to capture the tone of this moment than "foreplay," although the consummation we will witness comes in the form of Sawyer's mockery of mad Anne Ratcliffe and the simple command she now gives Dog: "Touch her" (4.1.203). The next thing we hear of Ratcliffe is the report of her suicide.

I do not think that a coherent view about witchcraft can be extracted from *The Witch of Edmonton.* A coherent view is trying very hard to assert itself in Goodcole's pamphlet, but the play offers a series of hypothetical explanations and appears to be unable to decide between them. Still, for all of the differences which separate pamphlet and play, the two accounts seem to agree on one point: in Elizabeth Sawyer's case, privacy offered no protection to the heterodox. Sawyer's exposure to the ill will of others may be in part the result of her membership in a fundamentally rural community, Edmonton being situated seven miles north of London. Here everyone is expected to know everyone else's business, and there is no escape from the cruelty of gossip. In part Sawyer's exposure is due also to her vulnerability: her village is a strictly hierarchical community, and she occupies the bottom rung of the ladder. And her exposure may be due in part to her failure to control what one commentator calls "that glibbery member," the tongue.[30] If Elizabeth Sawyer had been able to bridle her tongue, the citizens of Edmonton would have been more likely to ignore her, or, to put it another way, if she had not been in the habit of cursing and blaspheming, the devil might not have appeared to her in the shape of a Dog. As things turned out, in both versions of the story, her private space – what little she may have had of it – was easily permeated by her neighbours or her demons or both.

30 Richard Brathwait, *The English Gentlewoman, Drawne out to the Full Body* (London: B. Alsop and T. Fawcet, 1631), M4^{v}. I owe this reference to my colleague Christina Luckyj, who cites it adroitly and memorably in *"A Moving Rhetoricke": Gender and Silence in Early Modern England* (Manchester: Manchester University Press, 2002), 53.

The Love of Quietness: Sir Henry Slingsby

In August of 1641 Sir Henry Slingsby made a special trip to Skipton for the purpose of speaking with the earl of Pembroke, who at this time was Lady Anne Clifford's second husband (see chapter 5). Slingsby asked to be appointed Understeward of Knaresborough Castle, claiming that the post had been promised to him. But Pembroke had changed his mind, and Slingsby's request was denied. After he records this disappointment in his *Diary*, Slingsby stands back for a moment in the attempt to discover what he can about himself: "I have not yet learnt the way how to prevail, nor what weapons to bring to assail a wilful refusal, nor what more on my part to be seen than a clear intention & a thankful heart."[31] It may seem disingenuous, self-serving even, for an MP in the Long Parliament to declare that he's just too naive for this world, but I think that Slingsby was in some important ways right about himself. A seat in the House of Commons during the winter of 1640–1 must have been an excellent vantage point from which to watch the unfolding of Oliver Cromwell's career. Moderate, gentle, and fair-minded Slingsby must have gasped at the brilliance and audacity of the gifted politicians. Although he fought under the king's colours for the next five years, and although he was one of the fifty-nine MPs who voted against the attainder of Strafford, Slingsby was no knee-jerk royalist.[32] In response to the Root and Branch petition, he voted for political reform on the one hand, and for religious continuity on the other: he supported the bill to exclude bishops from the House of Lords, but voted against the abolition of bishops altogether (66–7). He stood for measured reform at a time when events were moving much more quickly than he was. History, like the earl of Pembroke, would be unkind to Sir Henry Slingsby; he was pushed aside to make room for those who could act decisively and confidently without second-guessing themselves.

Like Lady Anne Clifford, Slingsby read Montaigne. Indeed, he seems to have adopted Montaigne as a pedagogical and literary model of sorts. In July 1640, on returning from London to his home, Red House, on the

31 *The Diary of Sir Henry Slingsby, of Scriven, Bart.*, ed. Daniel Parsons (London: Longman, 1836), 72.

32 As he appears to be in Geoffrey Ridsill Smith's *Without Touch of Dishonour: The Life and Death of Sir Henry Slingsby, 1602–1658* (Kineston, Warwickshire: Roundwood, 1968), a book I have frequently consulted nonetheless.

Scagglethorpe Moor in Yorkshire, he appointed a Mr Cheney to serve as tutor and schoolmaster to his eldest son, Thomas. This decision prompted Slingsby to reflect on the educational experience and aptitudes of his five-year-old.[33] He remarks that last year, while not yet four, little Thomas was adept at using simple Latin words, such as the names for parts of the body. This year he finds him "duller to learn," and this naturally worries a careful father: "I think the cause to be his too much minding Play, which takes off his mind from his book; therefore they do ill that do foment & cherish that humour in a child, & by inventing new sports increase his desire to play" (53). The remedy for this lamentable decline in standards of education? Why, a Latin immersion program, in the manner of Michel de Montaigne. Slingsby notes that by age six Montaigne was fluent in Latin because he had "those about him that could speake nothing but Latin." He proposes that his son be taught Latin in the same way, "that is without Rule or grammer" (54), though he admits that he can't compete with Montaigne's father in surrounding his son with Latin speakers.[34]

Slingsby's *Diary* itself seems to be a project inspired by Montaigne. "I do likewise take his advise," Slingsby writes, "in Registering my daily accidents which happens in my house." Then, in an extended paraphrase of a passage from Florio's great translation of the *Essays*, Slingsby points out that Montaigne's father had one of his servants keep an account book of all household expenses, and that another servant "kept a journal Book, wherein he day by day register'd the memories of the historys of his house; a thing pleasant to read, when time began to wear out the Remembrance of them" (54).[35] Montaigne strongly recommends the practice of his father, and reproaches himself for having been unable to live up to this demanding model. Slingsby ventures forward optimistically

33 The boy's date of birth is given by Slingsby as 15 June 1636 (*Diary*, 3).

34 See Montaigne, *The Essayes: Or Morall, Politike and Millitarie Discourses*, trans. John Florio (London: Val[entine] Sims, 1603), H6^{v}: "the expedient my father found-out, was this; that being yet at nurse, and before the first loosing of my tongue, I was delivered to a Germaine (who died since, a most excellent Phisitian in *France*) he being then altogether ignorant of the French tongue, but exquisitely ready and skilfull in the Latine. This man, whom my father had sent-for of purpose, and to whom he gave very great entertainement, had me continually in his armes, and was mine onely overseer. There were also joyned unto him two of his countrimen, but not so learned; whose charge was to attend, and now and then, to play with me; and all these together did never entertaine me with other then the Latine tongue."

35 The similarity between this and Florio's Montaigne would, by today's standards, amount to plagiarism: "he appointed another journall-booke to one of his servants,

into the territory designated by Montaigne: "Hereupon I follow'd the advise of Michael de Montaigne to sett down in this Book such accidents as befall me, not that I make my study of it, but rather a recreation at vacant times, without observing any time, method, or order in my wrighting, or rather scribbling" (55). It would appear that Slingsby is trying to follow both Montaigne's precept and his example: on the one hand his *Diary* will be a faithful register of the events of his household, while at the same time it will be a work of whimsical and unsystematic bricolage. And perhaps Slingsby can be faulted for failing on both counts: he has neither the obsessive record-keeping mania of Montaigne the elder, nor the endless associative inventiveness of his famous son. But there is something attractive about Slingsby's book nonetheless, even if its virtues aren't the flashy ones. "My own disposition is to love quietness," he says of himself (118); his was a temperament especially suited to the cultivation of the private life.

On 7 July 1631 Slingsby married Barbara Belasyse, daughter of Thomas Belasyse, first Viscount Fauconberg. By the time Slingsby begins his *Diary* (in 1638), his wife is the mother of two small children (Barbara, age 5; Thomas, age 2) and is expecting a third. She is characterized repeatedly by her husband as a timid and fearful woman. Indeed, the *Diary* opens with an anecdote that leads to this characterization. The event in question is the accidental death of the eldest son of Sir Edward Osborn at the age of seventeen. On the morning of 31 October 1638, at 10 o'clock, the Osborn boy was studying French under the supervision of his tutor when an unusually powerful gust of wind "blew down with great violence 7 chimneys shafts upon the roof of that chamber in the mannor house, where he was at study." The tutor escaped with minor injuries, but the boy "was found dead and buri'd in a heap of rubbish" (1). This pathetic story had a particular resonance for Slingsby's wife because she was the dead boy's aunt: her older sister Margaret Belasyse, wife to Sir Edward Osborn, was the bereaved mother. The reaction of Barbara Belasyse to her nephew's death provides Slingsby with an opening for one of his most telling descriptions of her: "When my wife was told of this accident it did much trouble her, as she had reason, he being so near to her as

who was his clarke, wherein he should insert & orderly set downe all accidents worthy the noting, & day by day register the memories of the history of his house: A thing very pleasant to reade, when time began to weare out the remembrance of them, and fit for us to passe the time withall" (L2).

her sister's son. Having warning by this accident she would not let me rest till I had pull'd down a chimney that stood on the garden Side at Red House which was high built & shaken with the wind. She would often say how much we had cause to bless God, that hath given us this warning & not made us examples to give warning unto others. She is by nature timorous and compassionate which makes her full of prayer in the behalf of others" (2). There may be some affectionate irony in this portrait, but I don't believe there's any hostility. When Slingsby remarks that his wife wouldn't let him rest until he had pulled down the insecure chimney, he's not complaining about her shrewishness or confessing his own weakness but rather praising her persistence in taking every possible precaution to protect the domestic nest. When Slingsby calls her "timid and compassionate" I suspect him of picking out qualities that he finds particularly attractive in a woman. Her fearful reticence makes him feel all the more like he's the one in charge.

By the autumn of 1637 it was clear that Slingsby's wife was suffering from a recurrent and very painful physical ailment which Slingsby refers to as "her old dissease" (39). The Slingsbys consulted doctor after doctor, received a series of diagnoses, and were advised to try a veritable potpourri of treatments and cures. Dr Parker thought her ailment was a cholic; Dr Mickelthwayte believed it was jaundice; but Dr Fryer, a specialist from London, convinced everyone that the origin of her problem was a malfunction of the spleen. On 2 December 1639 the Slingsbys set out for London in the hope of getting the best possible medical advice. Slingsby's wife "was told of a skilfull woman for the Spleen" (47), a Mrs Kelway, but after a month of following her recommended treatments and noticing no improvements, "she gave her over, bestowing on her for her pains a Diamont ring" (48).

During his protracted stay in London in 1640, Slingsby continued searching for the cure for his wife's illness. He consulted the king's physician, Sir Theodore Mayerne, whose medicines were, in Slingsby's opinion, both more effective and more expensive than anyone else's. The relief was temporary, however; in November 1641 the Slingsbys were again on their way to London, again on the difficult mission of getting medical advice and treatment. This time the search ended in failure, for, in Slingsby's words: "The 31st of December my dear wife depart'd this life, after she had endur'd a world of misery" (73–4). This recording of a sad truth is followed by a tribute to Barbara Slingsby, née Belasyse, which may be conventional in both style and sentiment, but which is indubitably and entirely sincere. Slingsby mentions again his wife's timorous character, though now he stresses the sweetness of her disposition and the readiness with which she was able to forgive. But it is more than a collection of virtues that he's thinking of when he writes: "The loss of her by death is beyond expression, both to her children, & all that knew her; but chiefly to my self, who hath enjoy'd happy days in her company & society which now I find a want of" (74). Slingsby buried his wife in London and spent at least the next five months living with friends and relations. He couldn't bear to go home, "where I should find a miss of my dear wife, & where every room will call her to my memory & renew my grief" (76). For a man of Slingsby's temperament, the destruction of his private life was a devastating blow.

He now gave himself more and more ardently to the public work of defending the king. He received a commission to command a company of "trainbands" (76) whose special role was to guard the person of the king during his sojourn in the City of York. He raised a regiment of 200 volunteers to fight under the earl of Newcastle. He was with the royalist forces who surrendered the City of York in 1644, after the Battle of Marston Moor. He joined the army of the king now garrisoned in Oxford, fought in the Battle of Naseby, and participated in the surrender of Newark to the Scots in 1646. While still following the king, though now in the custody of the Scottish army, Slingsby records that "I was command'd by the King to return home" (179). His military career had come to an end, and he retired after a long absence to the diminished comforts of Red House.

Soon he became the object of various kinds of official harassment, such as the requirement that he take the "Negative oath" and subscribe to the "national Covenant." For Slingsby either of these gestures would have been repugnant: "The one makes me renounce my allegiance; the other my religion" (119). So he chose to retreat, to the confinement of a single secluded room within Red House, "where I spend my days in great sylence, scarce dare to speak or walk but with great heed taken least I be discover'd" (118). This is perhaps an exaggeration of his literal experience, but I have no doubt that it expresses something genuine about the pain of loss and diminution which Slingsby must have felt: about the paranoia, in short, of the politically expendable person he had become.

In March 1655 he was arrested on suspicion of being involved in a royalist plot. While being held in custody in Hull, he appears to have imprudently tested the sentiments of his guard, Major Ralph Waterhouse, to see if he could be drawn in on the royalist side. Waterhouse went straight to his superiors, and the rest of Slingsby's life was a series of tactics to delay the inevitable: his execution for high treason on 8 June 1658.

The published account of his trial and death is a moving document. The trial took place in Westminster Hall, presided over by Attorney General Edmond Prideaux, who read out at length the charges against Slingsby. When asked to enter a plea, "whether guilty or not guilty," Slingsby was immediately (and justifiably) evasive: "I desire to have Counsel assigned me."[36] When told that he could not have the assistance of counsel, he demanded to be tried by a jury, not by a court created by parliamentary commission. After all of his preliminary requests had been denied, Slingsby turned to Lord President Prideaux with what sounds like scorn: "I am (my Lord) of an opinion, (though you may account it a Paradox) that I cannot trespass against your Laws, because I did not submit to them" (A2). Brave though such rhetoric of resistance may be, this was hardly the place to deploy it; unless he were to show obvious signs of contrition, Slingsby was doomed.

The evidence against him included the sworn testimony of three witnesses, and a written document which Waterhouse claimed to have received from Slingsby. This document, purportedly in the hand of Charles Stuart, offered to appoint Waterhouse governor of the castle at Hull if he were willing to cooperate in the intrigue of restoring the monarchy. Slingsby's only line of defence was to claim that whatever he had done or said to Waterhouse "was but in jest" (A3^{v}); indeed, he argued that he had been "trepan'd" (i.e., framed) by the witnesses who were reporting in deadly earnest the very things that were "spoken in mirth between us" (A4). The judges were not convinced, and Slingsby was sentenced to be hanged, drawn, and quartered; subsequently, at the behest of the Lord Protector, the severity of the sentence was reduced to simple beheading. On 8 June 1658 he was led to the scaffold on Tower Hill. After kneeling to pray for a short while, he made a brief speech, in "a very low voice," claiming again that his intentions had been misunderstood: "what he spoke to them in private, was brought into evidence against him." He is reported to have shown little fear or sorrow, but to have declared himself ready for the end. "Then he addressed himself to private prayer again; and kneeling down to the Block, he prayed privately for a short space: Then laid his head upon the Block, and at the sign given,

36 *The Tryals of Sir Henry Slingsby K[nigh]t, and John Hewet D.D. for High Treason* (London: n.p., 1658), A2. The Slingsby portion of this document is reprinted as an Appendix in the *Diary* (418–41).

the Executioner severed his Head from his Body at one blow" (C2). As seventeenth-century executions go, this was a very restrained event; as a piece of theatre, it lacks everything except the very considerable power of understatement. For a man who declared his own predilection for quietness, this was a fitting end.

Slingsby had prepared for his execution in part by writing a letter of advice to his children entitled "A Fathers Legacy."[37] In this document he says with prudent regret that "the only way to be secure, is not to be active in the affairs of State." But even if someone follows this counsel, the outcome is by no means guaranteed: "*Privacy*, as it is the only recluse of safety; if Your Hours in it be not well *imployed*, it may become as dangerous as a place of Agency" (208). The way in which privacy becomes dangerous is through "too prodigal speech" (224) which delivers even private persons into the hands of their enemies. The only sure defence against such manipulation is complete silence. Did privacy protect the heterodox in the case of Sir Henry Slingsby? Obviously not, because no private space can yield absolute protection against the consequences of speech.

Before the outbreak of the Civil War, and before the death of his wife, Slingsby had been a soldier in the first Bishops' War (1639), on the side of Charles I against the Scottish Covenanters. This appears to have been Slingsby's first experience of military life, and in view of his advanced age (thirty-seven) he adapted remarkably well. After having spent only six weeks in uniform, Slingsby finds military life "a commendable way of breeding for a young Gentleman." The discipline "greatly improves" both body and mind: "by enabling his body to labour, his mind to watchfulness, & so, by a contempt of all things but that employment he is in, he shall not much care how hard he lyeth, nor how meanly he fareth; – whereas the independence of a private life, makes one insolent, & not easily brought under subjection" (38). If Slingsby is speaking about himself in this passage, then he's not being at all perceptive. He seems to me to have been a man far better suited to "the independence of a private life" than to the "employment of a soulgiers" (38). After marching all day in the hot sun of an early June day, the king's horse (including Slingsby) came face to face with the Scottish army. For various justifiable reasons (heat, fatigue, and the fact that the king's horse had left the infantry far

37 Printed as an Appendix to the *Diary* (195–229).

behind), the order was given not to fight but to retreat, at least for the night. The very next day Slingsby's butler arrived with the message that his wife "was in a great fit of sickness" and anxious to see her husband. "I instantly took post," Slingsby writes, "& without resting, in 24 hours, I got to her & found her well again" (37). With relief Slingsby turned his attention to a few other household matters, such as settling an old dispute with Mr Rhodes, the vicar of Knaresborough. Then Slingsby returned to the king's army, arriving at headquarters (in the village of Twizell, on the English side of the River Tweed) on 17 June, just one day before the two sides agreed to disband their troops. I think Slingsby should be commended for responding at once to the urgent message from his wife, and for getting whatever permission he needed for his absence from his superior officers. But my reason for praising this action is the value I place on "the independence of a private life." It seems to me that Slingsby was unusually dedicated to private values, even at times when public affairs were making heavy demands upon him. If privacy "makes one insolent, & not easily brought under subjection," as Slingsby claims, even this trajectory can be observed, though proleptically, in Slingsby's life. It's easy to surmise that the various parliamentary officials who had to deal with Slingsby after his arrest in 1655 would have found his behaviour at times "insolent"; it is certain, from the account of his trial, that he was "not easily brought under subjection." There's a sense in which Slingsby, unconvinced by the communal rhetoric of the Commonwealth, wanted to make privacy a principle worth dying for.

Privacy and Privilege

Under what circumstances was privacy likely to be an effective haven for the heterodox? Were scientific and religious unorthodoxy more likely to be tolerated, if confined to privacy, than political dissent? Did the social standing of the dissenter make a difference? Were there large numbers of ordinary dissenters who, because they kept their views private, were never called to account? Was the right to privacy ever used successfully as a defence against the officials who sought to exercise control? Was the private conscience more likely to be respected in Protestant England than in Catholic jurisdictions? At this point I ought to be drawing conclusions, and instead I'm asking questions. Even so, I now offer three general observations based on the instances cited and on what I know of some comparable cases, like those cited in chapters 2 and 5, for example.

1. Privacy was much more likely to protect you, in the early modern period, if you were willing to make some gesture of compliance or accommodation. I am thinking here of the highly public signals of conformity that Donne planted in his sermons, in contrast to the studied refusal to conform chosen by the Catholic martyrs of his generation. Even ordinary Catholics were required to make the public gesture of attending services in the Church of England, and if they did not comply, they could be fined for non-attendance. But this was not an issue restricted to religious controversy; notice that Slingsby, when offered what seem to be opportunities to recant, is unwilling to take the bait, whereas Galileo, at least outwardly, did as he was told.
2. The "early modern" is that period of cultural history in which the likelihood of being burned as a heretic is overtaken by the likelihood of being executed for high treason. Perhaps this is an inference that depends in part on accepting Protestant culture as normative. In England, at any rate, the rhetoric supporting execution becomes increasingly secular, even when religious issues are at stake. The contrast between Hugh Latimer's punishment (burned as a heretic in 1555) and Henry Slingsby's (executed for high treason in 1658) may seem perfectly understandable, given that Latimer was a preacher and Slingsby a Member of Parliament. But when we place Robert Southwell, SJ, between them, and notice that his crime (like Slingsby's) was high treason (for which he was hanged, drawn, and quartered in 1595), the situation becomes both more complicated and more interesting.
3. Privacy may have been a dangerous refuge, but it was a safer defence than irony. Privacy requires only the indifference of one's tormentors. Irony requires their collusion, and that's more than most of them can give. The records we have access to would suggest that both Elizabeth Sawyer and Sir Henry Slingsby allowed themselves the indulgence of irony at a time when silence would have been a far more prudent strategy. But when prudent silence seems to be required, even of the private adherent of a heterodox position, it soon becomes impossible to evaluate the success of such a strategy. Did silence work for Richard Barnfield? It would be difficult to say yes, without the uneasy feeling that his was a heterodox position subject to suppression.

Even if there isn't a single or univocal position that can be inferred from the evidence I have gathered here, there are provisional, tentative, interlocking conclusions that are important nonetheless, whether or not they can be rendered as the truth for all time. Did privacy protect the heterodox in early modern culture? Only if the person in question had enough influence, ingenuity, wealth, status, or patronage to ensure that the protection would work; it soon becomes difficult, under these circumstances, to attribute protection to privacy rather than to the influence of a powerful agent. In the absence of privilege in one of its many forms, privacy would not be enough; even if you allowed yourself only an indiscreet word, the appeal to privacy might not protect you from the ever dangerous risk of exposure.

Chapter Eight

"A Fine and Private Place": Andrew Marvell

What exactly did privacy mean to Marvell? The question arises, repeatedly and insistently, from his writing in both prose and verse. Although he was in many respects a public figure, serving both as Milton's assistant in the Cromwell government and as the "member for Hull" (in Eliot's famous phrase)[1] for nearly the last twenty years of his life, Marvell placed special value on whatever opportunities he could find to retreat from the public eye. In a letter to Sir Edward Harlay (3 May 1673) Marvell comments at some length upon the pamphlet war in which he is engaged, and wonders whether he should so much as acknowledge Samuel Parker's soon-to-be published attack on him. Then, as if reaching for a temporary respite from his most arduous public battle, Marvell writes as follows: "I intend by the end of the next week to betake my selfe some five miles of[f] to injoy the spring & my privacy."[2] This is an entirely typical turn for Marvell, and one he makes most memorably in "The Garden," as I will be arguing at some length.

The Private Retreat

"The Garden" has been greatly admired by many of Marvell's readers, and for perfectly legitimate reasons.[3] But the place occupied by this poem

1 "Andrew Marvell," *Selected Essays*, 3rd ed. (London: Faber, 1951), 292.

2 *The Poems and Letters of Andrew Marvell*, ed. H.M. Margoliouth, Pierre Legouis, and E.E. Duncan-Jones, 3rd ed. (Oxford: Clarendon, 1971), 2:328.

3 Some of these are described in thoughtful ways by Mary Thomas Crane; see "Marvell's Amazing Garden," in *Environment and Embodiment in Early Modern England*, ed. Mary Floyd-Wilson and Garrett A. Sullivan, Jr (Houndmills: Palgrave Macmillan, 2007), 35–54.

in the Marvell canon is rather different than it was a generation ago. The change is partly a simple matter of the poem's date, now generally thought to be 1668, ever since Allan Pritchard discovered in the text verbal echoes of poems (published in 1667 and 1668) by Katherine Philips and Abraham Cowley.[4] But a temporal change brings with it a geographical change: no longer are we being drawn in to the Fairfax estates where Marvell served as a tutor to young Mary Fairfax some twenty years earlier; we are on firmer ground now if we imagine Marvell spending the recess between sessions of Parliament at one of the Buckinghamshire residences (at Winchendon and at Wooburn) of his friend and political ally, Philip, fourth Baron Wharton, whose "houses and gardens were regarded as a source of wonder."[5] And, perhaps most telling of all, the later date of "The Garden" now opens up a chance for reassessing the relationship between this poem and Milton's Garden of Eden in *Paradise Lost.* This is a question I will return to shortly.

Marvell's poem begins with a rhetorical demotion of the accomplishments and efforts of public life:

How vainly men themselves amaze
To win the palm, the oak, or bays;
And their uncessant labours see
Crowned from some single herb or tree.[6]

Not that public achievements are without value, of course; but the speaker neatly places the exclusive search for success with the modifiers "vainly" and "uncessant." Competitive effort is made to seem both inflated and wearying, after which the reward offered (a "single" plant, even for the very best) is bound to look insubstantial. The emptiness of endless striving has disappointed the speaker; he prefers the plenitude of the garden, where "all flow'rs and all trees do close/To weave the garlands of repose."

4 See "Marvell's 'The Garden': A Restoration Poem?" *Studies in English Literature, 1500–1900* 23 (1983): 371–88.

5 Nigel Smith, *Andrew Marvell: The Chameleon* (New Haven, CT: Yale University Press, 2010), 219.

6 *The Poems of Andrew Marvell*, ed. Nigel Smith (London: Pearson Longman, 2003), 155. Subsequent references, unless otherwise noted, are to this edition, and are given parenthetically by page number only.

The word "privacy" is not used in this poem, but the idea is always present, variously named as "Quiet" and "solitude," or indirectly represented as a kind of withdrawal into pure spiritual being. This last notion motivates some of the most evocative language of "The Garden." The speaker has been describing, in terms that border on the comic, his passive immersion in the over-abundance of apples, grapes, nectarines, and peaches, all of which seem to be competing for his tactile and gustatory attention. The sequence of blandishments ends with the speaker in a most undignified position:

Stumbling on melons, as I pass,
Insnared with flow'rs, I fall on grass. (157)

What protects the speaker from outright ridicule is the fact that he's completely alone; he doesn't have to feel shame or embarrassment, because nobody is watching him. Furthermore, the excesses and confusions of the sensory world can, in the activity of private contemplation, be creatively rearranged:

Meanwhile the mind, from pleasure[7] less,
Withdraws into its happiness;
The mind, that ocean where each kind
Does straight its own resemblance find;
Yet it creates, transcending these,
Far other worlds, and other seas;
Annihilating all that's made
To a green thought in a green shade. (157–8)

Privacy gives the speaker access to an interior landscape of even greater pleasure than anything in the sensory world. The "green thought in a green shade" suggests endless mental fertility; here is a mind so clearly

7 Here I do not follow Smith's decision to print "pleasures" based on the manuscript annotation of a copy of the 1681 folio in the Bodleian Library. Smith's justification for sometimes (but not always) using the manuscript annotations seems to me unconvincing; see Smith's introduction, xiv. I am therefore printing the word "pleasure" as it appears in Andrew Marvell, *Miscellaneous Poems* (London: Robert Boulter, 1681), I1^{v} and most subsequent editions.

capable of transcendent flight that it can renounce the material culture which surrounds it ("all that's made") in favour of pure interiority.

The kind of privacy Marvell constructs here has nothing to do with either domesticity or sexual love. The possibility of admitting a female companion to the garden is mentioned, twice, only to be vigorously erased on both occasions. The lover who carves the name of a mistress into the bark of a tree is dismissed by the speaker as a fool; he ought to have known that the white and red of courtship are never "So am'rous as" the "lovely green" (156) of the garden: the colour, that is, of inspired contemplation. As to the Garden of Eden, the speaker incautiously suggests an improvement to the divine plan, namely the deletion of woman. "Such was that happy garden-state,/While man there walked without a mate." This indeed would have been the perfect scheme, the speaker argues, except that it would have been too good to be true:

> But 'twas beyond a mortal's share
> To wander solitary there:
> Two Paradises 'twere in one
> To live in Paradise alone. (158)

If, at the time of writing "The Garden" Marvell had recently read *Paradise Lost,* then it is an irresistible temptation to hear him expressing resistance to his old mentor's evocation of the perfect world. In Milton's Eden, even before the fall, Adam and Eve are active gardeners: they trim and dress the luxuriant vegetation of paradise so as to bring it into conformity with human needs and desires. In Marvell it's the fruits and plants that are active, and the speaker who is the object of their aggression. In keeping with this change in emphasis, the great mythic event of *Paradise Lost,* the Fall as we tend to represent it, capitalized as if to dress it in full theological splendour, is here just a trivially comic moment when the speaker falls "on grass" as he puts it, barely suppressing the thought that he's falling "on his ass," a variant that works just as well for the rhyme, though it disrupts the metre. And what of Marvell's attitude towards the construction of that love nest for Adam and Eve? The perfect harmony of their embrace is something he can't believe in. In view of the reputation of Renaissance gardens as meeting places for lovers, the exclusion here seems all the more striking. To insist on solitude, on a world that can't be shared, is to make this emphatically a poem about the garden of the mind. For Marvell, the place of rhapsodic mental fulfilment is by definition a place of wholeness: only one mind, one soul, and one sex is required to complete the perfection of oneness. Marvell's image of completion depends on the negation of everything except the self: whatever is socially constructed has to be annihilated; the vest of the body has to be cast aside; the bond between spousal partners has to be superseded, in order to arrive at the perfect state: "To live in Paradise alone."

Marvell is too good a poet to stop here, too clever an ironist to fall entirely into the transcendent green of solipsism. The final stanza of "The Garden" acknowledges the active designing intelligence of "the skilful gardner" (159) without whom none of the rhapsodic joys would be sustainable. Whether this figure is a servant of Lord Wharton or an image of Divine Providence doesn't matter all that much: the point is that private reverie does depend in the long run on the activity of a force external to it, from which it can retreat. Even nature contains the imprint of a designing intelligence: the "flow'rs and herbs" bear the shape of a sundial, and "th'industrious bee" carries out the act of reckoning which the mind has, in a moment of rapture, been able to escape. But if irony qualifies the pleasure of the garden by declaring it to be temporary, provisional, and contingent, the state of pure subjectivity is nonetheless the goal towards which all the yearnings of the poem are directed.

The word "privacy" and its cognates do occur elsewhere in Marvell's poetry, most notably in "To His Coy Mistress":

> The grave's a fine and private place,
> But none I think do there embrace. (83)

In these lines, as in the poem as a whole, there is a knowing worldliness in the speaker's tone of voice that borders on cynicism; and yet, despite the virtually audible sneer, the idea of "a fine and private place" remains a destination much to be desired: the trick is to get there before death gets you. The ironic effect is produced by referring to at least two kinds of privacy at the same time: explicitly to the wrong kind (the dark wooden box), and implicitly to the right kind (the bedroom, or perhaps the garden, but in any case the enclosure of love).

Except for the famous example just quoted, whenever the words "private" and "privacy" arise in Marvell's poems they do so in connection with the career of Oliver Cromwell. This is perhaps more surprising at first glance than it need be. Cromwell was, among many other things, a gigantic symbolic presence in Marvell's mind. Cromwell's characteristic movement, in Marvell's renderings, is the heroic quest: in "An Horation Ode upon Cromwell's Return from Ireland" (1650) he is pictured as leaving behind "his private Gardens" (274) in order to become a leader, a warrior, and certainly a public figure. When Marvell is most obviously celebrating the achievements of the hero, as in "The First Anniversary of the Government of His Highness the Lord Protector" (1654), his language nonetheless points again and again to the human costs of heroic striving:

> For all delight of life thou then didst lose,
> When to command, thou didst thyself depose;
> Resigning up thy privacy so dear
> To turn the headstrong people's charioteer. (293)

Nominally, Cromwell is being praised for the personal sacrifices he has made. But the terms in which this praise is cast imply that the authentic self is the private one, the one that has to be deposed in order to create the public self. And the image of "Resigning" one's "privacy" is a striking reversal of the established strand of meaning whereby a private person is someone who doesn't hold or no longer holds any public office (see the Introduction). Even in getting rid of Cromwell, in "A Poem upon the Death of His Late Highness the Lord Protector" (1658), Marvell sees the pattern being repeated, this time in the career of Richard Cromwell, the son:

> He, as his father, long was kept from sight
> In private, to be viewed by better light. (312)

Here the idea of privacy sounds more like a political ploy: rather like Prince Hal in *1 Henry IV*, young Cromwell has been lying low, it would seem, so as to be all the more visible when his opportunity arises. The notion of privacy is something altogether less grand than what is attributed to Cromwell senior, but there's a curious aptness even in this apparent decline; finding his father to be an impossible act to follow, Richard Cromwell was in the end unable to negotiate the change from private to public life.

Erotic Ambiguity

Taken together, "The Garden" and the Cromwell poems are enough to suggest that privacy occupied a special place in Marvell's mental geography. But a further question now needs to be addressed. Why? Why was privacy such a resonant idea in Marvell's mind?

Perhaps he had more than most of us to hide. This would be the answer suggested by recent studies of his sexual orientation. William Kerrigan makes the case as follows: "His famous lyrics are pedophilic ... Marvell yearned for innocence so acutely that he wanted ... to touch, embrace, make love to it."[8] This hypothesis has the advantage of accounting for (rather than explaining away) the unusual placement of the speaker in "The Picture of Little T.C. in a Prospect of Flowers." The little girl in the poem is clearly unaware of her own (prospective) sexuality, and hence of the power ("command severe") which she will "one day" wield over her suitors. The speaker therefore wants to take advantage of the moment, so as to form a relationship with her *before* she has knowledge of her own power. Perhaps it would be fair to add that, if T.C. is indeed Theophila Cornewall, as successive generations of editors believe, then she was between six and eight years old when Marvell encountered her at Nun Appleton and engaged (mentally) in the following negotiation:

> O then let me in time compound,
> And parley with those conq'ring eyes;
> Ere they have tried their force to wound,
> Ere, with their glancing wheels, they drive
> In triumph over hearts that strive,
> And them that yield but more despise.
> Let me be laid,
> Where I may see thy glories from some shade. (114–15)

But if the imagined relationship here is paedophilic, it is also voyeuristic, for reasons that I have described in detail in chapter 3. Here it should be enough to note that the speaker wants an unequal visual system in which the observer can see little T.C. displaying her "glories" unselfconsciously while he remains unobserved, protected by the covering of "some shade."

If "Little T.C." is a disconcerting poem, "Young Love" is downright disturbing. The difference arises in part because the speaker insistently and repeatedly asks the "little infant" whom he's addressing to reciprocate

8 "Marvell and Nymphets," *Greyfriar: Siena Studies in Literature* 27 (1986): 8. Kerrigan notices that Michael Long's *Marvell, Nabokov: Childhood and Arcadia* (Oxford: Clarendon, 1984) repeatedly gestures in the direction of the erotic (see 6–8), without acknowledging it explicitly.

his attentions. But I think "Young Love" is disturbing in another sense: it is always difficult to define precisely and with confidence what the speaker's tone of voice should be in a poem by Marvell, but here it's almost impossible to be sure what he's up to at all:

I

Come little infant, love me now,
While thine unsuspected years
Clear thine agèd father's brow
From cold jealousie and fears.

II

Pretty, surely, 'twere to see
By young Love old Time beguiled:
While our sportings are as free
As the nurse's with the child.

III

Common beauties stay fifteen;
Such as yours should swifter move;
Whose fair blossoms are too green
Yet for Lust, but not for Love.

IV

Love as much the snowy lamb
Or the wanton kid does prize,
As the lusty bull or ram,
For his morning sacrifice.

V

Now then love me: Time may take
Thee before thy time away:
Of this need we'll virtue make,
And learn love before we may.

VI

So we win of doubtful Fate;
And, if good she to us meant,
We that good shall antedate,
Or, if ill, that ill prevent.

VII

Thus as kingdoms, frustrating
Other titles to their crown,
In the cradle crown their king,
So all foreign claims to drown,

VIII

So, to make all rivals vain,
Now I crown thee with my love:
Crown me with thy love again,
And we both shall monarchs prove. (73–4)

We know that the infant is under fifteen, and therefore "too green … for Lust, but not for Love." Perhaps we should allow this distinction to carry the day, and to read the poem as a mature man's entreaty for affection only. But if we do so, what sense can we make of the suggestion that something furtive is going on: something that could awaken an "agèd father's" hostility, something that the speaker and the infant might do now "before we may"? Perhaps we should imagine the infant as very little indeed: so little as to declare sexual attraction irrelevant. This would be consistent with the "sportings" of nurse and child and with the image of a cradle containing a future monarch. But if sexuality is defined as off-limits in this way, why does it nonetheless linger in the language of the poem: in the image of "the lusty bull or ram," for example, or in the suggestion that potential "rivals" can be neutralized by acting now? Kerrigan is aware of these ambiguities but believes he knows what the poet is up to nonetheless: "Marvell … desires the green lady precisely because she is unripe" (7). He goes on to acknowledge that "Young Love" may well embody a fantasy never acted upon, but in a poem – by Marvell or anyone else – this should hardly be surprising.

Kerrigan assumes throughout that the little infant is a girl, even though no explicit mark of gender is offered. This reading, the default position in Marvell criticism, is challenged and presumably rendered untenable by Paul Hammond in "Marvell's Sexuality."[9] Hammond believes that Marvell was "carefully unspecific about the child's gender" (109), but that the imagery of the poem would suggest, if anything, that the infant is

9 *The Seventeenth Century* 11 (1996): 87–126.

a boy. The allusions to mature sexuality are blatantly masculine: the bull and ram, no less. And when the crown of love transforms the child into maturity, the simile evokes comparison with a "king." Hammond's point is an excellent one, and it is not an isolated detail. Rather, it is a small and careful step in an ingenious and comprehensive discovery of what he terms "Marvell's homosexual interests" (87). Reading Hammond's article is an exhilarating though at times an unsettling ride. It's a bit like showing up at a party where a great many of the attractive women you thought you knew turn out to be men in drag. The last to go is of course the "Coy Mistress" herself – no longer a mistress at all, but a completely manufactured sex toy, created by decorating a homoerotic pretext (the story of Narcissus and Echo) with spatterings of heterosexual imagery borrowed from such poets as Randolph and Herrick (112–14). As my description implies, I have a great deal of respect for Hammond's project as a whole, along with some reservations about particulars. I find myself eager to endorse his general conclusions: namely, that Marvell wasn't thought of as a man who fits easily into the heterosexual norm (99), and that his poems invite us "into new territory by finding a language for the ambiguities of sexuality" (117).[10]

This invitation is both transparently obvious and deliberately opaque in "The Definition of Love." I quote the whole poem here because it is short, and because it is not as well known as it deserves to be:

I

My love is of a birth as rare
As 'tis for object strange and high:
It was begotten by Despair
Upon Impossibility.

10 For thoughtful argument about this very question, see Michael John DiSanto, "Andrew Marvell's Ambivalence toward Adult Sexuality," *Studies in English Literature, 1500–1900* 48 (2008): 165–82. See also Derek Hirst and Steven Zwicker, who claim to discover in Marvell's poems "a program that deconstructs the very bases of heterosexuality and patriarchalism alike"; see "Andrew Marvell and the Toils of Patriarchy: Fatherhood, Longing, and the Body Politic," *ELH: A Journal of English Literary History* 66 (1999): 631. The same authors go on to outline what they believe is "a veritable etiology of the self: a dramatic and determining story of eros and abuse, and of wounding and incapacity, for which the transcendence of poetry was his counter and his solace"; see "Eros and Abuse: Imagining Andrew Marvell," *ELH: A Journal of English Literary History* 74 (2007): 371. These two articles reappear as chapters 2 and 3 in Hirst and Zwicker's *Andrew Marvell, Orphan of the Hurricane* (Oxford: Oxford University Press, 2012), 41–102.

II

Magnanimous Despair alone
Could show me so divine a thing,
Where feeble Hope could ne'er have flown
But vainly flapped its tinsel wing.

III

And yet I quickly might arrive
Where my extended soul is fixed,
But Fate does iron wedges drive,
And always crowds itself betwixt.

IV

For Fate with jealous eye does see
Two perfect loves, nor lets them close:
Their union would her ruin be,
And her tyrannic power depose.

V

And therefore her decrees of steel
Us as the distant poles have placed,
(Though Love's whole world on us doth wheel)
Not by themselves to be embraced:

VI

Unless the giddy heaven fall,
And earth some new convulsion tear;
And, us to join, the world should all
Be cramped into a planisphere.

VII

As lines so loves oblique may well
Themselves in every angle greet:
But ours so truly parallel,
Though infinite, can never meet.

VIII

Therefore the love which us doth bind,
But Fate so enviously debars,
Is the conjuction of the mind,
And opposition of the stars. (109–11)

The poem begins not with a claim about the nature of love in general, but with a personally inflected claim: "My love is ...". Frank Kermode pointed out many years ago that Marvell's text doesn't offer a definition "of love considered in the abstract"; rather, "it is the rarity, the unusual qualities, of his particular love, that the poem deals with." To put the matter epigrammatically, "it [the poem] distinguishes but it does not define."[11] The parents of Marvell's kind of love are two personifications: Despair and Impossibility. They are distinguished from the more conventional Hope, who, in Marvell's mental geography, has become both "feeble" and birdlike, and is caught in the ridiculous act of flapping "its tinsel wing."

Whatever Marvell's erotic preferences may have been, they seem to have led him to what he thought of as a confrontation with fate. Perhaps this was merely a confrontation with a normative morality that would be quick to judge and condemn, but such a force could have seemed only too much like "opposition of the stars." In any case, the parallel lines of the penultimate stanza imply that, for this speaker, love can never be consummated. The geometrical image here is often compared to Donne's conceit of the stiff twin compasses in "A Valediction: Forbidding Mourning."[12] The comparison is appropriate and telling: in Donne, the perfect circle with a fixed centre is the guarantee of a true spiritual love consummated in the flesh. The parallel lines can (by definition) never meet, and Marvell's perfect union can therefore happen only in the mind.

Marvell's most memorable use of the word "private," as his readers are likely to recall, occurs in a poem I have mentioned so far only in passing: "To His Coy Mistress." I am not going to offer a sustained reading of this text, but I do have a few observations to make. First, the poem seems to me to encapsulate a sense of frustration that is quite unusual in the libertine verse of the seventeenth century. This is in part the result of the one psychological characteristic attributed to the woman: she is forever "Coy." In this respect she is radically unlike the woman in Donne's "Elegy 19: To His Mistress Going to Bed," or the woman (identified as

---

11 "Definitions of Love," *Review of English Studies*, n.s., 7 (1956): 184.

12 See, for example, Rosalie L. Colie, *"My Ecchoing Song": Andrew Marvell's Poetry of Criticism* (Princeton, NJ: Princeton University Press, 1970), 45; and Robert Wilcher, *Andrew Marvell* (Cambridge: Cambridge University Press, 1985), 48.

Celia) in Carew's "A Rapture." True, there is a long Petrarchan tradition of the disdainful mistress, best represented in English literature by Stella in Sidney's *Astrophil and Stella.* But Stella is unavailable to Astrophil because she's married to someone else, and that's different from being – well, unreceptive.

If I'm right about the note of frustration in Marvell's poem, then this experience might help to motivate the speaker's increasingly violent rhetoric. He tries to begin with a fanciful blazon of the woman's attractions:

> An hundred years should go to praise
> Thine eyes, and on thy forehead gaze.
> Two hundred to adore each breast:
> But thirty thousand to the rest.

A language that begins by offering itself as playfulness soon slides into coercion: nobody, the speaker observes, can afford to spend all those hundreds and thousands of years in foreplay. The reason is both simple and incontrovertible:

> The grave's a fine and private place,
> But none I think do there embrace.

With his characteristic irony, Marvell has in fact cancelled out the possibility of mutual, private intimacy between the speaker and the woman spoken to. The concluding verse paragraph ("Now, therefore ...") offers not intimacy but aggression. The lovers are figured as "birds of prey" who "tear" their "pleasures with rough strife,/Thorough the iron gates of life" (81–4). The urgency here strikes me as a species of desperation: perhaps the desperation that accompanies a young man's lack of confidence in his own powers of persuasion, in his own sexual performances, and perhaps in his ability to conform to normative expectations as well.

Private Conscience

So it is entirely possible that Marvell valued privacy because he needed it: as a refuge from too glaring a search into the enigmatic territory of his own sexual proclivities, whatever these may have been. But to leave the matter there would be to do him an injustice. Marvell's lifelong interest in privacy may have been a protective strategy, but it was also a principled stand. His most visible public initiative was a protracted defence of the private conscience against the offers of church and state to control it. The Parliament in which Marvell served after the Restoration was taking a series of measures designed to inhibit the ways in which men and women might worship. These measures, collectively known as the Clarendon Code, were not in harmony with the wishes of the king, who had begun his reign by lending his authority to the Act of Indemnity, and thus in effect extending a pardon to all except named regicides. But the Anglican establishment was not satisfied with an unregulated spiritual marketplace; after the passage of the Conventicle Act (1670) it became illegal for five or more people, other than Anglicans, to assemble for purposes of public worship. "The terrible Bill against Conventicles is sent up to the Lords," Marvell wrote in a letter (21 March 1669/70) to his nephew William Popham; and he described the substance of the Bill as "the Quintessence of arbitrary Malice."[13]

Among the exponents of Anglican conformity was Samuel Parker, a young and ambitious clergyman, author of *A Discourse of Ecclesiastical Politie, wherein the Authority of the Civil Magistrate over the Consciences of Subjects in Matters of Religion is Asserted; the Mischiefs and Inconveniences of Toleration are Represented, and All Pretenses Pleaded in Behalf of Liberty of Conscience are Fully Answered* (London: John Martyn, 1670). The title doesn't quite say it all, but it certainly says a lot, and what it says is highlighted by means of typographical design choices. The word "*Toleration,*" for example, though it appears near the bottom of the title page, is printed in larger and bolder type than any other; "*Discourse*" comes a close second, but second nonetheless. We are being urged to beware of "*Toleration*" as if it were public enemy number one. Parker took the same high road when, two years later, he composed a long-winded preface to the late Bishop John Bramhall's *Vindication of Himself and the Episcopal Clergy from the Presbyterian Charge of Popery* (London: James Collins, 1672). Here Parker seems very quick to interpret any dissent as extremism: "For Fanaticism, howsoever useful it may be to the Designs of Rebels and Usurpers, is too untoward and intractable to be ever much doated upon by any setled Authority" (e7^{v}). Parker's preface was a provocation

13 *Poems and Letters*, ed. Margoliouth et al., 2:314.

which Marvell could no longer ignore, and he committed himself now to composing his satiric response, *The Rehearsal Transpros'd* (1672).

I will neglect the artistry of this text – its cunning exploitation of the popularity of *The Rehearsal* by Buckingham et al., its sheer dexterity at invective, and its very considerable verbal brio – in order to arrive at a simple but important destination: Marvell's defence of private conscience. He locates in Parker's writing a "grand Thesis,"[14] which he quotes, as I do now, from *A Discourse of Ecclesiastical Politie*, where Parker finds "it to be absolutely necessary to the peace and government of the World, that the supreme Magistrate of every Common-wealth should be vested with a Power to govern and conduct the Consciences of Subjects in affairs of Religion" (B5^{v}). To Marvell this is a position that makes a mockery of the very notion of conscience. Among the corollaries which follow from Parker's grand thesis Marvell lists "Publick Conscience" (*Discourse*, X2^{v}), a phrase he expects us to understand as oxymoronic, "for as to mens private Consciences he [Parker] hath made them very inconsiderable" (1:99). True enough, Parker allows that an individual can think whatever he likes, so long as he conforms to the established order in outward practice. But this proviso, Marvell points out, is little better than prescribed hypocrisy. And it is dangerous hypocrisy at that: "I ... would wish the Nonconformists to be upon their guard," Marvell warns, against a system that could, by means of "*Oaths* and *Renunciations*, and *Assents* and *Consents*," trick them into declaring themselves, "and then peach, & so hang them" (1:99–100). In view of the events Marvell had already lived through, and in the absence of a secure consensus on religious toleration, this was no idle fear.

Perhaps privacy was a political necessity for Marvell, given his record of conspicuously loyal service to apparently incompatible masters. Aubrey remarks that Marvell "had not a general acquaintance," by which he presumably means that Marvell lacked certain social gifts. He loved wine, but would rather "drinke liberally by himselfe" than under circumstances he couldn't control. Aubrey further reports Marvell as saying "he would not play the good-fellow in any man's company in whose hands he

14 *The Prose Works of Andrew Marvell*, ed. Annabel Patterson, Martin Dzelzainis, N.H. Keeble, and Nicholas von Maltzahn (New Haven, CT: Yale University Press, 2003), 1:91. Subsequent references to Marvell's prose, unless otherwise identified, are taken from this edition and are cited parenthetically.

would not trust his life."[15] Depending on your point of view, this rather obsessive need for privacy might be the neurosis of a solo alcoholic or the prudence of a social reformer looking far beyond the prejudices of his own time and place. But I don't want to imply that Marvell's political commitment to privacy is the trump card which captures and reduces the value of his other needs and desires. To do so would be in effect a denial of the privacy he worked so hard at negotiating and maintaining. Rather, I would suggest that Marvell's private place was, characteristically, multivalent. It included the aesthetic, spiritual, and erotic energies of his still unpublished poems, as well as a political commitment to defend another's privacy as if it were his own.

Supposition and Surmise

The question with which I began this chapter – namely, what exactly did privacy mean to Marvell – would therefore appear to have at least three separate if partly overlapping answers. First, privacy was an idea which he found attractive as a poet, and here he was thinking of a kind of privacy that comes very close to and is sometimes identical with solitude. Second, he thought of privacy as a kind of protection against the hostile judgments of persons who might find him insufficiently conventional, perhaps in his sexual behaviour, or at least in his erotic tastes, and in much of what we might refer to today as his lifestyle. Third, he thought of privacy as an endangered but indispensable matrix within the self where judgments of many kinds need to be made, and which is therefore worth defending with the best political and rhetorical powers he could muster. But even these answers, when added together, seem to me something short of a complete and satisfying solution. I am therefore going to propose a fourth answer which, I hope to demonstrate, grows out of and in a sense fulfils the needs of the other three. I am calling this fourth answer, somewhat cryptically, the grammar of supposition and surmise.[16] Why I

15 *Brief Lives*, ed. Oliver Lawson Dick (1949; repr., Harmondsworth: Penguin, 1972), 356.

16 For a critical position similar to mine, though worked out in an interpretation of *Appleton House* rather than the poems I've chosen to highlight, see Dorothy Stephens, "Caught in the Act at Nun Appleton," *The Limits of Eroticism in Post-Petrarchan Narrative: Conditional Pleasure from Spenser to Marvell* (Cambridge: Cambridge University Press, 1998), 178–209.

use this label will become apparent, I hope, when I attach it to some of the texts already mentioned, but also to a few so far neglected, especially "Mourning" and "The Nymph Complaining for the Death of Her Fawn."

A woman (Clora) is weeping and a male observer is watching her. That is the whole of the dramatic situation in "Mourning" (100–1). Everything that follows from it could be described as the man's attempts to interpret what he sees. Three different interpretations are offered, all of them hypothetical. The first is the closest to common sense, but it is not a sure thing; Clora's eyes are said to be "confused" in the sense that they "Seem bending upwards" while her tears are "suspended" before they "flow" downwards. So the first hypothesis begins with "As if" in order to signal that it stops short of certainty. Clora's weeping seems to the speaker

> As if she, with those precious tears,
> Would strow the ground where Strephon lay.

Strephon is later referred to as "her dead love," so the first interpretation, as the title of the poem suggests, is that Clora is engaged in an act of mourning.

But a second hypothesis is immediately offered, and attributed to observers who consider themselves to be too clever to take the common-sense view:

> Yet some affirm, pretending art,
> Her eyes have so her bosom drowned,
> Only to soften near her heart
> A place to fix another wound.

Clora stays in "her solitary bow'r" these observers declare, in order to indulge in the autoerotic pleasure of weeping: "She courts herself in am'rous rain," playing the parts of both Danaë and Zeus (as a shower of gold) in the mythological seduction story.

The third hypothesis is the cruellest one because it attributes hypocrisy to poor Clora:

> Nay others, bolder, hence esteem
> Joy now so much her master grown,
> That whatsoever does but seem
> Like grief, is from her windows thrown.

These others believe that Clora has already replaced Strephon with someone "new," and that the tears are her gifts to the man she now yearns for.

The penultimate stanza begins with "How wide they dream!" The interpretations offered are apparently not getting at the real truth, and the speaker now at last takes a stand in the concluding lines of the poem:

> I yet my silent judgement keep,
> Disputing not what they believe:
> But sure as oft as women weep,
> It is to be supposed they grieve.

The stand taken by the "I," in a move entirely typical of Marvell's poems, is that he won't take a stand. The best he can affirm is the impersonal "It is to be supposed," and in other respects the speaker's "judgement" will remain infuriatingly "silent." We are left, after all of the dexterously placed dance steps about interpretation, with no more than a surmise.

This reluctance to declare a position might easily be taken as the most distinctive mark of Marvell's various intellectual projects. His most famous poems draw attention to their own hypothetical suppositions. In "The Garden" an old-fashioned version of the subjunctive mood is the marker of what can be wished for, though it doesn't exist: "Two Paradises *'twere* in one/To live in Paradise alone" (*my emphasis*). And the opening gambit of "To His Coy Mistress" uses a more familiar form of the same grammatical trope: "*Had* we but world enough ..." (*my emphasis*). The speaker who admires little T.C. wants to observe her "from some shade" so as to prevent disclosure. The great "Horatian Ode" certainly praises Cromwell, in the sense that it recognizes his powers of military and political leadership, but on the most troublesome political question of the whole century – whether it be justifiable for a people to kill their king – Marvell's speaker certainly highlights the problem and then remains mute. Milton, by contrast, would have no trouble declaring exactly where he stood on this matter. And perhaps the great difference between these two is why Marvell's great tribute to his master, "On Mr Milton's *Paradise Lost*," sounds at times a trifle cool, as in the beautiful couplet where Marvell admits that, unlike Milton, he himself is a rhyming poet:

> I too transported by the mode offend,
> And while I meant to praise thee must commend. (184)

Even here, of course, Marvell isn't making a declaration of his own position so much as erasing what might be special about it.

I have earlier credited Marvell with initiating a vigorous defence of the private conscience in *The Rehearsal Transpros'd,* and I am certainly not going to withdraw my admiration now. But it is worth pointing out that the first edition of this text carries no sign of who the author was. Marvell's friends of course knew, and his enemies suspected that it was he. Before long he was obliged to admit his authorship of the book, and when *The Rehearsal Transpros'd: The Second Part* was published in 1673 it bore Marvell's name on the title page and it included a narrative in which he acknowledged authorship of the original *Rehearsal Transpros'd* (1:251). Still, even when Marvell becomes visible in this way, and even when he's polemically engaged, there's a sense in which his ultimate allegiance remains undeclared or, perhaps it would be more accurate to say, disguised. As he looks back over the well-remembered political events which led to the deposition of Charles I and at length to the Protectorate of Cromwell, he writes again in the idiom of supposition and surmise: "Whether it were a War of Religion, or of Liberty, is not worth the labour to enquire. Which-soever was at the top, the other was at the bottom; but upon considering all, I think the Cause was too good to have been fought for. Men ought to have trusted God; they ought and might have trusted the King with the whole matter" (1:192). That Marvell's political affiliations changed during his lifetime, though certainly true, is less remarkable than the brilliant phrase he devises to prevent partisans on either side from seeing exactly where he now stands. The "Cause ... too good to have been fought for" can be read as an endorsement of republican idealism (if you're a republican) or as a critique of Cromwell's ruthlessness (if you're a royalist).

I don't have world enough and time to deal with Marvell's writing comprehensively, so I will conclude this chapter by commenting on just one more text: a poem that is both strikingly unlike anything else Marvell wrote, and yet encapsulates a great many of his most distinctive qualities. "The Nymph Complaining for the Death of Her Fawn" is the only poem by Marvell in which the "I," who speaks all of its lines, is represented as female. This opening remark would (I think) be endorsed by every critical reader of the poem, but I can think of no other statement about this text that would gain widespread assent. In fact, the critical archive which this poem has brought into being is nothing short of astonishing, especially as a register of numerous incompatible readings.

The critical archive I refer to has been described with great care and intelligence by Matthew C. Augustine.[17] Instead of repeating Augustine's work, I will report some of the highlights of his account, and then remark on the ways in which my approach to Marvell differs from his. "Critics almost always have assumed that allegory is the key to interpreting" this text, Augustine observes (256), and he goes on to cite claims that the fawn should be read as representing Christ, the Anglican Church, or the beheaded Charles I.[18] He might have added that the fawn has also been identified as the Holy Ghost, the Nymph's virginity (which Sylvio didn't take though she wanted him to), the Nymph's illegitimate child (fathered by Sylvio), and a fetus which the Nymph has been unable to carry to term.[19] Jonathan Goldberg identifies the problem by remarking that "the poem has long baffled criticism," and then solves it by offering an allegorical reading of his own: "The poem defies referentiality. It is only, and entirely, self-referential, 'about' itself, about how the text comes to be, how it relates to antecedent texts, what it represents in the world."[20] Considered by itself and on its own merits, each of these positions can be made to sound quite plausible. It's only when you put them all together that they start to look ridiculous. So Augustine rather cautiously but quite rightly asks, "Could it be the case that the poem invites but also deflects such a form of interpretation?" (257). And here I am completely with him. The poem teases us into reading allegorically if by

17 "'Lillies Without, Roses Within': Marvell's Poetics of Indeterminacy and 'The Nymph Complaining,'" *Criticism* 50, no. 2 (2008): 255–78.

18 See, respectively, M.C. Bradbrook and M.G. Lloyd Thomas, *Andrew Marvell* (Cambridge: Cambridge University Press, 1940), 46–50; Douglas Bush, *English Literature in the Earlier Seventeenth Century* (Oxford: Clarendon, 1946), 161; and Yvonne Sandstroem, "Marvell's 'Nymph Complaining' as Historical Allegory," *Studies in English Literature, 1500–1900* 30 (1990): 92–114.

19 See, respectively, Geoffrey H. Hartman, "'The Nymph Complaining for the Death of Her Fawn': A Brief Allegory," *Essays in Criticism* 18 (1968): 113–35; James Reeves and Martin Seymour-Smith, eds, *The Poems of Andrew Marvell* (London: Heinemann, 1969), 164–5; Evan Jones, "Marvell's 'The Nymph Complaining for the Death of Her Faun,'" *Explicator* 26 (1968): item 73; and John J. Teunissen and Evelyn J. Hinz, "What Is the Nymph Complaining For?" *ELH: A Journal of English Literary History* 45 (1978): 410–28.

20 "Marvell's Nymph and the Echo of Voice," *Voice Terminal Echo: Postmodernism and English Renaissance Texts* (New York: Methuen, 1986), 14.

allegory we mean the "dark conceit" mentioned by Spenser in the letter to Ralegh appended to the first instalment of *The Faerie Queene*.[21] The problem is, however, that Marvell's poem is not a "*continued* allegory" (my emphasis), to quote again from the same source. So the lilies and roses in the Nymph's garden might plausibly send a reader to The Song of Solomon, but that isn't enough to sustain the allegory for even the 122 lines of Marvell's text: there is neither a bride nor a bridegroom in Marvell's poem, nor a sister nor a dove nor any mention of the cedars of Lebanon. Augustine has raised a question of great interest when he claims that the poem invites allegorical reading only to deflect it.

So it is with some ambivalence that I follow Augustine in the construction of his own allegorical interpretation: "I would go even further and contend that pleasure in Marvell's text also resembles the pleasure *of* the text – that is, if an allegory is present in the poem, it is an allegory *of reading*, that of Marvell and those figures who inhabit his poems, but also perforce our own" (257). On the one hand, I find this description of Marvell's artistic practice consistent with everything I have said about him so far. On the other hand, it is a little disappointing (or should I say "predictable"?) to find that the strangeness of Marvell's poem can be so systematically pressed into service as an affirmation of *The Pleasure of the Text* by Roland Barthes. This is a book I greatly admire, and that I think deserves more attention than it has been given in recent critical thinking. But if Augustine thinks Barthes has helped him escape the trap of allegory into which other readers have fallen, then I think he's more optimistic than he should be.

I want to end, however, not with the critical archive, but with Marvell's poem. In particular, I want to ask what (if anything) it has to tell us about the experience of privacy. To look at this question from the point of view of the Nymph would suggest that privacy is both possible and desirable, but also precarious. On two occasions she has her privacy encroached upon, both times by men. First there is "Unconstant Sylvio" (69), who gives her the fawn in the first place and who prefaces his gift with a ludicrous bit of bravado which the Nymph remembers exactly: "Look how

21 *Books I and II of "The Faerie Queene," the "Mutability Cantos," and Selections from the Minor Poetry*, ed. Robert Kellogg and Oliver Steele (Indianapolis: Odyssey Press, 1965), 74.

your huntsman here/Hath taught a fawn to hunt his dear." Then, at some unspecified time after Sylvio abandons her, the Nymph has to endure the violation of her privacy recorded in the opening couplet: "The wanton troopers riding by/Have shot my fawn and it will die."

In between these two events, the Nymph says that she retreated into her garden, taking the fawn with her of course, where she would have been happy "to play/My solitary time away/With this." She can think of herself as solitary because the fawn is not a human being: it's a pet which has some anthropomorphic qualities, but which is referred to (very seldom) as "thee" and far more frequently as "it."[22] And she can therefore indulge in a banquet of sensory pleasures that bring her and the fawn into wonderful and intimate proximity without requiring the ceremonies and regulations which apply, for example, to human sexual interaction. Privacy is clearly an ecstatic form of escape for the Nymph, even though it is an escape that she can enjoy only under the shadow of surmise. Of the fawn she says:

> Had it lived long, I do not know
> Whether it too might have done so
> As Sylvio did: his gifts might be
> Perhaps as false or more than he.

This is supposition, and she cancels it a few lines later with another, and far more congenial, surmise:

> Had it lived long, it would have been
> Lilies without, roses within. (70)

Like the speaker of "The Garden," the Nymph has achieved her state of blessedness "without a mate." But this is a dream too magnificent to last. In the final moments we learn that the fawn has died and gone to "Elysium," where it will spend its time "With milk-white lambs, and ermines pure" (71). The Nymph meanwhile promises to commission an "unhappy statue" of herself weeping for the fawn, and an "image" of the fawn too, "of purest alabaster made." But even this act of commemoration is subjected to a species of grammatical cancellation. Should the statue

22 See Goldberg, *Voice Terminal Echo*, 26–8.

of the Nymph be weeping? Not really: "there/Th'engraver sure his art may spare," because the Nymph herself will continue to weep, "though I be stone." As to the whiteness of the alabaster image, it shouldn't be absolute white: "For I would have thine image be/White as I can, though not as thee." The whiteness of the fawn is all the more wonderful if no simulacrum, not even the one posited and wished for by the Nymph herself, could possibly match it. Where then does Marvell himself stand in relation to all of this? Is he celebrating the Nymph's ostentatious work of mourning? Is he reflecting ironically on her emotional immaturity? The answer is that we will never know. Marvell valued his own privacy too much to allow us into his confidence here. Reading Marvell offers us a temptation that we must learn to both pursue and resist.

Conclusion

Readers who have followed me all the way in this long search for early modern privacy will agree, I hope, that they have discovered something of great interest, even if they might find it difficult to describe with precision exactly what it is they have seen. Each of the eight preceding chapters ends with a summing up of results, but this action is characteristically qualified as either provisional or tentative. So observing privacy turns out to be a little like watching a mirage: just when you think you've seen it, and have formed what you hope is a definite impression, it slips away and the exploration has to start all over again.

There are, as I see it, three reasons for this state of affairs, and I will comment briefly on each of them. One reason arises from the nature of the enquiry itself, and I have already drawn attention to it (in the introduction and elsewhere) as the paradox of privacy. Strictly speaking, privacy lasts only so long as it goes unobserved; the act of observing privacy, therefore, is bound to destroy (or at least diminish) the very thing it sets out to observe, as the discussion of voyeurism has shown in detail (chapter 3). We have all heard the painfully familiar complaint from celebrities who have decided (when under duress) that they want their privacy to be respected, even though it appears to us that they have lived their whole lives in a quest for maximum publicity. This is one expression of the paradox of privacy in the celebrity culture that we all in various ways consume. In early modern culture the spread of information about others was neither instantaneous nor electronic, and it was therefore subject to certain kinds of management, even restraint. I'm thinking here, for example, of people who chose to record their textual messages in manuscripts rather than printed books. And I would also say that the historical gap of some 400 years protects early modern people from a certain kind of exploitation, no matter how diligently researchers enquire into their privy lodgings. But it is true nonetheless that every private thought or feeling that we can recover from the age of Shakespeare had to be recorded in some way, and is therefore in danger of opening the door, however narrow the crack, to the closet that privacy needs to be protected by.

The second reason is the result of what I referred to at the end of the introduction as the texture of this book. Literary interpretation is not an exact science, and as I practise it, not a social science either. If it must be described as a science I would prefer to include it under the French designation, *les sciences humaines*, so as to imply that it is indeed a body of knowledge but one that has developed its own conventions and procedures. Among these I would list (1) the detailed and loving explication of the textual object, (2) the mapping of possible relationships between the textual object and its cultural setting, (3) accounting for anomalies or contradictions in the textual object, and (4) framing a persuasive but not dogmatic argument in favour of the interpretation(s) that one believes to be most plausible. If this list comes close to describing my own practices, then it will account for the prominence of the textual object in my work, and for the provisional status of inferences that can be drawn about it.

There is a third reason for the somewhat nebulous image of privacy that emerges from the eight separate explorations of the subject collected here, and this third reason is the most important one: it should be read as the thesis statement of my conclusion as a whole. Early modern privacy is difficult to pin down because it is not a static and unchanging construct; on the contrary, *privacy is an emerging expectation within early modern culture, and therefore will always be a moving target.* By way of contrast, it would be fair to observe that many assumptions remain stable over long periods of time; for this reason it is unavoidable and indeed essential that, when we read the literature created in historical periods other than our own, we bring with us some knowledge of the culture in which it is situated. Thus, when we read Shakespeare's plays (or Jonson's or Webster's) it may be useful to know that psychological thinking was still based in large measure on the theory of the humours: four bodily fluids (blood, yellow bile, black bile, and phlegm) were thought to be responsible for yielding within human beings the sanguine, choleric, melancholic, and phlegmatic temperaments. This system had been in place since Hippocrates and Galen invented it, and it was therefore a largely unchanging construct. Moreover, in its claim to account for variations in psychological orientation and behaviour, this theory makes no mention of privacy as a factor. Does this mean that early modern thinkers didn't care about privacy? Nothing of the sort. It means that the model they had inherited for talking about temperaments had not yet developed sufficient flexibility to include the dynamic and emergent category of privacy. Even if it's hard to pin down exactly what Montaigne or Marvell or Sir Henry Slingsby are identifying when they advance the claims of a private life, that does not diminish the importance of what they have to say. Rather, it implies that the full value of privacy has yet to be appreciated because too many of the static constructs inhibiting privacy are still firmly in place. One of the real pleasures of this enterprise has been to observe the many ways in which privacy gains credibility and authority in the century and a half under review.

New Directions

With these reservations in mind, then, it should now at last be possible to draw meaningful conclusions. Without requiring that privacy be a stable entity, and in full awareness of its dynamic mobility within early modern culture, we should be able to infer something about the directions in which privacy was moving. Any thoughtful reflections on the many texts and narratives and situations described in the eight preceding chapters will yield answers of genuine merit to this large overall question. Without losing sight of this large objective, I propose (in order to make it manageable) to divide it into four smaller questions, namely: Did the expectations of privacy in early modern culture inflect the sexual, spiritual, ethical, and political experience of those people who were able to leave behind records of how they thought and felt?

Sexual experience first. In a world without privacy, as depicted in More's *Utopia*, sexual experience will merit very little attention, and it certainly won't resemble what came to be thought of as love. Marriage is a transparent social contract in *Utopia*, and very little more. I think the same could be said of Lady Anne Clifford's marriages, the first of which left her feeling "like an owl in the Desert" (*Diary*, 48), the second of which ended in acrimonious separation. But the marriage of Simonds D'Ewes to Anne Clopton, though it certainly began as a social contract, was capable of growing into a genuine partnership. The courtship of John Hutchinson and Lucy Aspley, as told later by Lucy Hutchinson, was characterized by mutual admiration and respect. Both the D'Ewes/Clopton alliance and the Hutchinson/Aspley connection developed into companionate marriages, doubtless in part because of the willingness of both sets of partners to cultivate and value the kind of privacy that Adam and Eve are simply given by Milton and by God. It might be a crude overstatement to say that marriages contracted before and during Shakespeare's lifetime were lacking the sexual intimacy of those contracted after his death. But it would be an error of a greater magnitude to fail to notice the signs of change. If *Much Ado about Nothing* is telling us, in various ways, that society constructs the loving couple who then create a marriage, *The Duchess of Malfi* adds the proviso that only a partner freely chosen will feel like the right one. The Duchess and Antonio come to a tragic end because they are ahead of their time and are therefore denied the privacy which their intimacy requires. The aristocratic culture which surrounds and inhibits them is not yet ready for the claim to privacy that they are in every way advancing.

Spiritual life in the age of Shakespeare is characterized overwhelmingly by a turn inward. This is too complicated a process to describe in a single paragraph, but it needs at least to be acknowledged as another of the moving targets that participates in the efflorescence of early modern privacy. My discussion of devotional practices in both prose and verse (chapter 2) makes many explicit references to the turn inward, memorably invoked by Francis Rous, for example, who claims that "There is a chamber within us" (*The Mysticall Marriage*, A3) designed specifically for private communion between the Christian soul and God. Although it is unusual to find a statement so explicit, it is easy to identify devotional texts of many kinds, composed by authors from the whole spectrum of Christian affiliation, that are moving in a similar direction. A selection of such texts and authors occupies centre stage in chapter 2, but there are many more whose search for God within themselves can be observed elsewhere: Henry Vaughan (chapter 5) and Milton's newly fallen human couple (chapter 6) are good examples. And although I am thinking of spiritual experience as a largely religious category, it was not exclusively so. That is why my study of private devotions makes a concluding gesture towards René Descartes, whose *Meditations*, while not explicitly religious at all, certainly shared with religious writing of many kinds the striking turn inward that I have been trying to describe.

When ethical experience is defined as unquestioning obedience to authority, then privacy is not a required element within it. But to the extent that ethics becomes a field for the exercise of genuine choice, privacy will become a prerequisite. The most telling example of this principle, as I will argue in a moment, is *Hamlet*. But in parallel if less spectacular ways privacy is required by the ethical dilemmas which confront Lady Anne Clifford, Sir Simonds D'Ewes, Margaret Cavendish, and Andrew Marvell. When Lady Anne Clifford is under maximum pressure to sign an agreement that will in effect deprive her of financial independence, she leaves the male-dominated court in which she has been forced to negotiate and travels north to be with her mother for a couple of months. Each of the other persons just mentioned could be shown to gain ethical courage from a private retreat, but I will restrict my further comments to the celebrated Shakespearean example, Hamlet. Partly because everyone at Elsinore is trying to claim him in one way or another, Hamlet feels a profound need for privacy, or so it would appear in any case from his soliloquies, those brilliant theatrical enactments of interiority. "To be, or not to be – that is the question" (3.1.55). Before any serious ethical debate can begin, the question has to be proposed, and that is what Hamlet is doing here. He is able to do so because he believes he is alone: he is unaware that Claudius and Polonius are hiding behind the arras, or that Ophelia will soon be stalking him. So Hamlet assumes the protections that privacy ought to give him while he looks into himself for answers to the ethical question which troubles his "will" (79) and is troubled in turn by his "conscience" (82). Two profoundly antagonistic ethical scenarios are unfolding here: one is the debate within Hamlet's mind, a debate that he could not give himself to if he thought he was being observed; the other scenario is the treachery of his antagonists who may claim to be defending the kingdom but are breaking all ethical standards in order to do so. The privacy that Hamlet's ethical thinking requires is in fact never extended to him by a regime that wants not his independence of mind but only his submission.

And this point dovetails at once with the notion that privacy is part of a political structure too. Not of course if you live in a tyrannical order, as the citizens of Macbeth's Scotland do, or even if you live in a completely regulated stasis, as More's Utopians do. But if you live in Richard Barnfield's Shropshire, or Elizabeth Sawyer's Edmonton, or Sir Henry Slingsby's Yorkshire, it would be a great advantage to you if privacy were considered a territory that could be secured against political invasion. For the dissidents just mentioned, no such outcome was possible. But I think that, in the years immediately following, Andrew Marvell was dedicating his very considerable energies to ensuring that privacy would one day protect people like the three identified as dissidents and discussed at length in chapter 7. That seems to me the reason why he responds to Samuel Parker's attack on toleration with such tenacious energy. The private conscience was, for Marvell, an element of the political structure that he would defend at any cost. He too was engaged in designing a moving target; religious toleration would not be explicitly identified as a political good until John Locke took up the cause in the generation after Marvell's death. But before Locke there were dissidents who died for want of a private space to protect them, and for want of at least one brave advocate of the value of the private conscience.

The Private Self

And now, by way of a coda, I am going to introduce one more author and one more text. The author is Sir Thomas Browne (1605–82), the English writer of his generation who may be most plausibly described as having chosen privacy, and the text is his most private work, *Religio Medici.* I will quote some telling fragments from this text, and one extended passage, but before doing so I offer a few words of explanation.

Religio Medici was first printed in 1642, by Andrew Crooke, without any mark of authorship. Browne was apparently taken aback by this event and soon began preparing a second edition which would declare his authorship and remedy some of the deficiencies of the first printing. Before he could complete this project, Browne learned that Sir Kenelm Digby had read the unauthorized text and had written a detailed critique of it, already in press.[1] Browne wrote to Digby on 3 March 1642/3 acknowledging his authorship, and describing his text as a "piece contrived in my private Study, and as an exercise unto my self, rather than exercitation for any other."[2] Digby sent Browne an overtly reassuring reply, but went ahead with his critique nonetheless. There are of course many ways of interpreting this controversy, but I think we should give due weight to the claim, advanced by Browne in the address "To the Reader" of the authorized text, that it was written "about seven yeares past,"[3] which would give us a date of ca 1636. In support of Browne's claim, we should

1 For a more detailed account of Digby's critique and Browne's response to it, see Ronald Huebert, "The Private Opinions of Sir Thomas Browne," *Studies in English Literature, 1500–1900* 45, no. 1 (2005): 118–21.

2 *The Works of Sir Thomas Browne*, ed. Geoffrey Keynes, 2nd ed. (London: Faber, 1964), 4:235. Quotations from *Religio Medici* are from this edition, and will be made in parentheses (by part and section numbers only).

3 *Religio Medici* ([London]: Andrew Crooke, 1643), A1^{v}.

notice that eight extant manuscript copies of this text were in circulation presumably before any printed document was available. I am inclined to believe that Browne, a young doctor of not yet thirty years of age, wrote this text as a gesture of affiliation with like-minded people: that is, he was explaining to other members of his profession why, despite his extensive scientific training and orientation, he still values his religious beliefs and practices. He is quite sincere when he says that, seven years ago, he wrote many things that are no longer "agreeable unto my present selfe" (A2), and that, because of his habitual use of metaphor, "there are many things to be taken in a soft and flexible sense, and not to be called unto the rigid test of reason" (A2–2^{v}). Not all readers will extend to Browne the generosity he asks for here; but the important point is that he asks for his text to be thought of as a representation of his private self.

Readers already familiar with *Religio Medici* will understand why he makes this claim. Indeed, if my preliminary remarks have identified Browne as someone who, in the circumstances of authorship, was inclined to choose privacy, it would be fair to say that something similar was true of the *style* of authorship which he chose. Virginia Woolf was making a similar claim when, in attempting to define "the sublime genius of Sir Thomas Browne," she wrote the following tribute: "His immense egotism has paved the way for all psychological novelists, autobiographers, confession-mongers, and dealers in the curious shades of our private life. He it was who first turned from the contacts of men with men to their lonely life within."[4]

Browne's stated project is to understand himself: "The world that I regard is my selfe, it is the Microcosme of mine owne frame, that I cast mine eye on; for the other, I use it but like my Globe, and turn it round sometimes for my recreation" (2.11). But this objective, which he may be said to have shared with introspective thinkers from Socrates to Montaigne, becomes also a principle of style in Browne. I could illustrate this claim by choosing any of a number of passages: the one in which, when pondering what he calls the mysteries of Christianity, he says at last "me thinkes there be not impossibilities enough in Religion for an active faith" (1.9); the one in which he hopes to find a pathway to salvation for the virtuous pagans by surmising "methinks amongst those many subdivisions of hell, there might have bin one Limbo left for these" (1.54); or the one

4 *The Common Reader: First Series*, ed. Andrew McNeillie (New York: Harcourt, 1984), 45.

in which he acknowledges "That Miracles are ceased," a development he admits he "can neither prove, nor absolutely deny" (1.27). Each of these passages would in various ways exhibit Browne thinking through a problem. An idea for him is never just an abstract concept, but something he holds in his mind. And the distinctive way in which Browne holds an idea – the way he works and plays with it – is what makes his prose memorable.

Though the choice of a passage is in one sense arbitrary, because any passage will illustrate Browne's style, I have in fact selected a sequence of clauses that I think of as magnificent. Browne is reflecting on the meaning of the microcosm/macrocosm trope:

> but to call our selves a Microcosme, or little world, I thought it onely a pleasant trope of Rhetorick, till my nearer judgement and second thoughts told me there was a reall truth therein: for first wee are a rude masse, and in the ranke of creatures, which only are, and have a dull kinde of being, not yet priviledged with life, or preferred to sense or reason; next we live the life of plants, the life of animals, the life of men, and at last the life of spirits, running on in one mysterious nature those five kinds of existences, which comprehend the creatures not of the world, onely, but of the Universe; thus is man that great and true *Amphibium*, whose nature is disposed to live not onely like other creatures in divers elements, but in divided and distinguished worlds. (1.34)

In one sense this is a very conventional passage: it's yet another account of the Great Chain of Being. But the moment this observation has been made, it sounds inadequate. Browne is not stating a truism, but testing what we mean when we "call our selves a Microcosme"; he then reports on what he thought initially about this topic, and then on how he revised his thinking ("nearer judgement and second thoughts") until he arrived at something he can now regard as "reall truth." Though Browne is ostensibly describing properties of the whole created universe, from undifferentiated matter ("a rude masse") at the bottom to angels ("the life of spirits") at the top, he does so in a way that is utterly and unmistakably distinctive. The more he says about the world out there, as he sees it, the more he reveals about his inner self. If early modern privacy is indeed a moving target, Browne has found a way of using his prose style to give a new voice to the elusive private self; and this innovation is what has enabled his voice to be heard and admired over the many generations that separate his private ruminations from our own. He seems to have identified, intuitively, the direction in which privacy is moving, and he is therefore able to point ahead to developments about to unfold.

Bibliography

Manuscripts

Bodleian Library, Oxford University

MS Ashmole 38
MS Douce 280
MS Eng poet c 50
MS Eng poet e 97
MS Eng poet f 10
MS Eng poet f 25
MS Eng poet f 27
MS Rawl poet 85
MS Rawl poet 117
MS Rawl poet 148
MS Rawl poet 199

British Library, London

Add MS 21433
Add MS 25707
Add MS 30982
Add MS 44963
Egerton MS 2421
Harley MS 646
Harley MS 6057
Harley MS 6910
Harley MS 6931
Lansdowne MS 99
Lansdowne MS 777
Sloane MS 104
Sloane MS 542
Sloane MS 1446
Sloane MS 1792
Stowe MS 962

Cambridge University Library

Add MS 4138
Add MS 5778

Folger Shakespeare Library, Washington, DC

MS V a 89
MS V a 97

MS V a 103
MS V a 124
MS V a 125
MS V a 245
MS V a 319
MS V a 322
MS V a 345
MS V b 43

Newcastle University Library, Newcastle-upon-Tyne

MS Bell-White 25

Rosenbach Museum and Library, Philadelphia, PA

MS 239/18
MS 239/22
MS 239/27
MS 240/7
MS 243/4.2
MS 1083/16
MS 1083/17

Trinity College Cambridge

MS R 3.12

Printed Texts

Aleman, Matheo. *The Rogue: Or the Life of Guzman de Alfarache.* Translated by James Mabbe. London: Edward Blount, 1623.

The Apocrypha. Oxford: Oxford University Press, 1895.

Aubrey, John. *Brief Lives.* Edited by Oliver Lawson Dick. 1949; Reprint, Harmondsworth: Penguin, 1972.

Bacon, Francis. *The Letters and the Life.* Edited by James Spedding. 7 vols. London: Longmans, 1861–74.

– *The Major Works.* Edited by Brian Vickers. Revised ed. Oxford: Oxford University Press, 2002.

Barnfield, Richard. *The Complete English Poems.* Edited by George Klawitter. Selinsgrove, PA: Susquehanna University Press, 1990.

– *The Complete Poems of Richard Barnfield.* Edited by Alexander B. Grosart. London: J. B. Nichols, 1876.

– *The Life and Selected Writings of Richard Barnfield, 1574–1627.* Edited by Fred Clitheroe. Newcastle: The Lymes Press, 1992.

– *The Poems of Richard Barnfield.* Edited by Montague Summers. London: Fortune Press, [1936].

Bernard, Saint. *Cantica Canticorum: Eighty-Six Sermons on the Song of Solomon.* Translated by Samuel J. Eales. London: Elliot Stock, 1895.

Boccalini, Trajano. *I Ragguagli di Parnasso: Or Advertisements from Parnassus.* Translated by Henry Carey, 2nd earl of Monmouth. London: Humphrey Moseley and Thomas Heath, 1656.

The Booke of Common Praier, and Administration of the Sacramentes, and Other Rites and Ceremonies in the Churche of Englande. London: Richard Jugge and John Cawood, 1559.

Brathwait, Richard. *The English Gentlewoman, Drawne out to the Full Body.* London: B. Alsop and T. Fawcet, 1631.

Browne, Sir Thomas. *Religio Medici.* [London]: Andrew Crooke, 1643.

– *The Works of Sir Thomas Browne.* Edited by Geoffrey Keynes. 2nd ed. 4 vols. London: Faber, 1964.

Camden, William. *Remaines, Concerning Britaine: But Especially England, and the Inhabitants Thereof.* 2nd ed. London: Nicholas Okes for Simon Waterson, 1623.

The Catholic Hymnal. Edited by William L. O'Farrell. Cambridge: Office of the University Journal, 1926.

Cavendish, Margaret, duchess of Newcastle. *The Life of the Thrice Noble, High and Puissant Prince William Cavendishe, Duke, Marquess, and Earl of Newcastle.* London: A. Maxwell, 1667.

– *Paper Bodies: A Margaret Cavendish Reader.* Edited by Sylvia Bowerbank and Sara Mendelson. Peterborough, ON: Broadview, 2000.

– *Playes.* London: John Martin, James Allestrye, and Thomas Dicas, 1662.

– *Plays, Never Before Printed.* London: A. Maxwell, 1668.

Chamberlain, John. *The Letters of John Chamberlain.* Edited by Norman Egbert McClure. 2 vols. Philadelphia: American Philosophical Society, 1939.

Chaucer, Geoffrey. *The Works of Geoffrey Chaucer.* Edited by F.N. Robinson. 2nd ed. Boston: Houghton Mifflin, 1957.

Clifford, Lady Anne. *The Diary of Anne Clifford, 1616–1619.* Edited by Katherine O. Acheson. New York: Garland, 1995.

– *A Summary of the Records and a True Memorial of the Life of Me the Lady Anne Clifford.* In *Lives of Lady Anne Clifford Countess of Dorset, Pembroke and Montgomery (1590–1676) and of Her Parents,* edited by J.P. Gilson, 33–166. London: Roxburghe Club, 1916.

Corbett, William. *The Poems of Richard Corbett.* Edited by J.A.W. Bennett and H.R. Trevor-Roper. Oxford: Clarendon, 1955.

Crashaw, Richard. *The Poems: English, Latin and Greek.* Edited by L.C. Martin. 2nd ed. Oxford: Clarendon, 1957.

Davy, Sarah. *Heaven Realiz'd: Or the Holy Pleasure of Daily Intimate Communion with God, Exemplified in a Blessed Soul (Now in Heaven).* [London]: A.P., 1670.

Descartes, René. *Selected Philosophical Writings.* Translated by John Cottingham, Robert Stoothoff, and Dugald Murdoch. Cambridge: Cambridge University Press, 1988.

D'Ewes, Sir Simonds. *The Autobiography and Correspondence of Sir Simonds D'Ewes, Bart., During the Reigns of James I and Charles I.* Edited by James Orchard Halliwell. 2 vols. London: Richard Bentley, 1845.

Digges, Leonard. *An Arithmeticall Militaire Treatise, named Stratioticos.* London: Henry Bynneman, 1579.

Donne, John. *The Complete English Poems.* Edited by A.J. Smith. Harmondsworth: Penguin, 1971.

– *Poems of John Donne.* Edited by E.K. Chambers. 2 vols. London: Lawrence & Bullen, 1886.

– *The Poems of John Donne.* Edited by Herbert J.C. Grierson. 2 vols. London: Oxford University Press, 1912.

– *Selected Prose.* Edited by Evelyn Simpson, Helen Gardner, and Timothy Healy. Oxford: Clarendon, 1967.

– *The Sermons of John Donne.* Edited by Evelyn M. Simpson and George R. Potter. 10 vols. Berkeley: University of California Press, 1953–84.

Eliza's Babes: or The Virgin's Offering (1652): A Critical Edition. Edited by Liam Semler. Madison, NJ: Fairleigh Dickinson University Press, 2001.

Featley, Daniel. *Ancilla Pietatis: Or, the Hand-Maid to Private Devotion: Presenting a Manuell to Furnish Her with Instructions, Hymnes and Prayers Fitted to the Christian Feasts and Fasts, the Weeks of the Yeere, the Daies of the Weeke.* 2nd ed. London: Nicholas Bourne, 1626.

Foxe, John. *Ecclesiastical Historie: Containing the Acts and Monuments of Martyrs.* London: John Daye, 1583.

Gifford, George. *Fifteene Sermons upon the Song of Salomon.* London: Felix Kingston for Thomas Man, 1598.

Goethe, Johann Wolfgang von. *Wilhelm Meister's Apprenticeship.* Translated by Thomas Carlyle. 2 vols. London: John C. Nimmo, 1903.

Goodcole, Henry. *The Wonderfull Discoverie of Elizabeth Sawyer a Witch, Late of Edmonton, Her Conviction and Condemnation and Death: Together with the Relation of the Divels Accesse to Her, and Their Conference Together.* London: William Butler, 1621.

Gosson, Stephen. *Playes Confuted in Five Actions.* London: Thomas Gosson, [1582].

Gouge, William. *Of Domesticall Duties.* London: John Haviland for William Bladen, 1622.

Greer, Germaine, Susan Hastings, Jeslyn Medoff, and Melinda Sansone, eds. *Kissing the Rod: An Anthology of Seventeenth-Century Women's Verse*. London: Virago, 1988.

Hall, Joseph. *The Arte of Divine Meditation: Profitable for All Christians to Knowe and Practise; Exemplified with a Large Meditation of Eternal Life*. London: Samuel Macham and Mathew Cooke, 1606.

Harington, Sir John. *The Letters and Epigrams of Sir John Harington together with "The Prayse of Private Life."* Edited by Norman Egbert McClure. Philadelphia: University of Pennsylvania Press, 1930.

– *A New Discourse of a Stale Subject, Called the Metamorphosis of Ajax*. Edited by Elizabeth Story Donno. London: Routledge, 1962.

Herbert, George. *The English Poems of George Herbert*. Edited by C.A. Patrides. London: Dent, 1974.

Herbert, Thomas. *A Relation of Some Yeares Travaile, Begunne Anno 1626*. London: William Stansby and Jacob Bloome, 1634.

Herrick, Robert. *The Poetical Works of Robert Herrick*. Edited by L.C. Martin. Oxford: Clarendon, 1956.

Heylyn, Peter. *Cosmographie in Four Books: Containing the Chorographie and Historie of the Whole World, and All the Principal Kingdoms, Provinces, Seas, and Isles Thereof*. 2nd ed. London: Henry Seile, 1657.

Hoby, Lady Margaret. *The Private Life of an Elizabethan Lady: The Diary of Lady Margaret Hoby, 1599–1605*. Edited by Joanna Moody. Thrupp, Stroud, Gloucestershire: Sutton, 1998.

Horsey, Sir Jerome. *His Travels, Imploiments, Services and Negociacions*. In *Russia at the Close of the Sixteenth Century*, edited by Edward A. Bond, 153–266. London: Hakluyt Society, 1856.

Hutchinson, Lucy. *Memoirs of the Life of Colonel Hutchinson*. Edited by Julius Hutchinson. 3rd ed. 2 vols. London: Longman, 1810.

Hyde, Edward, earl of Clarendon. *The History of the Rebellion and Civil Wars in England, Begun in the Year 1641*. 3 vols. Oxford: Printed at the Theater, 1702–4.

Ignatius, Saint. *The Spiritual Exercises of Saint Ignatius*. Translated by Thomas Corbishley, SJ. London: Burns & Oates, 1963.

Isidore of Seville. *Étymologies* 12. Edited and translated by Jacques André. Paris: Les Belles Lettres, 1986.

James I, King of England. *Daemonologie* (1597): *News from Scotland* (1591). Elizabethan and Jacobean Quartos. Edited by G.B. Harrison. 1922; Reprint, Edinburgh: Edinburgh University Press, 1966.

Jonson, Ben. *Ben Jonson*. Edited by C.H. Herford, Percy Simpson, and Evelyn Simpson. 11 vols. Oxford: Clarendon, 1925–52.

– *Every Man in His Humor.* Edited by Gabriele Bernhard Jackson. Yale Ben Jonson. New Haven, CT: Yale University Press, 1969.

Lanyer, Aemilia. *The Poems of Aemilia Lanyer: "Salve Deus Rex Judæorum."* Edited by Suzanne Woods. New York: Oxford University Press, 1993.

The Life of St Cuthbert in English Verse. Edited by J.T. Fowler. Publications of the Surtees Society 87. Durham: Andrews, 1891.

Marlowe, Christopher. *Edward the Second.* Edited by Charles R. Forker. Revels Plays. Manchester: Manchester University Press, 1994.

Martin, Randall ed. *Women Writers in Renaissance England.* London: Longman, 1997.

Marvell, Andrew. *Miscellaneous Poems.* London: Robert Boulter, 1681.

– *The Poems of Andrew Marvell.* Edited by James Reeves and Martin Seymour-Smith. London: Heinemann, 1969.

– *The Poems of Andrew Marvell.* Edited by Nigel Smith. London: Pearson Longman, 2003.

– *The Poems and Letters of Andrew Marvell.* Edited by H.M. Margoliouth, Pierre Legouis, and E.E. Duncan-Jones. 3rd ed. 2 vols. Oxford: Clarendon, 1971.

– *The Prose Works of Andrew Marvell.* Edited by Annabel Patterson, Martin Dzelzainis, N.H. Keeble and Nicholas von Maltzahn. 2 vols. New Haven, CT: Yale University Press, 2003.

Meres, Francis. *Palladis Tamia.* London: P. Short, 1598.

Milton, John. *The Complete Poetry and Essential Prose.* Edited by William Kerrigan, John Rumrich, and Stephen M. Fallon. New York: Modern Library, 2007.

Montaigne, Michel de. *The Essayes: Or Morall, Politike and Millitarie Discourses.* Translated by John Florio. London: Val[entine] Sims, 1603.

Moravia, Alberto. *The Voyeur.* Translated by Tim Parks. 1985; Reprint, London: Abacus, 1991.

More, Sir Thomas. *A Frutefull Pleasaunt, and Wittie Worke, of the Beste State of a Publique Weale, and of the Newe Yle, Called Utopia.* Translated by Ralph Robinson. 2nd ed. London: Abraham Vele, [1556].

Mulcaster, Richard. *Positions, Wherein Those Primitive Circumstances Be Examined, Which Are Necessarie for the Training Up of Children, Either for Skill in Their Booke, or Health in Their Bodie.* London: Thomas Vautrollier for Thomas Chare, 1581.

Ovid. *Ovid's Metamorphoses.* Translated by Arthur Golding. Edited by Madeleine Forey. Harmondsworth: Penguin, 2002.

Pepys, Samuel. *The Diary of Samuel Pepys.* Edited by Robert Latham and William Matthews. 11 vols. London: G. Bell, 1970–83.

Petrarca, Francesco. *De vita solitaria/La vie solitaire.* Edited by Nicholas Mann and Christophe Carraud. Grenoble: Éditions Millon, 1999.

– *The Life of Solitude.* Translated by Jacob Zeitlin. [Urbana]: University of Illinois Press, 1924.

– *Songs and Sonnets from Laura's Lifetime.* Translated by Nicholas Kilmer. San Francisco: North Point Press, 1987.

Plot, Robert. *The Natural History of Staffordshire.* Oxford: The Theater, 1686.

Rainbow, Edward. *A Sermon Preached at the Funeral of the Right Honorable Anne Countess of Pembroke, Dorset, and Montgomery.* London: R. Royston and H. Broom, 1677.

The Revenger's Tragedy. Edited by R.A. Foakes. Revels Student Editions. Manchester: Manchester University Press, 1996.

Rous, Francis. *The Mysticall Marriage: Or, Experientall Discoveries of the Heavenly Marriage betweene a Soule and Her Saviour.* 2nd ed. London: Jasper Emery, 1635.

Rowley, William, Thomas Dekker, and John Ford. *The Witch of Edmonton.* Edited by Peter Corbin and Douglas Sedge. Revels Student Editions. Manchester: Manchester University Press, 1999.

Rutherford, Samuel. *Christ Dying and Drawing Sinners to Himselfe, Or a Survey of our Saviour in His Soule-Suffering, His Lonelynesse in His Death, and the Efficacie Thereof.* London: Andrew Crooke, 1647.

Saltmarsh, John. *Free-Grace: Or the Flowings of Christs Blood Freely to Sinners.* London: Giles Calvert, 1645.

– *Groanes for Liberty.* London: Giles Calvert, 1646.

– *Holy Discoveries and Flames.* London: Phillip Nevill, 1640.

– *Poemata Sacra, Latinè & Anglicè Scripta.* Cambridge: Thomas Buck and Roger Daniel, 1636.

– *Wonderfull Predictions Declared in a Message, as from the Lord, to His Excellency S[i]r Thomas Fairfax and the Councell of His Army.* London: Robert Ibbitson, 1648.

Scot, Reginald. *The Discoverie of Witchcraft.* Edited by Montague Summers. 1930; Reprint, New York: Dover, 1972.

Shakespeare, William. *As You Like It.* Edited by Alan Brissenden. Oxford Shakespeare. Oxford: Clarendon, 1993.

– *The Complete Sonnets and Poems.* Edited by Colin Burrow. Oxford Shakespeare. Oxford: Oxford University Press, 2002.

– *Hamlet.* Edited by Ann Thompson and Neil Taylor. Arden Shakespeare. London: Methuen Drama, 2006.

– *Henry IV,* Part 1. Edited by David Bevington. Oxford Shakespeare. Oxford: Clarendon, 1987.

– *Henry V.* Edited by Gary Taylor. Oxford Shakespeare. Oxford: Clarendon, 1982.

– *Henry VI,* Part 1. Edited by Michael Taylor. Oxford Shakespeare. Oxford: Oxford University Press, 2003.

– *Julius Caesar.* Edited by Arthur Humphreys. Oxford Shakespeare. Oxford: Clarendon, 1984.
– *King Henry VIII, or All Is True.* Edited by Jay L. Halio. Oxford Shakespeare. Oxford: Oxford University Press, 1999.
– *Much Ado about Nothing.* Edited by Sheldon P. Zitner. Oxford Shakespeare. Oxford: Oxford University Press, 1993.
– *Othello, the Moor of Venice.* Edited by Michael Neill. Oxford Shakespeare. Oxford: Oxford University Press, 2006.
– *The Tragedy of Coriolanus.* Edited by R.B. Parker. Oxford Shakespeare. Oxford: Clarendon, 1994.
– *The Tragedy of King Richard III.* Edited by John Jowett. Oxford Shakespeare. Oxford: Oxford University Press, 2000.
– *Troilus and Cressida.* Edited by Kenneth Muir. Oxford Shakespeare. Oxford: Clarendon, 1982.
– *Twelfth Night, or What You Will.* Edited by Roger Warren and Stanley Wells. Oxford Shakespeare. Oxford: Clarendon, 1994.
– *The Two Gentlemen of Verona.* Edited by Roger Warren. Oxford Shakespeare. Oxford: Clarendon, 2008.
– *The Works of William Shakespeare.* Edited by Richard Grant White. 12 vols. Boston: Little Brown, 1859–65.

Shirley, James. *The Lady of Pleasure.* London: Tho[mas] Cotes, 1637.

Sidney, Sir Philip. *The Poems of Sir Philip Sidney.* Edited by William A Ringler, Jr. Oxford: Clarendon, 1962.

Sleidan, Johann. *A Famouse Cronicle of Oure Time, Called Sleidanes Commentaries, Concerning the State of Religion and Common Wealth, During the Raigne of the Emperour Charles the First.* Translated by John Daus. N.p.: n.p., [1560].

Slingsby, Sir Henry. *The Diary of Sir Henry Slingsby, of Scriven, Bart.* Edited by Daniel Parsons. London: Longman, 1836.

Southwell, Robert, SJ. *The Poems of Robert Southwell, SJ.* Edited by James H. McDonald and Nancy Pollard Brown. Oxford: Clarendon, 1967.

Spenser, Edmund. *Books I and II of "The Faerie Queene," the "Mutability Cantos," and Selections from the Minor Poetry.* Edited by Robert Kellogg and Oliver Steele. New York: Odyssey Press, 1965.

Stapleton, Thomas. *A Fortresse of the Faith First Planted Amonge Us Englishmen, and Continued Hitherto in the Universall Church of Christ: The Faith of Which Time Protestants Call, Papistry.* Antwerp: Jhon Laet, 1565.

Teresa of Avila, Saint. *The Lyf of the Mother Teresa of Jesus, Foundresse of the Monasteries of the Descalced or Bare-footed Carmelite Nunnes and Fryers of the First Rule: Written by Her Self, at the Commandment of Her Ghostly Father, and Now Translated into English, out of Spanish.* Translated by W.M. Antwerp: Henry Jaye, 1611.

The Tryals of Sir Henry Slingsby K[nigh]t, and John Hewet D.D. for High Treason. London: n.p., 1658.

Truth Brought to Light and Discovered by Time, or a Discourse and Historicall Narration of the First XIIII Yeares of King James Reign. London: Richard Cotes, 1651.

Vaughan, Henry. *The Works of Henry Vaughan.* Edited by L.C. Martin. 2nd ed. Oxford: Clarendon, 1957.

Villa-castin, Thomas. *A Manual of Devout Meditations and Exercises, Instructing how to Pray Mentally: Drawne for the Most Part, out of the Spirituall Exercises of B.F. Ignatius.* Translated by [Henry More]. [St. Omer]: English College Press, 1618.

Virgil. *The Aeneid of Virgil.* Edited by R.D. Williams. 2 vols. London: Macmillan, 1972.

– *The Aeneid.* Translated by Robert Fitzgerald. New York: Vintage Classics, 1990.

Webster, John. *The Duchess of Malfi.* Edited by John Russell Brown. Revels Student Editions. Manchester: Manchester University Press, 1997.

Wetenhall, Edward. *Enter into Thy Closet: Or, a Method and Order for Private Devotion* 5th ed. London: John Martyn, 1676.

Wood, Anthony à. *Athenae Oxoniensis.* Edited by Philip Bliss. 3 vols. London: Rivington, 1813–20.

Critical and Cultural Studies

Alpers, Svetlana. *The Art of Describing: Dutch Art in the Seventeenth Century.* Chicago: University of Chicago Press, 1983.

Amussen, Susan Dwyer. *An Ordered Society: Gender and Class in Early Modern Europe.* Oxford: Blackwell, 1988.

Augustine, Matthew C. "'Lillies Without, Roses Within': Marvell's Poetics of Indeterminacy and 'The Nymph Complaining.'" *Criticism* 50, no. 2 (2008): 255–78.

Baker, Moira P. "'The Uncanny Stranger on Display': The Female Body in Sixteenth- and Seventeenth-Century Love Poetry." *South Atlantic Review* 56, no. 2 (May 1991): 7–25.

Baldwin, T.W. *The Organization and Personnel of the Shakespearean Company.* Princeton, NJ: Princeton University Press, 1927.

Barkan, Leonard. "Diana and Actaeon: The Myth as Synthesis." *English Literary Renaissance* 10 (1980): 317–59.

Barker, Francis. *The Tremulous Private Body: Essays on Subjection.* London: Methuen, 1984.

Beal, Peter et al. *Index of English Literary Manuscripts.* 10 pts in 4 vols. London: Mansell, 1980–97.

Belsey, Catherine. *John Milton: Language, Gender, Power.* Oxford: Blackwell, 1988.

– *The Subject of Tragedy: Identity and Difference in Renaissance Drama.* London: Methuen, 1985.

Bennett, Lyn. *Women Writing of Divinest Things: Rhetoric and the Poetry of Pembroke, Wroth and Lanyer.* Pittsburgh, PA: Duquesne University Press, 2004.

Benson, Sean. "'Perverse Fantasies'? Rehabilitating Malvolio's Reading." *Papers on Language and Literature* 45, no. 3 (2009): 261–86.

Berry, Ralph. "*Twelfth Night*: The Experience of the Audience." *Shakespeare Survey* 34 (1981): 111–19.

Boesky, Amy. *Founding Fictions: Utopias in Early Modern England.* Athens, GA: University of Georgia Press, 1996.

Bonin, Erin Lang. "Margaret Cavendish's Dramatic Utopias and the Politics of Gender." *Studies in English Literature, 1500–1900* 40 (2000): 339–54.

Booth, Stephen. "On the Value of *Hamlet*." In *Reinterpretations of Elizabethan Drama: Selected Papers from the English Institute,* edited by Norman Rabkin, 137–76. New York: Columbia University Press, 1969.

Borris, Kenneth, and George Klawitter, eds. *The Affectionate Shepherd: Celebrating Richard Barnfield.* Selinsgrove, PA: Susquehanna University Press, 2001.

Bourcier, Élisabeth. *Les journaux privés en Angleterre de 1600 à 1660.* Paris: Publications de la Sorbonne, 1976.

Bradbrook, M.C., and M.G. Lloyd Thomas. *Andrew Marvell.* Cambridge: Cambridge University Press, 1940.

Bradley, A.C. *Shakespearean Tragedy: Lectures on "Hamlet," "Othello," "King Lear," "Macbeth."* 2nd ed. London: Macmillan, 1905.

Brown, Nancy Pollard. "Southwell, Robert [St Robert Southwell] (1561–95), writer, Jesuit, and martyr." *Oxford Dictionary of National Biography* (2008).

Burrow, Colin."Rous, Francis (1580/81–1659), religious writer and politician." *Oxford Dictionary of National Biography* (2008).

Bush, Douglas. *English Literature in the Earlier Seventeenth Century.* Oxford: Clarendon, 1946.

Carey, John. *John Donne: Life, Mind and Art.* London: Faber, 1981.

Chambers, E.K. *Sir Henry Lee: An Elizabethan Portrait.* Oxford: Clarendon, 1936.

Chapman, Christopher. "Goodcole, Henry (bap. 1586, d. 1641)." *Oxford Dictionary of National Biography* (2004).

Chapman, H. Perry. "Inside Vermeer's Women." In Marjorie F. Wieseman et al., *Vermeer's Women: Secrets and Silence,* 64–123. Cambridge: Fitzwilliam Museum, 2011.

Chartier, Roger, ed. *Passions of the Renaissance.* Translated by Arthur Goldhammer. Vol. 3 of *A History of Private Life.* Gen. eds. Philippe Ariès and Georges Duby. Cambridge, MA: Harvard University Press, 1989.

Coffey, John. "Rutherford, Samuel (c. 1600–1661), Church of Scotland minister and political theorist." *Oxford Dictionary of National Biography* (2009).

Coiro, Ann Baynes. *Robert Herrick's "Hesperides" and the Epigram Book Tradition.* Baltimore: Johns Hopkins University Press, 1988.

Coleridge, Samuel Taylor. *Shakespearean Criticism.* Edited by Thomas Middleton Raysor. 2nd ed. 2 vols. London: Dent, 1960.

Colie, Rosalie L. *"My Ecchoing Song": Andrew Marvell's Poetry of Criticism.* Princeton, NJ: Princeton University Press, 1970.

Comensoli, Viviana. *"Household Business": Domestic Plays of Early Modern England.* Toronto: University of Toronto Press, 1991.

Cooper, Tarnya. *Searching for Shakespeare.* New Haven, CT: Yale University Press, 2006.

Crane, Mary Thomas."Marvell's Amazing Garden." In *Environment and Embodiment in Early Modern England,* edited by Mary Floyd-Wilson and Garrett A. Sullivan, Jr, 35–54. Houndmills: Palgrave Macmillan, 2007.

Cressy, David. *Birth, Marriage, and Death: Ritual, Religion, and the Life-Cycle in Tudor and Stuart England.* Oxford: Oxford University Press, 1997.

Crum, Margaret, ed. *First-Line Index of English Poetry 1500–1800 in Manuscripts of the Bodleian Library Oxford.* Oxford: Clarendon, 1969.

Curran, Jane V. *Goethe's "Wilhelm Meister's Apprenticeship": A Reader's Commentary.* Rochester, NY: Camden House, 2002.

Davies, Stevie. *Henry Vaughan.* Border Lines Series. Bridgend, Mid Glamorgan, Wales: Seren, 1995.

Davis, J.C. *Utopia and the Ideal Society: A Study of English Utopian Writing, 1516–1700.* Cambridge: Cambridge University Press, 1981.

DeLong, Linwood R. "Reflections on a Remarkable Performance of *Hamlet*: A Re-examination of the Hamlet Scene in Goethe's *Wilhelm Meisters Lehrjahre.*" *Man and Nature/L'homme et la nature* 5 (1986): 73–83.

Diamond, William. "Wilhelm Meister's Interpretation of Hamlet." *Modern Philology* 23 (1925–6): 89–101.

DiSanto, Michael John. "Andrew Marvell's Ambivalence toward Adult Sexuality." *Studies in English Literature, 1500–1900* 48, no. 1 (2008): 165–82.

Dolan, Frances E. "'Can this be Certain?': The Duchess of Malfi's Secrets." In *The Duchess of Malfi: A Critical Guide,* edited by Christina Luckyj, 118–35. London: Continuum, 2011.

Doughtie, Edward. "John Ramsey's Manuscript as a Personal and Family Document." In *New Ways of Looking at Old Texts: Papers of the Renaissance English Text Society, 1985–1991,* edited by W. Speed Hill, 281–8. Binghamton, NY: Renaissance English Text Society, 1993.

Doyle, Tony. "Privacy and Perfect Voyeurism." *Ethics and Information Technology* 11 (2009): 181–9.

Eliot, T.S. "Andrew Marvell." In *Selected Essays*, 3rd ed., 292–304. London: Faber, 1951.

Evans, John. "Extracts from the Private Account Book of Sir William More, of Loseley." *Archaeologia* 30 (1855): 284–310.

Everett, Barbara. "Donne and Secrecy." *Essays in Criticism* 51 (2001): 51–67.

– "*Much Ado about Nothing*: The Unsociable Comedy." In *English Comedy*, edited by Michael Cordner, Peter Holland, and John Kerrigan, 68–84. Cambridge: Cambridge University Press, 1994.

Fahie, J.J. *Galileo: His Life and Work*. London: Murray, 1903.

Feinberg, Anat. "Observation and Theatricality in Webster's *The Duchess of Malfi*." *Theatre Research International* 6 (1980–1): 36–44.

Ferry, Anne. *The "Inward" Language: Sonnets of Wyatt, Sidney, Shakespeare, Donne*. Chicago: University of Chicago Press, 1980.

– "Milton's Creation of Eve." *Studies in English Literature, 1500–1900* 28 (1988): 113–32.

Finocchiaro, Maurice A., ed. and trans. *The Galileo Affair: A Documentary History*. Berkeley: University of California Press, 1989.

Fitter, Chris. "Henry Vaughan's Landscapes of Military Occupation." *Essays in Criticism* 42 (1992): 123–47.

Fleming, James Dougall. *Milton's Secrecy: And Philosophical Hermeneutics*. Aldershot: Ashgate, 2008.

Foisil, Madeleine. "The Literature of Intimacy." In *Passions of the Renaissance*, edited by Roger Chartier, translated by Arthur Goldhammer, 327–61. Vol. 3 of *A History of Private Life*. General editors Philippe Ariès and Georges Duby. Cambridge, MA: Harvard University Press, 1989.

Freud, Sigmund. *The Interpretation of Dreams*. Translated by Joyce Crick. Oxford: Oxford University Press, 1999.

Fried, Charles. "Privacy [A Moral Analysis]." In *Philosophical Dimensions of Privacy: An Anthology*, edited by Ferdinand D. Schoeman, 203–22. Cambridge: Cambridge University Press, 1984.

Friedman, Michael D. "The Editorial Recuperation of Claudio." *Comparative Drama* 25 (1991–2): 369–86.

Frye, Northrop. *A Natural Perspective: The Development of Shakespearean Comedy and Romance*. New York: Columbia University Press, 1965.

Frye, Roland Mushat. *Milton's Imagery and the Visual Arts: Iconographic Tradition in the Epic Poems*. Princeton, NJ: Princeton University Press, 1978.

Fumerton, Patricia. *Cultural Aesthetics: Renaissance Literature and the Practice of Social Ornament*. Chicago: University of Chicago Press, 1991.

Garrard, Mary D. "Artemisia and Susanna." In *Feminism and Art History: Questioning the Litany*, edited by Norma Broude and Mary D. Garrard, 147–71. New York: Harper, 1982.

Gerstein, Robert S. "Intimacy and Privacy." In *Philosophical Dimensions of Privacy: An Anthology*, edited by Ferdinand D. Schoeman, 265–71. Cambridge: Cambridge University Press, 1984.

Gibson, Marion, ed. *Early Modern Witches: Witchcraft Cases in Contemporary Writing*. London: Routledge, 2000.

Goldberg, Dena. "'By Report': The Spectator as Voyeur in Webster's *The White Devil*." *English Literary Renaissance* 17 (1987): 67–84.

Goldberg, Jonathan. *Voice Terminal Echo: Postmodernism and English Renaissance Texts*. New York: Methuen, 1986.

Goulemot, Jean Marie. "Literary Practices: Publicising the Private." In *Passions of the Renaissance*, edited by Roger Chartier, translated by Arthur Goldhammer, 363–95. Vol. 3 of *A History of Private Life*. Gen. eds. Philippe Ariès and Georges Duby. Cambridge, MA: Harvard University Press, 1989.

Graham, Elspeth. "'Vain Desire,' 'Perverseness' and 'Love's Proper Hue': Gender, Sexuality and Feminist Interest in *Paradise Lost*." *Critical Survey* 4 (1992): 133–9.

Greenblatt, Stephen. *Hamlet in Purgatory*. Princeton, NJ: Princeton University Press, 2001.

– *Will in the World: How Shakespeare Became Shakespeare*. New York: Norton, 2004.

Greer, Germaine. *The Obstacle Race: The Fortunes of Women Painters and Their Work* 1979; Reprint, London: Picador, 1981.

– *Shakespeare's Wife*. London: Bloomsbury, 2007.

Grote, David. *The Best Actors in the World: Shakespeare and His Acting Company*. Westport, CT: Greenwood Press, 2002.

Guibbory, Achsah. *Ceremony and Community from Herbert to Milton: Literature, Religion, and Cultural Conflict in Seventeenth-Century England*. Cambridge: Cambridge University Press, 1998.

– "'No Lust There's Like to Poetry': Herrick's Passion for Poetry." In *"Trust to Good Verses": Herrick Tercentenary Essays*, edited by Roger B. Rollin and J. Max Patrick, 79–87. Pittsburgh: University of Pittsburgh Press, 1978.

Gurr, Andrew. *The Shakespeare Company, 1594–1642*. Cambridge: Cambridge University Press, 2004.

Habermas, Jürgen. *The Structural Transformation of the Public Sphere: An Inquiry into a Category of Bourgeois Society*. Translated by Thomas Burger and Frederick Lawrence. Cambridge, MA: MIT Press, 1989.

Halley, Janet E. "Versions of the Self and the Politics of Privacy in *Silex Scintillans*." *George Herbert Journal* 7 (1983–4): 51–71.

Hammond, Paul. "Marvell's Sexuality." *The Seventeenth Century* 11 (1996): 87–126.

Hammons, Pamela. "Robert Herrick's Gift Trouble: Male Subjects 'Trans-Shifting' into Objects." *Criticism* 47, no. 1 (2005): 31–64.

Harris, William O. "Herrick's 'Upon Julia's Clothes.'" *The Explicator* 21, no. 4 (December 1962): item 29.

Hartman, Geoffrey H. "'The Nymph Complaining for the Death of Her Fawn': A Brief Allegory." *Essays in Criticism* 18 (1968): 113–35.

Henderson, Andrea. "Death on the Stage, Death of the Stage: The Antitheatricality of *The Duchess of Malfi*." *Theatre Journal* 42 (1990): 194–207.

Henry, Nat. "Herrick's 'Upon Julia's Clothes.'" *The Explicator* 14, no. 3 (December 1955): item 15.

Hibbard, G.R. "Love, Marriage and Money in Shakespeare's Theatre and Shakespeare's England." *Elizabethan Theatre* 6 (1975): 134–55.

Hirst, Derek, and Steven Zwicker. "Andrew Marvell and the Toils of Patriarchy: Fatherhood, Longing, and the Body Politic." *ELH: A Journal of English Literary History* 66 (1999): 629–54.

– *Andrew Marvell, Orphan of the Hurricane.* Oxford: Oxford University Press, 2012.

– "Eros and Abuse: Imagining Andrew Marvell." *ELH: A Journal of English Literary History* 74, no. 2 (2007): 371–95.

Hockey, Dorothy C. "Notes Notes, Forsooth …" *Shakespeare Quarterly* 8 (1957): 353–8.

Hodgetts, Michael. "Owen, Nicholas [St. Nicholas Owen, called Little John, Little Michael] (d. 1606), carpenter and Jesuit lay brother." *Oxford Dictionary of National Biography* (2008).

Holmes, Martin. *Proud Northern Lady: Lady Anne Clifford, 1590–1676.* Chichester: Phillimore, 1975.

Huebert, Ronald. *The Performance of Pleasure in English Renaissance Drama.* Houndmills, Basingstoke: Palgrave Macmillan, 2003.

– "The Private Opinions of Sir Thomas Browne." *Studies in English Literature, 1500–1900* 45, no.1 (2005): 117–34.

– "'Study our Manuscripts': John Donne's Problems with Privacy." *The Seventeenth Century* 26, no.1 (2011): 1–21.

Hutton, Sarah. "Science and Satire: The Lucianic Voice of Margaret Cavendish's *Description of a New World Called the Blazing World*." In *Authorial Conquests: Essays on Genre in the Writings of Margaret Cavendish*, edited by Line Cottegnies and Nancy Weitz, 161–76. Madison, NJ: Fairleigh Dickinson University Press, 2003.

Jagodzinski, Cecile M. *Privacy and Print: Reading and Writing in Seventeenth-Century England.* Charlottesville: University of Virginia Press, 1999.

Jardine, Lisa, and Alan Stewart. *Hostage to Fortune: The Troubled Life of Francis Bacon.* London: Victor Gollancz, 1998.

Jones, Ernest. *Hamlet and Oedipus.* 1949; Reprint, Garden City, NY: Doubleday Anchor Books, 1954.

Jones, Evan. "Marvell's 'The Nymph Complaining for the Death of Her Faun.'" *The Explicator* 26 (1968): item 73.

Jordan, W.K. "Sectarian Thought and Its Relation to the Development of Religious Toleration, 1640–1660." *Huntington Library Quarterly* 3 (1939–40): 197–223, 289–314, 403–18.

Kermode, Frank. "Definitions of Love." *Review of English Studies*, n.s., 7 (1956): 183–6.

Kerrigan, William. "Kiss Francies in Robert Herrick." *George Herbert Journal* 14 (1990): 155–71.

– "Marvell and Nymphets." *Greyfriar: Siena Studies in Literature* 27 (1986): 3–21.

Krier, Theresa M. *Gazing on Secret Sights: Spenser, Classical Imitation, and the Decorums of Vision.* Ithaca, NY: Cornell University Press, 1990.

Kunin, Aaron. "From the Desk of Anne Clifford." *ELH: A Journal of English Literary History* 71 (2004): 587–608.

Lamb, Mary Ellen. "The Agency of the Split Subject: Lady Anne Clifford and the Uses of Reading." *English Literary Renaissance* 22 (1992): 347–68.

Levy, Eric P. *Hamlet and the Rethinking of Man.* Madison, NJ: Fairleigh Dickinson University Press, 2008.

Lewalski, Barbara K. *Protestant Poetics and the Seventeenth-Century Religious Lyric.* Princeton, NJ: Princeton University Press, 1979.

– "Re-writing Patriarchy and Patronage: Margaret Clifford, Anne Clifford, and Aemilia Lanyer." *Yearbook of English Studies* 21 (1991): 87–106.

Liddell, Mark H. "A New Source of The Parson's Tale." In *An English Miscellany Presented to Dr Furnivall in Honour of His Seventy-Fifth Birthday*, 255–77. Oxford: Clarendon, 1901.

Linthicum, M. Channing. *Costume in the Drama of Shakespeare and His Contemporaries.* Oxford: Clarendon, 1936.

Long, Mary Beth. "Contextualizing Eve's and Milton's Solitudes in Book 9 of *Paradise Lost.*" *Milton Quarterly* 37 (2003): 100–15.

Long, Michael. *Marvell, Nabokov: Childhood and Arcadia.* Oxford: Clarendon, 1984.

Longfellow, Erica. "*Eliza's Babes*: Poetry 'Proceeding from Divinity' in Seventeenth-Century England." *Gender and History* 14 (2002): 242–65.

Love, Harold. *Scribal Publication in Seventeenth-Century England.* Oxford: Clarendon, 1993.

Luckyj, Christina. *"A Moving Rhetoricke": Gender and Silence in Early Modern England.* Manchester: Manchester University Press, 2002.

M., "Wiltshire Members of the Long Parliament," *Wiltshire Notes and Queries* 1 (1893–95): 329–32.

MacNeil, Shaun. "A Philosophical Definition of Privacy." *The Dalhousie Review* 78 (1998): 437–57.

Marotti, Arthur F. "The Cultural and Textual Importance of Folger MS V.a.89." *English Manuscript Studies 1100–1700* (2002): 70–92.

– *Manuscript, Print, and the English Renaissance Lyric.* Ithaca, NY: Cornell University Press, 1995.

Martz, Louis L. *The Paradise Within: Studies in Vaughan, Traherne, and Milton.* New Haven, CT: Yale University Press, 1964.

– *The Poetry of Meditation: A Study in English Religious Literature.* Revised ed. New Haven, CT: Yale University Press, 1962.

Maus, Katharine Eisaman. "Horns of Dilemma: Jealousy, Gender, and Spectatorship in English Renaissance Drama." *ELH: A Journal of English Literary History* 54 (1987): 561–83.

– *Inwardness and Theater in the English Renaissance.* Chicago: University of Chicago Press, 1995.

Metz, Christian. "Story/Discourse (A Note on Two Kinds of Voyeurism)." Translated by Celia Britton and Annwyl Williams. In *The Imaginary Signifier: Psychoanalysis and the Cinema*, translated by Celia Britton, Annwyl Williams, Ben Brewster, and Alfred Guzzentti, 91–8. Bloomington: Indiana University Press, 1982.

Morton, A.L. *The World of the Ranters: Religious Radicalism in the English Revolution.* London: Lawrence and Wishart, 1970.

Moss, Ann. *Printed Common-Place Books and the Structure of Renaissance Thought.* Oxford: Clarendon, 1996.

Myhill, Nova. "Spectatorship in/of *Much Ado about Nothing.*" *Studies in English Literature, 1500–1900* 39 (1999): 291–311.

Nelson, Alan H. "Vere, Edward de, seventeenth earl of Oxford (1550–1604), courtier and poet." *Oxford Dictionary of National Biography* (2004).

Nicholl, Charles. *The Lodger: Shakespeare on Silver Street.* London: Allen Lane, 2007.

Norbrook, David. "Hutchinson [née Apsley], Lucy (1620–1681), poet and biographer." *Oxford Dictionary of National Biography* (2008).

Nordlund, Marcus. *The Dark Lantern: A Historical Study of Sight in Shakespeare, Webster, and Middleton.* Gothenberg Studies in English 77. Göteborg, Sweden: Acta Universitatis Gothonburgensis, 1999.

Nuttall, A.D. *Why Does Tragedy Give Pleasure?* Oxford: Oxford University Press, 1997.

Nyquist, Mary. "The Genesis of Gendered Subjectivity in the Divorce Tracts and in *Paradise Lost.*" In *Re-Membering Milton: Essays on the Texts and Traditions*, edited by Mary Nyquist and Margaret W. Ferguson, 99–127. London: Methuen, 1987.

O'Connor, Mary. "Representations of Intimacy in the Life-Writing of Anne Clifford and Anne Dormer." In *Representations of the Self from the Renaissance to*

Romanticism, edited by Patrick Coleman, Jayne Lewis, and Jill Kowalik, 79–96. Cambridge: Cambridge University Press, 2000.
Ohlmeyer, Jane. "MacDonnell [née Manners; other married name Villiers], Katherine, duchess of Buckingham and marchioness of Antrim (1603?–1649), noblewoman." *Oxford Dictionary of National Biography* (2008).
Orlin, Lena Cowen. *Locating Privacy in Tudor London*. Oxford: Oxford University Press, 2007.
– *Private Matters and Public Culture in Post-Reformation England*. Ithaca, NY: Cornell University Press, 1994.
Panofsky, Erwin. *Problems in Titian, Mostly Iconographic*. Wrightsman Lectures. New York: New York University Press, 1969.
Pearson, Jacqueline. "The Least Certain Boundaries: Gendered Bodies and Gendered Spaces in Early Modern Drama." *Sederi* 3 (2003): 163–81.
Peter, John. "Keep It in the Family." Review of the Cheek by Jowl Production of *The Duchess of Malfi*. *Sunday Times*, 7 January 1996, 10.19.
Plowden, Alison. "Grey [married name Dudley], Lady Jane (1537–1554), noblewoman and claimant to the English throne." *Oxford Dictionary of National Biography* (2008).
Pollock, Griselda. *Differencing the Canon: Feminist Desire and the Writing of Art's Histories*. London: Routledge, 1999.
Pooley, Roger. "Saltmarsh, John (d. 1647), preacher and religious controversialist." *Oxford Dictionary of National Biography* (2004).
Pritchard, Allan. "Marvell's 'The Garden': A Restoration Poem?" *Studies in English Literature, 1500–1900* 23 (1983): 371–88.
Puttfarken, Thomas. *Titian and Tragic Painting: Aristotle's "Poetics" and the Rise of the Modern Artist*. New Haven, CT: Yale University Press, 2005.
Rachels, James. "Why Privacy Is Important." In *Philosophical Dimensions of Privacy: An Anthology*, edited by Ferdinand D. Schoeman, 290–9. Cambridge: Cambridge University Presss, 1984.
Rambuss, Richard. *Closet Devotions*. Durham, NC: Duke University Press, 1998.
– *Spenser's Secret Career*. Cambridge: Cambridge University Press, 1993.
Reiman, Jeffrey. *Critical Moral Liberalism: Theory and Practice*. Lanham, MD: Rowman and Littlefield, 1997.
Rollin, Roger B. "Robert Herrick and the Erotics of Criticism." In *Renaissance Discourses of Desire*, edited by Claude J. Summers and Ted-Larry Pebworth, 130–42. Columbia: University of Missouri Press, 1993.
Ross, Richard J. "Herrick's Julia in Silks." *Essays in Criticism* 15 (1965): 171–80.
Rudinow, Joel. "Representation, Voyeurism, and the Vacant Point of View." *Philosophy and Literature* 3 (1979): 173–86.
Sackton, Alexander. "Donne and the Privacy of Verse." *Studies in English Literature, 1500–1900* 7 (1967): 67–82.

Sanders, Julie. "'The Closet Opened': A Reconstruction of 'Private' Space in the Writings of Margaret Cavendish." In *A Princely Brave Woman: Essays on Margaret Cavendish, Duchess of Newcastle*, edited by Stephen Clucas, 127–40. Aldershot, Hampshire: Ashgate, 2003.

Sandstroem, Yvonne. "Marvell's 'Nymph Complaining' as Historical Allegory." *Studies in English Literature, 1500–1900* 30 (1990): 92–114.

Schanfield, Lilian. "'Tickled with Desire': A View of Eroticism in Herrick's Poetry." *Literature and Psychology* 39 (1993): 63–83.

Schlegel, August Wilhelm von. *Vorlesen über dramatische Kunst und Literatur.* Vol. 6 of *Kritische Schriften und Briefe.* Stuttgart: W. Kohlhammer Verlag, 1966.

– *Course of Lectures on Dramatic Art and Literature.* Translated by John Black and A.J.W. Morrison. 2nd ed. 1846; Reprint, New York: AMS Press, 1965.

Schneider, Elisabeth. "Herrick's 'Upon Julia's Clothes.'" *The Explicator* 13, no. 5 (March 1955): item 30.

Schoeman, Ferdinand D., ed. *Philosophical Dimensions of Privacy: An Anthology.* Cambridge: Cambridge University Press, 1984.

Schoenbaum, S. *William Shakespeare: A Documentary Life.* New York: Oxford University Press, 1975.

Schoenfeldt, Michael C. "The Art of Disgust: Civility and the Social Body in *Hesperides.*" *George Herbert Journal* 14 (1990): 127–54.

Scott-Warren, Jason."Harington, Sir John (bap. 1560, d. 1612) courtier and author." *Oxford Dictionary of National Biography* (2008).

Semler, Liam. "The Creed of *Eliza's Babes* (1652): Nakedness, Adam, and Divinity." *Albion* 33 (2001): 185–217.

– "Who Is the Mother of Eliza's Babes (1652)? 'Eliza,' George Wither, and Elizabeth Emerson." *Journal of English and Germanic Philology* 99 (2000): 513–36.

Shullenberger, William. "Love as a Spectator Sport in John Donne's Poetry." In *Renaissance Discourses of Desire*, edited by Claude J. Summers and Ted-Larry Pebworth, 46–62. Columbia: University of Missouri Press, 1993.

– "Wrestling with the Angel: *Paradise Lost* and Feminist Criticism." *Milton Quarterly* 20 (1986): 269–85.

Slights, Camille Wells. *Shakespeare's Comic Commonwealths.* Toronto: University of Toronto Press, 1993.

Slights, William W.E. *The Heart in the Age of Shakespeare.* Cambridge: Cambridge University Press, 2008.

Smith, Geoffrey Ridsill. *Without Touch of Dishonour: The Life and Death of Sir Henry Slingsby, 1602–1658.* Kineston, Warwickshire: Roundwood, 1968.

Smith, Nigel. *Andrew Marvell: The Chameleon.* New Haven, CT: Yale University Press, 2010.

Snow, Edward A. *A Study of Vermeer.* Berkeley: University of California Press, 1979.

Steinberg, Leo. *The Sexuality of Christ in Renaissance Art and in Modern Oblivion.* New York: Pantheon, 1983.

Stephens, Dorothy. *The Limits of Eroticism in Post-Petrarchan Narrative: Conditional Pleasure from Spenser to Marvell.* Cambridge: Cambridge University Press, 1998.

Stewart, Alan. "The Early Modern Closet Discovered." *Representations* 50 (Spring 1995): 76–100.

Summers, Claude J., and Ted-Larry Pebworth, eds. *Renaissance Discourses of Desire.* Columbia: University of Missouri Press, 1993.

Teunissen, John J., and Evelyn J. Hinz. "What Is the Nymph Complaining For?" *ELH: A Journal of English Literary History* 45 (1978): 410–28.

Theodore, David. "'Gay' Is the Right Word: Montague Summers and the Replevin of Richard Barnfield." In *The Affectionate Shepherd: Celebrating Richard Barnfield,* edited by Kenneth Borris and George Klawitter, 265–79. Selinsgrove, PA: Susquehanna University Press, 2001.

Toulalan, Sarah "'Private Rooms and Back Doors in Abundance': The Illusion of Privacy in Pornography in Seventeenth-Century England." *Women's History Review* 10, no. 4 (2001): 701–19.

Turner, James Grantham. *One Flesh: Paradisal Marriage and Sexual Relations in the Age of Milton.* Oxford: Clarendon, 1987.

Usher, Brett. "Gifford, George (1547/8–1600), Church of England clergyman and author." *Oxford Dictionary of National Biography* (2004).

Vickers, Nancy J. "Diana Described: Scattered Woman and Scattered Rhyme." *Critical Inquiry* 8, no. 2 (Winter 1981): 265–79.

Wabuda, Susan. "Latimer, Hugh (c. 1485–1555), bishop of Worcester, preacher, and protestant martyr." *Oxford Dictionary of National Biography* (2009).

Walker, Claire. "Clitherow [née Middleton], Margaret [St Margaret Clitherow] (1552/3–1586), Roman Cathoic martyr." *Oxford Dictionary of National Biography* (2004).

Watson, Andrew G. *The Library of Sir Simonds D'Ewes.* London: British Museum, 1966.

Watt, Diane. "Askew [*married name* Kyme], Anne (c. 1521–1546), writer and protestant martyr." *Oxford Dictionary of National Biography* (2004).

Wieseman, Marjorie F. et al. *Vermeer's Women: Secrets and Silence.* Cambridge: Fitzwilliam Museum, 2011.

Wilcher, Robert. *Andrew Marvell.* Cambridge: Cambridge University Press, 1985.

Wilcox, Helen. "Private Writing and Public Function: Autobiographical Texts by Renaissance Englishwomen." In *Gloriana's Face: Women, Public and Private, in the English Renaissance,* edited by S.P. Cerasano and Marion Wynne-Davies, 47–62. Hemel Hempstead: Harvester Wheatsheaf, 1992.

Williamson, George C. *Lady Anne Clifford, Countess of Dorset, Pembroke and Montgomery: 1590–1676.* Kendal: Tits Wilson, 1922.

Wilson, Edmund. *Europe without Baedeker: Sketches among the Ruins of Italy, Greece and England.* Garden City, NY: Doubleday, 1947.

Wolf, Edwin, 2nd. "'If Shadows Be a Picture's Excellence': An Experiment in Critical Bibliography." *PMLA* 63 (1948): 831–57.

Wolfe, Heather. Commentary on "Elizabeth (Tanfield) Cary, Vicountess Falkland, to Susan (Villiers) Fielding, Countess of Denbigh (c. December 1626)." In *Early Modern Women: An Anthology of Texts in Manuscript and Print, 1550–1700,* edited by Helen Ostovich and Elizabeth Sauer, 211–14. London: Routledge, 2004.

Woolf, Virginia. *The Common Reader: First Series.* Ed. Andrew McNeillie. New York: Harcourt, 1984.

Worrall, Andrew. "Biographical Introduction." In *The Affectionate Shepherd: Celebrating Richard Barnfield,* edited by Kenneth Borris and George Klawitter, 25–38. Selinsgrove, PA: Susquehanna University Press, 2001.

– "Richard Barnfield: A New Biography." *Notes and Queries* 237 (1992): 370–1.

Wright, Joanne H. "Reading the Private in Margaret Cavendish: Conversations in Political Thought." In *British Political Thought in History, Literature and Theory, 1500–1800,* edited by David Armitage, 212–34. Cambridge: Cambridge University Press, 2006.

Zagorin, Perez. *Francis Bacon.* Princeton, NJ: Princeton University Press, 1998.

Ziegler, Georgiana. "'My Lady's Chamber': Female Space, Female Chastity in Shakespeare." *Textual Practice* 4 (1990): 73–100.

Index

www.ingramcontent.com/pod-product-compliance
Lightning Source LLC
LaVergne TN
LVHW041112090826
844660LV00061B/729/J

* 9 7 8 1 4 4 2 6 4 7 9 1 6 *